THIRD EDITION

Social Work Macro Practice

F. Ellen Netting
Virginia Commonwealth University

Peter M. Kettner
Arizona State University

Steven L. McMurtry
University of Wisconsin–Milwaukee

PEARSON

Boston   New York   San Francisco
Mexico City   Montreal   Toronto   London   Madrid   Munich   Paris
Hong Kong   Singapore   Tokyo   Cape Town   Sydney

Series Editor: *Patricia Quinlin*
Editorial Assistant: *Annemarie Kennedy*
Marketing Manager: *Taryn Wahlquist*
Editorial-Production Administrator: *Annette Joseph*
Editorial-Production Coordinator: *Holly Crawford*
Editorial-Production Service: *Lynda Griffiths, TKM Productions*
Composition Buyer: *Linda Cox*
Artist: *Asterisk, Inc.*
Electronic Composition: *Publishers' Design and Production Services, Inc.*
Manufacturing Buyer: *JoAnne Sweeney*
Cover Administrator: *Linda Knowles*
Cover Designer: *Susan Paradise*

For related titles and support materials, visit our online catalog at www.ablongman.com

Between the time Website information is gathered and then published, it is not unusual for some sites to have closed. Also, the transcription of URLs can result in typographical errors. The publisher would appreciate notification where these errors occur so that they may be corrected in subsequent editions.

Library of Congress Cataloging-in-Publication Data

Netting, F. Ellen.
    Social work macro practice / F. Ellen Netting, Peter M. Kettner, Steven L. McMurtry.—
3rd ed.
        p.   cm.
    Includes bibliographical references and index.
    ISBN 0-205-38069-7
    1. Social service.   2. Social service—United States.   3. Macrosociology.   I. Kettner,
    Peter M.   II. McMurtry, Steven Lloyd.   III. Title.

HV41.N348 2004
361.3′2—dc21   2003051823

Printed in the United States of America

10 9 8 7 6 5 4 3 2 1   RRD-IN   08 07 06 05 04 03

In memory of my father, Millege H. Daniel, who taught me to value the printed word
FEN

In hopes of a better world for Megan, Colleen, Braydon, Mackenzie, Brooklynn, and Noah
PMK

To G-Y, Caitlin, and Alex
SLM

CONTENTS

11 Planning, Implementing, Monitoring, and Evaluating the Intervention   367

PREFACE

Macro practice has come to mean many different things to different people, so we feel it is important to share our perspective at the outset. Over the years, we were intrigued to learn that previous editions of our text were being used in courses on human behavior and policy practice, as well as in community analysis and organization analysis courses at both graduate and undergraduate levels.

It is likely that a wide variety of curriculum designs and different ways of dividing curriculum content accounts for the varying perspectives on how this text can be used. We are pleased that so many faculty have found a variety of uses for the book and its content, but we would also like to take this opportunity to clarify our perspective about the purpose of the book.

We are aware that the history of social work as a profession has been marked by shifts in the dominant focus from intervention with individuals to intervention with and within larger systems. Early perspectives on the latter tended to focus primarily on policy-level involvements (especially legislative processes) and community organizing (using Rothman's classic models of locality development, social planning, and social action). As the need for social work administration content was recognized and incorporated into the curriculum of many schools of social work, this topic was also embraced as an area of concentration for those who preferred to work with and within larger systems.

However, as we taught our required foundation-level courses on community and organizational change, and as we worked with students and professionals in the field, we became aware of the changing dynamics of practice and expectations for practitioners. Students as well as practitioners were working with populations such as homeless persons, members of teen street gangs, victims of domestic violence, chronically unemployed persons, and other disenfranchised groups. Although social workers will always need casework and clinical skills to help people in need on a one-to-one basis, it was becoming increasingly evident to us that they were also expected to intervene at the community level. Typical activities included promoting the development of shelters, developing neighborhood alternatives to gang membership and juvenile incarceration, and addressing chronic unemployment as a community problem.

These activities are not new; many closely mirror the work of settlement-house workers in the early days of the profession. Yet, many social work students have traditionally seen themselves as preparing strictly for interventions at the individual or family level. It is unexpected and disconcerting when they find themselves being asked to initiate actions and design interventions that will affect large numbers of people and attack problems at the community or organizational level. A major goal of this book, then, is to recapture a broader definition of *social work practice* that recognizes the need for workers to be able to bridge these distinctions if they are to provide effective services.

When social work practice with macro systems is seen as solely the realm of administrators, community organizers, program planners, and others, a vital linkage to millions of people who struggle daily with environmental constraints has been severed. We believe that social workers who see clients every day are the ones who are most aware of the need for macro-level change. Macro practice, understood within this context, defines the uniqueness of social work practice. Many disciplines claim expertise in working with individuals, groups, and families, but social work has long stood alone in its focus on the organizational, community, and policy contexts within which its clients function. The concept of the person-in-environment is not simply a slogan that makes social workers aware of environmental influences. It means that social workers recognize that sometimes it is the *environment* and not the *person* that needs to change.

Macro-level change may, but does not necessarily always, involve large-scale, costly reforms at the federal and state levels or the election of candidates more sympathetic to the poor, neglected, and underserved members of society. Sometimes useful macro-level change can involve organizing a local neighborhood to deal with deterioration and blight, sometimes it may mean initiating a self-help group and stepping back so that members will assume leadership roles. The focus of this book is on enabling social work practitioners to undertake whatever types of macro-level interventions are needed in an informed, analytical way and with a sense of confidence that they can do a competent job and achieve positive results.

Organization

Social Work Macro Practice is organized into five parts. In Part One, we begin by highlighting examples of macro practice in the interest of acquainting students with the rich traditions of macro-level change that all social workers inherit when they enter the profession. We address ethical dilemmas that social workers may face when using micro-level strategies, and provide a historical overview of macro practice and the diverse population groups served.

Part Two is a new section in this edition, focusing on two components critical to planned change: understanding both problems and populations. We introduce the concept of analyzing macro systems, and we guide the student through the early phases of the process. Guidelines for problem and population analysis are incorporated into the chapters in this section, and students are referred to available literature and other resources to complete these analyses.

Parts Three and Four focus on community content and organizational content, the components that we have referred to as analysis of arena. These sections of the book are more comprehensive because the content is provided in the text itself. The content is designed to walk a student through a community and/or organizational analysis in preparation for proposing change that is relevant to the arena within which it will take place.

Finally, in Part Five we have designed a practice model for planned intervention that we believe is applicable to both communities and organizations, and that we sincerely hope addresses the realities of practice. We recognize the fact that when a caseworker or administrator becomes involved in a change effort, clinical or administrative responsibilities do not stop. The sharing of organizing responsibilities with others and the clear definition and analysis of the problem, population, and arena for intervention are critical. We believe the busy practitioner can bring about organizational and community change necessary to improve the quality of life for the intended beneficiaries of the change.

A familiar dilemma we faced in preparing the book concerned organizing the material for the purpose of teaching in contrast to organizing it in ways that reflect the realities of daily practice. One comment we received on the first edition was that it went too far in cautioning the reader to consider all alternatives and perspectives before proceeding with planned change. Certainly, we recognize that social movements and societal change would not occur if passion and risk taking did not incite people to action. However, we must always be mindful that we are attempting to reach an audience of new professionals who are just entering the field of social work. We would be remiss if we did not suggest that they critically consider the implications of their actions, for we believe that professionals have to be responsible for what they do. It is difficult to embrace this responsibility without recognizing the potential implications of one's actions. As in one-to-one practice, new professionals engaging in macro-level interventions need to act methodically early in their careers, in contrast to the practiced professional who can more swiftly accomplish the analytical work and move to action. We hope that the content of this book is helpful in developing that professional, analytical mindset. It is also our wish that social workers at all levels throughout organizations and communities are able to move skillfully from interventions with clients to interventions at the organization and community levels, depending on need.

Features New to This Edition

The third edition of *Social Work Macro Practice* has been thoroughly updated and revised to make it an even stronger and more user-friendly text.

- We reframed and reordered the materials in early chapters with the intent of emphasizing that practitioners are proactive learners who bring various needs and strengths to a variety of planning interventions amid the inevitability of value conflicts.
- We updated references and materials throughout the book, and at the end of each chapter, we added discussion questions and exercises designed to integrate chapter content.
- We developed a new Part Two, which expands material that was originally in Chapter 3. Now, Part Two consists of two chapters that focus on problems and populations, respectively. This new focus on understanding populations is designed to emphasize the importance of recognizing diversity among population groups involved in change efforts.

- We revised material originally in three chapters in Part Three on community, integrating this content into two chapters that more closely parallel the presentation of organizations as arenas in subsequent chapters.
- We reemphasized that task lists are not exhaustive and that students should use these only as guides, and we consolidated tasks wherever possible. In addition, we are more intentional in explaining the iterative nature of planned change and the necessity of preparing oneself for conflict in any change effort.
- We added a final chapter that focuses on the implementation of a planned change intervention.

In our earlier editions, students and faculty alike seemed to find that the frameworks we provided were "user-friendly" and easy to follow. We have kept those frameworks throughout the book and have strengthened them. However, we caution the reader to recognize that in our attempt to make these tools easy to use, we may falsely imply that step-by-step completion of all tasks will inevitably lead to success. Obviously, the world is far too complex for "cookbook" approaches that are followed in lockstep. Our intent is to provide tools and frameworks that have records of success and that offer a reasonable likelihood for future successes if used appropriately. We readily recognize that ours is not the only approach nor necessarily the best in all circumstances. We remain interested in any approach that provides students and practitioners with viable alternatives.

As with the first edition, this book will mesh well with a variety of contemporary policy texts. We have made every attempt to remind the reader that planned change approaches, such as the one presented herein, occur within a political environment that is constantly changing. We hope readers will always use our planned change approach with an eye to the political environment as well as to the iterative nature of how change processes occur.

ACKNOWLEDGMENTS

As we finish this third edition, much has changed since our original 1993 publication. We are now scattered in three different geographical locations: Virginia, Arizona, and Wisconsin. We are indebted to colleagues at the three universities where we have worked over the last decade who have given us constructive feedback.

At Virginia Commonwealth University, special appreciation is due to David Fauri, Mary Katherine O'Connor, Robert Schneider, Beverly Koerin, and Joseph Walsh, who shared their own and their students' insights with us after using our book in the classroom. We are especially grateful to King Davis for granting us permission to use his definition of *social justice,* to Elizabeth "Lib" Hutchison for sharing her work on community theory, to Stephen F. Gilson for his assistance in integrating content on disabilities into our book, and to Frank R. Baskind who has always supported our efforts. We wish to acknowledge with thanks and appreciation the important contribution of Dan Stanton, Arizona Local Documents Librarian, who was very helpful in identifying data sources and websites of use to social workers.

We are also indebted to colleagues who provided feedback as they used our text at other universities. Deep gratitude goes to Diane Kaplan-Vinokur at the University of Michigan, who sent us extensive feedback, along with copies of course materials into which she integrated our book. We are especially grateful to the reviewers of this edition for their helpful comments: Theresa J. Early, Ohio State University; Theresa L. Roberts, Indiana University; and James E. Rollin, University of Illinois at Chicago. We appreciate, as well, the efforts of a number of anonymous reviewers who provided careful and thoughtful assessments of earlier drafts.

To our editor, Patricia Quinlin, and her editorial assistant, Annemarie Kennedy, we express our appreciation for their oversight, interest, and assistance as we revised our text. To our former editors, David Estrin and Janice E. Wiggins, we are grateful for the support both provided in making our first and second editions a success.

Most of all, we thank those students and practitioners who, often in the face of seemingly insurmountable barriers, continue to practice social work the way it was intended. They intervene at whatever level is needed. They persist with what may appear to be intractable problems and work with clients who have lost hope until hope can be rediscovered and pursued. Their spirit and dedication continually inspire us in our efforts to provide whatever guidance we can for the next generation of social workers.

PART ONE

Values and Historical Perspectives

The first part of this book is intended to provide the definitions, background information, and context for the subsequent parts. Chapter 1 offers a definition of *macro practice*, explains the rationale for preparing social workers to undertake macro-practice activities, introduces the values and ethics of the profession, presents case vignettes to illustrate the fit between macro and micro social work practice, and discusses professional identity.

Chapter 2 takes the reader through a review of the historical development of traditional macro-practice roles, examines how changes in society have affected these roles, and identifies contemporary trends that may be important for the future evolution of macro practice.

1 An Introduction to Macro Practice in Social Work

OVERVIEW

Macro Practice in Context

This book is intended for all social workers, regardless of whether they specialize in micro or macro tracks within schools of social work. It is also designed to be an introduction to the macro practice roles social workers play. Although some practitioners will concentrate their efforts primarily in one arena more than another, in some situations all social workers will engage in macro-level interventions as the appropriate response to a need or a problem. Therefore, we define *macro practice* as *professionally guided intervention designed to bring about planned change in organizations and communities.*

This book is not designed to prepare practitioners for full-time agency administration, program planning, community organization, or policy analysis positions. Social workers who assume full-time macro roles will need a more advanced understanding than this text will provide. This is also not a book on specialization. Instead, the roles discussed in this and the following chapters are ones that all competent social work practitioners will play during their professional careers.

Experiences of Former Students

In preparation for each new edition of this book, we talk with former students who are practicing social workers, some of whom work directly with clients and some of whom are planners, coordinators, managers, administrators, organizers, or policy analysts in the United States and other parts of the world. We also save emails from former students who keep us up to date and pose questions to us. We then include some of these comments that illustrate the differences between students' expectations of social work practice and their actual experiences once they are working in the field.

A social worker employed by a community-based agency on an Indian reservation shared these thoughts: "Culture is so important to the work we do. I constantly have to ask indigenous people for advice so that I do not make assumptions about the people with whom I work. The concept of community and what it means to this tribe, even the value of the land as a part of their tradition, is so crucial. It is much more complex than I had assumed when I was in school."

Another former student reinforced the importance of community. "The thing that has surprised me is how much I need to know about the community—people's values, where funding comes from, how to assess community needs. Even though I do direct practice, I am constantly pulled onto task forces and committees that have to deal with the broader community issues."

One of our graduates, who decided to try a new location, sent an email from Australia where she, too, was recognizing the complexity of culture. She wrote, "Well, I got a job as a family counselor in the Northern Territory here and it's way out in the bush, as they call it. If you're wondering how remote it is, look it up on the Web. My main job duties are to work with Aboriginal youth and families, especially those who have been affected by past government policies of assimilation—[where] government officers took Aboriginal or part Aboriginal people from their homes and placed them with white families or institutions simply because of their race. They call this population of people 'The Stolen Generation.' It's clinical-type work, but I'm in a new community-based organization, and we are desperate for books and reading materials on grant writing and fundraising. Can you help?"

Whereas these social workers focus heavily on local community concerns, others find themselves in policy-making arenas. One student who began her social work career with a burning interest in working in state government sent this message: "I've been with the State Assembly for just over a year now, doing bill analyses in the areas of Aging, Social Services, Housing, Local Government, and Labor and Employment. It has been an interesting job, and I've definitely learned how the legislative process works here, but I really am looking for more of a challenge. I've applied and interviewed for the position of Government Program Analyst with the State Commission on Aging. In this position, I'll need to use lots of the skills that I learned in the macro classes. My current supervisor here at the legislature can testify to my policy and bill analysis skills, but I know that I can do more in-depth writing and research than anyone has had the opportunity to see. I'm excited about this new possibility."

A recent graduate who landed a position in a County Department of Social Service reported the following: "I'm hoping I'll eventually have enough wiggle room to go from child and adult protective services to the welfare-to-work area, which is my main interest. I think the political system is primarily involved in major policy issues and not implementation. They passed the welfare reform legislation and then expected the state and local delivery systems to implement the policy decision. I think on a micro level, legislators are concerned about the delivery of services to constituents, particularly if they receive a call. At the macro level, I am not as sure that there is a commitment to customer satisfaction. I believe more often social services are viewed as a social control program. Do I sound cynical?" This practitioner recognizes how policy intent is often hard to implement in agency and community arenas.

Another child protective services worker added: "It's really hard to describe. Within a few days last year in my caseload there was a death of a child, another of my kids was abandoned in our waiting room, and there were threats of violence against our staff from people who think we just indiscriminately take children away from their parents. I often think of going into other lines of work, but there are lots of intangible rewards in social work, and other professions have their headaches, too."

One of our former students, originally from Nigeria, returned to her country of origin to establish a Mission House designed to improve the welfare of elders. She wrote, "From our preliminary studies here, poverty and health-related problems are the two most prevalent issues for elders. Then, add widowhood and you'll have a grim picture. There are cases of neglect arising primarily from the economic situations of family members. It is a case of being able to share what you have. If you have no food to eat, you cannot offer another person food. This is what we are trying to address in our programs here."

Compare this to what the director of a social services unit in a U.S. hospital told us about elder care. "I have been here long enough to see the advent of diagnostic-related categories. This is the Medicare system's way of making sure older patients are discharged efficiently, and if they are not, the hospital has to pick up the tab." She went on to explain how social workers in health care are struggling to understand their roles, which are often limited by the services for which funding sources will authorize reimbursement. Understanding the way in which health-care organizations are changing, diversifying, and turning outward to the community has become critical for social workers who are encountering other professionals in roles similar to their own. As social work departments are decentralized into cost centers, social workers must understand why these administrative decisions are being made and find ways to influence future decision making. Many of these social workers entered health-care systems with the idea of providing counseling, but what they are doing is advocacy, solution-focused and crisis intervention, case management, and discharge planning. These roles require an in-depth understanding of macro issues.

Another student had this to say: "What makes this profession worthwhile for me is that there is a core of very committed people who really live up to the ideals of the profession. They're very talented people who could make a lot more money elsewhere, but they believe in what they're doing, and it's always a pleasure to work with them. Our biggest frustration has been that there are so many people (like state legislators, for example) who wield so much power over this profession but have no understanding of what social problems and human needs are all about. Even though professionals may have spent the better part of their careers trying to understand how to deal with people in need, their opinions and perspectives are often not accepted or respected by decision makers."

The clinical director of a private for-profit adoption agency added this view: "Unlike a lot of social workers, I work in a for-profit agency, and business considerations always have to be factored into our decisions. We have a fairly small operation, and I think the agency director is responsive to my concerns about how clients are treated, but I've still had to get used to the tension that can arise between making a profit and serving clients."

On a final note, a direct-practice student who recently graduated made this statement: "My education in social work taught me how little I know. I feel as if I have just scratched the surface. Learning is a long, ongoing process. I work in a head injury center and what I learned from having had exposure to macro practice roles is that you have to know the organization in which you work, particularly the philosophy behind what happens there. This is more important than I ever imagined."

These quotations tell their own stories. The issues facing social workers in their daily practice are not limited to client problems. If social workers are to be effective in serving their clients, many problems must be addressed at the agency or community level. Some of these problems require changing the nature of services, programs, or policies. Most require an understanding of funding issues. We're grateful to our former students for helping us illustrate these issues.

What Is Macro Practice?

As stated earlier, macro practice is professionally guided intervention designed to bring about planned change in organizations and communities. Macro practice, as all social work practice, draws from theoretical foundations while simultaneously contributing to the development of new theory. Macro practice is based on a variety of practice models, and it operates within the boundaries of professional values and ethics. Macro-level activities engage the practitioner in organizational, community, and policy arenas. In today's world, macro practice is rarely the domain of one profession. Rather, it involves the skills of many disciplines and professionals in interaction.

Macro activities go beyond individual interventions but are often based on needs, problems, issues, and concerns identified in the course of working one-to-one with clients. There are different ways to conceptualize the arenas in which macro social work practice occurs. Rothman, Erlich, and Tropman (2001) identify three arenas of intervention: communities, organizations, and small groups. We have selected communities and organizations as the arenas on which we will focus the majority of this text, folding in small group work as a critical part of most interventions in both communities and organizations. *Small groups* are defined as "a tangible collection of people who can discuss matters personally and work together in close association" (Rothman et al., 2001, p. 13). It is our contention that small groups are often the nucleus around which change strategies are developed in both communities and organizations, and they are therefore more logically conceptualized as part of the strategy or medium for change rather than the focus of change.

Other writers highlight the policy context in which macro intervention occurs (Gilbert & Terrell, 2002; Jansson, 1999; Karger & Stoesz, 2002; Popple & Leighninger, 2001). Organizational and community arenas are deeply embedded in political systems. Fundamental to macro change is an understanding of overriding ideologies and values that influence local, state, and national politics.

Levels of Involvement in Social Work Practice

Social work practice is broadly defined and allows for intervention at the micro (individual, group, or domestic unit) level and at the macro (organization and community) level. Social workers who undertake macro-level interventions will often be engaged in what is called "policy practice" (Jansson, 1999), since policy change is so integral to what happens in organizations and communities. Given this division of labor, some professional roles require that the social worker be involved full time in macro practice. These professional roles are often referred to by such titles as planner, policy analyst, program coordinator, community organizer, manager, and administrator.

The micro service worker or clinical social worker also bears responsibility for initiating change in organizations and communities. The micro service worker is often the first to recognize patterns indicating the need for change. If one or two clients present a particular problem, a logical response is to deal with them as individuals. However, as more and more persons present the same difficulty, it becomes evident that something is awry in the systems with which these clients are interacting. It then becomes incumbent on the social worker to help identify the system(s) in need of change and the type of change needed. The nature of the system(s) in need of change may lead to communitywide intervention or inter-vention in a single organization.

Take, for example, the discovery by the staff of a senior center that a number of elders in the community are, because of self-neglect, socially isolated and possi-bly malnourished. A caseworker could follow up on each person, one at a time, in an attempt to provide outreach and needed services. This leads to hit-or-miss results and takes a very long time to reach everyone in need. An alternative would be to deal with the problem from a macro perspective—to invest time in organiz-ing agency and community resources to identify older people who need the senior center's services and to ensure that these are provided through a combination of staff and volunteer efforts.

This may seem a complex task for someone who came into social work expecting to work with clients one at a time. Although it is true that macro-level interventions can be complicated, we will provide a systematic approach that attempts to make such undertakings more manageable. Remember, too, that these efforts are typically accomplished with the help of others, not alone.

A Systematic Approach to Macro Social Work Practice

Figure 1.1 illustrates an approach that can be used by social workers to identify, study, and analyze the need for change and eventually to propose solutions. A problem may be brought to a social worker's attention by a client. A group of res-idents within a neighborhood may present issues and concerns that need to be addressed. Issues in the workplace, such as the quality of service to clients, may

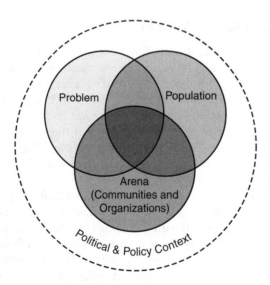

FIGURE 1.1   Macro Practice Conceptual Framework: Understanding Problem, Population, and Arena

surface and require organized intervention. Community problems may be so glaring that the need for change comes from many different directions. Regardless of how social workers identify change opportunities, they function in a political environment that cannot be ignored.

In Figure 1.1 there are three overlapping circles that illustrate the focal points of a social worker's efforts in undertaking a macro-level change episode. We will refer to these focal points as (l) problem, (2) population, and (3) arena.

Good social work practice requires understanding. A social worker cannot expect to help a client who is addicted to alcohol, for example, if the social worker does not understand both the phenomenon of alcoholism and the background of the person addicted. To engage in macro practice, the social worker must understand not only the problem (alcoholism) and the population (elderly, retired males, for example) but also the arena (community or organization) within which the problem occurs. Understanding communities and organizations adds a dimension of complexity to macro practice, but this understanding is a critical precursor to successful macro-level intervention.

In the course of developing an understanding of problem, population, and arena, the social worker will inevitably focus on the areas of overlap depicted in Figure 1.1. Continuing with the example of alcoholism among elderly, retired males, it would be important to review the literature on the phenomenon of alcoholism and on the population of elderly, retired males. But as the change agent builds a body of knowledge about problem and population, it becomes especially important to focus on the overlap between the two areas: alcoholism and its unique impact on elderly, retired males.

Likewise, it is important to understand how the phenomenon of alcoholism affects the local community (the overlap between problem and arena), and to what extent the needs of the population of elderly, retired males are understood and addressed in the local community (overlap between population and arena). Ultimately, in an episode of macro practice, the objective is to work toward an understanding of the area where all three circles overlap (alcoholism and its impact on elderly, retired males in XYZ town).

As the social worker and other change agents study the situation, they will gain at least some level of understanding of (1) basic concepts and issues surrounding alcoholism; (2) elderly, retired males; (3) the local community and/or relevant organizations; (4) alcoholism as it affects elderly, retired males; (5) alcoholism and how it is addressed in the local community; (6) how the needs of elderly, retired males are addressed in the local community; and finally (7) the problem and needs of elderly, retired males in the local community who are addicted to alcohol.

Social and community problems and needs must also be addressed within a larger context that examines the problem, the population, and the community or organization. Dealing with social and community problems and needs effectively requires an awareness of the political environment within which the change episode will be undertaken. For these reasons, we have placed the three circles (problem, population, and arena) within a large dotted outer circle intended to depict the political environment. The importance of and the need for understanding the political and policy contexts cannot be overemphasized.

The Interrelationship of Micro and
Macro Social Work Practice

Given the complexity of macro interventions, practitioners may begin to feel overwhelmed. Is it not enough to do good direct practice or clinical work? Is it not enough to listen to a client and assist in identifying options? Our answer is that professional practice focusing only on an individual's intrapsychic concerns does not fit the definition of social work. Being a social worker requires seeing the client as part of multiple, overlapping systems comprising the person's social and physical environment. The profession of social work is committed to seeking social justice in concert with vulnerable and underserved populations, and macro-practice skills are necessary to confront these inequalities. If the social worker is unwilling to engage in some macro-practice types of activities relating to these environments, he or she is not doing social work.

Similarly, social workers who carry out episodes of macro practice must understand what is involved in the provision of direct services to clients at the individual, domestic-unit, or group level. Without this understanding, macro practice may be carried out in the absence of an adequate grounding in client problems and needs. The interconnectedness of micro and macro roles is the heart of social work practice. In short, it is as important for social workers to understand the nature of individual and group interventions as it is to understand the nature of organizational, community, and policy change.

Because we believe that all social workers are professional change agents, we use the terms *social worker, professional,* and *change agent* interchangeably throughout this book. Social workers are always change agents because they are constantly identifying changes necessary to make systems more responsive or sensitive to target population needs. Indeed, change is so much a part of social work practice that one cannot separate the two. Other professionals may also see themselves as change agents, and it is important for the contemporary macro practitioner to collaborate and partner with those from other disciplines so that the knowledge of diverse fields can be used in planning effective change. *Professional* is a term that implies identification with a set of values that places the interests of the client first and relies on knowledge, judgment, and skill to act on those values. Later in this chapter we will discuss the meaning of professional values that unite social workers across roles, arenas, and areas of specialization.

The Foundation of Macro Practice

Understanding the professional mission of social work is essential to recognizing why macro practice is important. In a provocative argument, Specht and Courtney (1994) challenge social work's contemporary interest in the popular psychotherapies that have diverted social work from its original mission and vision of the perfectibility of society. There is a yet unfulfilled mission for social work: to deal with the enormous social problems under which our society staggers, the social isolation of the aged, the anomie experienced by youth, the neglect and abuse of children, homelessness, drug addiction, and the problem of those who suffer from AIDS.

Our mission should be to build a meaning, a purpose, and a sense of obligation for the community. It is only by creating a community that we establish a basis for commitment, obligation, and social support. We must build communities that are excited about their child care systems, that find it exhilarating to care for the mentally ill and the frail aged, and that make demands upon people to behave, to contribute, and to care for one another. (p. 27)

Similarly, the person-is-political perspective underscores the belief that individuals cannot be viewed separate from the larger society. The actions, and even the inactions, of individuals influence those around them and may have broad implications for others within an organization or community. Bricker-Jenkins and Hooyman (1986) explain:

Just as no "private realities" exist apart from political processes, there are no private solutions. Given that we are interconnected and the sum of our individual actions create the social order, we are thereby responsible to each other for our actions. Accordingly, failure to act is to act; likewise, failure to work to transform social and political realities is to support the status quo. (p. 14)

For those social workers who do feel a sense of commitment to bring about positive change not only for individual clients but for whole neighborhoods, organizations, and communities, the question becomes: How is it possible to meet all the expectations of a job and still be involved in dealing with larger issues?

In Chapters 3 through 11 of this book we will attempt to present building blocks of a planned change model that makes it both possible and manageable to carry out episodes of change. But before we focus on a change model, it is necessary first to develop a foundation for macro practice. That foundation, we believe, is based on an understanding of the relevance of theories and models, of values and ethics, of roles and expectations of a professional, and of the historical roots of macro practice. In the remainder of this chapter we will introduce theories and models, values and ethical dilemmas, and professional identity. Chapter 2 will be devoted to a review of the history of macro practice in social work.

Theories and Models

Theories are sets of interrelated concepts and constructs that provide a framework for understanding how and why something works or does not work. *Models* provide guidance and direction for the practitioner. Theories provide the tools for thinking about a problem or need, whereas models provide guidelines for action and intervention. Human behavior theories, for example, help one to understand why some human beings behave the way they do. A practice model would then draw on particular theories to suggest an approach to resolving client problems. Sociological theories may describe how communities, organizations, or societies function. A practice model for initiating change in communities and organizations (such as the planned change model presented in this book) would show how these theories can lead to specific actions.

Systems theory guides the planned change approach in this book. Early work on organizations (Katz & Kahn, 1966; Thompson, 1967) and on communities (Warren, 1978) laid the groundwork for an open-systems view of these arenas. Warren (1978) contends that social systems theory holds great promise for understanding communities. He built on the work of Talcott Parsons, a sociologist known for defining the characteristics of social systems. He also incorporated the work of others who described how community systems would differ from the groups and formal organizations to which systems theory had previously been applied.

Warren (1978) sees the community as not just one system but a system of systems in which all types of formal and informal groups and individuals interact. Given the diversity among groups and subgroups, communities have a broad range of structural and functional possibilities that do not conform to a centralized goal. The beauty of a community system is that it is a complex arena in which multiple groups and organizations with differing values can exist simultaneously. Warren defined a *social system* as

> a structural organization of the interaction of units that endures through time. It has both external and internal aspects relating the system to its environment and its units to each other. It can be distinguished from its surrounding environment, performing a function called boundary maintenance. It tends to maintain an equilibrium in the sense that it adapts to changes from outside the system in such a way as to minimize the impact of the change on the organizational structure and to regularize the subsequent relationships. (p. 138)

Several elements of Warren's definition are critical for understanding both communities and organizations as practice arenas. His contention that a system endures through time speaks to social work practitioners who work with groups that are committed to maintaining their communities and are grieving over the loss of what their communities used to be. For example, the physical land and the interactions that occurred on that land may render it sacred to First Nations People. Similarly, an elderly widow who has lived on the same street corner for 60 years may hesitate to move even when increasing crime threatens her physical safety.

In an organizational arena, a systems approach reveals the incredible complexity involved in recognizing multiple groups (e.g., professional staff, clerical staff, management, administration, board, clients, funding sources, neighbors, and others in the community) that have a stake in what the organization does and whom it serves. This theoretical perspective reminds the practitioner that organizations are complex systems embedded in larger community systems, all of which are interacting on a daily basis.

Warren also identifies the structure of internal and external patterns, which he labels vertical and horizontal community linkages. Vertical linkages connect community units (people, groups, organizations) to units outside the community. These linkages are exemplified by human service agencies with headquarters in a different community, by local chapters connected with state and national umbrella organizations, and by public agencies having a central office external to the community from which they receive instruction. The concept of *vertical community* calls attention to the fact that many important decisions may be made by parent organizations outside the boundaries of the local community, and these decisions may or may not be in the best interests of that community. The *horizontal community* is geographically bounded and is represented by many linkages between and among organizations and neighborhoods that are located within the area, and, in most cases, serve the community. For example, the local nursing home may work with the neighborhood school to develop an intergenerational program for residents and children. This effort may also include a local bookstore that provides children's books, a bus driver who provides transportation, and a staff member from the local multigenerational center. These types of collaborative efforts, which are becoming increasingly common, illustrate the importance of the horizontal community as a useful concept. By distinguishing between types of relationships, Warren acknowledges the complex array of possible interactions within the community and with the larger society.

Boundary maintenance is also part of systems theory. Establishing boundaries is critical to system survival. If boundaries become blurred or indistinguishable, the community as a spacial set of relationships or the organization as a distinct entity can become less viable. For example, as congregations in local communities contract with government to provide services to persons in need, the boundaries between what is an agency and what is a ministry can blur. Also, boundaries between long established faith-related nonprofit organizations and congregations within the same faith may begin to overlap in unanticipated ways. Macro practitioners will witness the struggle for boundary maintenance in their work with communities and organizations. For example, residents in a neighborhood that has just altered school-attendance boundaries may face major changes in how they view their community. The annexation of previously unincorporated areas into the city limits may bring protesters to city hall. The reconfiguration of a planning and service area that alters a regional agency's boundaries may mean that clients formerly considered part of one's community will no longer be eligible for services.

Systems theory recognizes the importance of formal groups and organizations. For example, in dealing with child maltreatment, child protection workers, law-enforcement officers, hospital emergency staff, teachers, public prosecutors, and others combine their efforts within a horizontal community to ensure that vulnerable children receive the highest levels of protection possible. However, it is equally important to recognize and acknowledge informal linkages. For example, the social support that a female caregiver of an aged parent receives from other caregivers may not be formalized or highly visible in the community. Yet, this linkage is vital to whether caregivers will be able to continue the caregiving role.

Systems thinking, therefore, is value-based thinking in that what is selected for consideration will determine what is considered important. Since communities are complex, thinking of them as social systems involves balancing a number of variables that are in dynamic interaction.

Systems theory, then, provides a set of assumptions that guide the planned change model in this book. It is important to note that there are multiple approaches to systems theory, some more open to change than others. Building on the work of Burrell and Morgan (1979), Martin and O'Connor (1989) encourage social workers to be aware that there are five analogies used by social scientists to view social systems: (1) mechanical, (2) organismic, (3) morphogenic, (4) factional, and (5) catastrophic (p. 54). Mechanical analogies see social systems as machines; organismic approaches emerged in reaction to this machine-like view. Organismic analogies are grounded in fields such as ecology and biology, and social systems are compared to living organisms. Both mechanical and organismic analogies are fairly conservative in that systems are seen as working toward stability, seeking to reestablish equilibrium, preserving the status quo, and focusing on order over conflict. Critics who argue that systems theory is weak on change and strong on status quo are typically reacting to these analogies of social systems.

However, morphogenic, factional, and catastrophic analogies to social systems assume that conflict is not only inevitable but is to be expected. *Morpho* means "structure" and *genesis* means "change," thus this analogy assumes that social systems (e.g., organizations and communities) can change in fundamental ways. From this perspective, social systems are always changing. A factional analogy views social systems as comprising competing subgroups that are contentious and uncooperative. Finally, a catastrophic analogy sees systems as in continual flux, changing so much that they appear chaotic (Martin & O'Connor, 1989).

Martin and O'Connor (1989) encourage social workers to be aware of the analogies they are using when approaching systems. For example, if a community is viewed as highly factional, attention to creating linkages among groups may be necessary before any planned change can occur. Alternatively, if one's organization is fairly closed and machine-like, attention will be focused on internal operations and the environment may be seen as a threat. This requires a different approach to change because change may not be welcomed.

The planned change model in this book is grounded in systems theory. We assume that social workers will encounter systems of every type—mechanical, organismic, morphogenic, factional, and catastrophic. Some organizations or communities will be more amenable to change than others. Some will be more closed and others more open to conflict. Being able to assess these arenas and their openness to change is central to the planned change process.

Underlying the planned change process is a recognition of the values and ethical dilemmas that occur in macro practice. We now turn to a brief review of these.

Values and Ethical Dilemmas

Values are fundamental to social work practice, and we define *values* as those norms and principles perceived to be important. In some ways, values are similar to theories—they provide a framework for understanding and analyzing situations. Ethics are similar to models—they provide guidelines for practice. One can feel strongly about something, but acting on that feeling involves ethical behavior, which is the operationalization of the value.

Because codes of ethics serve as guidelines for professional practice, it is imperative that students know the content and the limitations of written codes. For example, principle values in the NASW Code of Ethics include (1) service, (2) social justice, (3) dignity and worth of the person, (4) importance of human relationships, (5) integrity, and (6) competence. The NASW Code of Ethics is intended to introduce a perspective that drives practitioners' thinking, that establishes criteria for selecting goals, and that influences how information is interpreted and understood. Regardless of which role the social worker plays—whether it is community organizer, political lobbyist, or direct practitioner—these professional actions are not value free.

In many situations, social work practice presents ethical dilemmas. A dilemma implies that one is faced with a situation that necessitates a choice between equally important values. For example, a social worker who values a child's right to a safe and secure environment must also value the parents' rights to have a say in their child's future. The public housing administrator who values the freedom of a disruptive resident must also value the importance of being responsive to the larger resident community. Inherent in both situations are dilemmas. A choice between equally important values may have to be made where there are no easy or obviously "right and wrong" solutions.

Reamer (1995) notes that, although social workers' views of values and ethics have matured, it would have been difficult in the profession's early years to predict the types of dilemmas contemporary society poses. For example, practitioners may deal with clients who are child molesters, spouse abusers, drug pushers who sell to children, skinheads who commit hate crimes, and a host of other persons who act on values antithetical to social work. Fortunately, the field of professional and applied ethics in social work emerged during the 1970s, and today there is growing literature and energetic dialogue addressing the complex value issues that arise in social work practice (Reamer, 1995, 1998).

Jansson (1999) emphasizes ethical principles that are critical in analyzing policy practice decision making, including beneficence, social justice, and fairness. He also identifies other principles often discussed by ethicists, such as autonomy, freedom, preservation of life, honesty, confidentiality, equality, due process, and societal or collective rights (p. 45). Depending on the ethicist or philosopher one reads, different principles may take precedence. Realizing that many of these have relevance to social work macro practice, we select three principles to illustrate ethical dilemmas that social workers face: autonomy, beneficence, and social justice.

Autonomy. Autonomy is based on self-determination and freedom. It implies that each person should have the right to make his or her own life choices. Concepts such as empowerment are built on the principle of autonomy, implying that power or control over one's life means seizing the opportunity to make one's own decisions. As an example, pro-choice proponents in the abortion controversy advocate for autonomy, a woman's right to choose. This stance conflicts with a number of religious codes arguing the immorality of abortion and stating that rights of the unborn child must be considered as well. Although autonomy may be perceived as individualistic and therefore more relevant to direct-practice situations, one has only to be involved in the heated debate over abortion to realize the ethical dilemma involved in situations where the autonomy of both parties cannot be equally respected.

Beneficence.   Beneficence is based on the concept of doing good for others, as well as not doing harm. This principle tends to be a primary motivator for professionals who work in health and human service settings, reflecting their goal of finding ways to assist others in making life more meaningful.

Beneficence requires that the professional view clients holistically. Jansson (1999) uses examples of a physician who treats a woman's presenting medical problem but does not consider her inability to afford a healthy diet, and an attorney who assists with a divorce but does not consider the financial implications for the divorcee. Beneficence requires that the physician recognize the woman's broader needs and refer her to a food bank or Meals on Wheels program, or that the attorney refer the client to a financial counselor.

Beneficence, then, means that all professionals must consider multiple client needs. This is particularly important for social workers, who are expected to bring a person-in-environment perspective to all their interactions with clients. If social workers fail to perceive clients' broader needs, they have neglected the principle of beneficence.

Social Justice.   Social justice is a complex ethical principle. Ideally, social justice is achieved when there is a fair distribution of society's resources and benefits so that every individual receives a deserved portion. Social work is in the business of distributing and redistributing resources, whether they are as tangible as money and jobs or as intangible as self-efficacy or a sense of self-worth. Undergirding the distribution of resources in society are value considerations that influence the enactment of laws, the enforcement of regulations, and the frameworks used in making policy decisions.

Social justice is a value addressed explicitly in the NASW Code of Ethics. Davis (1995) defines it as follows:

> Social justice is a dynamic goal or condition of democratic societies and includes equitable access to societal institutions, resources, opportunities, rights, goods, services, responsibilities for all groups and individuals without arbitrary limitations based on observed or interpretations of differences in age, color, culture, physical or mental disability, education, gender, income, language, national origin, race, religion or sexual orientation.

Given the vast range of social justice issues encompassed in this definition, it is clear that macro practitioners are constantly facing justice-related dilemmas.

Jansson (1999) points out that social justice is based on equality. Given the many entrenched interests one encounters in local communities, it is likely that social workers will focus their efforts on particularly oppressed target population groups and will always be discovering new inequalities.

Concerns about justice are exacerbated when clients cannot pay for services. As long as clients can pay, professional decision making may not conflict with the larger society because resources do not have to be redistributed. Conceivably, as long as clients can pay for professional services, professions can operate within the market economy. Private practice and fee-for-service agencies conform to this approach. Quality care is exchanged for economic resources, often in the form of third-party payments. The key to this approach is that the client has insurance coverage or access to sufficient personal funds.

This approach breaks down, however, when clients cannot pay. Most social work clients are in problematic circumstances because their income is inadequate to meet their needs and other resources are not available. An AIDS patient may find himself unable to pay for his care at the same time his needs increase because he is fired from his job when news about his disease becomes known. An older woman could avoid institutional care by hiring an in-home caregiver, but despite having considerable lifetime savings, medical expenses from her husband's terminal illness have left her with too few funds to meet her own needs. A youth who has grown up in poverty knows exactly what it means when the model breaks down. For him, a broken model has been a way of life, and he has no expectation nor any reason to strive for a better standard of living.

Health and human service systems are driven by considerations of whether resources are available to pay for (or to subsidize) the services clients need. If resources are not available, the AIDS patient and the older woman may be forced to expend all their own resources before ending up in public institutions, and the minority youth may continue in a cycle of insufficient education, housing, health care, and job opportunities. In this resource-driven system, social workers may have difficulty maintaining a vision of the compassionate community in which mutual support is provided to all those in need. These dilemmas face social workers because the profession is enmeshed in issues of redistribution.

Balancing autonomy, beneficence, and justice demands an analytical approach to decision making and intervention. Inevitably, the macro practitioner will face ethical dilemmas that go beyond the bounds of the Code of Ethics. This requires that he or she have a strong professional identity.

Three Case Examples

Some aspects of social work macro practice that need to be understood by the student and the beginning practitioner can be illustrated by case examples. We selected the following examples because they contain similar themes but focus on different target population groups: children, elderly and disabled persons, and women. As these cases and the workers' thoughts are presented, we encourage the reader to think about how macro-level change might be approached by beginning with a study of the *problem,* the *population,* and the *arena* within which change might take place. We also hope that these examples will illustrate both the systemic nature of social work macro practice and the types of value dilemmas confronting social workers.

Case Example 1: Child Protective Services

Child protective services (CPS) workers have responsibility for dealing with the abuse and neglect of children. When reports of alleged abuse or neglect come to the unit, the CPS worker has the responsibility for investigating the report and making decisions about the disposition of the case. It is a very demanding and emotionally draining area of specialization within the field of social work. One CPS worker several years ago took the time to record the details of a particular case, and also shared with us a list of dilemmas and contradictions he had encountered over the years, in the interest of helping new workers prepare for what they will face as they enter practice.

> **Friday, 10:40 AM**   Supervisor called to inform me about a report of neglect. She felt it should be checked out today because it sounded too serious to be left over the weekend (as agency rules allow with some neglect allegations). According to the neighbor's report, parents have deserted and abandoned three minor children.
> **11:10 AM**   Got in my car and headed for the address on the intake form. I know the neighborhood well. It is the poorest in the city and unsafe at night. A high percentage of families receive some kind of assistance. Homes are run down, streets are littered, any sense of pride has long been abandoned.
> **11:40 AM**   The house at the address given is among the most run-down in a seriously deteriorating neighborhood. It has no front steps, just a cinder block placed in front of the door. Window casings are rotting out for lack of paint. There is no doorbell. I knocked. There was rustling inside, but no answer. I waited and knocked again. I walked around and peered through a window and saw a small child, about three years old I guessed, curled up in a chair. An older girl, about age eight or nine, peeked out from behind a doorway.
> I remembered that the oldest child was named Cindy, so I called out to her. After a bit of conversation I persuaded her to let me in. I quickly recognized that this would not be an ordinary case. A foul smell hit me so hard it made my eyes water. I used a tissue to filter the air. The worst odors were coming from the bathroom and kitchen. The water had evidently been shut off—toilets were not working and garbage was piled up. The kitchen was littered with fast-food containers, possibly retrieved from the dumpsters of nearby shops.
> There were three very frightened children: Cindy, age 9, Scott, age 6, and Melissa, age 3. None would talk.

12:35 PM   I made arrangements to transport them to the shelter and went back to the office to do the paperwork.

2:15 PM   A previous neglect report revealed the following:

Father: Stan, age 27, unemployed, in and out of jail for petty theft, public intoxication, and several other minor offenses. Frequently slept in public parks or homeless shelters. Rarely showed up at home any more. Several police reports of violence against wife and children. Admits paternity for only the oldest child.

Mother: Sarah, age 25. TANF recipient, high school dropout, never employed. Tests performed in connection with one attempt at job training revealed borderline retardation. Child care skills have always been minimal, but there is no previous history of abandonment of children. Whereabouts at this time are unknown.

3:35 PM   Filed the appropriate forms with agency and the police. Dictated case for the record. Children placed at Vista Shelter until a more permanent placement can be arranged.

Over the years as this CPS worker dealt with similar cases, he had kept a running list of the kinds of dilemmas, frustrations, and contradictions he and his colleagues regularly faced. These are excerpts from his list:

1. Abused and neglected children are the saddest victims of all. They brought nothing on themselves, yet their chances of success are extremely limited. Success, to a large extent, correlates with a child's ability to perform in school. A child's performance will be hindered by moving from shelter to foster home to home, changing schools, missing many days, lacking consistent parental support and help, having inadequate clothing and diet, lacking self-esteem, and other barriers. We can predict failure, but we can't seem to do anything to change it. Could a macro-level preventive effort be launched that focuses on success for these children?

2. A disproportionally high percentage of lower socioeconomic status teens get pregnant and drop out of high school, go on welfare, parent poorly, and recycle many of their problems to the next generation. How can we interrupt this pattern? Current programs seem to focus primarily on survival in terms of shelter, food, clothing, and medical care, but do not change the behavior patterns. Can we organize an intensive effort to help young women make informed decisions during this highly vulnerable time in their lives?

3. Lots of people in this wealthy country are worse off than lots of animals in this country. There ought to be minimum standards for food, clothing, housing, and medical care below which no one should be allowed to fall. Governments at all levels claim lack of resources and legislators seem bent on blaming the victims, when it is clearly a matter of priorities. Could we focus attention on this issue by organizing a panel of

experts to establish these types of standards for our community and give them maximum publicity?

4. The corporate sector has reaped enormous benefits from our economic system. Gross national product continues to grow and many corporations are moving from a national to an international market. As a sort of a "return" or "payback" for their success, the corporate sector donates a few dollars to charitable organizations. Rarely do they get involved directly in the habilitation or rehabilitation of human beings, even though they control the means to self-sufficiency and success. If all employable people were somehow tied to a job with benefits, the need for income assistance and human services would be greatly reduced. Perhaps a few community-minded business owners would be willing to experiment with "adopting" families by providing employment, training, and scholarships.

5. Bureaucracy has a tendency to become an end in itself. Its manuals become a way of life for many of its employees. People in severe emotional pain bring their needs to our agency and we look up an answer in the manual and quote it to them. Sometimes all they want is to make contact with a human being, and they are unable to do so in our agency. Can we change this agency to make it more responsive to those it serves even though it is a large bureaucratic organization?

Case Example 2: Case Management with Elderly and Disabled Persons

Case managers work in a variety of public and private settings. They are responsible for screening potential clients, assessing client needs, developing care plans, mobilizing resources to meet identified needs, and monitoring and evaluating services provided. The case manager in this example works for a nonprofit agency in an inner-city neighborhood, where many of her clients have lived all their lives. She is assigned to the home and community-based long-term care unit, and carries a caseload of about 60 elderly and disabled clients. As part of the program evaluation, she was asked to keep a diary of what happened during a typical day. The following are excerpts from her diary.

Wednesday, 7:30 AM   Arrived early to catch up on paperwork. Organized documents from eight cases, including two new care plans and five medical reports.

8:00–8:10 AM   Mrs. Garcia, a 79-year-old woman, called. She was distraught over a letter received from the Social Security office, thinking it meant her benefits would be cut off. Explained that it was a form letter, indicating a routine change, not affecting the amount of her check. Knowing that she is often forgetful and has a hearing problem, made a note to make home visit tomorrow to be certain she understands what was said.

8:10–8:30 AM Met with Jim from In-Home Support Services. Mr. Thomas, a 93-year-old man, had fallen last night and was in Mercy Hospital. Homemaker had found him when she arrived at 7:00 this morning. He is not expected to live. Homemaker is very upset. Called his daughter and will plan to meet her at hospital later this morning.

8:30–9:30 AM Staff meeting regarding 10 clients discharged from City Hospital with inadequate discharge plans. Discussed how to work better with discharge planners from hospital since this situation continues to be a problem. As I left meeting, another case manager told me that one of my clients, Mrs. Hannibal, had refused to let the home health nurse into her apartment.

9:30–9:45 AM Called Mrs. Hannibal, no answer. Called the lifeline program to meet me at her apartment.

9:45–10:00 AM Drove to Mrs. Hannibal's apartment. No one answered my knock, so got manager to let me in. Mrs. Hannibal had been drinking and was acting paranoid. Threw bottle at me and screamed "No one is going to get me out of here. I'll never go to a home. I'll die first." Worked with lifeline staff to get Mrs. Hannibal calmed down. She is a 67-year-old widow. She goes in and out of the hospital every two months. Has a severe drinking problem.

10:00–11:00 AM Arrived at Mercy Hospital. Met Mr. Thomas's daughter. She was in tears, saying it was all her fault, that if he had been living with her this would have never happened. Talked with her regarding her father's desire to live alone, that this had been his choice. Contacted hospital social worker to work with daughter.

11:15–12:00 AM Back to office. Wrote up visits to Mrs. Hannibal and Mr. Thomas. Called two new referrals and set up appointments to do assessments tomorrow. Received call from Ms. Roman, age 83. She is lonely and wondered when I would be seeing her. Her partner of 40 years died last week and she is crying. Has no family. Assured her I would come see her on Friday.

12:00–12:30 PM Ate lunch with Adult Protective Services (APS) worker. Discussed abusive relationship of Mr. and Mrs. Tan, a couple in their 60s living in public housing. Agreed to work closely with APS regarding this situation.

12:45–2:00 PM Conducted in-home assessment for new client, Ms. Johnson. She was released from the hospital yesterday and is receiving home-delivered meals and in-home nursing. Small house is a mess, roaches everywhere. Needs chore and housekeeping services, but there's a long waiting list. Called and cajoled volunteers at senior center to help her temporarily. Ms. Johnson was too weak to complete full assessment, will come back tomorrow.

2:30–3:30 PM Attended public hearing preceding the planning process for the area agency on aging. Presented written and verbal documentation of problems in working with my caseload. Discussed the need for more flexibility in providing services to disabled clients under age 60. Gave examples of three clients on caseload who are in their 40s and have severe mobility problems.

3:45–4:15 PM   Stopped by Sunnyside Nursing Home to see Mrs. Martinez. Has been my client for five years and was just admitted to Sunnyside. Doesn't know me and seems confused. Checked with facility social worker regarding what medications she is on and agreed to call physician regarding potential drug interactions. Made note to check with local long-term care ombudsman about any complaints against this facility. Also made mental note to check on Mrs. M's disabled daughter who is still in the home and will need supportive services previously provided by her mother.

4:45–5:15 PM   Returned to office, found out Mr. Thomas had died. Called his daughter. Called physician about Mrs. Martinez's medications. He was angry and told me it's none of my business. Received call from home health aide referring client to us. Had to tell her that the client did not qualify for our services, but referred her to a for-profit agency in town. Returned a call about assistive technology that might help several clients with disabilities.

5:00–5:30 PM   Tried to clean up desk. Decided to stop by and check on Mrs. Garcia on my way home.

Just as the CPS worker had kept a running list of the kinds of dilemmas he faced through the years, the case manager had kept a list of her dilemmas as well. In preparation for the public hearing on the area agency on aging, she had updated the list in hopes something could be done to address her ongoing frustrations, particularly about persons with disabilities who were not yet 60 years old. Excerpts from her list follow:

1. So many of the older people I see have had problems all their lives. You can almost tell what's going to happen in their old age by what happens to them as they go through life. Drug and alcohol problems only seem to get worse. If someone had intervened when they began having these problems, it would have been much easier, because the behavior patterns are set by the time I encounter them. I know people can change at any age, but it seems harder when one is under stress or facing hard times. Is there some way we could organize a prevention effort to prepare middle-aged people for their senior years?

2. Although some of our resources can be used to serve any older person in need, most of our funding is tied to income eligibility. Slots for people who aren't destitute are quickly filled and there is a long waiting list. So clients above the income eligibility level are referred to for-profit agencies or to other nonprofits that have sliding fee scales. The irony is that the ones who have set a little money aside are usually the same ones who get left out in the cold. These "notch group" clients can't afford to pay the full cost of services but fall just above our eligibility guidelines. It seems that in our society if you aren't really poor or really rich, you had better hope your health holds out or you'll have nowhere

to turn. Couldn't we organize this group to help each other and advocate for their own needs?

3. I'm concerned about our younger clients who have disabilities. So many of the places that claim to have their best interests at heart are not complying with the Americans with Disabilities Act. Water fountains aren't accessible, elevators are out of order, and ramps are poorly lit at night. I'm constantly reminding people who should know better that these policies are important. The problems caused by noncompliance are very demoralizing to our clients.

4. Working with Ms. Roman has reminded me how insensitive people are when partners die. I know there is new research on same-sex caregiving and resources on gay, lesbian, bisexual, and transgendered persons, but I haven't had time to fully explore these areas. I just know that when Ms. Roman went to the hospital to see her partner before she died last week that she was not treated as a family member and that her relationship was not respected as it should have been. What do I need to know in order to be more sensitive to diverse caregiving situations? How can I better advocate for my clients?

5. I'm learning some revealing things about case management. Case managers attempt to coordinate what is really a nonsystem of services. If we had a real system we wouldn't need to pay people like me and we could put those resources toward client services. Even our professional organizations have bought into it. The National Association of Social Workers and the National Council on Aging have developed guidelines and standards for case management. There is even a journal on case management. We are investing a lot in institutionalizing case management when often it just covers up the real problem—that we don't have a service delivery system in place. Until we get agencies in this community to collaborate in establishing a coordinated and accessible system of services, case management efforts will be of limited use. How can I work toward a more integrated system of care?

6. How does one maintain a client-centered perspective in a cost-obsessive environment? Working closely with health-care organizations has shown me the contrasts between the ideal and the reality of managed care. Ideally, managed care is supposed to view clients as whole people, recognizing that their psycho-social as well as medical needs must be addressed. In reality, many people view managed care simply as a mechanism for containing costs. As a case manager in a managed care environment, it's really hard to explain to higher-ups that case management can be intensive and long term and that it requires balancing advocacy and gatekeeping roles. How can I show administrators the effect that cost decisions have on clients' lives? What kind of documentation can I keep so that decision makers will benefit from what I know about my clients?

7. Old people are not a homogeneous group. There are vulnerable sub-populations that get lost when one talks about "the aged." Most clients in my caseload are women who live alone and are often members of oppressed groups. Because many have been oppressed all their lives, they are practically "invisible" now. How do we familiarize policy-makers with the unique needs of these clients?

Case Example 3: Displaced Homemaker Services

Many communities have designed programs and services to address the special needs of women. One such program targets displaced homemakers—persons who have experienced sudden and often traumatic change in their lives through separation, divorce, or widowhood. Having devoted their time to homemaking, they often encounter emotional and financial distress when their relationships change.

A social worker was hired by a coalition of community groups interested in women's issues. This coalition was housed in a community center dedicated to grass-roots organizing and getting people involved in strengthening their communities. Her task was to assess the status of displaced homemakers within the community and to make recommendations to the coalition. Excerpts from her field notes follow.

Tuesday, 8:00–9:00 AM   Met with representatives from two state agencies to locate data on women in the workforce. Very productive meeting, which resulted in identification of three studies on workforce characteristics. In addition, was referred to two groups that had conducted needs assessments on women's concerns in adjacent communities.

9:30–11:00 AM   Drove to the community center to observe a support group for women experiencing divorce. Group was led by a member of the coalition. Twelve persons attended. Topics discussed were no work experience outside the home and the accompanying economic fears, problems as single parents with sole responsibility for taking care of children, emotional distress and grief over relationship breakup, and lack of marketable skills and/or education needed to locate employment.

This meeting made me aware of how uncertain and vulnerable these women feel. Several of the women had been married for over 20 years. Many emotions were expressed during the meeting. Some women said they were angry; others indicated they felt depressed.

11:30–1:00 PM   Left support group to meet with five representatives from the TANF program. We discussed the results of a recent survey of TANF recipients. Although many of the women interviewed had been separated and divorced after only five years, 20 percent were teen mothers who had never married. We discussed the concept of displaced homemakers and whether the TANF respondents could be described in this way. Certainly many of their needs for marketable skills, education, and money paralleled the needs of the morning's support group. However, the workers felt that they could not be described as displaced homemakers because they had seldom had the opportunity to be in a homemaking role for extended periods of time. This precipitated a long discussion regarding how we should define the target group.

1:30–3:00 PM Drove to the senior citizens center to meet with the widows' support group. They had requested a speaker from the coalition. After my brief presentation, the group discussed its concerns. Of the 20 people present, 5 had worked outside the home all their lives and another 8 had worked outside the home part time. The remaining 7 described themselves as displaced homemakers who had been widowed in their fifties and had experienced severe financial problems when their spouses had died. They encouraged the coalition to focus on preparing women to understand finances and to obtain skills that would make them more marketable.

3:15–4:30 PM Tried to collect my thoughts. Returned several phone calls and began reading the state reports obtained this morning. The reports focused on the menial jobs filled primarily by women, often without adequate benefits.

4:30–6:30 PM Drove across town to a dinner meeting with representatives from the gay, lesbian, bisexual, and transgendered (GLBT) alliance. They indicated that the design of our programs would need to include those lesbian women who were often raising children on their own or with partners. Although some were struggling with financial issues, their primary concerns were around dealing with public attitudes that were often hostile toward their raising their own children.

The dilemmas experienced by this social worker are somewhat different from the previous two case examples. This professional was hired to assess a community situation described to her by members of a coalition. Her direct practice background gave her considerable insight in understanding women's issues, yet her first days on the job required a great deal of reflection. She outlined a number of questions and concerns.

1. Defining a target group or population sounds simple enough, but it isn't always clear. As I met with various community groups I realized that many population groups—young mothers, middle-aged widows, women of divorce at all ages, and lesbian women—were in need of varying degrees of support. The coalition needs to remain open to various groups, but must recognize that with limited resources there are often trade-offs of depth for breadth. Having a sincere commitment to serving all in need does not help to resolve the dilemma. How can we make an informed decision about who is most in need of what we have to offer and how can resources be invested to get the best possible return?

2. Not only is it difficult to define the problem, but there will be continued danger as we analyze the problem. Too often we view women's issues

in a "we-they" context that would really alienate men and some women. Can we frame the problems and issues we confront so that we don't impose dichotomous thinking on the process—as if everyone who doesn't think like us is against us?

3. There are themes that seem to emerge across all the groups. Women keep talking about how devalued they feel and support groups focus on finding one's voice. Why does it take a crisis before we socialize women to find their voices and to value who they are? Should we consider, as one element of this coalition effort, a prevention and early intervention component?

4. Coalition building is essential to community ownership of a problem. The coalition that wants to assess the status of women is composed of community-based women's groups. Where are the men? Many of the powerful leaders and groups in the community are not part of this coalition. What other groups should be involved? How can we build a base that assures broad support from the community?

5. The coalition is housed in the community center, but I can't quite figure out who it is I work for. The coalition has 22 members, ranging from large service provider agencies to small, grassroots community groups. All have their own interests but have agreed to participate in coalition building for a cause. My supervisor is a coalition member who works at the community center, but the entire advisory group for the coalition seems to think I'm its employee. I'm not sure what my role is and how I should relate to the advisory group or to individual coalition members. How do I define my role and the roles of others in this grassroots community effort?

6. In the women I've observed I have seen tremendous strength. Yet we always focus on the weaknesses of their economic and social dependency. Is it possible that helping professionals may see deficits before they see strengths? How can we develop the strengths of women in this community and build leadership in spite of the fact that some community members are not encouraging women to assume leadership roles?

Surviving the Dilemmas

We have presented these rather lengthy scenarios and the accompanying observations of the workers in an attempt to characterize the kinds of issues and problems social workers face almost every day. The nature of a capitalist economy is that some people are able to compete and to succeed while others are not. For the most part, social workers deal with those who are not able to care for at least a part of their own needs. It should be clear by this time that direct-practice interventions alone cannot address large-scale community problems. Social workers must also master the skills involved in organizing people who may want change and have good intentions but need coordination and direction. Faced with these contrasts, Sherman and Wenocur (1983) say that a practitioner has a number of options. We agree that certain choices are available and we categorize them as follows:

1. *Burn out and leave.* Frustrated and burned-out practitioners may decide to leave the organization in which they work or to leave social work altogether. Unable or unwilling to continue to deal with the ambiguities inherent in their professional practice, leaving becomes their most viable option. For some persons, this is an appropriate way to look for new challenges and to recognize when it is no longer productive to remain in a situation.

2. *Burn out and stay.* Some practitioners may burn out but remain on the job. Social workers can get caught in believing that they are working at impossible jobs. They stay in the system and feel powerless, accepting that they, too, are victims of the things they cannot control. They may do the basics of what has to be done with clients and ignore the larger issues, which means that they accept organizational norms and relinquish the advocacy role. This is a tempting option because taking on the larger issues can add many hours of work to an already busy week for what often seems like an impossible task. The profession, then, ceases to be a calling and becomes "just a job."

3. *Develop tunnel vision.* Even social workers who are not burned out may develop a sort of tunnel vision. These practitioners may remain very committed to clients but choose to ignore conflict or to engage certain issues by focusing on a narrow area of expertise or assuming a set of responsibilities that establishes an independent base of power within the organization. Although this is similar to option 2, the difference is that the social worker remains committed to clients as individuals. They acknowledge the problems and concerns that arise, but typically stay out of the central life of the organization and community. Thus, they do keep a client-centered focus, but are not active in addressing broader-scale change.

4. *Channel energies elsewhere.* Some social workers become activists, joining as many organizations and efforts as time and energy will allow. Rejecting the norms of what are viewed as flawed organizations, these persons try to effect systemic change through any means possible. Adopting an independent stance from the organization in which he or she works, the social worker quickly becomes a maverick or "house radical." Often, these persons become labeled as uncooperative and immature, losing credibility as they fight for change. Yet they can also be a reminder of the broader issues, even to colleagues who are frustrated by their attitudes.

5. *Initiate change.* Together with concerned colleagues, clients, and citizens, practitioners can apply professional knowledge and skill toward a systematic change effort designed to resolve at least a part of a problem and, hopefully, work toward its reduction and eventual elimination. This is an approach that

can be taken by social workers who are committed to clients, community, career, and profession. Together with colleagues, workers form committees and task forces with the intent of changing organizational and community problems. Initiating feasible change means that the social worker must be selective, recognizing that not every problem is solvable and that choices must be made as to which will be addressed. Working toward change calls for sound judgment and discretion. To their activist colleagues, these social workers may seem guilty of focusing on incremental change to the neglect of larger issues.

Much of the work done by social workers who seek to bring about change is what we refer to as macro practice, and it is carried out with widely varying degrees of skill. The purpose of this book is to present a theoretical base and a practice model designed to assist the professional social worker in bringing about change in organizations and communities. Not only do we encourage readers to become change agents within the organizations and communities in which they will work but we also believe that the value base of social work demands it. We believe, too, that surviving the dilemmas requires a strong professional identity. We now turn to an exploration of what that means.

Professional Identity

Lengthy lists of characteristics have been proposed to describe a *profession*. Gustafson (1982) identifies three principal characteristics common to all professions: (1) people-oriented purpose, (2) an extensive knowledge base, and (3) mechanisms of control.

First, professions "exist to meet the needs of others" within the larger community (Gustafson, 1982, p. 508). Professions are therefore client oriented and conform to a set of values that encapsulate the community good that is to be served. Activities designed only to serve the political or economic needs of powerful community members, even though they may be carried out by skilled individuals, do not qualify as professional endeavors.

Second, professions require mastery of a large body of theoretical, research-based, and technical knowledge. Professional judgment derives from the ability to skillfully apply knowledge in a workable manner. Gustafson argues that professional practitioners prefer guidelines rather than rules because guidelines offer direction rather than rigid formulation. They allow professionals to exercise discretion and to use their judgment. However, professionals also carry enormous responsibility because what they decide and how they act will affect both their clients and the multiple constituencies previously discussed. Every choice is a value judgment.

Gustafson's third characteristic of professions is that they place many social controls on professional activities. In social work, these controls include the accreditation activities carried out by the Council on Social Work Education (CSWE) to ensure the quality and consistency of degree programs in social work; the sanctioning capacity of the National Association of Social Workers (NASW); the NASW Code of Ethics, which provides basic value guidelines through which professional judgment is applied; and the credentialing and licensing requirements in various states. In short, there are many mechanisms for overseeing what occurs under the rubric of professional practice.

Professional identity, according to Gustafson (1982), is built on the sense of calling that draws individual social workers to professional practice. "A profession without a calling lacks moral and humane roots, loses human sensitivity, and restricts the vision of the purposes of human good that are served" (p. 501). Quality of motivation and an in-depth vision of the needs to be served are the distinguishing characteristics that make a profession a calling (Gustafson, 1982).

Certainly, each practitioner will have a vision of what the social work profession can be. The vision may be as broad as a higher quality of life for all and a better society, and may never be achieved as fully as one would like. Gustafson (1982) and Sullivan (1995) suggest that one major barrier to a shared vision is professional specialization. As the social work profession has developed (and as human service organizations have become larger and more bureaucratized), multiple specialties have emerged. For example, it is not uncommon to have social workers describe themselves as *psychiatric social workers, geriatric specialists, child welfare workers,* and so on. These specialties denote the target populations with whom these practitioners work. Just as common are terms such as *medical social worker* or *behavioral health specialist,* indicating a setting in which these professionals are employed. Terms such as *planner, community organizer, case manager,* and *group worker* describe actual functions performed by social workers. Specialization can lead to tunnel vision, in which one begins to focus on specific areas of expertise to the exclusion of broader concerns.

Bureaucratization can be a barrier to professional vision. As professional organizations have developed and grown, as settings in which social workers function have become multipurpose and diversified in their programs, and as communities have established numerous mechanisms that structure interaction amid units within those communities, it is easy to lose one's professional sense of the broader vision. Sometimes there are so many impediments to instituting change in an organization or community that the change agent becomes frustrated.

Fabricant (1985) discusses the "industrialization" of social work practice, particularly in large public welfare agencies. In his discussion, he argues that social work is losing its aspects of "craft." A craft implies that the person responsible for beginning the professional task continues it until the end. For example, if a social worker provides intake for the client, that same social worker assesses the client, contracts with the client regarding a care plan, and persists in working with the client until the goals of that plan are achieved. This provides both the worker and the client with a sense of continuity, with ownership of the entire process, and with a shared understanding of the desired outcome.

As the nation's health and human service delivery systems have become more and more complex, as new actors enter the arenas, and as professionals specialize, it becomes rare for the practitioner to see an intervention from beginning to end. Many tasks have become standardized and routinized, thus social workers may feel bound by rules rather than directed by flexible guidelines that allow discretion and judgment. These changes can jeopardize the maintenance of a professional vision that transcends individual organizations and communities.

Although there are barriers to achieving an in-depth vision, we believe it is built on a commitment to serve diverse persons within a society in which basic human needs are not always met and that at times actually denies support to some populations. The challenge is to work toward the development of comprehensive, effectiveness-oriented health and human service systems within local communities. This often requires the practitioner to understand situations without accepting "what is," to analyze dilemmas with the full realization that an ethical response is a choice among values, to envision competent and compassionate alternatives to what currently exists, and to skillfully use a macro practice model to change "what is" to "what could be."

In many ways it is this commitment to the understanding and changing of larger systems that defines social work. Sullivan (1995) argues that the very nature of professionalism implies a responsibility to the larger society. "The professions are important because they stand for, and in part actualize, the spirit of vocation. Professionalism promises to link the performance of specific tasks with the larger civic spirit" (p. 10). He goes on to say that professional "integrity is never a given, but always a quest that must be renewed and reshaped over time" (p. 220). Professional integrity means that those persons who call themselves professionals will remember that the center of their practice is always the client. Social work is only one of many helping professions, but its unique contribution is to serve as a constant reminder that people are multidimensional and must be viewed in the context of their environments.

Assumptions about Planned Change

Having examined theories and models, values and ethics, case examples, and professional identity, we end this chapter with a set of assumptions that guide the planned change model in this book. These assumptions will be discussed more fully in future chapters, so we will only briefly describe them here.

Using an Informed Systems Approach

We recognize that there are multiple ways to regard systems, and it is important to carefully assess each arena in which social workers plan to carry out an episode of change. The macro practitioner approaches the need for change with an understanding and expectation that decisions will be based on as complete a set of data and information as time and resources allow. Informed decision making is pursued in a systematic and scholarly manner, utilizing the best available theoretical, research-based, and practice-based knowledge.

Valuing Consumer Input and Participation

Although it may be more time consuming and take more energy to include clients in change processes, the NASW Code of Ethics is a reminder that the dignity and worth of the person and the importance of human relationships are core professional values. This means always looking for client involvement. Finding new and meaningful ways to facilitate consumer as well as citizen participation in organizational and community arenas is an ongoing challenge for the dedicated professional.

Thinking Critically

Fitting problems to solutions is based on thorough analysis. Defining the problem to be changed requires integrating what clients have to say with what is known from scholarly research and practice results. This analytical process is dynamic and interactive, often causing the change agent to reframe the original problem statement. This process is iterative, meaning that new information constantly requires rethinking. But once the problem statement is agreed upon, social workers must ascertain that their interventions make sense in relation to the problem at hand. Interventions often require a creative imagination that goes beyond traditional approaches bound by mechanical and organismic analogies, and that seek more fundamental change.

Identifying Goals and Outcomes

Systems theory implies that there will be goals and outcomes, both of which are important steps in the planned change process. *Goals* are broadly defined aims toward which practitioners guide their efforts. They are usually long term and sometimes idealistic. However, goals provide a vision shared by clients and colleagues—a hope of what can be—and they assist the practitioner in maintaining a focus.

Outcomes are defined as quality-of-life changes in clients' lives, based on the interventions planned by practitioners. Much of the history of social work practice has been focused on process—what the social worker does. Interventions of the future will be driven by outcomes—what change is expected to be achieved by and for the target population as a result of this change effort. Balancing the importance of process and the push for accountability through outcome measurement is part of contemporary practice. It is also key to planned change intervention.

Social workers have the opportunity to make change occur. Based on an understanding of theory, a set of values, and a recognition of one's professional identity, macro social work practice progresses in an informed manner, incorporating clients into the dynamic process, designing interventions to meet well-analyzed problems. Broad goals and specific outcomes provide the focused direction. These assumptions guide the planned change approach in this book.

Summary

In this chapter we have provided the basic foundations on which students can build an understanding of social work macro practice. We defined *macro practice* as professionally guided intervention designed to bring about planned change in organizations and communities, and we began a discussion of the circumstances leading to the need for planned change. A conceptual framework was provided.

We used comments from former students who are now practicing social workers to illustrate how circumstances that are often most important or troubling to social workers are not only client needs but also issues such as the management of their own organizations or resources available within their communities.

Systems theory guides the planned change model that will be elaborated in subsequent chapters. Critics of systems theory have typically focused on mechanistic and organismic analogies in which systems are seen as attempting to preserve the status quo. Yet more dynamic, open systems analogies focus on conflictual, even chaotic, views of how social systems perform. Social workers are encouraged to recognize the diversity among systems approaches and select the appropriate analogy to understand the uniqueness of each organization and community encountered.

The value base of social work is summarized most succinctly in the NASW Code of Ethics, which embodies the profession's orientation to practice. Intervening at any level presents ethical dilemmas that must be faced by the practitioner. In many cases, no right or wrong answer is present, and the appropriate course of action is not at all clear. In such cases, the practitioner's job can be facilitated by analyzing the situation in terms of three or more basic, though sometimes conflicting, ethical principles. *Autonomy* refers to the value ascribed to an individual's right of self-determination. *Beneficence* refers to the value of helping others. *Social justice* is assuring equal access to resources and equitable treatment. Social workers engaged in macro practice may find that their job is one of balancing these values. In micro practice, for example, one must often temper the desire to help (and notions of how best to solve a client's problem) with a recognition of the client's need for personal autonomy. From a macro-practice perspective, social justice considerations may demand that one focuses not on individual helping but on attempts to alter macro systems that fail to distribute resources in a fair manner. These points were reinforced through three case vignettes showing how policies, program structures, resource deficits, and other macro-related criteria have much to do with social workers' ability to be effective in their jobs.

One way that social workers sometimes respond to these realities is to give up fighting against them. This may be done through burning out and leaving the profession, burning out and staying in the profession, using tunnel vision, or redirecting one's energies beyond the employing agency. However, social workers who are skilled in macro practice have another option—to use their understanding of macro systems to bring about needed changes in these systems. The skills are not and should not be limited to those who are working in traditional macro-practice roles such as administration or planning. Instead, they are critical for all social workers to know, including those engaged mostly in micro practice.

Working through these dilemmas aids in the development of a professional identity that incorporates both micro- and macro-practice aspects. Just as the profession must be built on social workers who are committed to making a difference in the lives of individual clients, these same workers must also be committed to making a difference in the systems within which clients live and upon which they depend.

Parts Two through Five of this text will provide a macro practice model to guide social workers in undertaking change processes. But first, Chapter 2 will complete this part of the book by reviewing the historical background of social work macro practice.

DISCUSSION QUESTIONS AND EXERCISES

1. Case Example 1 in this chapter focused on child protective services. The child protective services worker raised a number of questions in his running list of the dilemmas he encountered. How would you respond to the questions he asked:

   - Could a macro-level preventive effort be launched that focuses on success for children such as the three encountered in this case? Why or why not?

   - Could an intensive effort be organized to help young, pregnant women and teen mothers make informed decisions during this highly vulnerable time in their lives? Explain.

   - How could attention be focused on the fact that some people in this country do not have their basic needs met? Would a viable intervention be to organize a panel of experts to establish standards for a community and give maximum publicity to their efforts? Why or why not?

   - How could the social worker in this case change the large bureaucratic organization in which he works to make it more responsive to clients?

2. Case Example 2 examined a case management program designed for elderly and disabled persons. In this case, the social worker raised a number of questions. How would you answer these:

   - How might one organize a prevention effort to prepare middle-aged people for their senior years?

   - Could a group be organized to help clients advocate for their own needs? Explain.

   - How might the implementation of the Americans with Disabilities Act (ADA) be better enforced for disabled clients?

   - What does this social worker need to know about her gay, lesbian, bisexual, and transgendered clients in order to be more sensitive to their diverse caregiving needs? How can she better advocate for them?

   - How could this case manager work toward a more integrated system of care?

   - How does one maintain a client-centered perspective in a cost-obsessive environment? How could a case manager show administrators the effect of cost decisions on clients' lives?

- How can social workers familiarize policymakers with the unique needs of diverse clients?

3. The third case example presented in this chapter examined the work of a newly hired social worker who is trying to assess the status of displaced homemakers in a community. From her field notes, these questions arise:

- How can this social worker make an informed decision about who is most in need? How can resources be invested to get the best possible return?

- How can problems and issues be framed so they do not alienate persons with whom one wants to join in a community change effort?

- Should an element of the coalition's effort be a prevention and early intervention component? Explain.

- What other groups need to be involved in this change effort? How can a broad base of support be assured in this community?

- How does working for a grass-roots coalition differ from being an employee of one agency? How might the social worker go about clarifying roles

and relationships in this community situation?

- How might social workers focus on strengths in this situation? How can strengths of women in this community and their leadership capabilities be used in developing a stronger coalition?

4. For each of the three cases, answer the following questions:

- Do you think this social worker is burned out, has tunnel vision, is channeling his or her energy, and/or initiating change? If you were the social worker in this situation, how would you feel?

- How might systems theory influence the actions of this social worker? Do you think the system in which the social worker is employed can be assessed as mechanical, organismic, morphogenic, factional, or catastrophic, and why?

- What value and ethical dilemmas arise in this situation and how might a social worker handle them?

- How would you describe the professional identity of this social worker? Does this person have vision? Explain.

- Are there assumptions about planned change that would be helpful if used in this situation? Explain.

SUGGESTED READINGS

Austin, M. J., and J. I. Lowe. (1994). *Controversial issues in communities and organizations.* Boston: Allyn and Bacon.

Daley, A. (Ed.). (1998). *Workplace diversity issues and perspectives.* Washington, DC: National Association of Social Workers.

Fauri, D. P., S. P. Wernet, and F. E. Netting (Eds.). (2000). *Cases in social work macro practice.* Boston: Allyn and Bacon.

Foreman, K. (1999). Evolving global structures and the challenges facing international relief and development organizations. *Nonprofit Voluntary Sector Quarterly, 28,* 178–197.

Gibbs, L., and E. Gambrill. (1999). *Critical thinking for social workers: A workbook* (2nd ed.). Thousand Oaks, CA: Pine Forge Press.

Gutiérrez, L. M., and E. A. Lewis. (1999). *Empowering women of color.* New York: Columbia University Press.

Hess, P. M., and E. J. Mullen (Eds.). (1996). *Practitioner-*

researcher partnerships: Building knowledge from, in, and for practice. Washington, DC: National Association of Social Workers Press.

Inglehart, A. P., and R. M. Becerra. (1995). *Social services and the ethnic community.* Boston: Allyn and Bacon.

Kondrat, M. E. (1999). Who is the "self" in self-aware: Professional self-awareness from a critical theory perspective. *Social Service Review, 73,* 451–477.

Lakey, B., G. Lakey, R. Napier, and J. Robinson. (1995). *Grassroots and nonprofit leadership.* Philadelphia: New Society Publishers.

Mayers, R. S., F. Souflee, and D. J. Schoech. (1994). *Dilemmas in human service management: Illustrative case studies.* New York: Springer.

Perlmutter, F. D. (Ed.). (1994). *Women and social change.* Washington, DC: National Association of Social Workers Press.

Schneider, R. L., and L. Lester. (2001). *Social work advocacy.* Belmont, CA: Brooks/Cole.

Tropman, J. E., J. L. Erlich, and J. Rothman. (2002). *Tactics and techniques of community intervention* (4th ed.). Itasca, IL: F. E. Peacock.

REFERENCES

Bricker-Jenkins, M., and N. R. Hooyman. (1986). *Not for women only.* Silver Spring, MD: National Association of Social Workers.

Burrell, G., and G. Morgan. (1979). *Sociological paradigms and organisational analysis.* London: Heineman.

Davis, K. (1995). *Definition of social justice.* Unpublished paper.

Fabricant, M. (1985). The industrialization of social work practice. *Social Work, 30*(5): 389–395.

Gilbert, N., and P. Terrell. (2002). *Dimensions of social welfare policy* (5th ed.). Boston: Allyn and Bacon.

Gustafson, J. M. (1982). Professions as "callings." *Social Service Review, 56*(4): 501–515.

Jansson, B. S. (1999). *Becoming an effective policy advocate: From policy practice to social justice* (3rd ed.). Pacific Grove, CA: Brooks/Cole.

Karger, H. J., and D. Stoesz. (2002). *American social welfare policy: A pluralist approach* (4th ed.). Boston: Allyn and Bacon.

Katz, D., and R. Kahn. (1966). *The social psychology of organizations.* New York: Wiley.

Martin, P. Y., and G. G. O'Connor. (1989). *The social environment: Open systems applications.* New York: Longman.

Popple, P. R., and L. Leighninger. (2001). *The policy-based profession: An introduction to social welfare policy analysis for social workers* (2nd ed.). Boston: Allyn and Bacon.

Reamer, F. G. (1998). *Ethical standards in social work: A critical review of the NASW code of ethics.* Washington, DC: National Association of Social Workers Press.

Reamer, F. G. (1995). *Social work values and ethics.* New York: Columbia University Press.

Rothman, J., J. L. Erlich, and J. E. Tropman. (2001). *Strategies of community intervention* (6th ed.). Itasca, IL: F. E. Peacock.

Sherman, W. R., and S. Wenocur. (1983). Empowering public welfare workers through mutual support. *Social Work, 28*(5): 375–379.

Specht, H., and M. E. Courtney. (1994). *Unfaithful angels.* New York: The Free Press.

Sullivan, W. M. (1995). *Work and integrity: The crisis and promise of professionalism in America.* New York: HarperCollins.

Thompson, J. D. (1967). *Organizations in action.* New York: McGraw-Hill.

Warren, R. L. (1978). *The community in America* (3rd ed.). Chicago: Rand McNally.

2 The Historical Roots of Macro Practice

OVERVIEW

Trends Underlying the Emergence of Social Work Roles

As noted in Chapter 1, social workers carry out their tasks in a complex and rapidly changing society. To understand better the problems and opportunities they face, it is important to understand historical trends that have shaped the development of current social systems, along with forces that will shape how they evolve in the future. A framework for analyzing these influences is provided by Garvin and Cox (2001), who call attention to (1) social conditions, (2) ideological currents, and (3) oppressed populations. We will examine each of these in our review.

Social Conditions

Population Growth and Immigration.   The first U.S. census in 1790 revealed a national population of less than 4 million. By 1900, this number had grown to almost 92 million, and current estimates place the nation's population at about 285 million (U.S. Bureau of the Census, 2002a). The period of fastest growth was in the 1800s, when the nation's population increased by more than one-third every 10 years throughout the first half of the century and, despite the death and destruction of the Civil War, continued to grow by more than 25 percent per decade during the century's second half. The rate of growth moderated after 1900, with increases diminishing to about 11 percent per decade since 1960. Still, in raw numbers, the nation continues to add about 25 million people to its population every 10 years.

Immigration has always been a critical element in population growth in the United States. One of the first great waves of immigrants occurred in the 1840s. To the East Coast came Irish and German immigrants fleeing famine and political upheaval, while to the West Coast came Chinese workers seeking employment during the California gold rush. Successive waves followed from Southern and Eastern Europe as well as Asia, reaching a peak during 1900 to 1910 when immigrants totaled over six million and accounted for almost 40 percent of the nation's population growth. Though arrivals slowed after 1920, the proportion of population growth accounted for by immigration has again risen. For example, in 1970, there were 9.6 million foreign-born persons in the population, whereas by 2000, the number had almost tripled to 28.4 million. This means that at present about 10 percent of individuals in the United States were born outside its boundaries. Mexico is the most common external birth country, accounting for roughly 25 percent of the total, and the next three most frequent countries of origin—China, India, and Korea—are all Asian nations (Schmidley, 2001).

Industrialization.   Accompanying the country's population growth was a rapid shift toward industrialization of its economy. Axinn and Stern (2001) use the production of cotton in the South to illustrate the effects of this shift. Total cotton production was only 6,000 bales the year before the invention of the cotton gin in 1793, after which it grew to 73,000 bales by 1800 and to almost 4,000,000 bales near the start of the Civil War in 1860. In less than 70 years, mechanization helped to effect an almost 700-fold increase in production. This type of dramatic change transformed working life throughout the country. In 1820, for example, nearly 3 of every 4 workers in the nation were employed in agriculture, whereas today only 1 in 250 labor-force members works in the combined areas of farming, fishing, and forestry. Instead, the largest single occupational category now is "Office and Administrative Support," which accounts for 23 million workers, or about 1 of every 6 persons in the labor force (U.S. Bureau of Labor Statistics, 2002).

The economic opportunity produced by rapid industrialization was a key enabling factor for the rapid growth of the nation's population. This is because the wealth generated by an expanding industrial economy meant that many more people could be supported than in previous agricultural economies. Trattner (1999) calls particular attention to the vast growth in national wealth that occurred following the Civil War. In just the 40 years between 1860 and 1900, for example, the value of all manufactured products in the country grew sixfold and total investment in industry grew by a factor of 12.

Urbanization. The combination of population growth and industrialization brought about increased urbanization. As recently as 1910, more than half the population still lived in rural areas, whereas by 2000 more than 80 percent lived in urban areas (U.S. Bureau of the Census, 2001a). Community researcher Roland Warren (1978) noted that no U.S. city had a population of 50,000 as of the 1790 census, yet almost 400 such cities existed by 1970. As of the year 2000, this number had grown still further, to a total of 601 cities (U.S. Bureau of the Census, 2001a). Initially, most population growth occurred in the urban core of large industrial cities, whereas more recent increases have taken place in suburbs and medium-sized cities. Still, no city in the United States reached a population of one million until the 1880s. Today, however, almost 6 of every 10 U.S. residents (59 percent) live in the 49 metropolitan areas having populations of one million or more (U.S. Bureau of the Census, 2001a).

Change in Institutional Structures.   Accompanying these trends were fundamental changes in the institutional structure of society, especially the system of organizations that meet people's needs. In the early 1800s, these organizations tended to be few in number, informal, and small in scope (e.g., families, churches, and schools). Engaged primarily in agriculture and living in rural areas, people were mostly self-sufficient and depended on organizations for a limited range of needs. With the advent of industrialization, however, new technologies were linked with advances in methods of organizing, and a new social structure began to emerge. The hallmark of this structure is a complex system of highly specialized organizations designed to meet very specific needs. Such organizations range from accounting firms to computer manufacturers to adoption agencies, and they exemplify the huge diversity and complexity of modern society. Their specialization allows them to do a few tasks very efficiently and in great quantity. However, this makes them dependent on other organizations for resources such as power, raw material, and trained personnel, even if they may not always recognize this dependence.

BOX 2.1

Historical Trends at a Glance

- **Population Growth and Immigration.** From less than 4 million in 1790, the U.S. population reached 285 million in the 2000 census. About 1 in 10 residents in that year were persons who were born outside the United States.
- **Industrialization and Urbanization.** Most Americans 200 years ago were farmers living in rural areas. Now, fewer than one in 250 works in agriculture, 80 percent are urban dwellers, and three-fourths of those live in metropolitan areas of more than one million residents.
- **Institutional Structures.** Although largely self-sufficient when the nation was an agrarian society, Americans now live in a highly interdependent economy and social system. Most workers are extremely specialized, and relatively young professions such as social work have developed in response to the increased complexity of society.

People in today's society benefit enormously from the vast production of these organizations, but like the organizations themselves, they, too, are more specialized in their roles. Instead of learning the range of tasks necessary for basic self-sufficiency, individuals in society now concentrate on learning specific skills that will allow them to carry out specialized functions—such as social work—that usually occur within or are provided by an organization. This allows both individuals and organizations to do particular tasks better and more efficiently, meaning that society as a whole is more productive. But a corollary effect of specialization is that individuals and organizations are no longer self-sufficient, and the level of interdependence within society is greater than ever before. Moreover, when for various reasons individuals cannot meet their needs through the roles they are able to fill, they are much more dependent than in the past on assistance from societal institutions. This is a principal reason for the development of social work as a profession.

Changes in broad social conditions that contributed to the development of social work thus included population growth, industrialization, urbanization, and changes in the institutional structure of society that led to increased specialization and interdependence. The institutional changes were particularly relevant to social work because they most directly influenced the development of services to people in need.

Ideological Currents

Not surprisingly, changes in broad social conditions coincided with considerable ideological change. Garvin and Cox (2001) identify several viewpoints that arose during the late 1800s in response to these conditions. These include Social Darwinism, anticapitalist or "radical" ideologies, and liberalism. In the late 1800s, Herbert Spencer, an English writer, drew comparisons between Charles Darwin's biological theories and social phenomena. Applying the concept of "survival of the fittest," Spencer suggested that persons with wealth and power in society achieve this status because they are more fit than those without such resources. Moreover, he argued, while in the biological world the random appearance of favorable traits leads to the gradual supplanting of less favorable traits, in societies some individuals or groups remain inherently "inferior." Not surprisingly, this philosophy was embraced by many of the wealthy, who used it to contend that little should be done for the poor and dispossessed on the grounds that such help would simply perpetuate societal problems.

Social Darwinism also provided ideological support for the philosophy of manifest destiny, which helped to fuel westward expansion during the latter half of the 1800s. Coined by a democratic politician in 1845, this term described the belief that God had willed the North American continent to the Anglo-Saxon race to build a Utopian world. Such a world would fuse capitalism, Protestantism, and democracy, and in it, Anglo-Saxon peoples were not to dilute their superiority by marrying members of other races (Jansson, 2001).

Partly as a reaction to the racism and classism inherent in these views, but also in response to the growing influence of Karl Marx and other socialist writers, a so-called radical ideology developed. This view is closely associated with the rise of the labor movement, which drew its strength from the appalling workplace conditions facing many industrial laborers at the time. One goal of radical writers and activists was the transfer of industrial control from capitalists to trade unions. But the growing plight of the poor also led to broader organizing efforts designed to mobilize and empower all those in lower socioeconomic classes (Garvin & Cox, 2001).

BOX 2.2

Historical Ideologies, Ideas, and Definitions

- **Social Darwinism.** The belief that income differences between rich and poor are natural and arise because the rich are more fit. A corollary is that services should not be offered to the poor since this would perpetuate the survival of those less fit.
- **Liberalism.** A counterargument (in part) to Social Darwinism contends that, as societies become more complex and individuals less self-sufficient, government must act to ameliorate the problems faced by those less able to cope.
- **Manifest Destiny.** The belief that North America was divinely intended for white Europeans, especially Anglo Saxons, to inhabit and control.
- **Radical Ideology.** A broad term covering the philosophies of union organizers, anticapitalists, social progressives, and others who fought the excesses of the Industrial Revolution and advocated on behalf of laborers, immigrants, and the poor.

Liberalism was a complementary ideology that arose partly as a secular expression of Judeo-Christian values of egalitarianism and social responsibility, which were seen as ways to temper the excesses of laissez-faire economic systems.

In this view, human rights supersede property rights, and society is considered to have a responsibility for promoting the collective good. One of the expressions of liberalism was scientific charity, which advocated "a method of investigation and planned helping, case by case, that would build on and strengthen the informal or natural 'fountains of charity' and not displace or weaken them" (Leiby, 1987, p. 764). This view was to contribute powerfully to the rise of some of the earliest human service agencies—the Charity Organization Societies—in the late 1800s.

Oppressed Populations

New social conditions such as the changing face of the U.S. population and shifts in ideological currents often intensified prejudicial attitudes and discriminatory behavior toward certain groups. As is often the case, these beliefs and actions were commonly directed toward groups already suffering the harshest effects of rapid social change. The following review thus focuses on trends affecting populations whose members would later become important constituents for professional social workers.

Native Americans.   Among First Nations people in the 1800s and early 1900s oppression was literally governmental policy, enacted via war, forcible relocation, deliberate spread of disease, contravention of treaties, and confinement to reservations. The Removal Act of 1830 gave the federal government the right to relocate any native groups living east of the Mississippi River. For many tribes this move meant virtual genocide. Relocation of the Cherokee nation in 1838, for example, led to immense loss of life from disease and exposure, becoming known as the Trail of Tears. Beginning in the 1890s, generations of Native American youth, whose families had previously been forced onto reservations, were required to attend off-reservation boarding schools where they were forbidden the use of their own language and made to "think, act, look and be, in every way possible, like members of white society" (Beane, 1989, p. 38). Although the goal of this policy was to speed assimilation into white culture, the main effect was to damage Native American family life and alienate American Indian youth from their heritage.

Latinos.   More than 100,000 indigenous Spanish-speaking people in the Southwest became part of the United States following the Mexican-American War in 1848. The war had begun primarily as a result of U.S. military incursions into Mexico. The Treaty of Guadalupe Hidalgo that ended it included specific protections regarding property rights and civil liberties for those who became part of the United States. Nonetheless, many of these people were forced from their lands (Griswold del Castillo, 2001). Language was also a common tool of oppression, with Latinos being denied participation in voting and public education because they were not proficient in English. Following the Mexican Revolution in 1910, large waves of Mexican immigrants began to face similar barriers. During the Depression years of the 1930s, unemployment pressures led to large-scale deportations of supposedly illegal residents, as many as half of whom were in fact U.S. citizens (Curiel, 1995).

African Americans.   The Civil War won emancipation from slavery for African Americans, but equal treatment was slow to follow. The Freedmen's Bureau, set up in 1865 to assist the transition of freed slaves, was a rare example of federal involvement in the provision of social welfare services. In its brief, six-year life span, it assisted many former slaves in finding employment or gaining access to education and health care. But more typical of the Reconstruction era was the founding, also in 1865, of the Ku Klux Klan. Its reign of terror in the South lasted almost 100 years, effectively denying many freedoms African Americans had supposedly gained. In the courts, rulings supporting segregationist "Jim Crow" legislation had similar effects. For example, the U.S. Supreme Court's landmark *Plessy v. Ferguson* decision of 1896 upheld the doctrine of "separate but equal" facilities—in this case with regard to public transportation. Trattner (1999) notes that even in the Progressive Era and the New Deal years, social welfare gains had a much greater impact on poverty among white than among black Americans.

Asian Americans.   On the West Coast, Chinese immigrants were often exploited as cheap labor, but when economic conditions changed, they became targets of discrimination and hostility. An example is the 1882 Chinese Exclusion Act, which for more than 60 years outlawed all Chinese immigration to the United States (Garvin & Cox, 2001). Meanwhile, immigration from Japan increased between 1890 and 1907, resulting in changes to California state laws that restricted the ability of Japanese residents to own or even lease property. Finally, in one of the most egregious examples of governmental discrimination by race, hundreds of thousands of Japanese were forcibly relocated to internment camps during the Second World War.

Women.   Although the roots of feminism emerged during the 1800s, most women remained relegated to traditionally subordinate roles. Women's suffrage was identified as a central goal at an early national Women's Rights Convention in 1848. But despite ceaseless efforts by pioneers of women's rights, such as Elizabeth Cady Stanton and Susan B. Anthony, full voting rights for women were not achieved until the ratification of the Nineteenth Amendment to the U.S. Constitution in 1919. Meanwhile, viewed as keepers of the hearth and nurturers of the family, women were placed on a pedestal of romantic idealization that also served as a prison to constrain their ideas and actions (Jansson, 2001).

Persons with Disabilities.   Laws urging charitable and considerate treatment of persons with disabilities date from the Code of Hammurabi and ancient Judeo-Christian writings; in practice, however, many societies have dealt harshly with their disabled members. Even in the relatively enlightened Greek and Roman cultures, accepted practices included infanticide, enslavement, concubinage, and euthanasia (Trattner, 1999). More recent societies have renounced these practices, but their treatment of persons with disabilities has still been affected by long-standing tendencies to view a disability as somehow the fault of the individuals with disabilities or as punishment for unspecified sins. Terms such as *crippled* or *simple minded,* which have only recently faded from common usage, are instructive because (1) they describe disabilities through pejorative terms and (2) they define disability as some form of deficit vis-à-vis others in the population, though research has shown that persons with disabilities do not perceive themselves in terms of deficiencies (Wright, 1988).

In the United States after the Civil War, battlefield injuries were one of the few categories of disabilities receiving public attention. In 1866, Mississippi spent one-fifth of its state funds on artificial limbs for wounded veterans (Ward, 1990), yet at the same time, no public system existed in the state to serve the needs of persons with mental retardation. Even for veterans, available assistance was usually limited and did little to foster independence or integration with the rest of society. Not until the Veterans Rehabilitation Act of 1918 and the Civilian Vocational Rehabilitation Act of 1920 were federal programs established to promote greater participation and self-sufficiency. These were followed by income assistance programs created by the Social Security Act of 1935 (Percy, 1989).

Gay, Lesbian, Bisexual, and Transgendered Persons.   Due to long-standing and widespread persecution, members of the gay and lesbian communities, along with persons of other sexual orientations, have historically been the most hidden of oppressed groups. For centuries, homosexuality was viewed largely through the lens of religious taboos and considered sinful behavior. However, English law, unlike that of many other European countries, made homosexuality a crime as well; as recently as 1816, English sailors were executed for the crime of "buggery" (Marotta, 1981). English legal codes on homosexuality were adopted in the United States, and, though not always enforced, were often used selectively as means of harassment. More recently, drawing in part on theories advanced by Sigmund Freud, gay men, lesbians, and bisexual or transgendered persons were considered mentally ill and could be forcibly subjected to hospitalization or other measures designed to cure their "perversions" (Szasz, 1965).

The Development of Social Work

The oppression of ethnic minorities, women, and sexual minorities predated the development of the social work profession. The profession was thus born into an environment in which social change was needed. The effects of discrimination, ideological shifts, and broad social changes created social pressures that could not be indefinitely ignored, and the first organized efforts to respond to these pressures formed the basis for the creation of social work. Among such efforts were the Charity Organization Societies (COS) and the settlement house movement.

Local COS agencies, which began forming in the 1870s, were usually umbrella organizations that coordinated the activities of a wide variety of charities created to deal with the problems of immigrants and rural transplants who were flooding into industrialized northern cities in search of jobs. Ironically, Social Darwinism provided some of the philosophical base of the movement, and the "scientific charity" provided by COS agencies tended to be moralistic and oriented toward persons deemed able to become members of the industrial workforce (Axinn & Stern, 2001). Workers in the COS agencies were often volunteers, especially middle-and upper-class women, who served as "friendly visitors" to poor individuals and families. They tended to share idealistic goals of providing the poor with an opportunity to "better themselves," meaning that they typically viewed poverty as the result of individual failings and targeted their efforts toward reforming individuals rather than systems (Chambers, 1985).

Whereas the COS movement represented one response to human need, settlement houses adopted a different approach. Conditions in the crowded slums and tenement houses of industrial cities in the late 1800s were as dire as any in the nation's history, and the goal of the settlement houses was to attack these problems on a systemic level. This meant an approach that emphasized societal as well as individual and group reform. Many of the workers in settlement houses served as religious missionaries and, like the COS members, did their share of proselytizing and moralizing. Nonetheless, they were also more willing to meet their mostly immigrant constituents on their own grounds and to believe that chasms of class, religion, nationality, and culture could be spanned. In addition, their societal vision tended to be pluralistic—for instance, COS workers feared organized efforts such as the labor movement, but settlement leaders tended to support these endeavors. Members of settlement houses also played prominent roles in the birth of organizations, such as the National Association for the Advancement of Colored People, the Women's Trade Union League, and the American Civil Liberties Union (Brieland, 1987).

Women played a major role in building the foundations of social work in both the COS and settlement house movements. Benevolent work was viewed as compatible with women's nurturing roles in society, and, ironically, even the social change roles played by women were justifiable as "'civic housekeeping' [that] was but an extension of women's concern for family welfare into the public sphere" (Chambers, 1986, p. 13). Also, Trattner (1999) notes that since elected office was effectively denied to most women, an alternative chosen by many was to pursue their interest in social and political issues through involvement in the settlement houses and other efforts.

Early Social Work Education

Service responsibility gradually began to shift from volunteers to paid employees. Charity Organization Society workers emphasized the need for a systematic approach to the work, whereas settlement house workers demanded training on how to effect social change. Both traditions "developed and promoted neighborhood-based research" (Brieland, 1990, p. 135), and this need for education and research fostered the organization of schools of social work. The New York School of Philanthropy began in 1898 as a summer training program of the New York Charity Organization Society, and the Boston School of Social Work was jointly founded by Simmons and Harvard colleges in 1904, also in response to prompting from local COS agencies (Trattner, 1999). Meanwhile, persons involved with the settlement house movement helped establish the Chicago School of Civics and Philanthropy in 1907 (Jansson, 2001).

Accompanying these efforts, a debate ensued over whether the fledgling profession should focus on macro or micro social work models. Macro models, concerned with fundamental social policy issues, demanded an academic curriculum based on social theory and an orientation toward analysis and reform. A parallel movement, represented by Jane Addams, emphasized training for political activism and promoted not only economic reforms but also a pacifist agenda (e.g., advocating peace negotiations instead of military involvement in World War I). In contrast, micro models focused on case-by-case assistance and required that caseworkers learn how to conduct field work.

An important turning point in this debate was the 1915 meeting of the National Conference of Charities and Corrections, described as the "most significant event in the development of the intellectual rationalization for social work as an organized profession" (Austin, 1983, p. 359). Abraham Flexner, a prominent national figure in medical education, was asked to address the issue of whether social work was truly a profession. He argued that social work still lacked key characteristics of a profession and could more appropriately be called a semi-profession, a view that Austin says was typically applied to careers in which women predominated. Flexner's six characteristics of a true profession were (1) professionals operate intellectually with large individual responsibility, (2) they derive their raw material from science and learning, (3) this material is applied practically, (4) an educationally communicable technique exists, (5) there is a tendency toward self-organization or association, and (6) professions become increasingly altruistic in motivation (Austin, 1983).

In a more or less unquestioning response to Flexner's remarks, social workers hurried to adopt these characteristics. In 1917, Mary Richmond published *Social Diagnosis*, which brought one-on-one casework practice to the fore and cast it firmly in a traditional, professional mold. As Reisch and Wenocur (1986) argue, the book "redefined investigation as diagnosis and thereby linked social work to the occupational symbols of the medical and legal professions" (p. 77). The focus on diagnosis was further strengthened by the influence of Freudian psychotherapy, which became the dominant theoretical basis for casework practice throughout the next half-century.

Community Organization and Social Reform

Although inconspicuous and not specifically professionally focused, the development of macro-practice models continued. By 1920, the first social work textbook on community organization had appeared, and at least five more books on the subject were written within the next 10 years. Organizational theorists such as Mary Follett and social work educators such as Eduard Lindeman called attention to the potential role to be played by small primary groups working to strengthen local areas within larger communities (Garvin & Cox, 2001). However, differences had already begun to arise concerning the appropriate focus of macro-level interventions. On one side were those who advocated for grassroots efforts in effecting community change, while on the other were those who argued for greater involvement in policy development and agency-based provision of services.

In addition, a radical social work movement emerged in the mid-1920s that reached a peak in the New Deal Era and was embraced as a part of professional identity in the early 1940s. Unionization efforts in the late 1920s and early 1930s resulted in social workers such as Bertha Capen Reynolds collaborating with other professions to reduce management abuses and ameliorate the effects of workforce reductions and pay cuts. Social workers also marched side by side with residents of urban slums, demanding improved housing conditions. These social workers were mostly young, held low-level positions such as case managers and community action organizers, and did not strongly identify with "professional" social workers (Wagner, 1989).

Effects of the Great Depression

The Great Depression, which began with the stock market crash of 1929, became a watershed event in the history of macro practice. In the four-year period from 1929 to 1933, the gross national product of the United States fell by almost half, and unemployment reached 25 percent. The resulting impoverishment of vast segments of the population raised doubts about traditional notions that poor people were responsible for their own plight and should solve it through personal reform. As Axinn and Stern (2001) note:

> The depression brought forcibly to consciousness the point that one could be poor and unemployed as a result of the malfunctioning of society. The temporary relief programs developed to meet the exigencies of the depression acknowledged the existence of this kind of poverty and of a "new poor." The later permanent programs of the Social Security Act recognized the possibility of inherent societal malfunctioning. (p. 169)

This was the point that settlement leaders and social reformers had long argued, and it was to play an influential role in the development of Franklin D. Roosevelt's New Deal programs. A number of social workers and agency administrators who had supported New Deal-like reforms during Roosevelt's term as governor of New York later assumed key positions in his presidential administration. Harry Hopkins, head of the Federal Emergency Relief Administration (FERA), and Frances Perkins, Secretary of Labor, were the most visible of this community (Jansson 2001).

Social Work and Social Change

In an atmosphere of sweeping change, radical social workers cooperated with mainstream social work leaders during the late 1930s. The journal, *Social Work*

Today, began to pay attention to social work practice, muting somewhat its traditional view that casework constituted a "Band-Aid" approach to client problems. Radical elements within the profession remained identifiable as the left wing in social work, but they were less dramatically differentiated from the liberal social work professional leadership. These shifts were facilitated by the achievement of mutual goals such as the Social Security Act in 1935 and passage of the National Labor Relations Act, which ensured labor's right to organize, strike, and bargain collectively. The latter act marked the beginning of a period of great successes on the part of the labor movement in organizing much of the industrial workforce in the country.

After the mid-1930s, large governmental agencies began to dominate the provision of human services, and the battle of social work roles shifted to this arena. Reisch and Wenocur (1986) note that advocates of the casework model were well placed in many of these organizations and developed job specifications that largely excluded community organizers. However, members of the Rank and File Movement of radical social workers also became involved in the public services arena, and they brought with them an emphasis on large-scale social reform (Wagner, 1989).

These developments in the 1930s and 1940s set the stage for later social movements. Although the 1950s were not a time of great tumult, key events occurred during the decade that were to open the door for considerable social change in the 1960s. A landmark example was the 1954 Supreme Court decision that struck down "separate but equal" policies in public education. Ensuing efforts to overturn school segregation became the foundation of the Civil Rights Movement. Beginning with the Montgomery, Alabama, bus boycott the following year, Martin Luther King, Jr., and the Southern Christian Leadership Conference carried out a campaign of nonviolent resistance through sit-ins and demonstrations. Other groups such as the Congress on Racial Equality (CORE) and the Student Nonviolent Coordinating Committee sponsored "freedom rides" and trained young whites and blacks from elsewhere in the country to assist with organizing efforts in the South. Both the Voting Rights Act of 1964 and the Civil Rights Act of 1965 were passed largely as a result of these efforts.

In response to the struggles of blacks in the South and elsewhere, other social change movements began to address the interests of other traditionally oppressed groups. Cesar Chavez's United Farm Workers began organizing the predominantly Chicano field workers in the Southwest, and the La Raza movement sought to gain political power for Latinos through voter registration drives and other efforts that had worked well in the South. The American Indian Movement (AIM) called attention to governmental policies that had often worsened rather than ameliorated problems in Native American communities. Writings such as Betty Friedan's *The Feminine Mystique* (1963) became a catalyst for the Women's Movement, which sought to extend into the social and economic realms the type of equality women had gained in voting rights through the suffrage movement. Episodes of "gay-bashing" by citizens and police officers in New York led to a disturbance in 1969 called the Stonewall Riot, which became a catalyst for the Gay

Liberation Movement, the first large-scale effort to overcome prejudice and discrimination against homosexuals. Finally, the counterculture movement, student unrest (through groups such as Students for a Democratic Society), and protests against the Vietnam War combined to make the late 1960s the most turbulent period of the century in terms of mass social movements. Participation in these events provided on-the-job training for many community activists who later became professional social work practitioners.

Also in the 1960s, expanded governmental social programs, though sometimes ill-conceived, provided new opportunities for community-level interventions. One stimulus for these changes was renewed awareness of the plight of poor people, brought on in part by books such as Michael Harrington's *The Other America* (1962). John Kennedy's election in 1960 on a platform of social activism also played a part, resulting in programs such as Mobilization for Youth, inner-city delinquency prevention efforts, and the Peace Corps. On an international basis, these efforts helped refine models of community development (Trattner, 1999).

In 1964, Lyndon Johnson's call for a war on poverty led to the passage of a vast array of social welfare programs. These programs left a mixed legacy of results but provided an opportunity for testing macro-practice models. One of the most important examples was the Community Action Program (CAP), part of the Economic Opportunity Act of 1964, which was a keystone of antipoverty legislation. The goal of CAP programs was to achieve better coordination of services among community providers and to facilitate citizen participation in decision making through "maximum feasible participation of the residents of the areas and the members of the groups being served" (U.S. Congress, 1964, p. 9). Accordingly, CAP agencies were created in neighborhoods and communities throughout the country, recruiting residents to serve as board members or as paid employees alongside professionally trained staff members.

In their evaluation and critique of CAP initiatives, Peterson and Greenstone (1977) argue that the design and implementation of the programs largely undermined the first objective of improving coordination of services. However, they also contend that CAP agencies achieved considerable success in their second objective of facilitating citizen participation, particularly in African American communities. In their view, "the contribution of [CAP agencies] to the organizational resources of local black communities was substantial. CAP's distinctive mission began the formation of new political linkages between black Americans and the political order" (pp. 272–274). Other programs were less successful and in some cases resulted in harsh criticisms of social workers and their efforts. Within the field itself, however, accomplishments such as those of the CAP agencies helped to reestablish the importance of macro-practice roles.

Reflecting this trend, the Council on Social Work Education (CSWE) in 1962 recognized community organization as a method of social work practice comparable to group work and casework. In 1963, the Office of Juvenile Delinquency and Youth Development of the U.S. Department of Health, Education, and Welfare funded CSWE to develop a curriculum for training community organizers. Between 1965 and 1969, the number of schools of social work providing training in community organization rose by 37 percent, eventually including virtually every school in the country (Garvin & Cox, 2001). Community organization thus emerged as a legitimate part of social work practice.

Macro Practice in Organizations

The Organizational Context of Social Work

Communities are macro systems in which all social workers interact and for which practice models have evolved. However, communities themselves are composed in large measure of networks of organizations, and it is these organizations that usually hold the direct responsibility for carrying out basic community functions. As such, organizations are a second type of macro system with which social workers must be familiar. One important consideration regarding human service organizations is historical patterns of shifting emphasis between centralization and decentralization of agencies and services.

England's Elizabethan Poor Law of 1601, the first written law establishing a governmental system of services for the poor, adopted a decentralized approach to providing services. Under this law, assistance to the poor was a local function (as was taxation to pay for the assistance), and responsibility for service provision rested with an individual "overseer of the poor." This model was retained more or less intact in the American colonies, and, until the 1800s, relief efforts for the needy remained primarily local and small in scale.

The reformist movement of the early nineteenth century began a slow transition to larger-scale services in the form of state-run asylums for dependent children, the mentally ill, and others. Later, as population, urban concentration, and service needs increased, so did the diversity of both public and private programs. Eventually, it became apparent that some sort of coordinating mechanism was needed for these various efforts. Trattner (1999) notes:

> The situation in Massachusetts was typical. In 1859, the commonwealth had three state mental institutions, a reform school for boys, an industrial school for girls, a hospital, and three almshouses for the state or nonresident poor. In addition, four private charitable institutions—schools for the blind, the deaf and dumb, the feeble-minded, and an eye and ear infirmary—received state aid. Each of these was managed by its own board of trustees. So uncoordinated a system not only increased the cost of operation, but it did not provide for a channel of communication between institutions; a reform in one, then, might not be implemented in the others. The situation obviously called for some method of state supervision. (p. 86)

The result was the creation of what became known as the State Boards of Charities, first in Massachusetts in 1863, then in another 15 states by the mid-1890s. These boards represented the first real involvement of state governments in centralized coordination of welfare services, and they helped establish standards for the administration of human service organizations.

For roughly the next 65 years, much of the development of human service organizations took place in the private sector. The formation of the COS agencies and settlement houses was a partial recognition of the advantages of establishing standard service practices within the framework of a strong organizational base. Efforts toward developing more comprehensive public agency involvement in social welfare services occurred during the Progressive movement in the early 1900s. One example was the creation of the first state public welfare department in Illinois in 1917. Still, the focus remained very much on decentralized service provision. Relatively little growth occurred among human service organizations in the public sector.

It was not until the Great Depression that public organizations for the provision of human services were established on a large scale. Roosevelt's New Deal programs created an infrastructure of organizations at the federal level that became both the foundation of the welfare state and the first large, governmental human service bureaucracies. In addition, a key function of these agencies was to distribute relief funds to various states, and this in turn helped to spur the creation of state-level public welfare organizations. Some programs, such as the Federal Emergency Relief Administration (FERA) and the Work Projects Administration (WPA), were established to respond directly to Depression-era problems and thus were relatively short-lived. Others, such as the Social Security Administration, formed the institutional basis of ongoing federal social welfare programs, and they continue to play major roles. With the creation in 1956 of the Department of Health, Education, and Welfare (now the Department of Health and Human Services), most of these agencies were combined into a single, cabinet-level organization through which federal social welfare programs were administered.

Since its early development, most professional social work practice has been carried out from within some type of organizational base. However, these organizations have varied over time, and the skills needed for effective practice within them have also changed. For example, in the early years of social work education, attention toward models of practice in social work organizations focused primarily on preparing a limited number of macro practitioners to assume roles as administrators of small agencies, usually in the private sector. The goal was to provide skills such as fund raising, working with voluntary boards, and supervising direct-service workers.

With the growth of large public bureaucracies and nationwide networks of affiliated agencies in the private sector, the size and complexity of human service organizations changed. The role of macro practitioners within these organizations was also forced to change. For example, trends such as the growing size of human service organizations, their increased complexity and diversity of services, and changes in standard budgetary policies forced administrators to seek new skills. Lewis (1978) calls particular attention to the growth of concern for fiscal accountability that first became a dominant issue in the late 1960s. He argues that these concerns forced social work administrators to shift from "problem solvers" to "managers." Implicit in this shift was a change in administrative orientation, moving away from external considerations of how best to deal with specific social problems and toward internal considerations such as budgetary compliance, operational efficiency, and, more recently, information management. Considerable concern still exists that if social work administrators do not acquire these skills, leadership of human service agencies will pass to persons from other disciplines who do possess such training.

Concern also arose that administrative decisions in human service agencies were being dominated by operational concerns rather than consideration of client needs. In response, writers such as Rapp and Poertner (1992) began to support a *client-driven* model of administrative practice in which the achievement of desirable outcomes for clients is the primary criterion for decision making. The intent of this model is to view administrative practice in social work as a unique blend of managerial skills combined with broader knowledge of social problems and the means of addressing these problems. More recently, Patti (2000) argues that the role of administrators in human service organizations is to fulfill instrumental tasks common to all managers (budgeting, acquiring resources, hiring and directing personnel, etc.) while retaining an overarching commitment to "the basic mission of the organization, which is to change people's lives and social circumstances" (p. 23).

Contemporary Trends

At the beginning of this chapter, we discussed major historical trends affecting the development of the social work profession. Using the model of Garvin and Cox (2001) these are (1) social conditions, (2) ideological currents, and (3) oppressed populations. In this section, we examine these same areas in terms of their influence on contemporary developments in the field.

Social Conditions

The effects of population growth, industrialization, urbanization, and changes in institutional structures have created a society that is very different today from the early years of the profession. On one hand, these changes have fostered improvements in areas such as health, income, transportation, and others. On the other hand, not all aspects of the transformation are ones to which members of society can easily adjust, and in some cases this has led to new social problems.

Income Inequality.   Many observers are concerned by a growing income gap between high- and low-earning households nationwide. From 1979 to 1998, for example, comprehensive income among households in the wealthiest one-fifth of the population grew by 38.2 percent, whereas in the poorest fifth it grew by 9.8 percent, or about one-fourth as much. Meanwhile, the gap between the very wealthy—the top 5 percent of households—and the poorest fifth widened still faster. In 1979, the top 5 percent of households had earnings 18.6 times as high as households in the bottom fifth; by 1998, their earnings had risen to 32.9 times greater. Adjusting for taxes and inflation, only the top fifth of households had meaningful income increases during this period, while the middle three-fifths stayed largely unchanged and the bottom fifth experienced a net decrease of 12.5 percent. These disparities may produce a variety of problems. For example, some studies have shown that, as compared to others, countries with large income gaps are likely to experience poorer average health, slower economic growth, and greater political and community disengagement of low earners (Bernstein, Mishell, & Brocht, 2000).

Loss of Identification with Community.   In 1978, Roland Warren called attention to what he described as the "community problem," noting that

> discerning Americans have come to the uneasy realization that all is not right with their community living, that undesirable situations appear with growing frequency or intensity and that these are not the adventitious difficulty of one community or another so much as the parts of a general pattern of community living. (p. 14)

More recently, public policy observer Francis Fukuyama (1999) describes what he terms the "Great Disruption," which occurred during a period beginning in the 1960s and extending into the 1990s, within which there was an unexpected growth of social problems in countries within the developed world. Among these were rising disruptions in family systems (i.e., high divorce rates and high rates of births to single or very young mothers), increased crime, deterioration of inner cities, erosion of trust in traditional institutions and organizations, and generalized "weakening of social bonds and common values" (p. 56). The increasing disengagement by some members of society reflects this weakening of bonds. Among its consequences are alienation, antisocial behaviors, and dependency—factors that profoundly affect the overall health of society.

Some of these problems are attributable to the continuation of trends we have already discussed, such as *urbanization.* Although large, complex cities offer many benefits, they also breed large, complex problems, and the very size and complexity of a community can interfere with solving these problems. One casualty that can result from metropolitan growth is a sense of solidarity within the community. Shared views of the common good are possible in small communities because their populations are relatively homogeneous and because each person can be personally acquainted with many or all of the other residents. This sharing is much more difficult in large cities, where the average resident encounters most others simply as blurred faces passing by in vehicles or on busy sidewalks. Too often, identification with the community instead devolves into narrow parochialism based on units such as an apartment building, area of gang turf, ethnic enclave, or neighborhood defined by a particular employer or institution such as a factory, church, or college. The greater the number of these communities within communities, the more difficult it is to identify with the interests of the whole.

Closely tied to these consequences of urbanization is the *loss of geographic relevance* of many communities (Warren, 1978). In small-town America, communities were largely defined in terms of residents' physical proximity, as well as commonalities such as topography, soil conditions, water supply, and other correlates of geographic closeness. People lived in the same town in which they worked, often remained there throughout their lives, and shared with their neighbors both fortune and misfortune (droughts, floods, good and bad harvests, etc.). In contrast, many cities are now so immense that residents in one area may share little with those in another relative to their economic base, political environment, lifestyle, or even climate and terrain. Because geographic, legislative, and social borders often intermingle and evolve, it may be difficult even to define the boundaries of a given community.

Changing Patterns of Affiliation. Robert Putnam (2000), in his intriguingly titled book *Bowling Alone,* describes shifts in the ways Americans associate with each other, especially their decreasing participation in most forms of membership groups—from the neighborhood bridge club to the Eagle's Lodge to local college alumni groups. Citing results of national surveys, he notes that in 1993, as compared to just 20 years earlier, 40 percent fewer respondents reported participating in community activities such as serving as an officer of a club or organization or working for a local political party. Instead, people in current times are most likely to affiliate with what Putnam calls "tertiary associations," where

> the only act of membership consists [of] writing a check. . . . Few ever attend any meetings of such organizations—many never have any meetings at all—and most members are unlikely to ever knowingly encounter any other member. The bond between two members of [for example] the National Wildlife Federation or the National Rifle Association is less like the bond between two members of a gardening club or prayer group and more like the bond between two Yankee fans on opposite coasts. . . . Their ties are to common symbols, common leaders, and perhaps common ideals, but *not* to each other. (p. 52)

Such patterns of affiliation are made possible by formal regulations, expectations, and codes of conduct shared among members of society. Through these, individuals act reasonably toward others not because they know them personally but because they have learned and accepted rules of behavior that maintain basic levels of social cohesiveness. In the absence of such norms, nonlocal affiliations such as those described by Putnam could neither arise nor persist.

Warren (1978) notes that this shift of focus away from local areas toward *extracommunity affiliations* is seen not only in individual associations but in organizations and institutions as well. Consider an automobile assembly plant that may be the major employer and economic engine in a small community. Despite the plant's importance to the local area, its most important ties may be to the home office of its corporate owner in a city far away. A decision to close the plant would likely come from the home office, but it is the community that would bear the principal consequences of the decision. Communities and their institutions are thus highly interdependent, just as are individuals. Loss of control over decisions makes communities and their internal units vulnerable, yet an excessive orientation toward external affiliations can also blind community members to critical local needs.

Changes in Organizations.   In addition to community issues, historical and contemporary developments in the structure of organizations are also important. One parallel between communities and organizations is that both have continued to grow and become more complex. In the organizational realm, this gave rise to the *bureaucratization* of organizational operations. The term *bureaucracy* has taken on a number of mostly negative connotations that, as we shall discuss in Chapter 8, may or may not always be accurate. Here, we refer to bureaucratization as the growth in size and structural complexity of organizations, including those that provide human services. This has been especially true in public agencies, which have generally continued to expand since the New Deal.

Bureaucratic organization is a means of structuring tasks and relationships among organizational members in order to maximize operational efficiency. Specialization of task is one aspect of bureaucratization, and, as we discussed earlier, these sorts of changes coincided with the vast increase in productive capacity of modern industrial organizations. The problem with bureaucracies is that they sometimes become as machine-like as the tools they employ, and the result can be a rigid and dehumanizing environment. This tends to grow more pronounced as the organization gets larger, and vast governmental human service agencies have been among the more notorious examples of the negative aspects of bureaucratic structure.

Partly in response to this problem, *privatization* became a significant trend during the past 25 years. Although the term can be used in many ways, we define privatization as "the deciding, financing, or providing of human services by the private sector to clients for whom the public sector is responsible" (Netting, McMurtry, Kettner, & Jones-McClintic, 1990, p. 34). This trend may be more accurately called "reprivatization" because of its focus on returning to the private sector for responding to human need.

Beginning in the 1960s, recognition of the limitations of government bureaucracies prompted growth in *purchase of service (POS) contracting,* in which public organizations pay private agencies to provide services, often those formally offered by public employees. Driven by a desire to reduce the size of government and to encourage competition and cost control, the amount of money flowing into POS has grown enormously. Kettner and Martin (1987) estimate that $263 million dollars were spent on POS contracts to private, nonprofit agencies in 1973. As of 1997, counting contracts to both private nonprofit and private for-profit agencies, this amount had grown to an estimated $19 billion (DeHoog & Salamon, 2002). Within the POS model, decision-making and financing functions remain governmental responsibilities, but the actual delivery of services is shifted to the private sector. This arrangement can be attractive to service seekers, since going to a local nonprofit agency may be viewed as less stigmatizing than asking for "government relief." However, other trends accompanying the move toward privatization have complicated the community service delivery system.

In the early 1980s, for example, conservative views toward human services, in combination with an economic slowdown, led to decreased public funding and decentralization of decision making. This meant that many nonprofit agencies, which had previously grown larger on public dollars, were suddenly faced with stiff competition for very limited resources. In the health-care field, hospitals facing shortages of patients began diversifying into service areas other than primary health care, such as substance abuse centers, home health, and others. For-profit organizations also began providing human services, and both they and private hospitals especially sought clients who could pay the cost of services from their own resources or through insurance coverage. Meanwhile, nonprofit agencies had traditionally served low-income clients by offsetting their costs with revenues earned from paying clients. But with government funds more scarce and paying clients being siphoned off through competition from hospitals and for-profit providers, the frequent result was cutbacks in services that fell most heavily on clients most in need (McMurtry, Netting, & Kettner, 1991).

The Information Age.   Anyone who has used the Internet to make a purchase, schedule a flight, find a reference, send an email, or visit a chat room knows that in the span of only a few years, computers and information technologies have made dramatic changes in our lives. These changes continue to progress rapidly, and even to accelerate, and they portend still more far-reaching changes in society as well. Futurist Alvin Toffler predicted this trend more than 20 years ago, believing it represents a major new form, or "Third Wave" of human society (1980). In his model, the first type or wave of social organization was the development of agriculture and the formation of communities it supported. The second wave came about as a result of the Industrial Revolution, which contributed to rapid technological change, accelerated population growth, and the appearance of large cities. Each wave was also marked by a change in the most important commodity in society. In the first wave, this was agricultural products; in the second wave, it was manufactured goods; and in the third wave, it is information.

Information as a commodity comes in many forms, one example of which is knowledge, such as that acquired and used by professionals. If a farmer was the emblematic figure of the first wave and a manufacturing worker that of the second, in the third it is professionals, who, as opposed to farmers or factory workers, provide services rather than physical goods. The shift to services is becoming increasingly profound, and in the past 50 years the service sector of the economy has grown far more rapidly than any other. This can be seen in changes over time in the percentage of the gross domestic product (GDP) in the United States accounted for by the three principal economic sectors of agriculture, industry, and services. In 1947, the percentage of GDP accounted for by each of these sectors was, respectively, 10, 34, and 56 percent. By 1999, in contrast, these percentages were 2, 18, and 80 percent (U.S. Department of Commerce, 2002). Four of every five dollars of wealth produced in 1999 thus originated in the service sector, and it is here that the vast majority of new jobs have been created during the past few decades.

As the Information Revolution advances, the character of the workplace is also changing. For example, more and more workers are now staying home for part or all of the work week, carrying out their tasks over the phone via voice links or data lines linking them to national and international networks. Over time, these changes have the potential of dramatically altering the nature of community life. At the very least, such changes are likely to modify traditional commuting patterns, as more workers "go to the office" at home. Farther in the future they may even reverse urbanization trends, contributing to smaller and more decentralized communities.

Social workers' roles will inevitably be affected by these changes. Not only are income differences widening across socioeconomic strata, but in terms of actual numbers of persons some evidence also suggests that the most-affluent and least-affluent segments of society have each grown while the middle class has shrunk (Hacker, 1996). Those with the necessary education and skills to participate in the Information Revolution have tended to prosper, while others face increasing difficulty maintaining their standard of living. In particular, the diminished number and importance of manufacturing and other blue-collar jobs has closed off traditional routes to middle-class prosperity for many low-income workers. This will further complicate the task of social workers who are attempting to assist society's poorest members, because few will have the specialized technical skills necessary to qualify them for better-paying jobs.

The way social workers do their jobs is also changing. They compose reports, write progress notes, exchange messages with others internal and external to the organization, access client records, search for referral options, and perform numerous other functions that define the technical details of their professional roles. Computers are well suited for assisting in these tasks, and they are becoming everyday tools for many social workers. For example, many social workers now carry laptop computers when making home visits to clients, which they can use to take case notes, fill out forms, or administer assessment tools. Some have dial-in access to agency records or bibliographic sources, and upon returning to the office they can upload data into larger information systems used to monitor and evaluate agency services as a whole. Not all observers have welcomed the increasing presence of computers in social work practice (Fabricant, 1985; Harrison, 1992; Chaiklin, 1993), nor do all social workers have equal access to current technologies. Nonetheless, as in virtually all other fields, computers are changing and will continue to change the way social workers do their jobs.

Welfare Reform.   The Personal Responsibility and Work Opportunity Act of 1996 (PRWORA) brought about sweeping changes to public assistance ("welfare") programs. A major goal of the measure was to reduce welfare caseloads, and at least in the short term this has occurred. For example, the number of persons receiving welfare nationwide dropped by more than 56 percent between 1996 and 2001, from 12.2 million to 5.3 million. As a percentage of the total U.S. population, recipients dropped from 5.5 percent in 1993 to 2.1 percent in 2000, the lowest figure since 1964 (U.S. Department of Health and Human Services, 2002).

Critics, however, argue that caseload size is the wrong measure of the impact of PRWORA. For example, public assistance was designed primarily to benefit poor children, yet roughly one in six children in the United States still lives below the poverty line, and "a child is more likely to be poor today than 20 or 30 years ago" (Children's Defense Fund, 2001, p. 3). Among developed countries, the United States continues to have the largest percentage of children living in poverty, along with the second-smallest percentage of those who are raised above the poverty line by public assistance (United Nations Children's Fund, 2000).

Passage of PRWORA was fostered in part by conservative charges that the existing system promoted dependency and a bloated, bureaucratic service system. For example, Newt Gingrich, then Speaker of the U.S. House of Representatives, argued that effective reform required the elimination of "the bureaucracies that are exploiting [welfare children] instead of helping" (Gingrich, 1995). Even critics of PRWORA cited the organization of welfare services as a major source of problems. For example, *Newsweek* columnist Joe Klein wrote,

> The current welfare system is an abomination. It is inflexible, bureaucratic, heart-less. . . . It is a system based on an assumption that has proved mistaken: that social work is a profession. It isn't. It is a *calling.* The work of caring for the poor is best done by inspired individuals and institutions, not career government workers. . . . We have tried to bureaucratize charity and have failed miserably. (1996, p. 45)

As this quote suggests, the development of large organizations to respond to the equally large scale of human services has had the effect of associating the entire profession of social work with large-scale governmental organizations. Although this is an inaccurate perception, it is widely held, and both large organizational structure and the profession as a whole are being cast as failures because social problems such as poverty have not disappeared.

BOX 2.3

Contemporary Trends at a Glance

- **Income Inequality.** Income gaps between wealthy and poor are widening, with the richest one-fifth of families in the United States gaining earning power in the past 20 years and those in the poorest 20 percent having lower earnings. In 1999, the average family in the wealthiest 5 percent of families had 33 times as much annual income as the average family in the poorest 20 percent.
- **Loss of Community Relevance.** Members of society rely less on local relationships and are less closely tied to their communities than in the past. For example, they are less likely to join local membership groups or clubs and more likely to affiliate with national organizations whose other members they may never meet. Also, their

(continued)

organizations and communities are much more affected than in the past by decisions made outside the local area.

- **Organizational Changes.** Social workers are more likely than in the past to work
  in organizations, and these are more likely to have formal, bureaucratic structures.
  They are also more likely to be private rather than public agencies and to depend
  on purchase-of-service contracts.
- **The Information Age.** Computerization of many aspects of society means that the
  most valuable commodity is information. Also, most jobs now involve the production of services rather than food or manufactured goods. Just 1 of every 50 dollars
  in the economy now comes from agriculture, as compared to 4 of every 5 dollars
  that come from services. From computer programming to health care, to a variety
  of social work functions, services are increasingly information driven and computer dependent.
- **Welfare Reform.** Between 1996 (when major federal reforms were passed) and
  2001, the number of welfare recipients dropped by more than half. However, the
  United States continues to have high rates of child poverty, and children are more
  likely to be poor now than in the 1970s or 1980s.

Edwards, Cooke, and Reid (1996) argue that this perception will contribute to
trends such as the privatization movement discussed earlier, and it may also alter
the organizational character of human service agencies:

> This situation will likely accelerate management changes that are already apparent
> in response to the shift of social policy. Downsizing or "right-sizing" is occurring in
> many social services organizations, a process driven by both budget constraints and
> the necessity for organizations to compete on service-product cost. The result is
> smaller and flatter organizations in which fewer people supervise more workers.
> (p. 473)

Indeed, the "devolution revolution" has intensified as the decentralization
of federal and state services has progressed. Also, some managers of human service agencies have been forced to become more concerned with responding to
market forces affecting the stability of their funding than with the furtherance of
social policy goals. This may lead to agencies headed predominantly by administrators trained as professional business executives rather than as professional
social workers.

Ideological Currents

As with the discussion of broad social conditions, Warren's (1978) notion of "the
community problem" also provides a starting point for addressing contemporary
ideological trends. One issue concerns community members' increasing difficulty
in achieving a *sense of community*—the psychological feeling of belonging that
is critical to both individuals and communities. This feeling should arise from
individuals' awareness of the roles they play as useful contributors to the well-

being of the community. In historic times, such roles were easier to perceive, as when a person was perhaps the only grocer, teacher, baker, blacksmith, or midwife in the community. In complex modern communities, however, few people have unique roles, and their activities are often so specialized that their contribution to the community good is seldom apparent either to them or to other community members.

The loss of a sense of community in turn induces feelings of *alienation* from both the community and the larger society. Alienation is often described as a sense of rootlessness, whereby individuals perceive themselves as isolated from social groups with which they might naturally identify. Persons experiencing alienation feel estranged or set apart from social and cultural connections, and they tend to be both less productive and less able to cope with the strains of daily living. Sometimes a vicious circle occurs, in which the complexity and impersonality of community living breeds alienation, and its sufferers in turn feel even less able to manage such complexity. Feelings of separation that are also part of the experience of alienation fall especially hard on traditionally disadvantaged populations and those in the lower end of the income gap. After all, in affluent societies, monetary wealth is often seen as a primary measure of personal worth. Not surprisingly, one consequence of alienation appears to be a rise of self-serving and antisocial behaviors in which concern for community good (in the absence of a clear perception of the community and one's role therein) is subordinated to individual interests. It is this phenomenon that has been labeled by some social commentators and political figures as a breakdown in "civility" in social relationships.

Current writers also wrestle with the mounting tension between *individualism* and *collectivism* (the common good). This issue has gained increasing attention, and it greatly influences the way individuals, communities, and societal responses to social welfare are perceived. One issue involves the question of where decision-making authority for designing programs should reside. As noted earlier, this is being played out in debates concerning whether state and local versus national authorities should control public programs. In general, political conservatives argue that local governments are best situated to discern local needs and tailor appropriate responses. Those with more liberal views argue for broad-scale programs that reduce inequities existing between communities and establish general standards for services or benefits.

BOX 2.4

Contemporary Ideologies, Ideas, and Definitions

- **Sense of Community.** The degree to which community members identify with a community (either local or nonlocal) and feel a part of it.
- **Alienation.** A sense of estrangement from and lack of belongingness to the rest of one's society. The absence of a sense of community is a common aspect of alienation.

(continued)

- **Individualism versus Collectivism.** A continuum along which social policies may differ. Policies tilting toward individualism seek to place minimal constraints on personal freedom and individual volition, whereas policies favoring collectivism assume that some individual options must be limited to better serve the good of all.
- **Social Capital.** A public resource that is reflected in the willingness of individuals to behave in ways that further the cohesiveness of society and the well-being of its members. Social capital tends to be higher where alienation is low but people's sense of community is high.

A relatively recent concept that is gaining attention for its explanatory power is *social capital.* This refers to the store of beliefs, values, and practices that are adhered to by members of society and that contribute to the well-being of all. A society with high social capital, for instance, would be expected to have low crime rates because the majority of persons perceive the benefits that arise from not preying on each other. Like economic capital (e.g., investable funds) or human capital (education or expertise), social capital is a measurable resource that can be considered part of the wealth of a society. As Fukuyama (1999) notes, social capital in the form of "honesty, reciprocity, and the keeping of commitments are not worthwhile just as ethical values; they also have a tangible dollar value and help the groups that practice them to achieve shared ends" (p. 59). The role of social workers can be seen as preserving and promoting social capital, but there is a lack of consensus as to what it is or how its promotion should proceed. For example, both individualism and collectivism can be seen as aspects of social capital, but disagreements occur concerning the proper balance between the two. Also at issue is whether, in the face of social disruptions—such as those described by Fukuyama (1999) or the decline of forms of association noted by Putnam (2000)— the nation's overall store of social capital is rising or ebbing.

Oppressed Populations

Terminology. A valuable contemporary lesson that has emerged in dealing with oppressed populations is the importance of language. Social workers need to recognize that terms used to define and distinguish special populations can be applied adversely in ways that reinforce stereotypes or isolate the members of these groups.

Abramovitz (1991) provides a glossary of terms to increase awareness about "hidden messages conveyed in everyday speech" (p. 380). For example, she discusses the *feminization of poverty* as a phrase that calls attention to the economic concerns of women but may also imply that poverty is a new issue for women. She argues instead for the term *povertization of women,* which better reflects the long history of women's economic disadvantage. Similarly, the sociological term *underclass,* which has been suggested as a replacement for *multiproblem, disadvantaged,* or *hard to reach* poor people, may stigmatize the persons so described (pp. 380–381).

Since the 1950s, growing attention has been given to employing more accurate and less historically laden language when referring to special populations. For example, among ethnic and racial groups, blacks adopted the term *black* as a preferred descriptor in the 1960s and 1970s, supplanting the segregation-linked terms of *Negro* and *colored*. More recently, the term *African American* has become favored. Similarly, *Native American* has been promoted as more appropriate than the term *Indian*, though many native people continue to refer to themselves as *American Indians*, while others prefer *First Nations people*. The term *Latino* is used as a generic expression to represent persons of Latin American ancestry, including Puerto Ricans, Cuban Americans, Mexican Americans (who also use the term *Chicano*), and others. Gutiérrez and Lewis (1999) argue for use of *Latino* or *Latina* over the term *Hispanic,* reasoning that the latter is appropriately applied only to persons with links to Spain. The term *white,* despite its common usage, is poorly defined, yet it remains more broadly applicable than *Anglo* or *Caucasian.*

A study of these issues was conducted as a supplement to the Current Population Survey, a monthly telephone survey conducted on a sample of roughly 60,000 households for the U.S. Bureau of Labor Statistics in 1995. The study was designed to determine the preferences of individuals in various ethnic and racial groups regarding the term they prefer to be used to describe their group. The terms favored by a majority of each group are to be used henceforth in censuses and other government surveys. Results showed that, among blacks, the preferred self-descriptive term is *black,* which was favored by 44 percent of black respondents, followed by *African American* (28 percent) and *Afro-American* (12 percent). Among persons of Hispanic origin, the overwhelming choice was *Hispanic* (58 percent), followed by *of Spanish origin* (12 percent) and *Latino* (11 percent). American Indian respondents showed a moderate preference for the term *American Indian* (50 percent) over *Native American* (37 percent), but the term *First Nations People* was not addressed in the study. Finally, among whites, *white* was greatly preferred (62 percent) over *Caucasian* (17 percent). No information on preferred terms was collected for other ethnic or racial groups.

The term *persons with disabilities* is considered appropriate to refer broadly to individuals having different physical or mental capacities from the norm. Recently, the term *differently abled* has been advocated as a way to avoid categorizing members of this group in terms of their perceived limitations, but this phrase has not yet gained wide usage. With respect to sexuality, *gay* and *lesbian* have been preferred terms for at least the past two decades. Members of both groups were previously referred to as being distinguished by their *sexual preference,* but the term *sexual orientation* is now considered more appropriate because it reflects research indicating that sexuality is more a matter of biology than choice. With respect to gender, some feminist writers have argued for use of the terms *womyn* or *wimin* on the basis that they are less derivative of the word *men,* but as yet these terms have not been adopted into wide usage.

We recognize the importance of language, and it is our intent in this book to reflect that importance in our use of terms. In some instances, where the use of a more traditional term seems more appropriate, we use such terms as *black, white,*

Hispanic, and *American Indian.* In other cases, where newly emerging terms seem appropriate, we will use *African American, Native American,* and *Latino.* Our intention is to be sensitive to the convictions and wishes of as many people within diverse population groups as possible, and to offend as few as possible. We hope the reader is not confused by this mixed use, but instead recognizes it as evidence of the dynamic, evolving nature of modern language.

Relative to earlier periods in U.S. history, the recent past has been marked by significant gains by ethnic and racial groups, women, and gays and lesbians in their struggle to achieve equal standing in society. However, although progress has undoubtedly been made, the struggle has by no means been won. For example, success in reducing societal acceptance of prejudicial attitudes and overt acts of discrimination is tempered by the fact that these attitudes and behaviors have in some cases only become more covert and thus more difficult to confront. Also, hard-won political victories have not always been matched by comparable economic gains, and for some groups conditions have in fact worsened.

Native Americans.   Native Americans clearly benefited in important ways from the social upheavals of the 1960s, with groups such as the American Indian Movement (AIM) helping to focus attention on the troubled relationship between tribal organizations and the federal government. As a result, tribal governments were able to diminish the paternalistic influence of agencies such as the Bureau of Indian Affairs and gain greater autonomy over their own operations. For example, the Indian Child Welfare Act of 1978 gave jurisdiction of child welfare cases to tribal rather than state courts, thus placing tighter controls on practices such as the adoption of Native American children by non-Native American families. Other examples of helpful federal legislation include the 1978 Religious Freedom Act, which benefited members of the Native American Church, and the 1988 Gaming Regulatory Act, which confirmed that tribes may create gambling establishments on reservation land if gaming of any other form is allowed in the state.

Nonetheless, Native Americans have a more distinct cultural heritage than many other ethnic groups, and the struggle to simultaneously preserve this heritage and integrate with the rest of society has taken its toll. Poverty on some rural reservations is as pervasive and severe as anywhere in the country, and much remains to be done to improving economic conditions in these areas. Another major concern is health care. The Indian Health Service, which was created to meet treaty-based federal guarantees for health-care provision to First Nations people, has a record of inconsistent and sometimes dramatically inferior care. It currently faces both budgetary cutbacks and controversy over the extent of its responsibility for providing services to urban as well as reservation-based populations. One reason for the high level of concern about health care is the high rate of diseases, such as diabetes and heart ailments, to which members of some tribal groups may be genetically predisposed. It is for this reason that many tribes see gaming as a path toward economic development and reduced federal dependence. According to the National Indian Gaming Association (2002), for example, gaming on reservations is estimated to have created 300,000 jobs directly or indirectly related to the industry.

Latinos.   The Latino population is growing faster than any other ethnic or racial group in the country, and this trend is expected to continue well into the twenty-first century. By 2050, for example, Latinos are expected to account for 25 percent of the U.S. population, as compared to 9 percent in 1990 (Day, 1996). At present, Latinos tend to be younger than the rest of the population and mostly urban. Not quite two-thirds are of Mexican descent, 14 percent are from Central and South American countries, 13 percent are Puerto Rican in origin, and 5 percent are from Cuba (U.S. Bureau of the Census, 2001b). Population concentrations are in the West and Southwest for Mexican Americans, the Northeast for Puerto Ricans, and the Southeast for Cuban Americans. Based partly on historic inequality and partly on the effect of many recent immigrants still struggling to gain equal economic footing, income among Latinos is lower than for the population as a whole. For example, in 2000, Latino men and Latina women, respectively, had earnings 65.3 and 52.8 percent that of white men, which in each case is the lowest among major ethnic or racial groups (National Committee on Pay Equity, 2002).

Of equal concern are problems of high school dropout rates and persistent language barriers. These related concerns have been the source of considerable controversy. For example, voters in some southwest states have passed "English-only" initiatives designed to restrict official use of Spanish in areas such as public education and voting. The expressed goal of this movement is to force Spanish speakers to learn English and thus integrate more fully into society. Critics charge that it has had the opposite effect, especially among children who have greater difficulty in school because they must learn in an unfamiliar language.

African Americans.   For blacks, victories in the Civil Rights Movement of the 1950s and 1960s meant the rejection of segregationist practices that had prevailed since the Civil War. These gains helped spur electoral successes, particularly on the local level. Within the past 15 years, each of the nation's five most populous cities—New York, Los Angeles, Chicago, Houston, and Philadelphia—have been or are being led by African American mayors. A major goal has been to narrow the gap in economic well-being between African American families and others, and although progress is being made, available indicators suggest that parity remains elusive. For example, in 1999, the percent of African Americans living in poverty reached an all-time low of 23.6 percent, yet this figure is still twice the national average. Similarly, middle-class black families continue to improve economically, as evidenced by figures indicating that "51 percent of African American married-couple families had incomes of $50,000 or more, compared with 60 percent of their white, not Hispanic, counterparts" (U.S. Bureau of the Census, 2001c, p. x).

Unfortunately, from a social work perspective it is also important to consider African Americans who have not shared in these economic gains, especially inner-city poor. In 1999, for example, the median annual income for African American households was $27,910 as compared to $44,366 for non-Hispanic white households (U.S. Bureau of the Census, 2001c). Also troubling are the following statistics from the Children's Defense Fund (1990) concerning the plight of young African American children. Relative to white children, they are:

> Seventy-eight percent more likely to die at birth
> Twice as likely to be a low-birth-weight child
> Three times more likely to be born into a poor family
> Four times more likely to be born to an unmarried mother
> Four times more likely to experience nutritional deficiencies

Black children are also 30 to 50 percent more likely than white children to die of injuries due to fires or household accidents (Leashore, 1995). In addition, death by firearms claims 11 times more young black males than white males aged 15 to 19 years (Children's Defense Fund, 1994).

Events such as the Million Man March by African American men in Washington in 1995 illustrate the variety of efforts made to acknowledge and address these problems. It also points out the increasing emphasis within the black community on addressing problems through strengthening basic institutions such as families and neighborhoods. Efforts to highlight the unique African American heritage through holiday celebrations such as Kwanzaa are also a part of this movement.

Asian Americans. Public attention is often directed toward the educational achievements of Asian American youngsters, who, for example, lead all other ethnic groups in standardized test scores and rates of college completion (National Center for Educational Statistics, 2002). However, this success has sometimes masked problems facing other Asian Americans, particularly Southeast Asian immigrants whose numbers have increased rapidly in the past 25 years. Many are refugees who arrived penniless and without other family members. Once here, they had to cope with "(1) the great disparity between their culture and American society, (2) the lack of an already established ethnic community to help them adjust, and (3) the poor economic conditions in this country at the time of their arrival" (Kitano, 1987, p. 168). As a result, they are now struggling to overcome lingering problems of poverty, poor housing, and racial discrimination.

Women. Women's advancement has been marked by both progress and disappointment. One of the most important gains was the development of women's groups such as the National Organization for Women (NOW), which was organized in the mid-1960s. Basically, NOW and other organizations formed the core of the Women's Movement, which has had considerable success in calling attention to institutional sexism present in employment, government policy, and language. These efforts helped produce tangible gains, such as the narrowing of the difference in earnings between men and women. In the year 2000, women on average earned 73 percent as much as men, a slightly lower figure than the all-time high of 74 percent in 1994 (Bureau of the Census, 2002b). A significant defeat was the failed attempt to add an Equal Rights Amendment to the U.S. Constitution, which was designed to offer protections against gender-based discrimination. The amendment, however, drew vociferous opposition by some women's groups who felt that it would undermine traditional roles. In 1982, it failed due to lack of ratification by a sufficient number of states. Its downfall serves to illustrate that sexual stereotyping exists on the part of both men and women, and its elimination will require continued efforts on a societywide basis.

Persons with Disabilities.   The Rehabilitation Act of 1973 and the subsequent Rehabilitation Act Amendments of 1974 were for persons with disabilities what the Civil Rights Act had been for other groups. They prohibited discrimination against anyone who currently had or had in the past "a physical or mental impairment which substantially limits one or more of such person's major life activities" (Rehabilitation Act of 1973). The act also was the first to require that public facilities be made accessible to people with disabilities, and it laid the groundwork for the expansion of these requirements to all commercial properties through the Americans with Disabilities Act of 1990. Another example of related legislation was the 1975 Education for All Handicapped Children Act, which required children with developmental disabilities to be given access to mainstream public education rather than the traditionally segregated "special education" system. The unifying feature of these and other initiatives was that they had the goal of achieving the fullest possible participation in society by persons with disabilities. They also endeavored to do away with programs, practices, and attitudes that emphasized differences rather than commonalities between disabled persons and the rest of society.

Gay, Lesbian, Bisexual, and Transgendered Persons.   A combination of factors has helped to ease the isolation of and institutional discrimination toward gay men, lesbians, bisexuals, and transgendered (GLBT) persons. One factor has been research results providing evidence that homosexuality is a basic and possibly genetically inherited trait in many people. These results have reduced some of the fear and misunderstanding of gays and lesbians on the part of heterosexuals. Progress has been slower, however, in promoting the general social consensus that sexual orientation, whether innate or developed, should make no difference in how a person is treated. An important advancement has been the increase in political activism on the part of both gays and lesbians. Lesbians, for example, were an integral part of the Women's Movement and have both contributed to and benefited from its achievements. Marotta (1981) notes that many gay males were inspired by the work of black civil rights leaders in the 1950s and 1960s, and this helped lead to the formation of organizations such as the Gay Liberation Front. These organizations have been pointedly visible in their advocacy and lobbying efforts and have helped many men accept and acknowledge their sexual orientation. In addition, gay and lesbian activism has led to the repeal of antihomosexual laws and the passage of ordinances against discrimination based on sexual orientation.

On the other hand, lobbying efforts by GLBT groups have generally been more successful at the local level than at the state and national levels. For example, members of the armed forces remain under the threat of immediate dismissal for identifying themselves as homosexuals. Moreover, nonheterosexuals remain targets for individual acts of discrimination and violence, and in most states they remain subject to arrest and prosecution for consensual sexual behavior. Finally, the AIDS epidemic struck a severe blow to the gay male community, and irrational fear of the disease compounded the problem of discrimination experienced by members of the GLBT population.

Lingering Problems.   Overall, although public acts of discrimination were increasingly condemned during and after the 1960s, prejudicial attitudes toward sexual and ethnic differences and toward women remain. In addition, many overtly discriminatory laws were altered, but blatant acts of discrimination often gave way to more subtle forms. In particular, there is disagreement over whether efforts should be made to redress the consequences of past discrimination, and, if so, what forms this should take. One example is the ongoing and often divisive debate over affirmative action policies governing hiring, admissions, and other actions.

Health and human service programs often reflect the status quo because they address the symptoms of oppression rather than the causes. Professionals frequently assume they know the causes of oppression—and thus the needs of consumers—rather than asking the people they serve. During recent decades, however, efforts such as the social movements and citizen participation activities described in this chapter have taken steps to address the needs of special populations in a more comprehensive and consumer-involved manner. Still, the task for practitioners remains that of finding interventions that are sensitive to the needs of diverse populations.

The Importance of Change

The development of social work macro practice has been accompanied by a number of changes over the years. Indeed, change is one of the few constants in modern life. Nevertheless, change is not always seen as desirable or favorable, and resistance to change occurs as individuals, groups, and organizations attempt to hold on to the familiar. Brager and Holloway (1978) define three types of change that affect health and human service providers: people-focused change, technological change, and structural change.

People-focused change centers on alterations in values, knowledge, and skills. Because it involves the values that underlie our attitudes and perceptions, people-focused change is often very difficult. Yet, in dealing with trends such as oppression, social workers are commonly faced with the need to change people's values, knowledge, and skills.

Technological change refers to alterations in the process of service delivery, those activities and procedures that guide policy and program implementation. Since the days when COS staffers and settlement house workers demanded training to become more systematic in how they approached individuals, groups, and communities, professional technologies have evolved and changed. The current explosion in computers and information technology is another example of this change, and such advances have the capacity to make meaningful improvements in the provision of human services. At the same time, however, these changes tax practitioners' abilities to stay current in their methods, adapt to new service approaches, and apply new technologies in a humane way so that clients are not depersonalized in the process.

Structural change deals with how units within a system relate to one another. Reprivatization of services represents this type of change, in that it has the potential to fundamentally alter the process of meeting the needs of disadvantaged persons in society. However, its success requires that services not be driven solely by the criterion of expending the minimum resources possible. Instead, change must be managed in such a way that effectiveness is maximized at the lowest cost possible.

As can be seen in our description of these three types of change, each raises important professional questions. Should macro practitioners react to trends, attempting to respond as spontaneous changes occur within the environment? Should they seize opportunities to plan community changes to address human need by selecting and utilizing the available tools? Can new structures be created or existing structures be altered to improve a community's ability both to meet individual needs and to reinforce its own cohesiveness? We believe that a planned change model can be successfully applied by social workers to address problems in macro systems. Chapter 3 will introduce the basic elements of such a model by discussing how to identify macro-level problems.

Summary

The need for social workers to be able to understand and practice in macro systems is based on both the history of the social work profession and the society in which it evolved. The effects of immigration, industrialization, and rapid population growth led to concentrations of people in large urban areas, where, for the first time, modern institutional structures (e.g., highly specialized organizations) began to arise. So, too, did modern problems of urban poverty, alienation, loss of a sense of community, and others. The types of service that developed to address these problems were affected by new ideologies. Social Darwinism led to assistance that was often paternalistic and judgmental, but this was tempered by liberalism and even radical ideologies that led to much more proactive helping efforts.

The traditions of the COS agencies, with their emphasis on case-level practice, and the settlement houses, with their more community-oriented efforts, led to a dualistic professional model that continues today. Within this model, social workers must be able to perceive their clients not only as individuals with personal problems but also as members of larger community systems, and they must be prepared to intervene at the community level as well.

Moreover, social workers themselves typically work within formal organizations, and the actions of these organizations also have much to do with how well social workers can do their jobs. Over time, these organizations have tended to become more complex and more bureaucratized, meaning that they may be more efficient, but they may also be more rigid and less focused on client interests. Other organizational trends such as reprivatization and computerization similarly present both risks and opportunities for social workers practicing within them. Understanding these trends and acquiring skills in bringing about planned change within organizations are one approach for reducing the risks and maximizing the opportunities.

A critical point in this chapter was that a meaningful understanding of the development of modern macro systems and of the social work profession requires an awareness of the history of oppressed groups within society. Macro-level systems can either overcome or exacerbate institutionalized oppression, depending on how they are structured. For example, protections supposedly guaranteed to African Americans and Hispanics through the Emancipation Proclamation and the Treaty of Guadalupe Hidalgo were undermined by other economic and social policies that effectively continued the oppression. Complex urban, industrial communities produced vast wealth during the past century, but this was not always shared by ethnic groups segregated (formally or informally) in ghettos or on reservations. Highly bureaucratized organizations became very efficient at processing individual clients in standardized ways, but they did not reliably advance in their ability to meet specific individual needs or to avoid practices that institutionally discriminate against particular groups.

Traditional debates about whether social workers should pursue casework, group work, or community organization seem less important in light of these realities. Macro systems pervade all types of social work practice, and the ability to recognize and redirect their influence is critical to all social workers, regardless of their primary role.

DISCUSSION QUESTIONS AND EXERCISES

1. Americans have traditionally upheld values such as rugged individualism, autonomy, and self-sufficiency. Based on the material in Chapter 2, do you believe Americans today are more autonomous and self-sufficient than in the past, or less so? Support your answer. Is there evidence that other values have been more important to Americans than these? If so, identify and discuss these other values. Be sure to include the concept of *social capital* in your discussion.

2. Do you believe that conditions for traditionally oppressed populations discussed in Chapter 2 are better in current times than in the past? Why? Discuss the implications for social work macro practice of circumstances affecting these populations that still need improvement.

3. Some observers have argued that the professionalization of social work has hurt social work macro practice because of the one-on-one approach to practice that is predominant in most professions. Discuss your beliefs about whether macro practice is helped or hindered by the professionalization of the field.

4. Some writers argue that the goal of members of ethnic minority communities should be to assimilate as fully as possible into the larger culture. Others strongly disagree, arguing that people should not be expected to fit themselves into particular molds and that the maintenance of diversity strengthens society as a whole. Discuss these views in the context of the historical review of traditionally oppressed populations in Chapter 2. Explain how the choice of one or the other might lead you to take very different actions as a social work macro practitioner.

5. Grass-roots community organizations, in which social workers work closely with and on behalf of persons in poor neighborhoods, were probably much more common in the 1960s than today. Based on

the historical review provided in Chapter 2, discuss the forces you believe have contributed to this change.

6. Chapter 2 discusses community problems that have arisen from the changing nature of communities, and it also reviews examples of organizational problems associated with changes in organizations. Then, at the end of the chapter, there is a discussion of how the various changes occurring in society can be grouped into three categories: people-focused change, technological change, and structural change. Discuss whether and how the various historical changes discussed in the chapter can be classified using these categories. Give examples to illustrate your points, and indicate whether the categories are helpful in making sense of societal change.

SUGGESTED READINGS

Abramovitz, M. (1996). *Regulating the lives of women: Social welfare policy from colonial times to the present* (rev. ed.). Boston: South End Press.

Adam, B. D. (1995). *The rise of a gay and lesbian movement*. New York: Twayne Publishers.

Calloway, C. G. (1995). *The American revolution in Indian country: Crisis and diversity in Native American communities*. New York: Cambridge University Press.

Delgado, R. (1999). *When equality ends: Stories about race and resistance*. Boulder, CO: Westview Press.

Elshtain, J. B. (2002). *Jane Addams and the dream of American democracy: A life*. New York: Basic Books.

Fabricant, M., & R. Fisher. (2002). *Settlement houses under siege: The struggle to sustain community organizations in New York City*. New York: Columbia University Press.

Gonzalez, J. (2000). *Harvest of empire: A history of Latinos in America*. New York: Viking.

Hochman, A. (1994). *Everyday acts and small subversions: Women reinventing family, community, and home*. Portland, OR: Eighth Mountain Press.

Horton, J. O. (1993). *Free people of color: Inside the African American community*. Washington, DC: Smithsonian Institution Press.

Inglehart, A. P., and R. M. Becerra. (1995). *Social services and the ethnic community*. Boston: Allyn and Bacon.

Mansbridge, J. J., and A. D. Morris. (2002). *Oppositional consciousness: The subjective roots of social protest*. Chicago: University of Chicago Press.

Rivera, F. G., and J. L. Erlich. (1998). *Community organizing in a diverse society* (3rd. ed.). Boston: Allyn and Bacon.

Simon, B. L. (1994). *The empowerment tradition in American social work: A history*. New York: Columbia University Press.

Specht, H., and M. E. Courtney. (1994). *Unfaithful angels: How social work has abandoned its mission*. New York: The Free Press.

Suro, R. (1998). *Strangers among us: How Latino immigration is transforming America*. New York: Knopf.

Treanor, R. B. (1993). *We overcame: The story of civil rights for disabled people*. Falls Church, VA: Regal Direct.

Wilson, W. J. (1997). *When work disappears: The world of the new urban poor*. New York: Knopf.

Wu, F. H. (2001). *Yellow: Race in America beyond black and white*. New York: Basic Books.

REFERENCES

Abramovitz, M. (1991). Putting an end to double-speak about race, gender, and poverty: An annotated glossary for social workers. *Social Work, 36*(5): 380–384.

Austin, D. M. (1983). The Flexner myth and the history of social work. *Social Service Review, 57*(3): 357–377.

Axinn, J., and M. J. Stern. (2001). *Social welfare: A history of the American response to need* (5th ed.). Boston: Allyn and Bacon.

Beane, S. (1989). Indian child welfare social policy history. In E. Gonzalez-Santin (Ed.), *Defining entry-level competencies for public child welfare workers serving Indian communities*. Tempe: School of Social Work, Arizona State University.

Bernstein, J., L. Mishell, and C. Brocht. (2000). *Briefing paper: Any way you cut it—Income inequality on the rise regardless of how it's measured*. Washington, DC: Economic Policy Institute.

Brager, G., and S. Holloway. (1978). *Changing human service organizations: Politics and practice*. New York: Free Press.

Brieland, D. (1987). Social work practice: History and evolution. *Encyclopedia of social work* (19th ed., vol. 3, pp. 2246–2258). Washington, DC: National Association of Social Workers.

Brieland, D. (1990). The Hull-House tradition and the contemporary social worker: Was Jane Addams really a social worker? *Social Work, 35*(2): 134–138.

Chaiklin, H. (1993). Systems analysts are perilous for social welfare organizations. *Computers in Human Services, 9*: 479–487.

Chambers, C. A. (1985). The historical role of the voluntary sector. In G. A. Tobin (Ed.), *Social planning and human service delivery in the voluntary sector* (pp. 3–28). Westport, CT: Greenwood Press.

Chambers, C. A. (1986). Women in the creation of the profession of social work. *Social Service Review, 60*(1): 3–33.

Children's Defense Fund. (1990). *S.O.S. America: A Children's Defense Fund budget*. Washington, DC: Author.

Children's Defense Fund. (1994). *The state of America's children yearbook, 1994*. Washington, DC: Author.

Children's Defense Fund. (2001). *The state of America's children yearbook, 2001*. Washington, DC: Author.

Curiel, H. (1995). Hispanics: Mexican Americans. *Encyclopedia of social work* (19th ed., vol. 2, pp. 1233–1244). Washington, DC: National Association of Social Workers.

Day, J. C. (1996). *Population projections of the United States by age, race, and Hispanic origin: 1995 to 2050*. Washington, DC: U.S. Bureau of the Census, Current Population Reports, P25-1130, U.S. Government Printing Office.

DeHoog, R. H., and L. M. Salamon. (2002). Purchase-of-service contracting. In L. M. Salamon (Ed.), *The tools of government: A guide to the new governance* (pp. 313–339). New York: Oxford University Press.

Edwards, R. L., P. W. Cooke, and P. N. Reid. (1996). Social work management in an era of diminishing federal responsibility. *Social Work, 41*(5): 468–480.

Fabricant, M. (1985). The industrialization of social work practice. *Social Work, 30*(5): 389–395.

Friedan, B. (1963). *The feminine mystique*. New York: Norton.

Fukuyama, F. (1999). *The great disruption*. New York: Free Press.

Garvin, C. D., and F. M. Cox. (2001). A history of community organizing since the Civil War with special reference to oppressed communities. In J. Rothman, J. L. Erlich, & J. E. Tropman (Eds.), *Strategies of community intervention* (6th ed., pp. 65–100). Itasca, IL: F. E. Peacock.

Gingrich, N. (1995). *To renew America*. New York: HarperCollins.

Griswold del Castillo, R. (2001). *The Treaty of Guadalupe Hidalgo: A legacy of conflict*. Norman: University of Oklahoma Press.

Gutiérrez, L. M., and E. A. Lewis. (1999). *Empowering women of color*. New York: University of Columbia Press.

Hacker, A. (1996). Meet the median family. *Time, 147*(5): 41–43.

Harrington, M. (1962). *The other America: Poverty in the United States*. New York: Macmillan.

Harrison, T. (1992). Is social work being deskilled? A sociological analysis. *Canadian Social Work Review, 9*: 117–128.

Jansson, B. S. (2001). *The reluctant welfare state: American social welfare policies—Past, present, and future* (4th ed.). Belmont, CA: Wadsworth Thomson Learning.

Kettner, P. M., and L. L. Martin. (1987). *Purchase of service contracting*. Newbury Park, CA: Sage.

Kitano, H. H. L. (1987). Asian Americans. *Encyclopedia of social work* (18th ed., vol. 1, pp. 156–171).

Silver Spring, MD: National Association of Social Workers.

Klein, J. (August 12, 1996). Monumental callousness. *Newsweek*, 45.

Leashore, B. R. (1995). African Americans overview. *Encyclopedia of social work* (19th ed., vol. 1, pp. 101–115). Washington, DC: National Association of Social Workers.

Leiby, J. (1987). History of social welfare. *Encyclopedia of social work* (18th ed., vol. 1, pp. 755–777). Silver Spring, MD: National Association of Social Workers.

Lewis, H. (1978). Management in the nonprofit social service organization. In S. Slavin (Ed.), *Social administration: The management of the social services*. New York: Council on Social Work Education.

Marotta, T. (1981). *The politics of homosexuality*. Boston: Houghton Mifflin.

McMurtry, S. L., F. E. Netting, and P. M. Kettner. (1991). How nonprofits adapt to a stringent environment. *Nonprofit Management and Leadership*, 1(3): 235–252.

National Center for Educational Statistics. (2002). *Digest of Education statistics—2001*. Retrieved on July 22, 2002, from http://nces.ed.gov/pubs2002/digest2001/tables/dt134.asp

National Committee on Pay Equity. (2002). *2000 median annual earnings by race and sex*. Retrieved July 18, 2002, from http://www.infoplease.com/ipa/A0197814.html

National Indian Gaming Association. (2002). *Statistics on economic impact of Indian gaming*. Retrieved July 18, 2002, from http://www2.dgsys.com/~niga/stats.html

Netting, F. E., S. L. McMurtry, P. M. Kettner, and S. Jones-McClintic. (1990). Privatization and its impact on nonprofit service providers. *Nonprofit and Voluntary Sector Quarterly*, 19(1): 33–46.

Patti, R. J. (2000). The landscape of social welfare management. In R. J. Patti (Ed.), *The handbook of social welfare management* (pp. 3–25). Thousand Oaks, CA: Sage.

Percy, S. L. (1989). *Disability, civil rights, and public policy*. Tuscaloosa: University of Alabama Press.

Peterson, P. E., and J. D. Greenstone. (1977). The mobilization of low-income communities through community action. In R. H. Haveman (Ed.), *A decade of federal antipoverty programs: Achievements, failures, and lessons*. New York: Academic Press.

Putnam, R. D. (2000). *Bowling alone: The collapse and revival of American community*. New York: Simon & Schuster.

Rapp, C. A., and J. Poertner. (1992). *Social administration: A client-centered approach*. New York: Longman.

Rehabilitation Act of 1973, P.L. 93-112, 87 Stat. 335 (1973).

Reisch, M., and S. Wenocur. (1986). The future of community organization in social work: Social activism and the politics of profession building. *Social Service Review*, 60(1): 70-93.

Richmond, M. (1917). *Social diagnosis*. New York: Russell Sage Foundation.

Schmidley, A. D. (2001). *Foreign-born population in the United States: 2000*. U.S. Census Bureau, Current Population Reports, Series P23-206, Profile of the U.S. Government Printing Office, Washington, DC.

Szasz, T. S. (1965). Legal and moral aspects of homosexuality. In J. Marmor (Ed.), *Sexual inversion: The multiple roots of homosexuality*. New York: Basic Books.

Toffler, A. (1980). *The third wave*. New York: Morrow.

Trattner, W. I. (1999). *From poor law to welfare state: A history of social welfare in America* (6th ed.). New York: Free Press.

United Nations Children's Fund. (2000). *A league table of child poverty in rich nations*. Retrieved July 19, 2002, from www.unicef-icdc.org/publications/pdf/repcard1e.pdf

U.S. Bureau of Labor Statistics. (1995). *A Current Population Survey supplement for testing methods of collecting racial and ethnic information: May 1995*. Washington, DC: U.S. Department of Labor.

U.S. Bureau of Labor Statistics. (2002). *Occupational employment and wages, 2000*. Retrieved June 20, 2002, from www.bls.gov/news.release/ocwage.nr0.htm

U.S. Bureau of the Census. (2000). *Money income in the United States—1999*. Retrieved July 19, 2002, from www.census.gov/prod/2000pubs/p60-209.pdf

U.S. Bureau of the Census. (2001a). *Statistical Abstract of the United States* (121st ed.). Washington DC: U.S. Department of Commerce.

U.S. Bureau of the Census. (2001b). *The Hispanic population of the United States: Population characteristics*. Retrieved July 18, 2002, from www.census.gov/population/socdemo/hispanic/p20-535/p20-535.pdf

U.S. Bureau of the Census. (2001c). *The black population in the United States*. Retrieved July 18,

2002, from www.census.gov/population/www/socdemo/race/black.html

U.S. Bureau of the Census. (2002a). *Current population estimates.* Retrieved July 9, 2002, from http://eire.census.gov/popest/data/national/populartables/table01.php Population Profile of the United States.

U.S. Bureau of the Census. (2002b). *Income 2000.* Retrieved on July 22, 2002, from www.census.gov/hhes/www/income00.html

U.S. Congress. (1964). Act to Mobilize the Human and Financial Resources of the Nation to Combat Poverty in the United States, 188-452, 88th Congress, 2nd Session.

U.S. Department of Commerce, Bureau of Economic Analysis. (2002). *Gross Domestic Product by industry data.* Retrieved July 17, 2002, from www.bea.doc.gov/bea/dn2/gpo.htm

U.S. Department of Health and Human Services, Administration for Children, Youth and Families. (2002). *Temporary assistance for needy families (TANF): Percent of total U.S. population, 1960–1999.* Retrieved on July 19, 2002, from www.acf.hhs.gov/news/stats/6097rf.htm

Wagner, D. (1989). Radical movements in the social services: A theoretical framework. *Social Service Review, 63*(2): 264–284.

Ward, G. C. (1990). *The Civil War: An illustrated history.* New York: Alfred A. Knopf.

Warren, R. L. (1978). *The community in America* (3rd ed.). Chicago: Rand McNally.

Wright, B. A. (1988). Attitudes and the fundamental negative bias: Conditions and corrections. In H. E. Yuker (Ed.), *Attitudes toward persons with disabilities.* New York: Springer.

PART TWO

Understanding Problems and Populations

In Part II, we begin to examine how problems and opportunities can be understood in context. Chapter 3 details the process of analyzing community and organizational problems, and Chapter 4 focuses on understanding populations. Together, the two chapters provide an overview of how social workers prepare for macro-level interventions so that change can occur in organizations and communities.

Understanding Community and Organizational Problems

OVERVIEW

What Is Social Work Practice?

Social work is a profession oriented toward action and change. People who practice social work commit themselves to serve as a resource for those who are struggling with problems or needs. Poor and vulnerable populations often have limited or no control over the changes that need to be made in order to resolve their problems or meet their needs. When people with problems or needs request or are willing to accept help, social work intervention is appropriate.

Problems and needs emerge in many forms. Some are personal or family problems and can be resolved within an individual or family context; others can only be solved by changing something within a neighborhood, an organization, or a community.

The majority of social workers deal with change directly with clients, usually working with individuals, one on one, or with families or small groups. Some practitioners focus on communitywide problems. Others work in the areas of planning, management, and administration of organizations. Regardless of the professional social worker's practice orientation, it is crucial that all social work practitioners support the position that although some problems can be resolved at an individual or family level, others will require intervention that takes on a broader scope, including the need to effect changes in organizations and communities.

This broad focus on arenas for change is one of the factors that makes social work unique among helping professions. When the arena for change is limited solely to casework with individuals and families, an implied statement is being made. The implication is that causal factors associated with the problem or need can be found only in some deficit in the micro system—the client, couple, or family coming for help—or in their abilities to access needed resources. Broadening problem analysis to organizations and communities gives recognition to the possibility or likelihood that in some situations, the "pathology" or causal factors may be identified in the policies and/or practices of macro systems—communities and their various institutions. For example, an organization may fail to provide relevant and needed services, or may provide them in a narrow and discriminatory manner. Or some members of a community may find themselves excluded from participation in decisions that affect them.

Intervention at the organizational or community level is referred to as *macro-level change*. Managing macro-level change requires a good deal of professional knowledge and skill. Poor management and flawed decision making in the change process can result in serious setbacks, sometimes making things worse for those already in need. On the other hand, many very positive changes in organizations and communities have been orchestrated by social workers and others who have carefully planned, designed, and carried out the change process.

It is not unusual for direct practitioners to have clients ask for help with problems that appear to be individual or interpersonal but, upon further probing, turn out to be macro-level problems. A family that loses its primary source of income, is evicted, and finds that there is no low-income housing and a three-month waiting list to get into a homeless shelter represents a symptom of a community problem. Clearly, the family's immediate shelter problem must be resolved, but just as obviously, the communitywide lack of housing and emergency alternatives must be addressed.

A mother may describe the pressures put on her son to join a gang and become involved in the drug trade. The immediate need for this family can perhaps be met by building a support system for the boy designed to keep him in school, in a part-time job, and in constructive activities. However, this individual/family approach alone would not solve the problem for the many other families who must live daily with the same threats. More broadly, micro-level interventions are inefficient (and often ineffective) ways to address macro-level problems. For example, consider the benefits of vaccinating a population against a new flu strain as opposed to treating each individual sufferer after he or she contracts the disease.

The Role of the Social Worker in Macro Practice

Identifying and dealing with organizational and community conditions, problems, and needs presents a complex set of challenges to a social worker. Over the years, the image of the change agent has developed around some of the early social change pioneers—people such as Dorothea Dix and Florence Kelley who advocated for vulnerable populations. Others view change agents as super-organizers—for example, Saul Alinsky, Dr. Martin Luther King, Jr., and Cesar Chavez. Still others may look to high-profile advocates such as Ralph Nader and Jesse Jackson as role models who have had great success in bringing about social change through nationwide organization and exceptional political skill.

In reality, most social workers lack the resources, the media exposure, the charisma, the experience, the following, or the power that these leaders have had available to them. Yet, in spite of seemingly overwhelming challenges, social workers have been effective in bringing about positive changes in organizations and communities.

Effectiveness does not necessarily come from the power of personality or the ability to mobilize thousands to a cause. It comes from careful, thoughtful, and creative planning undertaken by a group committed to change, along with the tenacity to see it through to completion. The change effort may be guided, led, or coordinated by a professional social worker, but those involved will represent a broad range of interests.

Planned change is often incremental and cumulative. One particular episode of change may appear small and insignificant in view of the scope of the problem, but it should be recognized that others committed to positive change may be working on the same problem or need from a different perspective. Recovery from the terrorist attacks of September 11, 2001, is a good example. When faced with the enormity of the task, members of any one group could easily feel that their contributions to recovery were insignificant. But taken together, the work of the cleanup crews, the financial support to families, the church groups that helped clear away dust and debris in the surrounding neighborhoods, the social workers who provided counseling services, and many others all contributed to a renewal of the community and the city that would have been impossible if the tasks had not been shared.

The Social Worker's Entry into an Episode of Macro-Level Change

As noted in Chapter 1, social workers find themselves drawn into episodes of macro practice through a number of different avenues, which we will refer to as

(1) problem/need/opportunity, (2) population, and (3) arena. As the intervention becomes more clearly conceptualized and defined, political and policy contexts must also be taken into consideration. More will be said about these interacting factors later in this book, as the analytical and intervention phases of macro-level change are described. The following examples will illustrate these different points of entry into an episode of change.

- A social worker with a neighborhood service center may discover that among the many families served by the center are five or six single parents who have recently moved from welfare to work but are unable to find affordable child care. Working with this group's *problem or need* (children who need to be cared for while the parent is at work) as her point of entry into the episode of change, the social worker and others develop a plan for child care for the children of these single moms.
- A social worker finds that the housing agency he works for has not been responsive to requests for assistance from people with AIDS. In this instance, the worker's point of entry into the episode of change may be through the *population* of people with AIDS, helping them organize themselves to take their concerns to the city council or funding source.
- A school social worker makes a presentation at a meeting to orient parents to school programs and to meet school personnel. When she asks for questions and discussion, she finds the primary concern of parents is that their children are alone from the time school gets out until the parents get home from work. In this instance, the worker's point of entry into the episode of change may be the community or neighborhoods within the school's boundaries, perhaps beginning with a door-to-door or mailed survey of community residents to assess need. This represents an entry through the community *arena*.

The point is that in the practice of social work, one finds many avenues or points of entry that lead into the use of macro-practice skills. This chapter focuses on understanding *problem/need/opportunity*, one of the three domains through which social workers become involved in community and organizational change. Major tasks to be undertaken in understanding the problem/need/opportunity will be spelled out.

In Chapter 1, Figure 1.1, we presented problem, population, and arena as *separate circles*, each of which must be thoroughly explored in its own right. In other words, in order to be effective in bringing about macro-level change, first the social worker and collaborators must become knowledgeable about (1) the problem, need, or opportunity; (2) the population affected; and (3) the locality or arena where the change will take place.

These three domains can also be thought of as *intersecting circles* in which the most critical knowledge and information is at the points of overlap. Figure 3.1, originally presented in Chapter 1, illustrates how each of these domains has unique as well as overlapping elements.

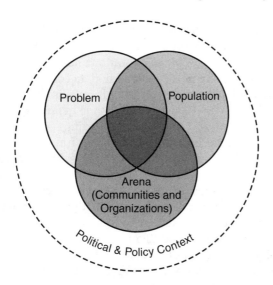

FIGURE 3.1   Understanding Problem, Population, and Arena

In this chapter, we will focus on one of the three circles: understanding the problem/need/opportunity. In following chapters, we will explore the remaining circles: understanding populations and understanding the communities and/or organizations in which macro practice is carried out. This chapter and the next will be used to guide the practitioner into a study of a particular social, community, or organizational problem or need, as well as a study of a selected population. Information gathered and people consulted will depend on the problem(s)/need(s) or opportunities and population(s) selected, and will be drawn from resources other than this book.

Understanding organizations and communities and preparing a plan for intervention requires an understanding of some of the theories and concepts that help to explain structure and function within these domains. Chapters 5, 6, 7, and 8, which focus on communities and organizations, will attempt to identify and describe some of the critical variables that must be understood and addressed in order to bring about change, regardless of the nature of the community or organization.

Guidelines for Planning Change

Initiating an episode of organizational or community change involves three different and distinct types of activities: (1) a brief review of theoretical and research literature on the topic, together with collection of relevant data and information; (2) gathering historical information and opinions from people affected by the problem or need; and (3) skillful organizing and coordinating of the various participants.

For change to be initiated, there must be an individual or small group that recognizes the need for change and is prepared to take action. Within this core group, early decisions must be made about collaboration and sharing of responsibility. Skills are needed in the areas of library research, data collection, interviewing representatives of affected populations, and informed analysis based on findings. Remember that it is likely that the case to be made in favor of change will be taken to a decision-making body and possibly to a funding source. People who accept responsibility for making decisions and allocating funds have a right to expect that those who come before them are knowledgeable, informed, and have done their homework.

Doing one's homework in this instance means taking a disciplined, methodical approach to understanding the problem, the population, the arena, and the political context of the proposed change. Returning to Figure 3.1 as a guide to the study of these domains, we first approached them as separate circles. This means that a social worker might, for example, look first at the problem/need/opportunity and attempt to understand everything he or she can about this domain within the limited time available. In the early phase of the process, data-collection efforts would have two goals—gathering information from local people familiar with the problem or need, and at the same time researching the topic in social work and other relevant literature.

For example, if a local neighborhood has been the site of increased teen violence, it is important to know as much as possible about the phenomenon of violence. What do experts understand about the etiology (cause-and-effect relationships) of violence? What does the research say about the importance of early nurturing experiences? About the need for an identity? About social skills? About previous encounters with authority?

At the same time, if resources are available, other participants can be gathering information from people in the organization or community that is the focus of the change effort. The intent is to understand as much as possible about the phenomenon itself—to explore the entire problem/need/opportunity circle from a scholarly perspective, while at the same time using information from those affected to help rule in or rule out various causal factors and other considerations.

Information on the overlapping areas of problem and population will often be found in the course of this study. While attempting to understand teens, for example, a social worker may come across studies on teen violence. In most cases (but not all), these studies or summaries of existing knowledge about problem and population will be even more valuable than studies of problem alone or population alone. Each new finding is a potentially valuable addition to a body of knowledge that brings the change agent closer to understanding the problem. In this manner, the change agent and others involved in the change effort gradually move toward understanding the problem and population as they currently exist in the local community, though keeping in mind the fact that their understanding will never be fully complete.

Information and knowledge that will be of greatest value to local decision makers will ultimately be that which is found where the three circles in Figure 3.1

intersect. In other words, knowledge of problem, population, and arena overlap will aid in understanding how these domains interact with each other to create the current situation and explain how that situation is unique to this local community.

In summary, the activities undertaken in the study phase of macro-level change include the following:

Problem

Explore relevant literature to:
- conceptualize and define the problem or need
- locate relevant literature on theory related to causes and consequences of the problem
- compile relevant quantitative data and other forms of information

Interview those affected by the problem or need to:
- understand historical development at the local level
- identify major participants and systems

Population

Explore relevant literature to:
- know as much as possible about the population affected
- understand cultures and ethnic groups represented
- understand gender issues

Interview those affected by the problem or need to:
- identify personal perspectives
- understand personal experiences in relation to the problem or need and the attempts to deal with it
- understand how the problem or need is perceived by various groups within the organization or community

Arena

Explore relevant literature to:
- compile demographic and other data on the organization or community
- create useful maps of the community
- compile data on the problem or need and how it has been addressed by the organization or community

Interview those affected by the problem or need to:
- identify past experiences with the organization or community
- establish boundaries for the proposed change
- identify key decision makers and funding sources
- understand the many different perspectives on the etiology of the problem or need

For all three studies (problem/need/opportunity, population, and arena), the core planning team will need to coordinate activities. These will include identifying various roles and responsibilities, assigning individuals according to their abilities, monitoring progress, and dealing with interpersonal, intergroup, and political dynamics.

We are not proposing here an exhaustive exploration that goes on for months or years. There is rarely time or resources for such study, and responding in a timely manner is often critical to success. However, plunging into a proposed solution without doing the necessary homework is equally risky. Our intent in this and the following chapters is to lay out a format for systematic study of each of the three circles in Figure 3.1 (as well as the political context, which will be discussed in Chapters 9 and 10) that can be accomplished within a reasonable amount of time (a few weeks to a few months, depending on the people and the skills involved) with a small core team of perhaps four or five people committed to bringing about needed change (together with others who are willing to carry out specifically assigned tasks).

Understanding Problems and Opportunities

Community political and civic leaders, activists, and others involved are often so anxious to make change happen that they begin at the point of proposing solutions. Increased incidence of drug abuse? Let's hire more police and increase penalties! More and more homeless families on the streets? Let's build a shelter. Increased numbers of teen pregnancies? Let's offer classes on the importance of sexual abstinence until marriage. These overly simplistic "solutions" will inevitably emerge in any episode of change, but it is the responsibility of the social worker in a professionally guided change effort to make certain that a range of alternative perspectives and possible causes is adequately explored before proposing a solution.

There are several reasons for exploring multiple perspectives on a problem. First, leaping to quick solutions without adequate study is the antithesis of professional practice. In one-on-one counseling, for example, telling clients exactly how to solve their problems after only a brief review of the facts violates many ethical and professional principles. Second, quick and easy solutions usually are based on the assumption that the problem in question has one primary cause. In fact, as we will discuss in greater detail later in this chapter, virtually no social problem has only one cause. Many different factors come into play in the development of a social condition, and changing that condition almost always necessitates addressing more than one of these factors.

Consider, for example, a community in which highway deaths due to alcohol have increased 37 percent in the past two years. How might the causes in this case be defined? One group will be convinced that the cause is lack of strict enforcement of existing laws prohibiting driving under the influence of drugs or alcohol. Another group will describe causes as easy availability of alcohol to teenagers. Others will see alcohol abuse as a symptom of increasing stress or family breakdown. These represent just a few of the perspectives that might be introduced in an attempt to understand some of the reasons behind driving under the influence of alcohol or drugs.

This initial analytical work is a very important part of the change process. We propose that change agents proceed with a set of tasks designed to gather as much useful information about the problem as is available. These tasks involve direct contact with those who have experienced the need or problem firsthand, as well as a systematic exploration of theoretical and research literature, data summaries, and perhaps some historical documents. This approach is designed to produce as thorough an understanding of the problem and population as possible in as short a time as possible.

These tasks can and should proceed simultaneously, which is where the coordinating work of the change agent becomes important. Those participating in the change effort who have the best credentials for entering the community or organization for the purpose of interviewing and data collection should be assigned to such tasks. Those who have demonstrated skill in library research and are best able to read and summarize relevant literature should carry out these tasks. Those who work well with data and information should plan to compile the necessary tables and charts. In the end, all these separate efforts will contribute to a clearer understanding of the problem, need, or opportunity and will provide the best chance for a well-designed plan of intervention that leads to a positive solution.

Task 1: Gather Information from Key Informants in the Community or Organization

Understanding a macro-level problem or need in all its complexity requires skillful eliciting of information from a variety of people who have experienced it. The type of interviewing needed requires knowledge and sensitivity. The work done in macro practice in social work is not like that of a newspaper reporter gathering information for an article. A trusting relationship must be built so that those indigenous to the community or organization will develop a commitment to the changes needed and will participate in the change effort.

A number of authors emphasize the importance of approaching the study of communities or organizations sensitively. Devore (1992) proposes six layers of understanding important to macro practice in social work:

1. Understanding how social work values relate to understandings about people and about how people relate to their environment
2. Building basic knowledge about the community and an understanding of interrelationships among key community representatives, community history, community expectations, roles, values, and norms
3. Building a basic knowledge of local, state, and federal policies and programs related to the problem or need as well as other local resources such as the church or other significant organizations
4. Examining self-awareness and insights into one's own ethnicity and an understanding of how that may influence practice and perceptions of others
5. Considering the impact of ethnicity on the daily lives of people in the community
6. Adapting and modifying skills and techniques in response to the ethnic reality, listening carefully and following the lead as indicated by community members' responses

Lecca, Quervalu, Nunes, and Gonzales (1998) propose a number of cultural considerations when planning community or organizational changes. Some of the questions the authors raise include:

- Is there a history of having planned activities imposed on the community through negatively stated sanctions (educational, political, etc.)?
- Is there universal agreement among the cultural group on the individual result desired?
- Are there cultural standards? How can established standards be more inclusive?
- Are the overall goals and policies in line with the culture?
- What resources are available within the culture? (p. 229)

Gutiérrez and Lewis (1999) propose the following practice principles when working with women of color:

1. Learn about, understand, and participate in the women's community.
2. Serve as a facilitator and view the situation through the lens or vision of women of color.
3. Use the process of praxis to understand the historical, political, and social context of the organizing effort.
4. Through participation, learn about the women's ethnic community.
5. Begin with the formation of small groups.
6. Recognize and embrace the conflict that characterizes cross-cultural work.
7. Recognize and build on ways in which women of color have worked effectively within their own communities; build on existing structures.
8. Involve women of color in leadership roles.
9. Understand and support the need that women of color may have for their own separate programs and organizations. (p. 107)

The point illustrated by these three sets of strategies is an important one. The organizer or change agent cannot simply enter a community or organizational culture without preparation. People who live or work in the place that is seen as needing change may not perceive the situation as the change agent does. They may have important social-support structures or resources that are unknown to persons outside that group. Their positions in the community or organization and their perspectives need to be respected. Cues should be taken from indigenous people as to appropriate roles and responsibilities in initiating a change effort.

Many changes involve cultural and ethnic considerations. Therefore, these guidelines can be useful in efforts toward macro-level change. For example, in an extended care facility, there is a culture of care provision. In a high school, faculty, staff, students, and administrators have developed an organizational culture over time. In these and other situations where the change agent is perceived as an outsider, the preceding principles can help the organizer or change agent build credibility and avoid mistakes.

The task of gathering information from key informants involves a number of activities, including (1) identifying the major participants, (2) identifying and defining the community or organizational condition or problem, and (3) preparing a chronology of significant historical events leading to the current situation. These activities will be discussed in the following sections.

Identify Major Participants.   Questions to be explored for this activity include:

- Who first identified the problem? Are those initially involved still available? Are they still involved?
- What roles have local people played in past efforts at change?
- What individuals or groups support or oppose change?
- What individuals or groups have the power to approve or deny change?

At a later point in the process, after the community or organizational analysis has been completed, the change agent will organize a systematic assessment of the various systems involved and identify representatives of each of these systems. This is for the purpose of selecting a strategy for change and organizing participants in a way that will maximize effectiveness.

That type of thorough identification of all systems is not the focus of this early identification of major participants. Rather, this effort is intended to identify key informants so that those gathering information at the local level can be certain they have drawn on the experiences of the most knowledgeable individuals, as well as those best positioned to understand what has happened to date.

Those who first identified the problem are important to the change process. For example, a community activist may have taken the lead in the past to ensure the availability of emergency health care for illegal immigrants. If this issue is revisited at a later date, it is important to understand the experiences and perspectives of the first initiator. Was she successful? Why or why not? Did she alienate any critical decision makers? How would she evaluate her approach, and what would she do differently? Who else was involved, and what were their roles and perspectives on the proposed change? Change agents are not obligated to use the same method or to affiliate with an earlier change effort, but they should at least be aware of the approach taken and the results achieved.

Whether or not the current condition or problem has been addressed before, it is important that the change agent develop an understanding of which local individuals and groups support and which oppose the change effort being considered. For example, a small group of staff within an organization may want to promote an aggressive affirmative action approach to recruitment and hiring in order to better reflect the changing demographics of a community. It would be a mistake to assume that all staff, managers, and administrators will favor this change effort. Rather than plan only with those who agree, change agents should encourage opponents to express their opinions. Working with the opposition can present some difficult ethical issues, but the skillful change agent will find ways to identify key local participants who favor and who oppose the change effort, and will make every attempt to keep the process open to all.

The third group of local participants to be identified is those individuals who have the power or authority to approve or reject the change that ultimately will be proposed. Within an organization, this will most likely be the chief executive officer (CEO) or the board of directors, but others within the organization may have an important say, as well. In a community, the identity of decision makers will depend on the domain identified for change. If the focus is on a school or school district, decision makers will include principals, school board members, and others within the system. In a local neighborhood, key persons will include city council members or city staff. Some exploration will be needed to determine who has this type of authority. More will be said about this in Chapter 9.

Identify the Community or Organizational Condition.   Questions to be explored for this activity include:

- What is the difference between a condition and a problem?
- What does this community or organization consider to be its priority problems?
- In approaching an episode of change, how should the condition statement be framed?

A *condition* is a phenomenon that is present in a community or organization that may be troublesome to a number of people, but that has not been formally identified, labeled, or publicly acknowledged as a problem. It is important that social workers understand whether a phenomenon is a condition that has not been formally recognized or a problem that has been acknowledged by the organization or community. This status will affect where the social worker places her or his emphasis in early planning efforts. Ultimately, decision makers will have to acknowledge the existence of a problem (either willingly or reluctantly) if formal resources are to be dedicated to alleviating or eliminating the problem. An observer once noted that a condition becomes a problem when it is recognized by a significant number of people or a number of significant people.

Every organization and community is full of conditions as well as problems. Social consequences of urban living—such as traffic congestion, air pollution, unsupervised children, broken families, and suicide—can all be considered social or community conditions if no efforts have been mobilized to address them. Similarly, in rural communities, isolation, inaccessible health care, and a declining economic base can all be considered social conditions if they remain unrecognized by any formal or informal efforts toward resolution.

The same concept applies to organizations where troublesome phenomena are present but have not necessarily been formally identified or labeled as a problem. For example, staff in a long-term care facility for elders may be concerned about what they consider to be overmedication of some of the residents. Similarly, program managers may recognize a trend to extend services to those who can pay while offering only a waiting list to those who cannot.

To be defined as a *problem*, a condition must in some way be formally recognized and incorporated into the action agenda of a group, organization, or community. This may mean, for example, that an elected official proposes a study of elderly suicide, or that a group of parents concerned about inhalant abuse lobbies for legislation to require that spray-paint cans for sale be placed in locked display cases. It may mean that a task force within an organization is officially sanctioned to explore the effects of medication on residents in long-term care. Or it may mean that a neighborhood group experiencing high-speed traffic on their residential streets takes steps to bring about broader recognition of the presence of the condition and its problematic nature. Regardless of the form it takes, formal recognition is important for legitimization.

The distinction between a *condition* and a *problem* is significant to a social worker planning a macro-level intervention. If a condition has not been formally recognized in some way, the first task must be to obtain that formal recognition. For example, for many years, homelessness was dealt with as an employment problem, child maltreatment as a family matter, and AIDS as a personal health problem. Most communities simply viewed these as existing conditions, not as social or community problems. When these conditions began to affect greater segments of society and reached the point at which they could no longer be ignored, national, state, and local community leaders began to identify them as problems and to dedicate resources toward their resolution. Once formally recognized and acknowledged as problems (usually as a result of persistent media attention), these conditions become candidates for organized intervention efforts. The creation of task forces for the homeless in cities across the country, child abuse and neglect reporting laws, and federal funding for AIDS research and services are results of recognizing conditions and defining them as problems.

A first task in problem identification, then, is to develop a condition statement. A *condition statement* must include (1) a target population, (2) a geographical boundary, and (3) the difficulty facing the population. Statements should be descriptive, as objective as possible, and based on findings to date.

Statements should be adapted depending on whether the condition exists within a community or in an organization. For example, a condition statement might be, "Domestic violence in Preston County is increasing." Generally speaking, the more precise the statement, the greater the likelihood of a successful intervention. The above statement, for example, could vary from extremely general to very specific, as depicted in Figure 3.2.

A similar process within an organization would begin with a general statement. For example, an organizational condition might be that in a domestic violence shelter, resources are not being used efficiently, and many residents are returning to their abusers. Quantitative data and other information would then need to be compiled to help pinpoint the condition as precisely as possible.

Condition statements are made more precise through a process of research and documentation of the nature, size, and scope of the problem. As one proceeds with subsequent tasks in problem analysis, the condition statement will be refined many times as new facts and findings emerge. The statement may evolve into an identified problem on which there is consensus, or it may be perceived as a need or deficit. Some change efforts are developed around opportunities where there is no identified problem or need, but a funding or resource opportunity has

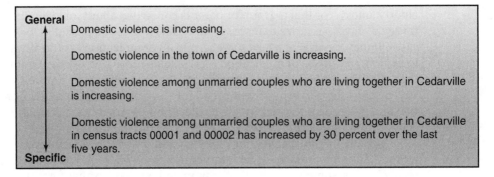

FIGURE 3.2   Sample Condition Statements

presented itself. We will therefore offer examples of changes arising from both problems and needs, since either may present social workers with a change opportunity. The change agent needs to recognize, however, that consensus building is important no matter how the change effort arose.

Identify Relevant Historical Incidents.   Questions to be explored for this activity include:

- Has the problem been recognized and acknowledged by any community or organizational members?
- If so, when was this condition, problem, or opportunity first recognized in this community or organization?
- What are the important incidents or events that have occurred from first recognition to the present time?
- What do earlier efforts to address this problem reveal?

The next task is to compile a chronology of significant events or milestones that promotes understanding the history of the community or organizational condition or problem. This shifts the focus to the area in Figure 3.1 where the problem and the arena overlap.

A condition or problem in any community or organization has its own history. This history can affect the ways in which people currently perceive the condition or problem. It is therefore important to understand how key people within the community or organization perceived the condition or problem in the past. If seen as a problem, how was it addressed? How effective were the attempts to alleviate the problem? Who were the major participants in any previous change efforts?

If one looks solely at the condition or problem as it is defined at present, much will be missed. Instead, it is crucial to determine the problem's history, particularly in terms of critical incidents that have shaped past and current perceptions of the problem. A task force, for example, might be concerned about a high dropout rate from the local high school. The following chronology of critical incidents could help the group better understand factors that influenced the origin and development of important issues in the high school over the years:

1992   Riverview High School was a predominantly lower-middle-class high school with an 82 percent graduation rate.

1994   School district boundaries were redrawn, and the student body changed. For 30 percent of its members, English was a second language.

1996   Enrollment dropped 20 percent, and the graduation rate fell to 67 percent.

1997   Riverview High School initiated a strong vocational training program designed to prepare high school graduates for post–high school employment; the college preparatory curriculum was deemphasized.

1999   Enrollment increased; attendance patterns improved.

2001   Local employers hired only 32 percent of the graduates; unemployment rates among Riverview graduates one year later were as high as 37 percent.

2003   Enrollment dropped back to 1988 levels; the dropout rate reached 23 percent, its highest mark yet.

2004   Riverview High School was written up in the local newspaper as one of the ten worst schools in the state in terms of quality of education, retention rates of students, and post–high school employment. A blue-ribbon panel was formed to make recommendations to improve the quality of education.

Tracing these historical events lends insight into some of the incidents experienced by the faculty, staff, administration, students, and families associated with Riverview High School. In this case, the task force should expect to encounter a discouraged and cynical response to any sort of a "Stay in School" campaign. The critical incidents list indicates that many of the arguments for staying in school simply did not prove true for those who graduated.

When employment, career, and financial incentives for remaining in high school are removed, the challenge to keep students in school is greatly increased. This means that the approach to organizational change needs to be adapted in relevant and meaningful ways to those who are intended to be the primary beneficiaries. This has clear implications for including in the change effort those who can, for example, positively influence the employment environment for graduates.

Exploring relevant historical incidents also helps establish the credibility of the change agent. Many people are simply not open to supporting change for their communities and organizations if those organizing the change effort are perceived as being "outsiders" who have not taken the time to become familiar with what has gone on in the past.

The types of critical incidents that have been described are generally gleaned from interviews or discussions with long-time residents, activists, community leaders, teachers, and social service agency employees. In tracing the history or antecedent conditions of an episode of change, what the change agent hopes to discover is (1) what happened in the past to call attention to the problem or need and (2) what was the community's (neighborhood, city, county, state, private sector) response to the attention focused on the problem or need?

Task 2: Review the Literature on the Condition, Problem, Need, or Opportunity

In addition to interviewing local people to help frame the condition or problem, those involved in a change effort are also expected to immerse themselves in relevant literature, including theory and research on the problem as well as quantitative data and other information. These types of activities should be assigned to participants who are skilled at library research and comfortable with collecting and compiling data. There are two types of literature to be explored here: (1) theoretical and research literature, including texts and journal articles on the problem to be studied; and (2) statistical data and information that can be used to document the existence of the problem or need, and that can help in understanding such factors as size, scope, trends, and other useful information. The Internet is an increasingly valuable source of information of this nature.

Explore Relevant Theoretical and Research Literature.   Questions to be explored for this activity include:

- What literature is considered key to understanding the condition, problem, need, or opportunity?
- What frameworks are useful in understanding the condition, problem, need, or opportunity?

The challenge to the change agent in this activity is to become as much of an expert on the condition, problem, need, or opportunity as possible in the time available. Few experiences are more embarrassing than to be making a public presentation to a decision-making or funding body and to be exposed as less knowledgeable than the audience.

Literature reporting empirical testing of theoretical and practice-related questions has increased dramatically in the social sciences in recent years. A number of journals are now devoted almost exclusively to reporting research in social work and related fields (e.g., *Social Work Research, Journal of Social Service Research, Research on Social Work Practice*). Others focus on special populations and/or social problems (e.g., *Child Welfare, Journal of Gerontological Social Work, Journal of Child Sexual Abuse, Journal of Poverty, Bulletin of HIV/AIDS & Social Work*, and many others). A computerized search of journal abstracts such as *Social Work Abstracts, PsycINFO,* or *Sociological Abstracts* should quickly produce a listing of relevant literature, and a scan of the titles will guide the change agent toward those articles that appear to be most useful in understanding a particular condition, problem, or opportunity.

Evaluations of existing social service programs can be informative, but they often lack the methodological rigor of organized research. Reports of practice findings tend to be the least formal in terms of their data collection, analysis, and reporting of findings, yet they can be helpful and informative as long as the user is cautious in interpreting findings and deriving applications.

One feature that can be useful in attempting to understand a phenomenon is the way in which the author has conceptualized the condition, problem, or opportunity. In compiling an article for publication, it is incumbent on the author to present some framework or format for analysis that sheds light on the topic under study. In a study of elder abuse, for example, does the author break the topic down by levels of severity? By classification of the perpetrators? By victims? What concepts (and what technical terms) are presented that aid in understanding the phenomenon of elder abuse? Information uncovered in the literature review should be constantly examined for its relevance to the current situation. Ultimately, a mix of potential causal or contributing factors will be selected as a framework for explaining the phenomenon under study. Achieving this beginning level of understanding of the condition, problem, or opportunity under study prepares the change agent for the next task—collecting supporting data.

Collect Supporting Data.   Questions to be explored for this activity include:

- What data are most useful in describing the condition, problem, or opportunity?
- Where can useful quantitative data and other types of information be found?

There was a time when a community could become sensitized to a condition and recognize it as a problem based on a few incidents. Churches started orphanages and counties started poor houses with little or no data beyond personal knowledge of a few people in need and the expectation that there would be more.

In the complex communities of today, however, with so many social and community problems competing for limited resources, data must be compiled to document the size and scope of a problem or need. Collecting data on a community social condition or problem can be a challenge. Ideally, in promoting a program to educate homeless children, for example, one would hope to find powerful statistics that clearly demonstrate something similar to the following:

- There are currently 3,279 homeless children in Clifton County.
- Lack of positive early school experience can be expected to result in about 2,000 of these children being unable to read at grade level.
- Inability to read at grade level can be expected to result in 1,500 of this group dropping out of school by the tenth grade.
- Of the 1,500 who drop out of school by the tenth grade, about 1,000 will eventually either be in trouble with the law and become incarcerated or otherwise be placed in a state-supported institution.

- Each person supported by the state costs, on average, $28,000 per year. The cost to the state for 1,000 incarcerated or institutionalized dropouts will be $28 million per year.
- An early intervention program for 2,000 homeless children will cost $6.5 million.
- About 1,800 of these children can be expected to improve their reading skills to grade level, resulting in improved opportunities for employment and self-sufficiency.
- If successful, this program offers a potential annual savings to the state of up to $21.5 million.

These kinds of figures make it clear that it is a case of paying something now for prevention or paying many times more than that amount later for care, maintenance, or perhaps rehabilitation. However, although these kinds of statistics are much desired and preferred, they have rarely been compiled in a usable format. Instead, individuals who initiate change must rely on what is available: census data; community needs assessments; levels of demand for service as reported by agencies; rates of service; and data generated by hospitals, schools, police departments, and any other reasonably reliable source available.

A few techniques can be helpful in cases in which quantitative data and other types of information are needed. One resource is national, regional, or state studies in which a percentage or an incidence rate (per thousand or sometimes per hundred thousand) has been established. If, for example, it has been found that 48.5 percent of marriages performed in a state end in divorce, one can apply this percentage to a city or town within that state to calculate the number of divorces that can be expected to occur over time. Obviously, the number will not be exact, but it provides at least a beginning point for projection.

Basic to all statistical support is a knowledge of the number of people in various demographic categories (e.g., gender, age, racial/ethnic groupings, etc.). Valuable information of this type is available in the *County and City Data Book* published by the Bureau of the Census (and now available online at www.census.gov/statab/www/ccdb.html). This resource includes such data categories (for both counties and cities) as ethnic breakdown, age, gender, the number of people with less than a high school education, the number of people in poverty, and other valuable information. Additional statistical references based on census data include *USA Counties, Statistical Abstract of the United States,* and *State and Metropolitan Area Data Book,* which in most cases are also available online. Other selected national and state resources are identified in Figure 3.3.

State and/or county departments of social services, health, mental health, and corrections also collect data that can be useful in documenting the existence of social conditions or problems. Other sources include local social service agencies, the United Way, community councils, centralized data-collection resource centers, centralized information and referral agencies, law-enforcement agencies, hospitals, and school district offices. The process of tracking down information is often similar to a scavenger hunt, where one clue leads to another until a point is reached

FIGURE 3.3   Resources for Data Collection

Monthly Catalog of United States Government Publications
Washington, DC: U.S. Government Printing Office
Available online as *Catalog of U.S. Government Publications*
http://www.access.gpo.gov/su docs/locators/cgp/index.html

American Statistics Index
Washington, DC: Congressional Information Service

Statistical Abstract of the United States
Washington, DC: U.S. Dept. of Commerce, Economic and Statistics Administration,
Bureau of the Census
Available online: http://www.census.gov/statab/www/

County and City Data Book
Washington, DC: U.S. Dept. of Commerce, Economic and Statistics Administration,
Bureau of the Census
Available online: http://www.census.gov/statab/www/ccdb.html

State and Metropolitan Area Data Book
Washington, DC : U.S. Dept. of Commerce, Economic and Statistics Administration,
Bureau of the Census
Available online: http://www.census.gov/statab/www/smadb.html

Health, United States
Hyattsville, MD: U.S. Dept. of Health and Human Services, Public Health Service,
Centers for Disease Control, National Center for Health Statistics
Available online: http://www.cdc.gov/nchs/products/pubs/pubd/hus/hus.htm

Mental Health, United States
Rockville, MD: U.S. Dept. of Health and Human Services, Substance Abuse, and Mental
Health Administration, Center for Mental health Survey
Available online: http://www.samhsa.gov/news/newsreleases/
011024nr.MH2000.htm

Sourcebook of Criminal Justice Statistics
Washington, DC : U.S. Dept. of Justice, Office of Justice Programs, Bureau of
Justice Statistics
Available online: http://www.albany.edu/sourcebook/

Digest of Educational Statistics
Washington, DC: U.S. Dept. of Education, Office of Educational Research and
Improvement, National Center for Educational Statistics
Available online: http://www.ed.gov/pubs/stats.html

where the quantity and quality of supportive data collected is sufficient to allow the persons initiating change to make their case.

In collecting supporting data, the change agent should think in terms of the entire "circle" of understanding of the presenting problem or condition. That means that data collection will not necessarily be limited to the *local* community, neighborhood, or organization that is the focus of the change effort. Although data on the smallest local units of analysis (such as the neighborhood or census tract) can be powerful in terms of supporting the argument that something must be done, data on the same conditions or problems at the county, state, or national levels can provide a basis of comparison for local data.

Make the Data Meaningful for Interpretation.   Questions to be explored for this activity include:

- What options could be used to display data?
- How should data be displayed in order to clearly and concisely make the case for change?

Comparative data are generally more useful than a single statistic, and several techniques can be used to collect and display comparative data. These include cross-sectional analysis, time-series comparisons, and comparisons with other data units. In addition to these data displays, techniques such as standard comparisons and epidemiological analysis can be useful (Kettner, Daley, & Nichols 1985). Displays should be prepared and presented in a way that will tell the story effectively. A number of graphic options are available, including line graphs, bar graphs, and pie charts. Thought should be given to which graphic display will have the greatest impact, given the data to be presented.

Cross-Sectional Analysis.   This approach focuses on a single population but provides a number of different perspectives on that population at a particular point in time. For example, a survey might focus on areas of need experienced by a particular target population and display the percentage of the population who report a problem in this area, as illustrated in Table 3.1.

The data presented in Table 3.1 can be used to create a more dramatic visual effect by translating the numbers into graphic formats. Figure 3.4 illustrates age distribution in the form of a bar graph, which presents a picture of an aging population.

Figure 3.5 uses a pie chart to illustrate ethnic distribution. Side-by-side pie charts using census data 10 years apart could be used as a cross-sectional analysis as well as a time-series analysis.

As community or organizational conditions are identified, subpopulations can usually be assessed by demographic characteristics such as age, gender, ethnic group, and others. The most serious limitation is that a cross-sectional analysis does not reveal changes over time.

Time-Series Comparisons.   When available, data from repeated observations over time are preferred because they display trends. Assuming data were collected on

TABLE 3.1   An Illustration of Cross-Sectional Analysis, Examining the Percentage of Each Population Experiencing a Problem

Variable	Percent of Population	Housing	Employment	Nutrition	Transportation
Age					
0–18	11%	5%	N/A	5%	N/A
19–30	21%	14%	7%	9%	16%
31–64	28%	17%	11%	8%	19%
65+	40%	19%	33%	15%	33%
Gender					
Female	52%	5%	7%	6%	18%
Male	48%	16%	24%	11%	17%
Ethnicity					
White	42%	10%	5%	4%	7%
Asian Amer.	6%	3%	4%	5%	9%
African Amer.	34%	17%	11%	12%	15%
Hispanic	14%	7%	10%	9%	11%
Native Amer.	4%	11%	23%	8%	14%

an annual basis, a time-series comparison would look at trends in the variable(s) of interest. For example, the number of nonduplicated individuals requesting overnight stays in homeless shelters in a given city might be displayed in a line graph, as shown in Figure 3.6.

Statistics such as these can help project need and cost into the future, based on assumptions about trends identified through a series of observations. Compar-

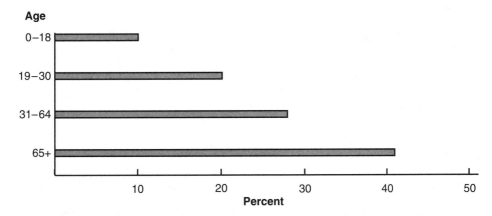

FIGURE 3.4   A Bar Graph Illustrating Age Distribution and Revealing an Aging Population

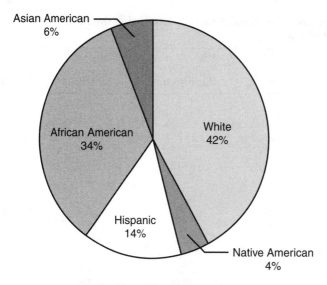

FIGURE 3.5   A Pie Chart Illustrating Ethnic Distribution

isons among these observations can provide the change agent with valuable information. For example, they can be used to document how client need is increasing, why additional resources are needed, and the projected dollars necessary to fill anticipated need.

Comparison with Other Data Units.   Even though cross-sectional analysis can provide a "snapshot" at a point in time, and time series can depict trends over time,

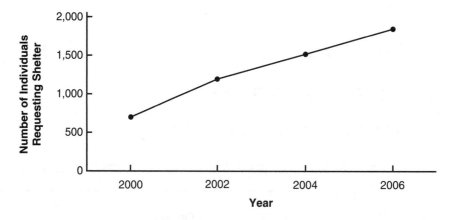

FIGURE 3.6   A Line Graph Illustrating a Time Series Analysis of the Number of Individuals Requesting Overnight Shelter by Homeless Persons

questions might still be raised about the legitimacy of a problem, especially when comparisons are being made with other communities or organizations. For example, if a change agent is able to document a current teen pregnancy rate of 22 percent in a community, and to show an upward trend over five years, a critic might reasonably ask if this rate is considered high or low. This is where comparison to other data units is helpful.

A wealth of both regularly and specially assembled information is available for use as supporting data. Over the past few decades, many federal, state, and local agencies have contributed to databases on rates per 1,000, 10,000, or 100,000 on a wide range of social, economic, and health problems. These statistics allow for comparison regardless of the size of the city or neighborhood in question. Studies have also identified state and local per-capita expenditures for various social and health problems. Based on these findings, states and cities can be ranked on the incidence and prevalence of problems or on their efforts to address the problems.

Comparisons are particularly useful in making a case that a disproportionate share of resources should go to a particularly needy community. By comparing census tracts within a county on selected variables, it becomes readily evident that problems and needs are not always equally distributed across communities and neighborhoods within the county, and therefore resources should not always be distributed on a per-capita basis.

Standards Comparisons.   This technique is particularly helpful when other comparative data are not available. A *standard* is defined as "a specification accepted by recognized authorities that is regularly and widely used and has a recognized and permanent status" (Kettner, Moroney, & Martin, 1999, p. 126). Standards are usually developed by accrediting bodies, governmental entities, or professional associations. For example, the Child Welfare League of America publishes comprehensive sets of standards related to community and agency programs for child abuse and neglect, adoption, and other child welfare services. Similarly, the National Council on Aging has developed case management standards. The National Association of Social Workers lists standards for social work services in a wide variety of settings.

Where governmental units, accrediting bodies, or professional associations have defined standards, conditions considered to be falling below health, education, personal care, housing, and other types of standards become more readily accessible as targets for change. Community leaders do not like the negative publicity that often results when services offered within their communities are described as being "below standard." These types of standards apply primarily to the quality of services being provided.

Standards of sorts may also be used to define a problem or population. For example, some cities have developed standardized criteria to define a homeless person or a gang member. Where such criteria have been established, they can be useful in interpreting existing records and compiling new quantitative data or other information.

Epidemiological Analysis.   This is a technique adapted from the field of public health, where an analysis of factors contributing to a disease helps to establish relationships even when a clear cause-and-effect relationship cannot be demonstrated. This approach can be applied not only to disease but to social problems as well. For example, Piven and Cloward (1971) established relationships among the variables of poverty, poor education, poor housing, and welfare dependency. Although it cannot be said that any of these conditions *cause* welfare dependency, the relationship of dependency to the combination of factors is well established.

An original study of the scope of Piven and Cloward's research is beyond the expectations of an episode of macro practice. It is mentioned here not to suggest that a social worker should attempt such studies, but so that existing studies will be recognized as viable resources. The American Public Health Association, the National Center on Child Abuse and Neglect, the American Public Welfare Association, the Urban Institute, and other such organizations have provided many sound epidemiological studies that can be used as resources by social workers.

A useful feature of epidemiological thinking is that in analyzing problems it can help avoid simplistic cause-and-effect thinking. Although a single causal factor (e.g., poor education, poverty, or child abuse) may explain current problems faced by a small portion of the population, multiple factors in combination frequently help explain the problem or phenomenon for a much larger portion of the population.

Task 3: Select Factors That Help Explain the Underlying Causes of the Problem

Questions to be explored for this task include:

- From interviews with key informants, identification of important historical events, review of theoretical literature, and compilation of data, what appear to be the major factors that help in understanding the problem?
- Which factors, at this point, appear to be the most logical ones to be addressed in this episode of change?

When those involved in the change effort have defined the problem, reviewed important historical events, completed a literature review, and compiled evidence, they should have at least a beginning understanding of what it is that is causing the problem. The next step is to determine what factors must be dealt with in order to bring about needed changes. Preliminary identification of these factors is a necessary step in clarifying the change effort. Before summarizing these factors, however, it is important to understand the types of issues or considerations to be identified.

When examining conditions or problems in the human services, there is often a strong temptation to identify lack of resources as the cause of a problem. For example, in studies focused on organizational problems, causal factors tend to be defined in terms of a lack of staff, lack of funds for new staff, lack of adequate equipment, inadequate facilities, and so on. In defining a community problem, causal factors tend to be seen in terms of lack of resources for new programs or expanded services, such as more day-care slots, more training, and so on. In many cases, genuine resource deficits may exist, but we caution against superficial assessments that look to dollars as the only solution to every problem. There are several reasons for a more thorough approach.

First, resources have to do with the intervention or the "solution," and they should be considered only after a specific approach has been proposed and resource issues can be addressed in detailed, not general, terms. Second, lack of resources is so universal that it is relatively meaningless as a part of problem analysis. Third, "lack of adequate resources" does not help to explain underlying causal or contributing factors. The statement simply assumes that more of whatever is already being done will solve the problem. Additional resources in macro-level change can be critical to success, but the issue should be addressed later in the change process.

The types of causal or contributing factors to be addressed are those fundamental factors that explain why the problem emerged and why it persists over time. They are substantive factors that prevent progress toward solutions. For example, in exploring a problem of unsupervised children after school in a community, interviews and library research may have led to identification of the following factors: (1) a high percentage of single working mothers in the community who cannot afford child care, (2) poor cohesion and weak sense of community in the neighborhood, (3) feelings of powerlessness to address the problem, (4) lack of community awareness of the problem, (5) feelings of reluctance to ask for help, and other such factors. The purpose of identifying these factors is to help clarify the complex nature of the problem. As greater understanding of problem, population, and arena is achieved, these factors will be used to develop a working hypothesis of etiology, or cause(s) and effect(s). This working hypothesis will then be used to guide the intervention.

Identification of causal or contributing factors is intended to help those who are exploring the need for change to focus their efforts toward a manageable number of contributing factors, thereby increasing the chances of success. In most cases, it is unlikely that all contributing factors will be addressed. Selection of explanatory factors may lead to a narrower, more limited focus or it may lead to collaboration with others, with agreement that each change effort will concentrate on different factors. In the preceding example, a local community center might agree to take responsibility for building mutual support systems among single mothers and strengthening the sense of community, while the local school may choose to work on developing constructive after-school activities. At this point, however, these decisions would be premature. The purpose of identifying contributing factors is to arrive at an understanding of the problem that is as clear as possible.

Summary of Steps Involved in Understanding the Problem

The following important points have been made about identifying a condition and creating an awareness that it is a problem.

1. *Identify a Problem.* Initiating macro-level interventions in organizations and communities begins with the recognition that a community or organizational problem exists.
2. *Identify Participants.* A change agent identifies participants in the change effort and coordinates the tasks and activities to be undertaken by various individuals and subgroups.
3. *Interview Key Informants.* Part of the data-gathering process involves interviews with key informants in the community or organization. Information gathered includes experiences and perspectives of major participants as well as a chronology of events to date, and it is used to help frame the condition or problem as seen by those who have experienced it.
4. *Review Relevant Literature.* When a condition or problem statement has been framed, relevant literature on the topic should be reviewed to gain an understanding of the concepts and issues involved.
5. *Collect Data and Information.* Relevant data should be collected to support the contention that a problem exists and to aid in understanding its nature, size, and scope. Data displays should be carefully constructed so that they are clear and easily understood by their intended audiences.
6. *Identify Contributing Factors.* Identification of contributing factors helps to make clear the complexity of the problem and serves to bring focus to a limited number of factors to be addressed.
7. *Understand the Problem.* The purpose of this problem-analysis exercise is to bring clarity to understanding the condition, problem, need, or opportunity, and to provide a foundation for later design of a solution or intervention.
8. *Recognize the Problem.* By this point, the change agent should either have succeeded in convincing the appropriate individuals and groups that the condition is a problem, or the focus of the change effort should be shifted to that task.

Summary

In this chapter we have presented an approach to orderly, systematic, professionally assisted change. Critics may say that this approach takes too long and fails to seize the moment, and we acknowledge that part of the responsibility of a change agent is to make judgments about how and when to act. The study process can be streamlined or extended, depending on the complexity and duration of the problem. But simply ignoring the need for current information and proceeding to action may prove to be irresponsible and detrimental to the very people the change is intended to serve. A change effort worth undertaking is worth approaching methodically and thoroughly. In the next chapter we will explore what needs to be understood about target populations.

DISCUSSION QUESTIONS AND EXERCISES

Case Example Exercise

You are a social worker in a domestic violence shelter. Your clients are young women, many of whom have small children. You provide intensive services during their stay at the shelter, including teaching them independent living skills, parenting skills, job readiness skills, and marketable skills for employment. After they have achieved an acceptable level of stability in their lives, they are discharged from the program, and follow-up services are provided until they are self-sufficient. In evaluating the success of the program, you find that of those who remain independent and do not go back to their abusers, 77 percent are able to make a successful transition to the community and remain free of subsequent incidents of abuse. Among those who do go back to their abusers, 85 percent return to the shelter within three months. The agency director has asked you to chair a task force to find ways to reduce the number of clients who return to their abusers.

Refer to the discussion questions below.

Discussion Questions

1. Draft a clear, one-sentence statement of the problem as you see it at this point, defining (a) the problem, (b) the target population, and (c) the geographical boundaries. Explain why you wrote this particular statement in the way you did.

2. Explain why a funding source (e.g., state legislature or private foundation) would care about this problem.

3. Write a one-sentence problem-resolution statement that expresses what outcome you expect to achieve if your intervention is successful.

4. Identify individuals (by title) in the target organization that you think should be interviewed in order to better understand local perspectives.

5. List a set of questions you would ask these individuals to help you in understanding historical perspectives.

6. Identify the types of data you believe would be useful if you wanted to do the following types of analyses:

   - Time-series analysis (changes or trends over time)

   - Cross-sectional analysis (comparison of a number of variables for the same population)

   - Comparison with other data units (comparison of your problem in your agency to the same problem in a comparable agency)

7. Explain how the variables you selected would be helpful in understanding the problem.

8. List key words you would use for a literature search to help you understand the condition, problem, or need.

9. Identify some of the factors you believe might contribute to the problem.

APPENDIX
Framework for Understanding Community and Organizational Problems

Task 1: Gather Information from Key Informants in the Community or Organization

Identify Major Participants
- Who first identified the problem? Are those initially involved still available? Are they still involved?
- What roles have local people played in past efforts at change?
- What individuals or groups support and oppose change?
- What individuals or groups have the power to approve or deny change?

Identify the Community or Organizational Condition
- What is the difference between a condition and a problem?
- What does this community or organization consider to be its priority problems?
- In approaching an episode of change, how should the condition statement be framed?

Identify Relevant Historical Incidents
- Has the problem been recognized and acknowledged by any community or organizational members?
- If so, when was this condition, problem, or opportunity first recognized in this community or organization?
- What are the important incidents or events that have occurred from first recognition to the present time?
- What do earlier efforts to address this problem reveal?

Task 2: Review the Literature on the Condition, Problem, Need, or Opportunity

Explore Relevant Theoretical and Research Literature
- What literature is considered key to understanding the condition, problem, need, or opportunity?
- What frameworks are useful in understanding the condition, problem, need, or opportunity?

Collect Supporting Data
- What data are most useful in describing the condition, problem, or opportunity?
- Where can useful quantitative data and other types of information be found?

Make the Data Meaningful for Interpretation
- What options could be used to display data?
- How should data be displayed in order to clearly and concisely make the case for change?

Task 3: Select Factors That Help Explain the Underlying Causes of the Problem

- From interviews with key informants, identification of important historical events, review of theoretical literature, and compilation of data, what appear to be the major factors that help in understanding the problem?
- Which factors, at this point, appear to be the most logical ones to be addressed in this episode of change?

SUGGESTED READINGS

Fellin, P. (1995). *The community and the social worker.* Itasca, IL: F. E. Peacock.

Hardcastle, D. A., S. Wenocur, and P. R. Powers. (1997). *Community practice: Theories and skills for social workers.* New York: Oxford.

Jansson, B. (2003). *Becoming an effective policy advocate: From policy practice to social justice.* Pacific Grove, CA: Brooks-Cole.

Rothman, J., J. L. Erlich, and J. E. Tropman (Eds.). (2001). *Strategies of community intervention* (6th ed.). Itasca, IL: F. E. Peacock.

Rubin, H. J., and I. S. Rubin. (2001) *Community organizing and development* (3rd ed.). Boston: Allyn and Bacon.

Tropman, J. E., J. L. Erlich, and J. Rothman (Eds.). (2001). *Tactics and techniques of community intervention* (4th ed.). Itasca, IL: F. E. Peacock.

REFERENCES

Devore, W. (1992). The African-American community in 1990: The search for a practice method. In F. Rivera and J. Erlich (Eds.), *Community organizing in a diverse society.* Boston: Allyn and Bacon.

Gutiérrez, L., and E. Lewis. (1999). *Empowering women of color.* New York: Columbia University Press.

Kettner, P. M., J. M. Daley, and A. W. Nichols. (1985). *Initiating change in organizations and communities.* Monterey, CA: Brooks/Cole.

Kettner, P. M., R. M. Moroney, and L. L. Martin. (1999). *Designing and managing programs: An effectiveness-based approach.* Newbury Park, CA: Sage.

Lecca, P., I. Quervalu, J. Nunes, and H. Gonzales. (1998). *Cultural competency in health, social, and human services.* New York: Garland.

Piven, F., and R. Cloward. (1971). *Regulating the poor: The functions of public welfare.* New York: Pantheon.

4 Understanding Populations

OVERVIEW

Populations

Problems affect people. Solutions, if they are to be effective, must reflect an understanding of the people affected. Much has been learned over the years about
human growth and development. Typical patterns of physical, emotional, cognitive, and social development have been established and can be used in a very general way to help in understanding behavior. Social workers know that the issues,
concerns, and needs of adolescents, for example, are not the same as those of
elders, and that experiences may affect people differently depending on characteristics such as ethnicity and gender.

If society hopes to understand why problems exist, people must understand the populations affected. For example, why do some individuals in response to feelings of despair commit acts of violence and others commit suicide? The answer is likely very different for teenagers than it is for adults or for older persons. How do people react to stress? The research may help explain that reactions can be affected not only by personal characteristics but also by social, cultural, and economic factors.

Identifying a Target Population

In many cases, a particular target population is implied or stated as a part of framing the problem. Focusing on a problem such as teen pregnancy immediately narrows the population to young women between the ages of approximately 11 and 19. Elder abuse narrows the population to people who are usually over age 65 and in a vulnerable and dependent situation. Identified populations lend themselves to study and understanding by the completion of a review of the literature, interviewing of key informants, and related measures.

In other cases, the population may not be as clearly defined. For example, an episode of change may focus on a neighborhood. In this instance, it may be necessary to identify several populations, such as preschoolers, children, teens, young families, adults, and elders. When intervening at the neighborhood level, it is likely that the analysis will be more heavily focused on "arena" (to be discussed in the following chapters), with less emphasis on a study of the population. For example, residents of a neighborhood are being organized to become more actively involved in the decisions that affect their lives. It may be helpful to compile a brief overview of factors such as political activism among adults in poor neighborhoods, but it will probably be more productive to focus on specific barriers to involvement in the neighborhood.

To conduct an analysis of the population in as efficient a manner as possible, we propose that the change agent engage in another series of tasks, which include the following:

1. Review the literature on the target population.
2. Seek diverse perspectives.
3. Select factors that help in understanding the target population.

When these three tasks have been completed, it is time to review the factors identified in relation to the problem together with the factors identified about the population in item 3 above. Then, speculation about possible cause-and-effect relationships occurs. We undertake these speculations in:

4. Develop a working hypothesis of etiology about the problem.

But first, we begin with a review of the literature in Task 1.

Task 1: Review the Literature on the Target Population

Task 1 involves defining a target population and researching a number of different content areas in order to better understand the population, thereby providing more useful information on which to base the intervention. Content areas should include at least an exploration of issues of growth and development of the population, of racial and ethnic considerations, and of gender issues.

In the model of problem analysis presented in Chapter 3, we proposed a review of the literature on the condition or problem. In many ways, the population analysis may overlap with this earlier effort. Studies often cover both a problem and a population, such as "the health needs of rural, elderly, African American women." Literature that covers both problem and population can be doubly useful. However, it is also important not to overlook relevant literature focused exclusively on the population.

In attempting to understand certain types of problems and populations, it may be useful to explore the literature on human growth and development. With other problems or populations, this literature may be less useful. If, for example, a social worker in a high school is asked to address a growing problem of eating disorders among high school girls, much can be learned from the literature on adolescence and gender. A different type of study emerges if a social worker working in a community center in an ethnic community is asked to deal with a persistent denial of health care from the local hospital's emergency unit. In this instance, a study of the population would probably draw on the actual experiences of community residents with the hospital, and perhaps explore experiences in comparable communities.

These decisions on selection of resources should be carefully weighed because information compiled can influence the direction of the analysis and the intervention. For example, analysis of the behavior of underutilization of medical care in a poor community could lead to a conclusion that the problem lies in the passive behavior of the poor, rather than recognizing the need to explore potential policy and programmatic barriers to medical care in this community.

Understand Concepts and Issues Related to Growth and Development.   Questions to be explored for this activity include:

- What literature is available on this population group?
- What factors or characteristics gleaned from the literature on this population will be helpful in understanding the target population?

This activity involves a review of relevant literature on the target population. When an understanding of target population behavior is determined to be necessary, texts on human growth and development and human behavior can be very useful. These texts are frequently divided into ages and stages of life. For example, Ashford, LeCroy, and Lortie (2000) have organized their text on human behavior in the social environment around a framework for assessing social functioning, including the biological, psychological, and social dimensions. The authors then explore phases of growth and development from pregnancy and birth through late adulthood. Hutchison (1999a, 1999b) introduces two volumes in which the changing life course and the person and environment are explored. Santrock (1998) uses the following chapter headings: Beginnings, Infancy, Early Childhood, Middle and Late Childhood, Adolescence, Early Adulthood, Middle Adulthood, Late Adulthood, and Death and Dying.

There is a rich body of knowledge about the population groups with which social workers interact. Understanding the needs and developmental patterns of the population to be served can be a critical ingredient to designing meaningful and relevant macro-level interventions.

Identify Relevant Theoretical Perspectives. Questions to be explored for this activity include:

- What theoretical frameworks are available that relate to the target population?
- What frameworks are particularly useful in understanding the target population?

An important part of the literature review should be devoted to identifying and applying relevant theoretical perspectives. Theories are intended to explain phenomena and to provide a framework for research and testing of hypotheses.

As opposed to the random listing of facts and observations, theories allow for categorizing one's findings, making sense out of them, and turning seemingly unrelated bits of information into explanatory propositions that lead to logical, testable hypotheses. For example, focusing on the population of high school dropouts, one might draw on the work of Skinner (1971), Erickson (1968), Gilligan (1982), or Maslow (1943) to understand the behavior of the target population.

Using some of Skinner's most basic concepts—such as reinforcement, extinction, and desensitization—one might examine the high school experience for selected students. It might be hypothesized that negative reinforcements in the form of poor grades and criticism lead to discouragement and poor attendance on the part of some students. These negative responses may also extinguish certain behaviors and limit the effort a student is willing to invest in academic success. Or perhaps school disciplinary experiences such as detention, suspension, or extra assignments systematically desensitize some students to organizationally imposed sanctions. In this case, efforts would have to be expended to discover what this group of students would consider positive reinforcement, and how the academic experience could be designed so that they could achieve success.

Erickson's concept of identity might cause one to focus on the needs of high school youth for a positive self-image. The high school experience might then be examined to determine the degree to which it supports the development of a positive identity for some and thwarts it for others. Activities would be designed to build self-esteem based on the hypothesis that increased self-esteem will act as a motivator to academic success.

Gilligan's work raises consciousness in understanding the psychological development of women and the effect of gender on how one views the world. If dropout rates for women are related to teen pregnancy, one may want to consider the importance of gender identity. Gilligan theorizes that women seek connection and affiliation as they develop, not having to separate from the mother in the same way that boys do. Becoming pregnant, which contributes to dropping out of school, may be a young girl's way of establishing intimacy and feeling needed.

Maslow, on the other hand, would examine the phenomenon of high school dropouts in terms of the congruence between the high school experience and students' needs. The pertinent question would be whether the educational programs were appropriately tailored to meet the social, esteem, and fulfillment needs of students. Each level of need, once met, is no longer a motivator, so new challenges would have to be designed to achieve the goal of self-fulfillment.

Still other theorists provide additional perspectives on how adolescents deal with issues of self-identity as they grow and develop (Kohlberg, 1984; Marcia, 1993; Piaget, 1972). Using theoretical frameworks is far more complex than illustrated here, and it is not our intent to trivialize the full depth and breadth of these explanatory theories through our brief examples. What we do hope to illustrate is that theory is an important ingredient in understanding the target population. Theoretical frameworks give the analysis internal consistency and ultimately contribute to a rationale for the intervention.

Different theories propose divergent explanations of the problem and may suggest widely varying interventions. Sometimes these explanations and potential interventions allow two different theories to merge and reinforce each other, but at other times each theory may conflict sharply with all the rest. The change agent should be prepared to weigh these differing views and choose among them based on factors such as which seems to best fit the setting and population, which one seems to have the greatest explanatory power, and which offers the richest range of testable hypotheses (usually in the form of possible interventions).

Theoretical principles should be critically evaluated for their biases and given credibility based on how thoroughly they have been tested, especially in relation to the problem and population being explored. Once selected as a framework for analysis, theoretical assumptions should be stated and shared with those involved in the change effort. This is intended to facilitate the achievement of a shared understanding of the problem and population(s) involved.

Task 2: Seek Diverse Perspectives

A full understanding of a social problem requires attention to a range of perspectives. Problems can be understood in a number of ways, including (1) experiencing the problem firsthand, (2) working closely with people who have experienced the problem, and/or (3) studying the literature on the problem. In considering these three approaches, it is necessary to distinguish between the understanding and insight gained by firsthand experience as contrasted with other methods of learning about a social problem. After having examined the literature, then, it is critically important to talk with persons who know about the problem firsthand.

Listen to Persons Who Have Experienced the Problem. Questions to be explored for this activity include:

- How do representatives of diverse groups affected by this problem view the problem?
- Have diverse voices and perspectives been included in articulating and understanding the problem? If not, why not?

When it comes to representing the perspectives of a population of people who have experienced a problem, it should be understood that those who have only secondhand experiences usually are not accepted as spokespersons by those who have direct experience with the problem. For example, people who have experienced day-to-day life on public assistance may not be willing to accept a social worker as a spokesperson to articulate their feelings and needs. Likewise, people living in a housing development may be more likely to turn to a fellow housing-project resident as a spokesperson. Describing the experiences that led to post-traumatic stress disorder in a Vietnam veteran can usually be done with credibility only by someone who was there. People of a particular ethnic group may be able to speak for the experiences of their own group, but not for another group. A person who is not transgendered may not be able to credibly represent a transgendered person.

For these reasons, it is important to find spokespersons who are accepted and supported by their peers and who can help articulate the perspectives of the group(s) involved. It is also important to locate literature that will help those involved in the change effort to understand important issues and perspectives of the target population.

The Importance of Culture. Green (1995) points out that "there are literally hundreds of definitions of culture in the professional literature of sociology and especially anthropology" (p. 14). The term *culture* may refer to the ways in which a group of people perceive and understand phenomena. It may be defined by the ways in which people behave and transmit customs from one generation to another. Green warns against attempting to understand a culture as simply an inventory of values and traditions. This, he says, risks leading to simplistic stereotyping. Instead, Green proposes that culture be understood as "a perspective that emerges when people engage one another across boundaries they recognize as significant" (p. 15). These concerns illustrate why it is important for a social worker engaging in macro practice to immerse herself or himself in literature on culture and ethnicity. It is also important for him or her to engage in face-to-face interactions with people representing a culture in the interest of pursuing a more complete understanding of what factors may be significant in the current situation.

The work of Lecca, Quervalu, Nunes, and Gonzales (1998) provides an example of ways in which literature alone can be limiting. The authors cite the work of Locke (1992), who identifies the following American values: (1) achievement and success, (2) activity and work, (3) humanitarian mores, (4) moral orientation, (5) efficiency and practicality, (6) progress, (7) material comfort, (8) equality,

(9) freedom, (10) external conformity, (11) science and secular rationality, (12) nationalism-patriotism, (13) democracy, (14) individual personality, and (15) racism and related group superiority (pp. 42–43). In contrast, the authors provide some generalizations about Native Americans, including the values of (1) sharing, (2) cooperation, (3) noninterference, (4) time orientation, (5) extended family orientation, and (6) harmony with nature (p. 39).

Although cultural values influence individuals, it should be clear from even a cursory review of the sets of values presented here that no assumptions can be made about a specific individual or group of people in a community. Some level of very general introduction can be accomplished through a review of the literature, but the usefulness and relevance of information can be determined only through interpersonal interactions with community members.

The Importance of Inclusion.   Diverse perspectives and their importance in assessing a population group are reinforced by Weil, Gamble, and Williams (1998): "Community practice that is done with, rather than on, communities can generate knowledge as well as empower and emancipate members, leading to a process of social change" (p. 251). The authors propose action research methods that involve "a simultaneous process of knowledge building, reflection, and action" (p. 252), along with four feminist-influenced approaches to community practice research:

Participatory Action Research
- Collaboratively involves members of the community in negotiating research topics, format, and data analysis
- Minimizes the distinction between the researcher and the "client"; the relationship is reciprocal, both teaching and learning from the other
- Action results from increased critical consciousness

Needs/Assets Assessment
- Provides data about the incidence of issues that are often "invisible"
- Provides data to be used by the community in advocacy work

Empowerment Evaluation
- Uses evaluation concepts, techniques, and findings to foster improvement and self-determination
- Assesses the effectiveness of different types of actions in meeting needs or solving problems
- Increases capacity to self-evaluate

Demystification
- Illuminates the "invisible"
- Gives voice to the "voiceless" (p. 253)

In the best of all possible worlds, in each episode of macro-level change there would be a change agent available who reflects the culture, ethnic group, gender, age group, and life experiences of the target population. This is seldom the case. Social workers find themselves the focal point or conduit for concerns representing many diverse perspectives, and it is expected that they will find ways to give visibility and voice to each legitimate perspective.

If a social worker happens to be 23 years old, white or Latina, and working with elderly African American people, it is incumbent on her to recognize that her experiences are not the same as those with whom she is working. Effective cross-cultural social work in this situation requires that the social worker be able to hear the voices of elderly African American persons and partner with them as they guide one another.

The Dual Perspective. A framework helpful in understanding and dealing with the complexities of characteristics such as ethnicity and gender is the dual perspective. Initially conceptualized by Norton (1978), the dual perspective views an individual as being at the center of two surrounding systems, which Norton calls the nurturing system and the sustaining system, shown in Figure 4.1.

The center of the diagram represents the *individual.* Immediately surrounding the individual is a *nurturing system,* represented by the values of parents and extended family or substitute family, by community experiences, beliefs, customs, and traditions with which the individual was raised. Surrounding the nurturing system is a *sustaining system* represented by the dominant society. The sustaining system also reflects beliefs, values, customs, and traditions.

The focus of analysis for the change agent is the degree of fit between an individual's, family's, or group's nurturing system and the sustaining system within which they function. The nurturing system may, for example, support the importance of family over individual, whereas the sustaining system emphasizes and rewards individual competition and merit.

Sustaining systems are made up of influential and powerful people—teachers, employers, elected officials, and others. Some segments of sustaining systems may reflect ageist, racist, sexist, or other prejudicial attitudes, and can therefore be perceived by diverse population groups as representing alien and hostile environments. Yet, these individuals frequently have little choice but to interact with the sustaining system environment.

For these reasons, those whose nurturing-system experiences, beliefs, and values are most dissimilar to those of the sustaining system may have the most difficulty crossing cultural borders. Individuals who represent the sustaining system

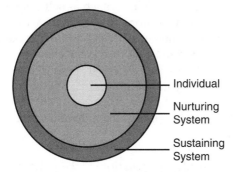

FIGURE 4.1 The Dual Perspective
Source: Based on Norton (1978).

in local communities may be insensitive to cultural differences and may assume that everyone wants (or should want) to adopt sustaining or dominant system values, beliefs, and language. This situation can set up an impasse, and it is incumbent on the social worker to understand the nature of the impasse and to develop a basis for better mutual understanding.

In attempting to improve the quality of cross-cultural and cross-gender communication, it is reasonable to assume that oppressed or ignored groups have a better understanding of the sustaining system than sustaining-system representatives have of oppressed and ignored people. People who live within a dominant society observe and experience, on a daily basis, the values, beliefs, traditions, and language of the dominant society through personal contact, television, newspapers, and other media. The reverse is not true. Representatives of the dominant society do not observe and experience the values, beliefs, and traditions of nondominant groups. Therefore, it makes sense for the social worker to concentrate on helping representatives of the dominant society to understand the needs of the target population.

Most programs and services, along with their underlying rationale, are designed from a sustaining-system or dominant-society perspective. Even the theories used to explain the problem and the research on which the practitioner builds hypotheses may reflect sustaining-system biases. Members of diverse ethnic groups, on the other hand, may have very different perspectives of the problem and how to resolve it.

Consider, for example, a situation in which some of a community's elders are experiencing a deteriorating quality of life. One culture may value the extended family and wish to maintain elderly parents in the home, but most family members cannot afford the expense of taking on another dependent. Another culture may value the independence and privacy of elderly parents, but its members cannot afford to pay retirement-community prices. The community's influential and powerful members may believe that government should not be involved, and that decisions about aging parents should be left to adult children. It is likely that these types of perceptions will be linked to factors relating to culture and/or gender and to nurturing-system/sustaining-system perspectives.

Resources available to the social worker in promoting better cross-cultural understanding include informal and mediating units such as self-help and voluntary associations, as well as formal organizations that represent themselves as speaking for cultural or ethnic groups. Whenever diverse groups make up a part of the target population and are expected to benefit from the change effort, credible expertise reflecting these different perspectives must be sought and incorporated into the problem analysis and intervention design.

Explore Past Experiences with the Target Population and Problem.   Questions to be explored in this activity include:

- What kinds of experiences has this population had in the past in their attempts to deal with this problem?

- How do representatives of this group perceive the sustaining system?
- Has this same group or population attempted to initiate change in the past? If so, with what results? If the results were positive, why is the change effort being repeated? If the results of the past efforts were negative, what happened?

Identifying and interviewing past spokespersons for the target population and past representatives of the community or organization should aid in understanding the history of experiences with the target population and problem. If there have been relevant past experiences with this population, the change agent should compile a list of key actors and a chronology of interactions between the target population and community or organizational representatives that leads up to the present. Interviews with some of these important actors will then help shape strategy and tactics later in the episode of change.

Cross, Bazron, Dennis, and Isaacs (1989) promote the notion of cultural competence when engaging in cross-cultural social work. They identify six points on a continuum of competency. Understanding this continuum can be helpful to social workers who need to explore past experiences from the perspective of persons who experienced or are experiencing the identified problem. The continuum is:

Cultural Destructiveness
- Attitudes, policies, and practices that are destructive to cultures and consequently to individuals within cultures.

Cultural Incapacity
- The system lacks the capacity to help members of a cultural or ethnic group.
- The agency does not respect the beliefs or traditions of the group being served

Cultural Blindness
- The belief that culture is not important; that all people are the same.
- The use of helping approaches are seen to be universally applicable.

Cultural Precompetence
- The agency or system recognizes its cultural deficiencies and begins to make attempts to address them through outreach or hiring practices.

Cultural Competence
- Acceptance and respect for differences.
- Self-assessment of staff, and policies in relation to culture.
- Expansion of cultural knowledge and resources.

Cultural Proficiency
- Holds culture in high esteem.
- Cultural practice is enhanced by research.
- Builds cultural knowledge.

These concepts can be helpful to a social worker engaging in an episode of macro-level change by strengthening self-awareness, understanding how culture may influence practice, and promoting adaptation of skills and techniques in response to diversity.

Task 3: Select Factors That Help in Understanding the Target Population

Questions to be explored in this task include:

- From review of relevant literature on the target population and from listening to key informants, what appear to be the major factors that help in understanding the population?
- Which factors, at this point, appear to be the most logical ones to be addressed in this episode of change?

When a literature review and interviews have been completed, a beginning profile or pattern of behavior should emerge. This profile will contribute to understanding important factors about why the target population has behaved or reacted as it has. Factors relating to this population's needs or behaviors that must be dealt with in order to bring about needed changes should begin to become evident.

For example, if the target population is preadolescents at risk of delinquency, some of the following factors have been identified as being associated with this population: (1) low expectations for education, (2) little participation in school activities, (3) low school achievement, (4) poor verbal ability, (5) truancy, (6) early stealing and lying, (7) heavy peer influence, (8) nonconformity, (9) hyperactivity or aggressive behavior, (10) lack of bonding with parents, (11) family history of violence, and (12) high-crime, high-mobility community (Ashford, LeCroy, & Lortie, 2000, p. 376).

Which, if any, of these factors is useful in understanding the target population in a particular episode of macro-level change? Only those directly involved can answer that question. Much will depend on the nature of the problem identified and the purpose of the intervention. When a list of relevant factors has been identified, the process is at a point where speculation can begin about etiology (cause-and-effect relationships).

Summary of Steps Involved in Understanding the Population

In summary, the following steps or tasks have been proposed as a means of understanding the target population.

1. *Review the Literature.* Complete a review of relevant literature in the interest of developing an understanding of population perspectives.
2. *Interview Those Affected by the Problem.* Identify local, indigenous spokespersons who represent diverse perspectives.

3. *Identify Factors That Contribute to the Problem.* Develop a consensus among those involved in the change effort as to the factors that contribute to understanding the needs and concerns of the population. The consensus should represent the best and most relevant information about the current situation, drawn from local people, experts, and relevant literature.

Having completed this effort to achieve the best possible understanding of the target population, those involved in the change effort may now turn their attention to refining the problem statement.

Understanding Problems *and* Populations

It is now time to pull together the material presented in Chapters 3 and 4. The purpose of Chapter 3 was to guide the social worker through an analysis of the problem. In this chapter, we have examined in detail the population group most involved in this identified problem. The next step is to turn to the development of a working hypothesis, based on everything that has been learned.

Task 4: Develop a Working Hypothesis of Etiology about the Problem

When the problem- and population-analysis phases have been completed, a good deal of relevant quantitative data and other types of information have presumably been compiled and prioritized. The final activities under Task 4 involve distilling this information into a focused, shared understanding of the reasons behind the continued existence of the problem.

Etiology is defined as "the underlying causes of a problem or disorder" (Barker, 1995, p. 125). Speculating about the etiology of a problem is an attempt to arrive at an understanding of cause-and-effect relationships. As one begins to move into this territory, it is important to keep an open mind and let quantitative data, related information, and the personal experiences of target population representatives inform an understanding of the problem. It is highly unlikely—in analysis of social, community, and/or organizational problems—that there will be simple, linear, cause-and-effect relationships. It is more likely that there will be multiple contributing factors, along with multiple views on what is relevant and applicable to the current situation.

Review What Was Learned in Both the Problem Analysis and the Population Analysis. The questions to be explored in this activity are:

- What are the major concepts, issues, and perspectives identified in the problem analysis?
- What are the major issues and perspectives identified in the population analysis?

Examination of a history of the problem, theory, and research on the population and problem come together at the point at which cause-and-effect relationships are postulated. The change agent looks for patterns of events or factors that seem to be associated so that a case can be made for a working hypothesis on selected causal or contributing factors.

In many cases, alternative explanations of cause and effect are all logical and, in a sense, "correct," but they may apply to different groups with a given population. For example, all the following statements are probably rational understandings about why groups of high school students drop out of school:

- Some students drop out because they believe that the structure of the program and the content of the curriculum are not relevant to their needs.
- Some students drop out because of inability to handle the academic demands, even though they see relevance to their needs.
- Some students drop out because income is needed by their families and they are the only resource at the time.
- Some students drop out because they suffer discrimination and rejection from their peers, and leaving the situation is a way of avoiding emotional pain.
- Some students drop out because there is such intense discord in their home and family lives that they are incapable of dealing with the added stress of academic demands.

The decision that must then be made is not one of choosing the "correct" perspective on etiology, but rather on selecting the subgroup(s) to be addressed. As with many (probably all) populations and problems, one understanding of etiology and one intervention does not fit all. There are multiple rational explanations, and ultimately one or more must be selected to serve as a framework for understanding the problem and the population.

The hypothesis of etiology should identify what the participants in the change process believe to be the most important and most relevant factors contributing to the problem. This may be different from what was identified in the literature or may lead to a particular part of the literature that needs reexamination.

Select Important Factors Explaining the Current Problem.   Questions to be explored in this activity include:

- What are the factors that explain the problem?
- What are the results of these factors?

Based on what was learned, statements itemizing contributing factors can be generated. The following is a series of statements about probable effects of each of these contributing factors. For example, in exploring the question of why some adolescents demonstrate antisocial behavior, including committing status offenses (acts that would not be offenses if they were adults, such as truancy or running away from home), a hypothesis of etiology emerges. For example:

Some adolescent first offenders who commit status offenses seem to present the following pattern:

Factor 1: Some parents of adolescents experience a range of personal problems and stresses, often including financial, interpersonal, and/or employment-related problems.

Factor 2: Under stress, some parents tend to focus on their own needs and neglect the needs of their children.

Factor 3: When adolescents do not get the attention they need from parents, they seek attention in other ways from other people.

Factor 4: One way that adolescents seek attention is to act out; first in a minor way, then in increasingly more serious ways.

Other factors could be added that focus on, for example, a specific subgroup of adolescent girls, or a group of Native American boys, in which case gender or cultural factors may be included in the hypothesis.

Once these factors have been selected from the many factors generated in the problem and population analyses, attention should turn to speculation on effects or results. Continuing with the example of adolescents demonstrating antisocial behavior, we might propose the following results:

Result 1: Personal problems and stresses for parents of at-risk adolescents increase the likelihood of neglect of the adolescent.

Result 2: Neglect from parents often results in anger, hostility, and acting out on the part of adolescents.

Result 3: Neglected adolescents may feel a need to call attention to themselves by rebelling against parents, teachers, and authority figures through antisocial acts.

Result 4: Acting out may take the form of committing status offenses that bring the adolescent into contact with police or other law-enforcement agencies and serve the function of getting them the attention they seek.

Prepare a Hypothesis. Questions to be explored in this activity include:

- Based on the foregoing analysis of problem and population, what seem to be the dominant themes in understanding cause-and-effect relationships?
- How should the hypothesis of etiology be framed?

The hypothesis of etiology frames a change effort in a way that makes it focused and manageable. Using the foregoing working hypothesis, a change agent will begin to think in terms of framing the intervention around (1) identifying at-risk adolescents, (2) working with their parents to reduce stress and develop more positive responses to their adolescent children, and (3) attempting to meet the adolescents' needs for positive attention and identity formation.

If, on the other hand, the problem and population analyses had led to a conclusion that the most important factors had to do with racism and discriminatory or bullying behavior against a group of adolescents in a high school, the hypothesis of etiology and the intervention would move in a different direction. It is important also to note that the hypothesis of etiology will be refined following analysis of arena, and a working intervention hypothesis will be developed.

Summary of Steps in Developing a Working Hypothesis of Etiology

The following steps complete the analysis and hypothesis-development phases of a macro-level change episode:

1. Review the major concepts, issues, and perspectives identified in both the problem analysis and population analysis.
2. Examine all factors contributing to an understanding of the population and the problem, and select those seen as most important and most useful in explaining the current problem.
3. Prepare a hypothesis of etiology that clearly identifies factors seen as contributing to the problem and that also identifies consequences or results of those factors.

Summary

This chapter and the previous one have proposed a method for understanding the problems and populations to be addressed by macro-level interventions in organizations and communities. The method begins with a thorough examination of the current condition in the organization or community that has led to the perception that a problem exists. Condition is seen as a more neutral term; its use recognizes that not everyone agrees on the existence of a problem (or negatively defined condition). Someone must first identify the negatives that make the condition a cause for concern. This is accomplished by developing a clear statement of the condition, by collecting quantitative data and other types of information about the condition, by reviewing the literature on the condition and the population(s) affected, and by identifying barriers to resolution.

A thorough analysis of all information gained about the condition/problem and population leads to a refinement of the problem statement, an identification of important statistical data supporting the existence of the problem, and a highlighting of factors that help to explain the etiology of the problem. Once a consensus is achieved on these issues (or concurrently with this achievement), an analysis of community and/or relevant organization(s) is undertaken. These topics will be covered in the next chapters.

DISCUSSION QUESTIONS AND EXERCISES

Case Example Exercise

You are a social worker in a homeless shelter for families. You have worked there for six months and are finding that very few children are able to have a positive experience with their local schools for a number of reasons. You find that schools are reluctant to enroll children from homeless families because they cannot verify that all enrollment criteria have been met. Often other children pick on homeless children and perpetuate a stereotype or stigma. Also, some homeless children get little support from their parents and do not have the resources to compete academically. It appears that, without some type of change, the children in the shelter are destined to repeat the patterns of their parents and have difficulty in school, difficulty later in employment, and difficulty bringing stability into their lives. For these reasons, you propose that the shelter address the problem of the school experience for children of resident families. The director appoints you as chair of a task force, and asks you to bring forward a proposal for consideration.

Discussion Questions

1. How would you describe the population affected by this problem (e.g., age range, gender, ethnic makeup, SES, geographic location, or any other factors that will help to understand the population on which you are focusing this change effort)?

2. From your knowledge of human behavior in the social environment, what factors can you identify from each of the following domains that may help you to better understand your target population?

   ■ *Biophysical.* What are the major biophysical concerns relative to stage of growth and development for your population?

   ■ *Cognitive.* Describe expectations for cognitive development that are relevant to your population and problem as conceptualized by the major theoretical frameworks related to cognition.

   ■ *Psychological/Emotional.* Select and apply relevant theoretical frameworks that will help in understanding the psychological or emotional growth and development or the developmental tasks of your population.

   ■ *Social/Interpersonal.* Select and apply relevant theoretical frameworks that will help in understanding the social growth and development of your population.

3. From your knowledge of culture and gender, what factors can you identify that may help you to better understand your target population?

   ■ *Culture.* Identify the major factors (values, perspectives, traditions, beliefs, practices, roles, and role expectations, etc.) that provide the context for growth and development of your target population.

   ■ *Gender.* Identify relevant gender-related factors as they apply to this population and problem.

4. Based on the information you have compiled, what mix of biophysical, cognitive, psychological/emotional, social/interpersonal, cultural, and gender-related factors do you consider to be most important or most relevant in helping to explain the behavior or response of your target population to the identified problem?

APPENDIX
Framework for Understanding
the Target Population

Task 1: Review the Literature on the Target Population

Understand Concepts and Issues Related to Growth and Development
- What literature is available on this population group?
- What factors or characteristics gleaned from the literature on this population will be helpful in understanding the target population?

Identify Relevant Theoretical Perspectives
- What theoretical frameworks are available that relate to the target population?
- What frameworks are particularly useful in understanding the target population?

Task 2: Seek Diverse Perspectives

Listen to Persons Who Have Experienced the Problem
- How do representatives of diverse groups affected by this problem view the problem?
- Have diverse voices and perspectives been included in articulating and understanding the problem? If not, why not?

Explore Past Experiences with the Target Population and Problem
- What kinds of experiences has this population had in the past in their attempts to deal with this problem?
- How do representatives of this group perceive the sustaining system?
- Has this same group or population attempted to initiate change in the past? If so, with what results? If the results were positive, why is the change effort being repeated? If the results of the past efforts were negative, what happened?

Task 3: Select Factors That Help in Understanding the Target Population

- From review of relevant literature on the target population and from listening to key informants, what appear to be the major factors that help in understanding the population?
- Which factors, at this point, appear to be the most logical ones to be addressed in this episode of change?

UNDERSTANDING PROBLEM *AND* POPULATIONS

Task 4: Develop a Working Hypothesis of Etiology about the Problem

Review What Was Learned in Both the Problem Analysis and the Population Analysis
- What are the major concepts, issues, and perspectives identified in the problem analysis?

- What are the major issues and perspectives identified in the population analysis?

Select Important Factors Explaining the Current Problem
- What are the factors that explain the problem?
- What are the results of these factors?

Prepare a Hypothesis
- Based on the foregoing analysis of problem and population, what seem to be the dominant themes in understanding cause-and-effect relationships?
- How should the hypothesis of etiology be framed?

SUGGESTED READINGS

Aguirre, A., Jr., and J. H. Turner. (2001). *American ethnicity: The dynamics and consequences of discrimination* (3rd ed.). Boston: McGraw-Hill.

Crawford, M. (1995). *Talking difference: On gender and language.* Thousand Oaks, CA: Sage.

Farley, J. E. (1995). *Majority-minority relations* (3rd ed.). Englewood Cliffs, NJ: Prentice-Hall.

Fong, T. P. (1998). *The contemporary Asian American experience: Beyond the model minority.* Upper Saddle River, NJ: Prentice-Hall.

Lum, D. (1996). *Social work practice and people of color: A process-stage approach* (2nd ed.). Pacific Grove, CA: Brooks/Cole.

Martin, E., & J. Martin. (1995). *Social work and the black experience.* Washington, DC: National Association of Social Workers.

Mindel, C. H., R. W. Habenstein, and R. Wright, Jr. (1998). *Ethnic families in America: Patterns and variations.* Upper Saddle River, NJ: Prentice-Hall.

Rosenblum, K. E., and T. C. Travis. (2000). *The meaning of difference: American constructions of race, sex and gender, social class, and sexual orientation* (2nd ed.). Boston: McGraw-Hill.

Sotomayor, M. (1991). *Empowering Hispanic families: A critical issue for the '90s.* Milwaukee, WI: Family Service America.

Tannen, D. (1990). *You just don't understand: Women and men in conversation.* New York: Ballantine Books.

REFERENCES

Ashford, J. B., C. W. LeCroy, and K. L. Lortie. (2000). *Human behavior in the social environment: A multidimensional perspective* (2nd ed.). Pacific Grove, CA: Brooks-Cole.

Barker, R. L. (1995). *The social work dictionary.* Washington, DC: National Association of Social Workers.

Barker, R. L. (1998). *The social work dictionary* (4th ed.). Washington, DC: National Association of Social Workers.

Cross, T. L., B. J. Bazron, K. W. Dennis, and M. R. Isaacs. (1989). *Towards a culturally competent system of care.* Washington, DC: Georgetown University Child Development Center, Technical Assistance Center.

Erickson, E. (1968). *Identity, youth and crisis.* New York: Norton.

Gilligan, C. (1982). *In a different voice.* Cambridge, MA: Harvard University Press.

Green, J. W. (1995). *Cultural awareness in the human services: A multi-ethnic approach* (2nd ed.). Boston: Allyn and Bacon.

Hutchison, E. D. (1999a). *Dimensions of human behavior: Person and environment.* Thousand Oaks, CA: Pine Forge.

Hutchison, E. D. (1999b). *Dimensions of human*

behavior: The changing life course. Thousand Oaks, CA: Pine Forge.

Kohlberg, L. (1984). *Essays on moral development: Vol. 2. The psychology of moral development.* San Francisco: Harper & Row.

Lecca, P. J., I. Quervalu, J. V. Nunes, and H. F. Gonzales. (1998). *Cultural competency in health, social and human services: Directions for the twenty-first century.* New York: Garland.

Locke, D. C. (1992). A model of multicultural understanding. In D. C. Locke (Ed.), *Increasing multicultural understanding—A comprehensive model.* Newbury Park, CA: Sage.

Marcia, J. E. (1993). The ego identity status approach to ego identity. In J. E. Marcia, A. S. Waterman, D. R. Matteson, S. L. Arcjer, and J. L. Orlofsky (Eds.), *Ego identity: A handbook for psychosocial research.* New York: Springer-Verlag.

Maslow, A. (1943). A theory of motivation. *Psychological Review, 50:* 370–396.

Norton, D. G. (1978). *The dual perspective: Inclusion of ethnic minority content in the social work curriculum.* New York: Council on Social Work Education.

Piaget, J. (1972). Intellectual evolution from adolescence to adulthood. *Human Development, 15:* 1–12.

Santrock, J. (1998). *Life-span development* (7th ed.). Madison, WI: Brown & Benchmark.

Skinner, B. (1971). *Beyond freedom and dignity.* New York: Knopf.

Weil, M., D. N. Gamble, and E. S. Williams. (1998). Women, communities, and development. In J. Figueira-McDonough, F. E. Netting, and A. Nichols-Casebolt (Eds.), *The role of gender in practice knowledge* (pp. 241–286). New York: Garland.

PART THREE

Communities as Arenas of Change

In the next two parts of the book we will provide information on the principal levels or "arenas" at which macro interventions take place: communities and organizations. Each of these parts begins with a review of theoretical literature relevant to the arena and the systems that characterize it, followed by a second chapter that provides a model for analyzing the arena in anticipation of a change effort. Part Three initiates these discussions by examining communities as an arena for macro-level practice.

5 Understanding Communities

OVERVIEW

Introduction

Communities are arenas in which macro practice takes place, yet they are so diverse that no one definition or theory will capture their total essence. Terms such as *global community* and *world community* are used in contemporary society to refer to the complex array of relationships among the people of the world. Yet, when most people think about communities that are important to them, they usually think less globally, remembering where they grew up, identifying with where they live today, or focusing on various relationships that transcend traditional geographical boundaries. These relationships may be bound by characteristics such as shared history, cultural values and traditions, concern for common issues, and frequent communication. Many people identify with multiple communities, thus making "the community" a misnomer. For many, affiliation with more than one community is part of who a person is.

Based on their life experiences, social workers will have their own perceptions of what a community is, along with expectations about what it should be. These perceptions and expectations will influence how they approach work in communities that are new to them. It is important to recognize that experiences with and feelings about community as a geographic locality vary. Some communities will be viewed nostalgically, as desirable places that evoke warm memories. Some communities will be seen as oppressive, restrictive, or even dangerous to the people who live there as well as to "outsiders." Sometimes these differing views will be held by different people about the same community, because every person's experience is unique. Community-based groups ranging from youth gangs to garden clubs represent attempts to create specialized communities of interest within a geographic community, sometimes in ways that intentionally run counter to the local culture.

Some observers and analysts believe that community as a geographically relevant concept began to erode with the emergence of suburbs in the 1950s and 1960s (Gerloff, 1992). Others see unlimited human potential lying dormant in inner-city communities that have been rendered dependent by overzealous provision of services (Kretzmann & McKnight, 1993). We believe that social workers have the responsibility to recognize that community can be a powerful medium for enfranchisement and empowerment when its potential is understood and skillfully brought to life. We also believe that social workers must recognize that problems and needs can often be addressed more effectively by dealing with them collectively than by approaching them individually. The major focus of this chapter will be on understanding communities from a theoretical perspective as a first step toward better-informed and more skillful community-level intervention.

Defining Community

There are many definitions of community, and we provide only a sampling here. As early as the 1950s, one scholar identified over 90 discrete definitions of community in use within the social science literature (Hillery, 1955). No matter what definition is selected, though, concepts such as "space," "people," "interaction," and "shared identity" are repeated over and over again.

Irrespective of changes to be made in community arenas, the social worker will want to be fully aware of how persons affected by the change define and perceive their communities. The social worker must understand alternative perspectives, recognize the assumptions and values that undergird these views, and understand how differing perspectives influence change opportunities (Netting & O'Connor, 2003). It is also important to recognize that even persons within the same community will differ in their perspectives of what that community is and of what changes are needed. For example, it is not unusual within the boundaries of a community for one ethnic or cultural group to believe that schools are relevant and city services adequate to meet local needs, while another ethnic or cultural group believes they are irrelevant and inadequate.

One of the most cited definitions of community was provided by Warren in 1978, and over the years many schools of social work have used Warren's book, *The Community in America,* as a basic text for courses with community content. Warren defines *community* as "that combination of social units and systems that perform the major social functions" relevant to meeting people's needs on a local level (p. 9). *Community,* according to Warren, means the organization of social activities that affords people access to what is necessary for day-to-day living, such as the school, the grocery store, the hospital, the house of worship, and other such social units and systems. We customarily think of social units as beginning with the domestic unit, extending to the neighborhood or to a voluntary association, and on to the larger community. A community may or may not have clear boundaries, but is significant because it performs important functions necessary for human survival.

Types of Communities

Fellin (2001) contends that community occurs when "a group of people form a social unit based on common location, interest, identification, culture, and/or activities" (p. 118). He distinguishes three dimensions of communities: (1) a place or geographic locale in which one's needs for sustenance are met, (2) a pattern of social interactions, and (3) a symbolic identification that gives meaning to one's identity. We will briefly examine each category.

Geographical, spacial, or territorial communities vary in how they meet people's needs, how social interactions are patterned, and how collective identity is perceived. Local communities are often called neighborhoods, cities, towns, boroughs, barrios, and a host of other terms. Smaller geographical spaces are nested within other communities, such as neighborhoods that are portions of towns or public housing developments within cities.

In earlier times, before people were so mobile and technology transcended space, communities were much more place bound. Today, however, considerations of space must be juxtaposed with other ways of conceptualizing community. Whereas one may operate within geographical jurisdictions, the influences of forces beyond spacial boundaries are limitless.

Communities of identification and interest are not necessarily geographically based. These "nonplace" communities are called names such as functional communities, relational or associational communities, communities of affiliation or affinity, and even communities of the mind. These nongeographical or functional communities bring people together based on "ethnicity, race, religion, lifestyle, ideology, sexual orientation, social class, and profession or workplace" (Fellin, 2001, p. 118).

Functional communities, which are examples of communities that are based on identification and interest, are formed when "people share a concern about a common issue, which ranges from advocacy for the needs of children with disabling conditions to environmental protection" (Weil & Gamble, 1995, p. 583). For the social work practitioner, it is important to recognize and understand communities that are formed around shared concerns, such as AIDS, gun control, terrorism, and political loyalties. It is even more critical to recognize that these communities reflect a mutuality of deeply held beliefs and values that may conflict with those of other communities. For example, faith-based communities or congregations that believe that being gay or lesbian is morally wrong may have a clash of values when encountering the gay and lesbian community. Similarly, professional communities that believe in social justice and advocacy for the poor may encounter political communities formed to reduce government spending and to terminate public assistance to those who are on welfare, regardless of need or capacity for self-sufficiency. Communities of interest are becoming increasingly politically active, and many people have warned of the polarizing effects of special-interest politics.

Fellin also identifies communities that are focused on *a collective relationship that gives meaning to one's identity.* In a complex society, people establish their own constellations of relationships based on both place and nonplace considerations. For example, a social worker is likely to be a member of the National Association of Social Workers (a nonplace community), live in a neighborhood (a place community), and have close relationships scattered around the world (a personal network). Because each person will have a particular constellation of relationships, each person's definition of community will be distinctive. Often viewed as networks or webs of formal and informal resources, these relationships and what they mean to the person's "sense of community" are very important for the change agent to recognize, respect, and understand. Methods such as network analysis and ecological mapping are intended to reveal how individuals perceive their communities. For example, if people find their "sense of community" or identity through disparate, scattered relationships in which members seldom meet, the change agent may have difficulty mobilizing them to want to address a local community need.

Community, then, can be seen as those spaces, interactions, and identifications that people share with others in both place-specific and nonplace-specific locations. Table 5.1 provides a summary of the types just discussed, their definitions, and examples of each. The planned change model presented in later chapters will be applicable to both place and nonplace communities.

Distinguishing Community Theories and Models

No understanding of community is complete without viewing the historical distinction between Tönnies's (1887) concepts of Gemeinschaft and Gesellschaft. *Gemeinschaft* is roughly translated to mean community and focuses on the mutual, intimate and common bonds that pull people together in local units. These bonds are based on caring about one another and valuing the relationships in the group

TABLE 5.1 Types of Communities

Type of Community	Definition	Example
Geographical	A community bounded by a geographically defined perimeter	Neighborhood, city, town
Identification and Interest	Nongeographical communities bound together by common interests and commitments	Political action groups, child welfare advocacy groups, right to choose/right to life groups, religious groups
Collective Relationships of an Individual	The constellation of relationships of an individual that gives meaning and identity	Professional colleagues, personal friends, neighbors

in and of themselves. The group is valued, whether or not its members are creating a product or achieving a goal. Examples are the domestic unit, the neighborhood, and groups of friends. The focus of Gemeinschaft is on intimacy and relationship.

In contrast, Tönnies's concept of *Gesellschaft* refers generally to society or association. Examples of this concept are the city or the state. Gesellschaft is an ideal type representing formalized relationships that are task oriented. In Gesellschaft-type relationships, people formally organize to achieve a purpose, a task, or a goal. Although they may benefit from the relationships that are established, the purpose of these social interactions are to achieve a particular end, create some product, or complete some task.

Sociologists of the late 1800s viewed Gesellschaft as representing all the negative forces pulling people away from traditional communities that were built on institutions such as the family and religion. It is important to recognize, however, that the contribution of Tönnies's ideal types is to call attention to the differences between informal and formal systems and to the richness of their interactions. Social workers doing macro practice will find elements of both concepts in the communities with which they work. As for Tönnies's work, it is considered a classic piece that became the base from which community theory emerged in the 1900s and is cited in most historical literature on community.

Warren's (1978) text on community synthesized community theory development prior to the early 1970s and is a valuable resource for identifying studies conducted up to that time. Warren characterizes community as:

1. Space
2. People
3. Shared values and institutions

4. Interaction
5. Distribution of power
6. Social system

These themes will recur frequently as we enter into a discussion of community theory.

Theories are sets of interrelated concepts that explain how and why something works or doesn't work. Sociological theories of community often describe how communities function, whereas community practice models are intended to provide direction or guidance for persons wanting to change or intervene in a community arena. In the remainder of this chapter we present an overview of community theories and perspectives, followed by an identification of practice models that have emerged from these efforts.

Community Functions

Communities are structured to perform certain functions for their members. Warren (1978) identified five functions carried out by locality-relevant communities:

1. Production, distribution, consumption
2. Socialization
3. Social control
4. Social participation
5. Mutual support

Production, distribution, and consumption functions are community activities designed to meet people's material needs, including the most basic requirements of food, clothing, shelter, and the like. In earlier times, families had to produce most or all of what they consumed, but this is seldom the case in today's society. People today are interdependent for such basic needs as food, clothing, shelter, medical care, sanitation, employment, transportation, recreation, and other goods and services. The generally accepted medium of exchange for these goods and services is money. Money, therefore, becomes an important factor in defining the limits of consumption, and it comes into consideration in almost all community change efforts.

A second function of community is *socialization* to the prevailing norms, traditions, and values of those with whom people interact. Young people growing up in severely deprived communities will develop value perspectives different from those growing up in affluent communities, for example. Socialization guides attitudinal development, and these attitudes and perceptions influence how people view themselves, others, and their interpersonal rights and responsibilities. To understand an individual or a population, it is important to understand the norms, traditions, and values of the community or communities in which the person's socialization occurred.

Social control is the process by which community members ensure compliance with norms and values by establishing laws, rules, and regulations, as well as systems for their enforcement. Social control is a function performed by institutions representing various sectors such as government, education, religion, and social services. Many social workers serve in practice settings in which they must constantly strive to achieve a balance between dual roles as helpers and agents of social control. Schools, correctional institutions, probation and parole offices, and employment and training programs are just a few examples of such settings.

Other settings and programs deal with more subtle forms of control, such as patterns of service distribution and eligibility criteria that govern access to resources on the part of vulnerable groups. For example, case managers often find they must deny services when faced with limited resources. Sensitivity to these limitations may spur the practitioner to work toward change, only to discover that key policymakers have chosen to constrain access to assistance rather than provide the level of assistance needed to combat the presenting problem. Recognizing how social control is manifested in social welfare policies, programs, organizations, and communities can be disillusioning, but is necessary for understanding the structure and process of service delivery.

Social participation includes interaction with others in community groups, associations, and organizations. Communities provide an outlet for people to express their social needs and interests as well as opportunities to build natural helping and support networks. People are assumed to need some form of social outlet. Some find this outlet through local churches, some in civic organizations, and some in informal neighborhood groups. Understanding the opportunities and patterns of social participation in a target population is helpful in assessing the extent to which a community is meeting the needs of its members.

Mutual support is the function that families, friends, partners, neighbors, volunteers, and professionals carry out in communities when they care for the sick, the unemployed, and the distressed. Most helping professions and government-sponsored programs developed in response to the inability of other social institutions (i.e., domestic units, faith groups, civic organizations) to meet the mutual support needs of community members. As society grew more complex and the supportive capacity of traditional institutions such as families and neighbors was increasingly strained, professions were established to address the resulting unmet needs. Some observers believe that the service mentality developed by government and the helping professions has undermined the mutual support function in neighborhoods and communities, and has weakened the capacity for collective community problem solving (Kretzmann & McKnight, 1993).

When Community Functions Fail

These five functions, according to Warren (1978), define the purpose of a community. If all functions were performed in a given community in a manner that met the needs of all its members (that is, if all consumption, socialization, social control, social participation, and mutual support needs were met in a healthy, positive, and constructive manner), then the existing natural structures of that community would represent all the resources needed to nurture and care for its members.

However, such an "ideal" community is rarely found. Some religious communities in rural areas have been able to fulfill most of these functions in a way that precluded the need for intervention and change, but these are clearly exceptions. It is far more common to find that these functions are carried out in a way that falls short of meeting the needs of at least some community members. There may be inadequate resources for distribution and consumption, or they may be distributed unevenly. Socialization may be to a set of values supported by some community members but not others. The social control function may not operate in a fair and even-handed manner for all. Social participation opportunities may be severely limited for some. Mutual support functions may be undermined by a dominant value system that places a premium on rugged individualism. In short, communities can be considered healthy or unhealthy, functional or dysfunctional, and competent or incompetent based on their ability to meet community needs. This may be particularly true for oppressed target populations within their boundaries. We hasten to say that rarely do we find a community that can be labeled so easily one way or another. Most communities are somewhere along a continuum between the sets of terms stated above.

Building on Warren's work, Pantoja and Perry (1992) provide a working model of community development and restoration. Citing production, distribution, and consumption as the economic functional area on which all other functions depend, they then list socialization, social control, social placement (participation), mutual support, defense, and communication. The areas of defense and communication are additions to Warren's list.

Defense is the way in which the community takes care of and protects its members. This function becomes very important in communities that are unsafe and dangerous. Some communities have even been labeled *defended communities*, in that they have to devote a great deal of effort toward looking after their members. This function is relevant to nonplace communities as well. For example, the function of defense may be critical among gays or lesbians because there are groups within the larger society that may seek to do them harm. Similarly, people of color in various communities have had to support one another in defending themselves against the violence of racial hatred.

Communication is also added by Pantoja and Perry to Warren's list of functions. Communication includes the use of a common language and symbols to express ideas. Although communication may have been assumed as part of all the functions originally identified by Warren, its identification as a separate function in contemporary society is very important. For example, the importance of language has been shown by debates that have raged over political correctness or English-only initiatives in various states. Written communication has also been revolutionized through the use of email and the ability to communicate instantly worldwide with the push of a computer key. Communication is a function that serves as a glue to hold people together, whether it is "verbal, written, pictorial [or an] expression through sound" (Pantoja & Perry, 1992, p. 230).

The assumption underlying the identification of functions is that communities serve the needs of members by performing these functions well. Conversely, when communities are dysfunctional (Pantoja & Perry, 1992) or incompetent (Fellin 1995), their members suffer and change needs to occur. According to Pantoja and Perry's theoretical framework, it is when the economic function breaks down that dysfunctional communities occur. Without a stable economic base, other functions, which are largely supportive, deteriorate or are impaired. Therefore, it is important for the social worker to carefully assess how communities are functioning and how the needs of people are or are not being addressed. Table 5.2 provides an overview of community functions.

Functional definitions and understandings of community can also be useful in communities that are not geographically specific. For example, some people may have their communication needs met by keeping in touch with persons in different geographical areas. It is not unusual to have adult children of elderly parents who live miles apart calling daily to check on how their parents are doing. In professional communities, long-distance communication is carried out through telephone, fax, email, or instant messaging on a regular basis. This assumes people have access to the technology that facilitates this communication. For many persons, these options are not available, however, and this raises questions about the competence of the community to meet members' needs (Fellin, 1995).

Functionalism "regards social structures (definable social entities that exist in relationship to other structures) and social functions (the roles, purposes, and uses of the entities) in a given social system as inextricably intertwined" (Harrison, 1995, p. 556). What this means is that *structures,* such as schools, synagogues, and political entities, are intermeshed with *functions,* such as teaching, providing leadership, and advocating for change. Understanding community requires analysis of structures and function *together*—not as separate entities. This is a notion that is

TABLE 5.2   **Functions of Community**

Warren's Functions of a Community	Pantoja & Perry's Functions of a Community
1. Production, distribution, consumption	1. Production, distribution, and consumption
2. Socialization	2. Socialization
3. Social control	3. Social control
4. Social participation	4. Social placement
5. Mutual support	5. Mutual support
	6. Defense
	7. Communication

Source: Warren (1978) and Pantoja and Perry (1992).

also relevant to social systems theory, so we now turn to the concept of social systems as it applies to community.

Systems Theory

In Chapter 1 we introduced Warren's (1978) contention that social systems theory holds great promise for understanding communities. We also indicated that the planned change model in this book is based predominately on systems theory.

Building on the work of Talcott Parsons (1971) and others, Warren applied social systems theory to communities. The functions identified earlier are viewed as being performed by various groups and organizations within local communities. These internal, horizontal relationships are complemented by vertical relationships in which communities connect beyond their own geographical boundaries. External linkages such as these provide mechanisms by which local communities reach out to other systems, including groups, organizations, and other communities. Each community system is composed of multiple interacting subsystems that perform functions for community members. Given the diversity among groups and subgroups, communities have a broad range of structural and functional possibilities regarding how they evolve.

Boundary maintenance is critical to system survival. If boundaries become blurred or indistinguishable, the community as a spacial set of relationships will be less vital. Macro practitioners may witness the struggle for boundary maintenance in their work with communities (Norlin & Chess, 1997), and it is likely that community practitioners will encounter conflict arising from boundary issues, whether it is a gay rights group seeking access to services for their members or a youth gang wearing its colors. It is important, then, to recognize that there are various analogies to systems theory, as originally introduced in Chapter 1. These are mechanical, organismic, morphogenic, factional, and catastrophic analogies (Burrell & Morgan, 1979; Martin & O'Connor, 1989).

The *mechanical analogy* views a social system as a machine in which all parts work closely together, are well coordinated, and are nicely integrated. When one part of the system changes, every attempt is made to reestablish equilibrium. In this analogy, order is emphasized over change and conflict. If the practitioner approaches a community using this analogy, there is an expectation that conflict needs to be reduced and a sense of connectedness restored. Practice models that derive from this systems analogy will seek to organize the local community toward making things pleasant and restoring order.

The *organismic analogy* comes from comparing social systems to biological organisms. Communities are viewed much as the human body, with each organ having a different function. If this sounds familiar, it is because we discussed the functions of community earlier in this chapter. Assuming that each unit within the community performs its assigned role, the community should progress toward a common good. Parson's work on structural functionalism is primarily grounded in this analogy. As long as community members can agree on what needs to happen, this systems analogy may work. However, many practitioners discover that it is not always easy to reach consensus among diverse community members.

What happens when there is conflict that cannot be overlooked or when communities do not work together? What happens to systems theory when there is seemingly no articulation of the parts or performance of the functions? When harmony does not exist or cannot be restored or when there are dynamics that require a great deal of change, other analogies apply.

A *morphogenic analogy* is applicable when change is ongoing and the structure of the system is continually emerging. Fundamental change can occur in this type of situation because there is no chance of returning to a former state of homeostasis (balance or equilibrium). This highly open approach to systems thinking means that change may be just as likely to be unpredictable as it is to be orderly. It is this unpredictability that requires the community practitioner to be open to clues about how things are changing and to be open to new possibilities.

Similar to the morphogenic analogy is the *factional analogy*, in which contentiousness is open and obvious. Conflict is so basic in this type of community system that change is likely to remain disorderly and subject to instability. Approaching this type of system with assumptions that order can be reestablished may be a setup for failure. On the other hand, for the practitioner who can face conflict head-on, this type community can be a stimulating challenge.

Last, a *catastrophic analogy* takes contentiousness and conflict to extremes, and such a community system will be characterized by deep fissures and distress. Without order or predictability, there will be a sense of chaos in which no one can determine future directions. Communication may have broken down in the process and subsystems are warring. Intervention in this type of community would look very different than it would from mechanical or organismic analogies.

Our point is that, depending on one's assessment of the community system and the degree of conflict, interventions will greatly vary. Table 5.3 provides an overview of the systems analogies just discussed.

Strengths and Weaknesses

An understanding of the possible structures and functions of community is valuable in providing ways of conceptualizing these arenas. Warren's work synthesized early research on communities, introduced the sociology of the community in America, and has become a classic in the field.

Of particular importance are the implications of systems theory for community practice. Hardina (2002) identifies these as

1. Changes in one aspect of a system produce alterations in other parts of the community;
2. Actions in community subunits not only influence what happens within the unit, but within the larger system;
3. Being able to identify how well a community functions means being able to compare its effectiveness to other communities; and
4. The push to return to a steady state in which everyone can participate in community life becomes a driving force in systems theory. (pp. 49–50)

TABLE 5.3   Systems Analogies

Systems Analogy	Definition	Example
Mechanical	All parts of the system work closely together—well coordinated and integrated.	A highly efficient, well-run city or town
Organismic	Each part of the system has a special function; if each performs as it should, the parts work together for the common good.	A commune where specialized roles are assigned
Morphogenic	Change is ongoing and the structure of the system is continually emerging.	A fast-growing school district with a multiethnic population
Factional	Conflict is basic; change and instability are ongoing.	A small town in conflict over growth versus no growth, where one group of residents favors growth and another group of residents favors no growth
Catastrophic		An environmental group that adopts a civil disobedience tactic to stop a chemical plant from moving into the community that desperately needs jobs; job seekers retaliate with violence

Source: Martin and O'Connor (1989).

Critics of systems theory are particularly concerned about the use of mechanical and organismic analogies in which assumptions are made about parts of systems working together to the benefit of the whole. Assumptions about common purposes fly in the face of unexplained change, conflict, and situations in which community members not only disagree but are deeply divided. These analogies are considered to be focused on preservation of the status quo and incremental change, attempting to return to harmony and consensus. Using these analogies is seen as an abdication of dynamics of power, conflict, and change inherent in community life (Martin & O'Connor, 1989). However, as pointed out earlier, there are other analogies of systems theory that do recognize conflict and change.

Even in systems approaches that recognize change and divisiveness as part of the human community, systems theory on the whole does not focus on power and politics. There are no directions provided for community practitioners who must face uncertain dynamics among diverse participants. There is no direction provided for how to engage community members, how to communicate, or how to use systems concepts to bring about change. Practice models derived from this theory base must therefore draw from other human behavior theories and perspectives to guide practitioners about power and politics, group dynamics, and interpersonal communication.

Stanfield (1993) contends that it is critical to revise sociological concepts that are based on viewing community as grounded in structural functionalism and social processes such as socialization. This orientation, he says, is based on a "monocultural system perspective" that views U.S. society from a singular value assumption in which conflict is seen as deviant. As long as there are set ways or familiar approaches to understanding community, associations and institutions created by population groups that do not conform to these accepted standards will be perceived as underdeveloped, dysfunctional, and pathological.

Human or Population Ecology Theory

Closely aligned with systems theorists are human ecology theorists, who also carefully examine structural patterns and relationships within place-based communities. In the mid-1930s, a group of sociologists under the leadership of Robert E. Park at the University of Chicago examined local community spacial relationships, and out of their work emerged human ecology theory. Human ecology theory was based on plant and animal ecology, with its roots in Darwin's biological determinism. This theoretical view of community was elaborated in the work of Hawley (1950, 1968) and characterized by Park (1983) as follows:

> Individual units of the population are involved in a process of competitive cooperation, which has given to their interrelations the character of a natural economy. To such a habitat and its inhabitants—whether plant, animal, or human—the ecologists have applied the term community.
>
> The essential characteristics of a community, so conceived, are those of (1) a population, territorially organized, (2) more or less completely rooted in the soil it occupies, (3) its individual units living in a relationship of mutual interdependence that is symbolic rather than societal, in the sense in which that term applies to human beings. (p. 29)

The human ecologists believed that if they studied one city well enough, what they learned could be applied with appropriate modifications to other cities. Two spacial concepts, the urban zone and the central city, became important elements of the ecology school. Zones were large concentric circles surrounding the central city, whereas natural areas (e.g., neighborhoods) were smaller arenas in which social relationships developed. Both zones and natural areas were considered changing and dynamic. However, subsequent studies in other metropolitan areas revealed just how difficult it is to generalize. Other cities did not always show the same structural patterns.

Today, ecological theorists focus on population demographics (e.g., age, gender, race), the use of physical space, and the structures and technology within communities. An ecological approach views communities as highly interdependent and teeming with changing relationships among populations of people and organizations. "From an ecological perspective a competent community enjoys a productive balance between its inhabitants and their environment, allowing for

change in an orderly, nondestructive manner and providing essential daily sustenance requirements for its citizens" (Fellin, 1995, p. 11).

Human ecologists are particularly concerned about how place-based communities deal with the processes of competition, centralization, concentration, integration, and succession. Each of these processes can be viewed along a continuum
(Fellin, 2001). For example, the degree of *competition* in a local community is primarily about the acquisition or possession of land among competing groups, moving from low to intense (even contentious) depending on the power dynamics. The
continuum from *centralization* to *decentralization* involves the degree to which
groups and organizations cluster in one location or disperse beyond the area. *Concentration* is a process in which persons enter communities, whether through immigration or migration, and those communities vary from great to small depending
on how many people or organizations stay within a particular locale. The continuum of *segregation* to *integration* of population groups occurs as diverse groups
either maintain or reduce their separation by characteristics such as race, religion,
age, or other variables. The degree of community change can be placed along a *succession* continuum determined by the rapidity with which one social group or set
of organizations replace one another within the geographical area. Table 5.4 high-
lights the characteristics of and issues associated with human ecology theory.

Advances in depicting these processes in geographical communities have
paralleled the development of management information systems in organizations.
Geographic information systems (GIS) use data to develop maps and graphics as
tools to problem-solve in local communities. Originally applied to planning and
development activities in environmental protection and natural resources management, this technology is being adapted for use in human service systems for
research, social planning, management, and administration. For example, a study
of youth gangs in Rockford, Illinois, demonstrates the use of technology to analyze
the structural dimensions of community in working toward change. An advisory
council appointed by the mayor gathered data from multiple sources, then used a
map of the area to plot what had been found. From the police department the
council obtained gang members' addresses, and these were laid over a map of city

TABLE 5.4   Human Ecology Characteristics and Issues

Human Ecology	Characteristics	Issues
Individual units of a population are in competition, but also must cooperate to ensure that the community can support all its inhabitants (including plant, animal, and human life)	An organized population, rooted in the soil it occupies, and mutually interdependent on other inhabitants	▪ Competition vs. Cooperation ▪ Centralization vs. Decentralization ▪ Concentration vs. Dispersion ▪ Segregation vs. Integration ▪ Succession vs. Status Quo

blocks. On the same map, schools and human service agencies were circled, then demographic information and reported crime statistics were overlaid. The final form of the map thus incorporated multiple data sources to allow the advisory group to have a visual representation for analyzing the problem.

> [The map] showed quite clearly that the areas suffering from the most gang-related crime and violence were in the southwest quadrant. In addition to suffering from poverty, low education levels, and the other demographic and social disadvantages . . . the southeast quadrant was very poorly served by schools, parks, and other recreational centers, and even by social service agencies. Overlay technique allowed [the advisory group] to demonstrate clearly the appropriate target population for improved services, and some of the area in which services should definitely be improved. (Hoefer, Hoefer, & Tobias, 1994, p. 120)

Elements such as population characteristics and geographical boundaries will be part of the framework presented in Chapter 6 to analyze a local community. Recognizing how the use of physical space can enhance access or create barriers to community resources is important, particularly in communities with diverse population groups.

Strengths and Weaknesses

Human and population ecologists are cousins of systems theorists. They, too, hope to find ways in which systems can become more harmonious and work better together. However, unlike their systems counterparts, they recognize competition as an ongoing process that includes a certain inevitable level of conflict. Hardina (2002) identifies three community practice implications of ecological theory:

1. Recognition that community groups are competing for limited resources, with survival of those with power
2. Realization that groups without power must adapt
3. Acknowledgment that social structures are heavily influenced by the physical environment, and changes in the physical can make a difference in the social

The recognition of multiple processes occurring simultaneously within communities is a major contribution of ecological theory. Acknowledging competition, centralization, concentration, integration, and succession as ongoing processes makes for a very dynamic, interactive understanding of how communities work. In addition, ecology theorists recognize organizations, populations, and communities as basic elements of ecological systems, thus reinforcing the importance of examining patterns and relationships.

Yet, recognizing relationships and their dynamics must be translated into ways to go about practice. Although competition is acknowledged and ecological theorists recognize power dynamics, they do not provide guidance regarding ways in which groups that do not currently have power can gain it. More important, assumptions that the physical environment influences social structures are somewhat deterministic, leaving the practitioner to wonder whether an individual or even a group has the potential to make change within environments that are not conducive to the desired change. As with systems theories, ecological theories are more likely to examine ways to establish harmony among populations, organizations, and communities. Accordingly, they can be accused of being inherently conservative and somewhat fatalistic by assuming that populations and sets of organizations must find ways to adjust within resistant environments.

Human Behavior Theories

Parallel to the issues of space, structure, function, and relationships among systems is the question of how people behave in communities—how they understand and find meaning in relationships, what values guide their actions, and how their needs are determined. There are many ways to examine these aspects of community, and we will address only a few here. However, human behavior theories can help social workers better understand why people do what they do.

Interactions

Beginning with rural communities and then expanding to urban environments, early anthropologists and sociologists explored how people relate to one another. The Lynds' 1929 study of Middletown and its 1937 follow-up offered a cultural anthropological view of a small American city (Lynd & Lynd, 1929, 1937). A subsequent study by West (1945) of the fictitiously named Plainville, Illinois, was similar to the Lynds' effort. These works were based on the assumption that rural communities were able to maintain traditional values while cities were moving closer to a mass-society orientation in which competing values made life more complex. These same distinctions and concerns are often expressed today.

Anthropologists attempted to understand the daily lives of people, their behavior patterns, and their belief systems. What emerged from these and other case studies was a recognition of the deeply held values that are inherent in community life.

Collective Identity

Clark (1973) proposes stepping back from the structural approaches in favor of examining the psychological ties that bind people in communities. He contends that *community* is a sense of solidarity based on psychological identification with others. Going beyond social interactions, community is deep seated in a sense of "we-ness" that can be place specific or can transcend place. This sociopsychological perspective (Martinez-Brawley, 1995) complements the structural approach to community in that it focuses on the meaning or "sense of community" that people feel in relationship to others.

MacNair, Fowler, and Harris (2000) develop what they call a framework of diversity functions based on previous work. Examining three social movements—the African American Movement, the Women's Movement, and the Lesbian, Gay, and Bisexual Movement—McNair and colleagues identify six functions: assimilation, normative antidiscrimination, militant direct action, separatism, introspective self-help, and pluralistic integration (p. 73). These approaches to organized change reveal how different people may identify with nonplace communities for different purposes.

In this model, *assimilation* occurs when identity is tied to mainstream culture and the purpose of being a part of a change effort is for the movement to result in the individual becoming a part of existing, oppressive communities in which he or she has previously been denied access. *Normative antidiscrimination* is a confrontational approach that stays within legal parameters and is used to gain access to community institutions that are oppressive. *Militant direct action* is used to catch people off guard through activism, still with the intent to gain a place within the community for persons involved in the movement. *Separatism* is an approach in which parallel communities are established and the identity of participants becomes tied to the alternative community. Since interaction with the mainstream is painful, norms emerge in association among members of the oppressed community and may be hidden from the mainstream. *Introspective self-help* is used when separatism is too difficult to maintain, thus community members focus on self-development and self-mastery. Finally, *pluralistic integration* occurs when groups that are confident in their own cultural identities do not give up their distinctiveness. They participate among and with persons from other cultures without losing a sense of who they are.

Values

Cohen (1985) views the community as ripe with symbols, values, and ideologies that people have in common with one another but that also distinguish them from those who hold different beliefs. For example, the colors that a youth wears may symbolize certain values not easily recognized to someone who is not part of a particular culture. Yet, wearing the colors into another community in which they are viewed as hostile can incite a violent response.

This relational view of community implies boundaries that are not necessarily tied to place. Boundaries may be physical, but they may also be racial, ethnic, linguistic, or religious. Boundaries can also be perceptual, and they may even vary among those who are part of the same relational community, just as persons who are not part of that community will perceive boundaries differently. Cohen (1985) explains that it is not the clarity of boundaries that is important (for they are always changing) but "the symbolic aspect of community boundary" (p. 12) that is most crucial. For example, even though people may move out of a local community, the key phrases and words that they used with others will remain as symbols of their close relationship. Similarly, when a person with disabilities moves into a long-term care facility, the ties that are maintained with persons outside the home become symbolic of returning home.

Unlike the functionalist perspective on community that focuses on culture as the integrating force that binds people together, Cohen (1985) suggests that

> the commonality which is found in community need not be uniformity. It does not clone behavior or ideas. It is a commonality of forms (ways of behaving) whose content (meanings) may vary considerably among its members. The triumph of community is to so contain this variety that its inherent discordance does not subvert the apparent coherence which is expressed by its boundaries. (p. 20)

Another way of expressing this perspective is that the secret of the successful community is to find unity amid diversity.

Needs

Amid these community interactions and values, community members have needs. Abraham Maslow developed a hierarchical framework for understanding lower- and higher-level needs. Maslow's hierarchy of needs moves from the most basic survival or physiological needs to a next level of safety and security needs, then social or belonging needs, esteem or ego needs, and finally the highest level of self-actualization needs, as depicted in Figure 5.1.

Maslow argued that lower-level needs must always be addressed before an individual can move to the next level. Any time a lower-level need is not being met, the person regresses down the hierarchy to satisfy that unmet need. Lower-level needs usually require a more immediate response and thus have higher urgency.

This framework can be useful in ranking and evaluating the needs of a target population, which can then be used to assess adequacy of services. The assessment

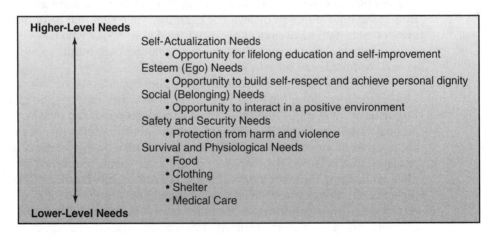

FIGURE 5.1   Maslow's Hierarchy of Needs

task is one of defining more specifically the problems faced by the target population at each level and identifying the extent of met and unmet need in relation to each problem.

In discussing a community development perspective, Pantoja and Perry (1992) examine the "nature of the human person [and] his/her dimensions and the needs these create" (p. 229). The authors begin, as does Maslow, with basic biological needs such as food, rest, and medicine. After this, they discuss the need for love and belonging (a second level of biological need); for groups and relationships, particularly in times of emergency (social); for self-expression through symbols such as art and language (cultural); for learning from the past (historical); for the use of power (political); for viewing the past, present, and future through action, words, and movement (creative/spiritual); and for explanations that connect what happens in one's world through investigation and experimentation (intellectual). Their list of needs follow:

1. *Basic biological needs* to have food, shelter, and clothing for survival and protection;
2. *Secondary biological needs* to have love, belonging, and identity as a human being;
3. *Social needs* to engage in relationships, mutual aid, and support;
4. *Cultural needs* to use language, norms, values, and customs;
5. *Historical needs* to record the past and to use the past to explore the future;
6. *Political needs* to gain power, order, and control;
7. *Creative/Spiritual needs* to use words, movements, and art to explain the unknown;
8. *Intellectual needs* to explore the nature of the environment, to investigate, and to experiment. (Pantoja & Perry, 1992, p. 229)

Table 5.5 summarizes these points and provides an overview of human behavior theories, their focus, and findings.

Strengths and Weaknesses

Human behavior theories that examine the relationships, interactions, values, and needs of individuals are helpful in understanding the dynamics that occur within populations, organizations, and communities. Without insight into why people feel and act as they do, community practitioners may see only the big picture, missing critical clues that will make the difference in whether trust and beneficial relationships can be established.

A subcategory of collective identity or interpersonal communities is the therapeutic community that some sociologists and social workers view with skepticism. In therapeutic communities, the purpose of coming together is for the good of the individual so he or she can be better, feel better, or do better. This quest for individualistic self-actualization carried to extremes can undermine the concept of community as a collective notion. Leading writers have questioned "if psychological sophistication has not been bought at the price of moral impoverishment" (Bellah, Madsen, Sullivan, Swidler, & Tipton, 1985, p. 139). Others call for a sense

TABLE 5.5 Human Behavior Theories: Foci and Findings

Human Behavior Theories	Focus	Findings
Interactions	The daily lives of people; behavior patterns and belief systems	Deeply held values are inherent in some communities.
Collective Identity	The psychological ties that bind people within a community	People feel a "sense of community" and a "we-ness" when there are psychological ties.
Values	Values bind people together but also distinguish them from those who hold different values	It is not the clarity of boundaries that is important; it is the symbolic aspect of the boundary created by common values.
Needs	Understanding needs in a hierarchy from lower-order needs to higher-order needs	Higher-order needs cannot be met until lower-order needs are satisfied.

of collectivism and community as a basis for social work practice (Specht & Courtney, 1994). The proliferation in the number of self-help groups is an example of how therapeutic collectivities develop around common concerns.

Human behavior theories look at the individual or the actions of individuals with others. However, critics of these theories caution that human beings are not robots and that actions are situational. Viewing needs, values, interactions, and relationships without a contextual understanding can lead to misunderstandings about what certain behaviors mean. Theories that focus on individuals must be used with an eye to context so that the person-in-environment remains paramount.

Theories about Power, Politics, and Change

Given the diversity within communities, the focus of much community literature has been on community building and creating bonds among people. However, it is vitally important to recognize political and social dynamics within communities as powerful forces that can be oppressive as well as supportive.

In her community practice work, Hardina (2002) reviews three theories related to the acquisition of power: power dependency theory, conflict theory, and resource mobilization theory. Although *power dependency theory* has been primarily applied to organizational arenas in which organizations become dependent on donors (Blau, 1964), Hardina sees important implications for community practice:

1. External funders may make demands that limit the abilities of local communities to initiate change,

2. Consumers may be fearful to bite the hand that feeds them, and
3. Change occurs within the boundaries of an exchange relationship in which people feel obligated to support the donor. (p. 52)

In other words, local communities and units within local communities become "beholden" to external funding sources.

Conflict theory typically views the community as divided into "haves" and "have-nots," all competing for limited resources. A Neo-Marxist view of conflict theory is that social services fulfill a social control function, providing just enough resources to keep the voices of dissent from becoming louder and maintaining the status quo (Hasenfeld, 1983). This casts social workers in the role of social control agents. However, Alinsky's perspective (1971, 1974) sees the role of social workers as organizing to use power to upset those in critical decision-making positions. Hardina identifies basic assumptions of conflict theory as:

1. There is competition for resources,
2. "Haves" hold power over the "have-nots,"
3. Oppression comes largely from the isms (e.g., racism, classism), and
4. Government as well as other vehicles of decision-making are controlled by the "haves." (p. 55)

Community organizers, then, must work with oppressed groups to access the system, to locate other power sources, and to gain a voice in community decision making.

Resource mobilization theory draws from conflict and power dependency theories with a focus on social movements and why they occur. In order to mobilize, one has to develop a collective identity (as was noted earlier under human behavior theories). Mulucci (1995) indicates that the construction of a collective identity requires three processes: a shared language in which the ends, means, and field of action are defined for the collective; an interacting network of active relationships with others who communicate, influence one another, and make decisions; and a certain amount of emotional investment that is needed for an individual to join the collective (p. 45). Hardina (2002) identifies basic assumptions of resource mobilization as it relates to community practice:

1. Social movements arise when groups are not represented in decision-making processes;
2. Public recognition occurs when there is protest;
3. Such a movement must develop an appropriate structure;
4. Success is dependent upon establishing a collective identity;
5. The better the organization's message, the more membership will increase; and
6. Fund raising is always a problem because members will have limited resources and accepting funds from others may lead to abandoning the radical nature of the cause. (p. 57)

Table 5.6 provides a quick overview of power dependency, conflict, and resource mobilization theory.

TABLE 5.6 **Themes and Implications of Power, Politics, and Change Theories**

Power, Politics, and Change Theories	Theme	Implications for Community Organizing
Power Dependency Theory	Organizations and communities are dependent on donors.	■ Consumers may limit change for fear of offending funders. ■ Change may be limited to boundaries established within the relationship. ■ Funders external to the community may limit change.
Conflict Theory	The community is divided into "haves" and "have-nots."	■ There is competition for resources. ■ "Haves" have power over "have-nots." ■ People are usually oppressed because of prejudice and discrimination. ■ Decision makers, including government, are controlled by "haves."
Resource Mobilization Theory	Social movements need a collective identity.	■ Groups not represented in decision making initiate social movements. ■ Public protests bring public recognition to an issue. ■ Movements need a structure. ■ Success depends on a collective identity for those involved in protest. ■ Strength depends on the quality of the message. ■ Funding without compromising the group's position is often a problem.

In an earlier chapter, we introduced a framework called the dual perspective, which views the individual in a nurturing system that functions within the context of a larger sustaining system. The nurturing system is made up of those traditions and informal relationships in which the individual feels most familiar. The sustaining system is made up of traditions, beliefs, values, and practices of the dominant society. This framework is important in understanding how communities contain built-in conflicts. Persons who experience divergence between nurturing and sustaining systems will be aware of community politics, power, and change as part of their daily experience. If there is congruence between nurturing and sustaining systems, there may be a false sense that communities are benign or supportive of all their members.

To illustrate how community norms are often taken for granted, Stanfield (1993) points to the importance of civic responsibility and civic cultures in African American traditions. Historically, these traditions have been supported by institutions such as "civic associations, fraternal orders, and churches rather than businesses and finance institutions" (p. 137). Whereas European American communities have prided themselves on a civic culture rooted in production, distribution, and consumption (the economic function of community), African American communities have been traditionally excluded from full participation in the dominant institutions within local communities. In addition, Stanfield points out that African American communities are not just formed in response to oppression, but they are based on unique cultural attributes that find expression through the development of community. Since civic society is treasured by dominant groups because it reflects the hallowed traditions of those in power, those same persons in power will resist the development of civil rights associations and other organizations dedicated to changing the status quo through political and economic empowerment.

Understanding the politics of different communities is critical to social workers as they interact with diverse groups. For example, volunteerism in traditional American communities usually involves a formalized process through which volunteers are organized and coordinated. Stanfield (1993) points out that volunteerism in African American communities is so much an integral part of the informal nature of caring that it becomes a way of life. Yet, there is no calculation of in-kind contributions or records of volunteer time in this latter definition of volunteerism. It is not captured in anyone's log or volunteer record book. Put simply, it is considered nonexistent because it cannot be defined as "volunteerism" in traditional U.S. communities.

Another example of communities that do not conform to dominant criteria is provided by Kayal (1991) in his study of gay men's health crises in New York City. Kayal analyzes how volunteerism among those in the AIDS community became necessary at a time when government support was not forthcoming. He explains that "the gay community's response to AIDS represents yet another chapter in the long American tradition of voluntary problem solving on the local level. For this reason, those most at risk were expected, even forced, to take on the burden themselves of responding to AIDS with any magnanimity, virtually alone" (p. 307). We could identify many more examples of groups that have formed locally and have responded to problems but whose work has not been recognized or valued within traditional understandings of community. Because social workers advocate with and for these groups, conflict is inevitable when intervening through macro practice.

Politics cannot be ignored as a part of community understanding. Feminist writers have long declared that the personal is political, indicating that every action or inaction that one takes is a political statement (Bricker-Jenkins & Hooyman, 1986). There are multiple examples of various interest groups, some more formalized than others, interacting within local communities. A political economy perspective recognizes this interplay of interest groups competing for resources within the community.

Strengths and Weaknesses

Understanding power and politics as part of community dynamics is critical to macro intervention. Theorists who focus on power, politics, and change are typically very appealing to social work because they recognize oppression and are aware that conflict cannot be ignored. Their language is compatible with social work values and ethical principles such as autonomy and social justice. These theorists are often appealing to social workers who want to make a difference.

Limitations within these theories are that they pit the community practitioner against the current power structure. Certainly this is appropriate at times, but these theories do not offer guidance on how to achieve one's ends without radical initiatives or how to judge when to act and when not to act. The nuances of finessing change are overwhelmed by the push to make change happen. There is little guidance for how to develop and use professional judgment so that targets of change are not alienated, since the assumption is that alienation will inevitably occur. "Although these theories offer some guidance about how power functions in society and the source of competition among various constituency groups, they do not present the organizer with a full range of strategic options for resolving community problems" (Hardina, 2002, p. 57).

Contemporary Perspectives

In the 1950s and 1960s, sociological interest in and research on communities suffered a decline. It was assumed that mass society had replaced the concept of community (Lyon, 1987), giving in to the fears that Tönnies's Gesellschaft had overwhelmed Gemeinschaft. Also, in recent years there has been a nagging fear among many writers, theorists, and citizens that community has been lost and that there must be a search to regain, revitalize, and reinforce community. This fear has been magnified in national, state, and local politics as persons campaigning for public office have reinforced the importance of decentralizing government, returning control to local communities, and reestablishing family values. "Community lost" has been a theme in the popular media when people use words such as *helplessness* and *disempowerment* to describe their feelings about what is happening to community life.

Putting this in perspective, however, these concerns have waxed and waned since the Industrial Revolution. Hunter (1993) points out, "For decades, social analysts have described the disappearance of the local community in modern society, and social pundits have decried the concomitant social decay, decadence, and deviance" (p. 121). Hunter goes on to say that a number of researchers have reminded practitioners of the resilience of the informal relationships and structures that maintained human relationships even prior to the advent of modern society. What is hopeful about Hunter's reminder is that he recognizes and validates what was once viewed as nonrational, short lived, unimportant, and invisible. Those relationships that women with children formed in local neighborhoods, the plethora of self-help groups that emerged in the last decades, the nurturing systems of racial and ethnic minorities, the voluntary associations to which people flocked, the efforts of natural helpers, and the human bonds that transcend time and space all maintain semblances of community when the formal structures suffer crises in credibility, integrity, or financial viability. Essentially, Hunter declares that those linkages that so carefully delineate as "micro" and "macro" are intricately interwoven, so that if one works with individuals, one will, by definition, have to understand community.

Resiliency, Empowerment, and Strengths Perspectives

In the mid-1980s and into the 1990s, community scholars regained what we believe to be a more balanced perspective, indicating that *both* mass society and community are relevant concepts. Communities, like people, have great *resilience* (Lyon, 1987). Breton (2001) ties resilience to neighborhoods, noting that "the stock of human and social capital characteristic of resilient neighborhoods consists of: (1) neighbor networks and the trust they generate, (2) active local voluntary associations through which residents mobilize for action, (3) stable local organizational networks, and (4) the services typical of an adequate social infrastructure" (p. 22). Of particular relevance is the rapidly increasing literature on the communal nature of people and the resiliency of "the commons" even in times of great change (see, for example, Lohmann, 1992).

Akin to resilience is the *empowerment perspective,* in which individuals, groups, organizations, and communities are seen as capable of gaining control over what they are doing by recognizing how social structures repress and influence everything they do (Solomon, 1976, 1987). Gutierrez and Lewis (1999) contend that "empowerment practice must be focused at three levels: the personal, the interpersonal, and the political" (p. 11). Mondros and Wilson (1994) identify four sources of literature that have contributed to the understanding of community power and empowerment:

1. Theoretical debates over social protest and discontent, when it arises and why
2. A growing body of literature that attempts to classify types of community organizations
3. A descriptive body of knowledge describing social protest movements
4. An extensive literature on community organizing skills providing practical guidance about how to go about organizing.

Closely related to an empowerment perspective is the *strengths perspective* offered by Saleeby (1997). Whereas communities may not appear to be as functional or competent as one might wish, social work practitioners must be careful to recognize and assess the strengths within the communities in which they work. When addressing terrible social problems such as homelessness and violence, it can become easy to write off entire communities as pathological and beyond assistance. Saleeby reminds practitioners of terms such as *empowerment, resilience,* and *membership* that can lift and inspire. *Empowerment* means assisting communities in recognizing the resources they have. *Resilience* is the potential that comes from the energy and skill required by ongoing problem solving. *Membership* is a reminder that being a member of a community carries with it civic and moral strength.

Kretzmann and McKnight (1993) use a strengths perspective to develop a model of practice that focuses on community assets rather than limitations. They advocate for strengthening local community networks and provide detailed guidance for how to do what they call *asset mapping*. Table 5.7 provides an overview of themes in resilience, empowerment, and strengths perspectives.

Capacity Building and Asset Mapping

Delgado (2000) reminds community practitioners that the strength of informal networks within ethnic communities is critical to organizing efforts. *Informal units* are those that are not publicly incorporated as legal entities to deliver health and human services. Often, these units have not been recognized for their importance in the service delivery system, whereas they actually perform a vast assortment of mutual support tasks. They include the household unit, natural support systems and social networks, self-help groups, and voluntary or grassroots associations.

Household Units.   The household unit consists of persons who share a common dwelling, whether they consider themselves families, significant others, friends, partners, or roommates. "The concept of the family is roughly equivalent to the household, but in recent decades more and more people have lived together in dwelling units without being related, making household a more broadly useful term" (Smith, 1991, p. 138). Service provision in this unit generally takes the form of caregiving and tends to fall heavily on women. The potential for caregiver bur-

TABLE 5.7   Contemporary Perspectives

Contemporary Perspectives	Themes	Characteristics
Resiliency	Communities have great potential to rebound and to cope.	■ Neighbor networks; trust ■ Active voluntary associations ■ Stable organizational networks ■ Adequate services
Empowerment	Communities can gain control over decisions that affect them.	■ People are excluded from decisions. ■ Resources go to the more powerful. ■ Leadership emerges and promotes an understanding of how decisions can be controlled locally.
Strengths	Communities are assessed in terms of their strengths rather than their deficits.	■ Community intervention may emerge around a problem or need. ■ Assessments identify community strengths (asset mapping). ■ Solutions come from community rather than from "services."

den or strain suggests that mutual support provided by the informal system may require assistance from others within the community. Respite services are often needed in the interest of sustaining the physical and mental well-being of the caregiver.

In assessing the extent of service provided in household units within a given community, one should look for indicators of what is happening within private dwellings of members of the target population. For example, are identified caregivers within the community overburdened? Is there an identified need for respite services for caregivers of physically disabled, developmentally disabled, elderly persons, and/or young children? Are requests for live-ins and shared housing increasing?

Of particular concern is identifying the importance of the household unit for the target population. For example, if the target population is frail widows living alone, the household unit does not contain others who can assist. Not only are caregivers not available, but formerly active older women may suddenly find themselves alone after years of providing care to children and spouses. On the other hand, target populations such as inner-city children, who often live in crowded households where privacy is limited and tension is high, may draw support from siblings, peers, and parents. Respite for single mothers may be difficult to locate and poverty may have reduced opportunities and life choices. Yet, the household unit can be a critical source of support for these children, fragile as it may be. Recognizing the household unit as a source of community strength and developing services to support this unit can produce a double benefit in strengthening families and reducing the need for other support services.

Natural Support Systems and Social Networks. Often an unstructured, informal approach to mutual support will evolve as natural or social support systems develop. Most people are part of social networks, but this in itself does not constitute a natural support system. A natural support system, according to McIntyre (1986), exists when resources have actually been exchanged.

The existence of natural support systems have been recognized for years. Recent studies and an emphasis on informal support have prompted a more intense examination, particularly among people of color and aging populations (Specht, 1986).

Because networks do not have established boundaries and depend on interaction between informal individuals and groups, they are likely to extend beyond the local community. Mutual support tasks may be provided by geographically dispersed, as well as geographically close, network members. Dispersed networks will depend on linkages such as transportation systems and telephones, and may therefore be vulnerable in times of crisis. Balgopal (1988) explains the importance of social networks:

> Social networks such as kin, friends, neighbors, and coworkers are supportive environmental resources that function as important instruments of help, especially during times of crisis. Social networks provide emotional resources and strength for

meeting the needs of human relatedness, recognition, and affirmation. They also serve as mutual aid systems for the exchange of resources such as money, emotional support, housing, and child care. Well-developed social networks often consciously and purposefully serve as helpers to families in crisis, making it unnecessary for these families to resort to institutionalized services through publicly and privately supported health and welfare agencies. The concept of a family's social network emphasizes the idea of the family with multiple affiliations, some of which overlap and some of which do not, as well as the idea of the family as an active selector, manipulator, and creator of its environment. (p. 18)

Within the local community there are indicators of the extent of informal neighborhood groups and support systems. Neighborhood associations, child-care exchanges, and neighbor-to-neighbor interaction are all indicators of the extent of support available within this unit.

The significance of natural support systems and social networks will depend on the target population. Networks that advocate for and provide ongoing support for the target population should be identified as a part of the human service system.

Self-Help Groups.   Self-help groups are one of the fastest growing elements of community support. They have been formed to deal with a variety of personal and social problems and needs, including substance use, bereavement and loss, depression, parenting, and many other issues. A number of self-help groups (probably the best known being Alcoholics Anonymous) have formed national and international chapters and are recognized vehicles of service delivery.

Hutcheson and Dominguez (1986) acknowledge the importance of ethnic self-help groups in their research on Latino clients. Because language and cultural barriers can arise in this and other ethnic populations, self-help groups assist in maintaining community identity and involvement.

Self-help groups are often viewed as being compatible with feminist perspectives. Such groups are directed toward widows, women who have been exploited or abused, and caregivers. Mutual support provided through self-help groups may assist in protecting the mental and physical health of caregivers.

Depending on the target population identified, self-help groups may be more or less important to their members and to the communities in which they operate. For example, groups that already have access to the service system and its resources may find them less necessary, whereas populations that are struggling to have their needs recognized may find them extremely helpful in supporting their efforts.

Voluntary Associations.   Smith (2000) identifies what he calls *grassroots associations* that form an interface between informal support groups and more structured service organizations. These associations are local in nature, largely autonomous, and composed of volunteers. Voluntary associations often serve as a bridge between the informal and formal components of a human service system. A *voluntary association* is defined as "a structured group whose members have united for the purpose of advancing an interest or achieving some social purpose. Theirs is a clear aim toward a chosen form of 'social betterment' " (Van Til, 1988, p. 8). Community groups such as neighborhood associations or local congregations fall within this category. Similar to self-help groups, voluntary associations vary in their degree of formalization. Since they are membership groups, a dues structure will often be in place. Therefore, their boundaries become more clearly defined than informal groups relative to those who are paying members and those who are not.

Voluntary associations have several characteristics. Members share a sense of community, which provides a collective identity. Social status may be enhanced by membership, and social control may be exercised over members. A function of the association may be to enhance the well-being of its members in a supportive manner. If the association is strong, it may exert a powerful influence on nonmembers that may be positive or negative (Williams & Williams, 1984). For example, associations such as the Ku Klux Klan are powerful yet destructive forces within certain communities.

Voluntary associations are also a study in both inclusiveness and exclusiveness. Williams and Williams (1984) discuss the importance of the black church in the development and growth of mutual aid societies. Historically, many mainstream activities beyond the church were closed to blacks who migrated to urban centers. "Blacks organized voluntary associations in the church in such forms as sick and burial societies, economic self-help groups, mission societies, and various secret and fraternal orders" (Williams & Williams, 1984, p. 21). Voluntary associations within the black church became an adaptive mechanism to deal with discrimination. Numerous studies report higher participation rates of blacks in voluntary associations than for any other groups (Florin, Jones, & Wandersman, 1986). In fact, ethnic groups, lesbians and gays, and other oppressed people may generally use informal and mediating units to a larger degree than other populations. Neighborhood groups, self-help groups, and voluntary associations serve as a means of mutual support, as a place for clarifying perspectives, and as a focal point for action. In some cases these activities lead to recognition and wider support, and to improved access to the existing formal units of human service delivery in a community.

In assessing available services for a target population, it is important that the macro practitioner identify voluntary associations. Churches, unions, and professional groups are all potential sources of support for the target population. These organizations may not be listed in human service directories, yet they may be the first source to which many people turn when in need (Wineberg, 1992). Table 5.8 provides an overview of informal community units.

Other Perspectives

In the communitarian movement, postmodernism and feminist theory converge to provide a new perspective from which to view communities, organizations, and societies. For example, communitarianism, spawned by concerns about weakening communities in U.S. society, appeals to people from diverse political persuasions (Harrison, 1995). Arguing that the common good must be reconsidered,

TABLE 5.8   Overview of Informal Community Units

Informal Community Units	Composition	Examples of Support Provided
Household Units	Persons who reside within the same dwelling	Caregiving
Natural Support Systems and Social Networks	People within a community who exchange resources	People who provide for a neighbor's need during a crisis
Self-Help Groups	People who come together to help each other with a problem or need that they share	Parents whose children have been killed by drunk drivers provide mutual support
Voluntary Associations	People who unite for the purpose of advancing an interest	Neighborhood associations

the communitarian movement proposes renewed community development efforts. Viewing social policies as critical to how people work together in a community, principles of communitarianism focus on the collective rather than the individual. A leading advocate of the communitarian movement, Etzioni (1993) explains the return to local control and responsibility as follows:

> The government should step in only to the extent that other social subsystems fail, rather than seek to replace them ... at the same time vulnerable communities should be able to draw on the more endowed communities when they are truly unable to deal, on their own, with social duties thrust upon them. (p. 260)

By now it should be clear that there are multiple theoretical perspectives and practice models emerging. Approaches to understanding communities, much less practicing in communities, are far from refined. There are multiple ways of viewing community, just as there are different and often conflicting views on how to proceed with social change. Marie Weil, the founding editor of the *Journal of Community Practice,* opened the first issue in 1994 with a call for clarity in connecting theory with reality. At this point, there is much room for theory development, based on what social work practitioners learn. Our advice to the reader is to recognize the complexity of community relationships and dynamics, and to look at communities from different perspectives rather than to search for one integrated way.

Overview of Community Practice Models

Whereas theories of community provide an understanding for why communities do what they do, community action and community development writers seek to prescribe how change can occur in communities. Numerous community practice models have been and are being used by social workers to effect community change. These models are heavily grounded in systems and ecological language. A summary of the theories that influence many of the community practice models appear in Table 5.9.

There are many ways to approach community and practice models that reflect those possibilities. Mondros and Wilson (1994) identify components typically found in practice models:

1. A change goal
2. Specific roles for staff, leaders, and members
3. A process for selecting issues,
4. An identification of the target of the change effort,
5. An assessment of how cooperative or adversarial the target will be,
6. A change strategy,
7. An understanding of resources needed to produce change,
8. An understanding of the role of an organization in the change process. (p. 240)

TABLE 5.9 Summary Contributions of Theories to Community Practice

Theories	Contributions to Community Practice
Social Systems	■ Reveals that changes in one community unit will impact other units ■ Indicates that changes in subunits also influence the larger community ■ Allows comparisons between how different communities function ■ Recognizes that the push to return to a steady state will depend on analogy used
Human or Population Ecology	■ Is particularly helpful with geographic communities intent on understanding relationships among units ■ Recognizes that community groups are competing for limited resources, with survival of those in power ■ Recognizes that groups without power have to adapt to community norms ■ Acknowledges the influences the interconnections and mutual shaping of physical and social structures
Human Behavior	■ Focuses on the individual within the context of community as the unit of analysis ■ Provides insight into relationships, interactions, values and needs of individuals ■ Provides community practitioners with critical clues about the difference that trust and relationship can make in community interaction
Power, Change, and Politics	■ Reveals the influence of external funders on local communities ■ Views the community as divided into "haves" and "have-nots" ■ Focuses heavily on the "-isms" ■ Recognizes the dynamics of social movements and their influence on community change

Hardina (2002) provides an excellent overview of community practice models, should the reader be interested in more detail.

Most well known are the Rothman models. Rothman (2001) builds on the three community practice models he originally developed in 1968, and he proposes a multimodal approach. His three intervention approaches are locality development, social planning/policy, and social action.

The goal of *locality development* is to develop community capacity and integration through self-help, based on the assumption that broad cross-sections of the community need to engage in problem solving. Empowerment in this mode occurs through collaborative efforts and informed decision making by community residents. The focus is on process, building relationships, and solving problems so that groups can work together. Locality development fits well with approaches like asset mapping, capacity building, strengths, resilience, and empowerment. Its limitations are its time-consuming nature and its assumptions that change can occur through consensus rather than confrontation. Its theoretical roots, therefore, fit well with mechanical and organismic analogies of social systems.

The more task-oriented goal of *social planning/policy* is to confront substantive community problems. Whereas locality development is more process oriented, social planning/policy engages participants in an interaction designed to address social problems with the hope of empowering consumers by hearing their needs and making them more informed in their service choices. Theoretically, social planners function in a rational manner as experts who guide change. In its purest form, there is an assumption that logic will prevail, without political bias. However, planners do not have to be politically naive, and modifications can be made in the rational planning approach to include political considerations and advocacy.

Social action is both process and task oriented in that participants seek to shift power relationships and resources in order to effect institutional change. Beneficiaries of this type of intervention are often perceived to be victims of an oppressive power structure. Empowerment is achieved when beneficiaries feel a sense of mastery in influencing community decision making. Although the language of social action is often espoused by social workers, it is important to realize that this approach to community practice is based in conflict, power-dependency, and resource-mobilization theories of power and politics. The confrontation required in this model is energy draining and time consuming, and sometimes the focus on task becomes so important that process is forgotten. We recommend that this approach be used when other approaches have failed to be effective.

Rothman (2001) is quick to point out that these models are "ideal types" and that there are multiple ways in which they can interrelate and overlap. Other writers have expanded on Rothman's models. For example, Mondros and Wilson (1994) identify three practice approaches that come under the rubric of the social action model: grassroots practice, lobbying practice, and the mobilizing approach. Political practice is added by Haynes and Mickelson (1999).

Weil and Gamble (1995) provide an overview of community practice models used by social workers. These include:

- Neighborhood and community organizing
- Organizing functional communities
- Community social and economic development
- Social planning
- Program development and community liaison
- Political and social action
- Coalitions
- Social movements

Each of these models is described and placed in a matrix according to the following comparative characteristics: desired outcome, system targeted for change, primary constituency, scope of concern, and social work roles (p. 581).

These models reflect the many different ways in which social workers engage in community work. They range from grassroots community organizing in which social workers participate with indigenous groups to make change, to social movements that occur across geographical communities. Social movements, such as the Disability Movement (Mayerson, 1993) or the Gay and Lesbian Movement (Adam, 1995), are usually broad based. They transcend geography and often include a wide range of people and perspectives. Social movements remind practitioners of Warren's distinction between vertical and horizontal relationships because they connect people from multiple communities (vertical) in addition to developing local chapters (horizontal).

A major concern is that the reader recognizes there is no single or "right" way to categorize models, strategies, and tactics. Planned community change is a mixture of various approaches and is based on a careful assessment of the situation to be changed. It is critical also to recognize that since situations and problems are constantly evolving, social workers must be flexible in altering their direction as new information emerges and reassessment occurs. Table 5.10 provides an overview of community practice models (Kettner, Moroney, & Martin, 1999; Rothman, 2001; Weil & Gamble, 1995).

Summary

This chapter provided a very general overview of community theory, perspectives, and practice models used by social workers. There are multiple definitions and types of communities. Three types that were briefly examined include (1) geographical, spacial, or territorial communities; (2) communities of identification and interest, and (3) personal networks or an individual membership in multiple communities. The planned change model presented in later chapters will be applicable to both place and nonplace communities.

An overview of community theory reveals that community structure and function have dominated how communities are viewed. When functions are not adequately performed, communities are seen as dysfunctional or incompetent in meeting the needs of their members. Five community functions were identified by

TABLE 5.10 Overview of Community Practice Models

Model	Basic Premise	Reference
Locality Development or Neighborhood and Community Organizing	Focuses on development of community capacity and integration through self-help; very process oriented; asset mapping and capacity building are used	Rothman (2001)
Organizing Functional Communities	Brings together people focused on a particular cause to change people's behaviors and attitudes; not necessarily place based; focus on empowerment	Weil & Gamble (1995)
Community Social and Economic Development	Prepares citizens at the grassroots level to focus on economic and social development; uses intensive asset mapping, particularly in the economic arena, and capacity building	Weil & Gamble (1995)
Social Planning	Engages participants in an interaction designed to address substantive social problems; uses skills of expert planners to guide process	Rothman (2001)
Program Development and Community Liaison	Uses organizational base in which programs are designed to address community needs; uses skills of professionals in program design and intervention	Kettner, Moroney, & Martin (1999)
Political and Social Action	Attempts to shift power relationships and resources in order to effect institutional change; strengths and empowerment perspectives dominate	Rothman (2001)
Coalitions	Joins multiple community units (e.g., organizations, groups) to build a power base from which change can occur	Weil & Gamble (1995)
Social Movements or Social Reform	Works outside existing structures toward social justice goals that will change existing societal structures; oriented toward broad-scale change	Weil & Gamble (1995)

Warren: (1) production, distribution, and consumption; (2) socialization; (3) social control; (4) social participation; and(5) mutual support. Pantoja and Perry added two additional functions: (6) defense and (7) communication. According to their approach, it is most commonly when the economic function breaks down that failing communities occur. Under structure and functional approaches, community systems theory was introduced.

Human ecology theory, originating with the work of Robert E. Park, views communities as highly interdependent and changing. Community people, values, and interactions include human behavior within communities that was studied by early anthropologists and sociologists. The emergence of community as a collective identity reveals that communities are ripe with symbols, values, and ideologies that people hold in common.

Community power, politics, and change are hallmarks of social work practice. Social workers often view communities as political arenas in which the power of dominant groups necessitates a change so that underserved population needs can be addressed. Understanding the politics of different communities is critical to social workers as they interact with diverse groups.

Finally, contemporary community theory and practice reveal a new interest in rethinking the value of community as an arena for future study. Resilience, empowerment, and the strengths perspectives were followed by capacity building and asset mapping approaches to community practice. Various practice models were presented as a way to introduce the reader to the multiple strategies used to foster community change.

DISCUSSION QUESTIONS AND EXERCISES

1. Multiple definitions of *community* appear in the literature. The definition often cited in social work texts was developed by Roland Warren. Warren states that a *community* is "that combination of social units and systems that perform the major social functions" relevant to meet people's needs on a local level. Critique this definition. Does it help a macro social worker to understand community? What is your definition? Does it encompass all types of communities?

2. In this chapter we point out that there are several types of communities. What types of communities can you identify and how would you classify them?

3. There are seven functions of community identified in this chapter. These functions are typically used to understand what a geographical community does for its members. Select a nonplace community with which you are familiar and use these functions to analyze this nonplace community.

4. Communities do not always live up to the expectations of their residents. Focus on a community with which you are familiar and discuss its competence in serving people in need. What strengths does this community have? What are its limitations? What changes need to be made?

5. *Collective identity* implies that people have common rituals, symbols, and values. Think about examples of how collective identity develops. What are the common rituals, symbols, and values that hold these examples together?

6. Social workers are often faced with community politics, power, and the need for change. Discuss how you perform in situations that are highly politicized. Do you embrace these situations or are they somewhat overwhelming? What do think social workers need that will give them more confidence in approaching these types of situations?

7. Identify a community in which conflicts of values lead to power and politics issues. Give examples of how value conflicts emerge. Give examples of how value conflicts arise in communities and what practice models you might use to address these conflicts in values.

SUGGESTED READINGS

Bailey, D., and K. M. Koney. (2000), *Creating and maintaining strategic alliances: From affiliations to consolidations.* Thousand Oaks, CA: Sage.

Castelloe, P., and J. Prokopy. (2001). Recruiting participants for community practice interventions: Merging community practice theory and social movement theory. *Journal of Community Practice,* 9(2): 31–48.

Ewalt, P. L., E. M. Freeman, and D. Poole (Eds.). (1998). *Community building: Renewal, well-being, and shared responsibility.* Washington, DC: National Association of Social Workers.

Figueira-McDonough, J. (1995). Community organization and the underclass: Exploring new practice directions. *Social Service Review, 69*(1): 57–85.

Inglehart, A. P., and R. M. Becerra. (1995). *Social services and the ethnic community.* Boston: Allyn and Bacon.

Mancoske, R. J., and J. M. Hunzeker. (1994). Advocating for community services coordination: An empowerment perspective for planning AIDS services. *Journal of Community Practice,* 1(3): 49–58.

Mary, N. L. (1994). Social work, economic conversion, and community practice: Where are the social workers? *Journal of Community Practice,* 1(4): 7–25.

Mizrahi, T., and J. D. Morrison (Eds.). (1993). *Community organization and social administration: Advances, trends and emerging principles.* New York: Haworth.

Odendahl, T., and M. O'Neill (Eds.). (1994). *Women and power in the nonprofit sector.* San Francisco: Jossey-Bass.

Perlmutter, F. D. (Ed.). (1994). *Women and social change.* Washington, DC: National Association of Social Workers.

Rosenthal, S. J., and J. M. Cairns. (1994). Child abuse prevention: the community as co-worker. *Journal of Community Practice,* 1(4): 45–61.

Schneider, R. L., and L. Lester. (2001). *Social work advocacy.* Belmont, CA: Brooks/Cole.

REFERENCES

Adam, B. D. (1995). *The rise of a gay and lesbian movement.* New York: Twayne Publishers.

Alinsky, A. (1971). *Rules for radicals.* New York: Vintage.

Alinsky, A. (1974). *Reveille for radicals.* New York: Vintage.

Balgopal, P. R. (1988). Social networks and Asian Indian families. In C. Jacobs and D. D. Bowles (Eds.), *Ethnicity and race: Critical concepts in social work* (pp. 18–33). Silver Spring, MD: National Association of Social Workers.

Bellah, R. N., R. Madsen, W. M. Sullivan, A. Swidler, and S. M. Tipton. (1985). *Habits of the heart: Individualism and commitment in American life.* New York: Harper & Row.

Blau, P. (1964). *Exchange and power in social life.* New York: Wiley.

Breton, M. (2001). Neighborhood resiliency. *Journal of Community Practice,* 9(1): 21–36.

Bricker-Jenkins, M., and N. R. Hooyman. (1986). *Not for women only.* Silver Spring, MD: National Association of Social Workers.

Burrell, G., and G. Morgan. (1979). *Sociological paradigms and organisational analysis.* London: Heineman.

Clark, D. C. (1973). The concept of community: A reexamination. *Sociological Review,* 21: 397–416.

Cohen, A. P. (1985). *The symbolic construction of community.* London: Routledge & Kegan Paul.

Delgado, M. (2000). *Community social work practice in an urban context.* New York: Oxford University Press.

Etzioni, A. (1993). *The spirit of community: Rights, responsibilities, and the communitarian agenda.* New York: Crown Publishers.

Fellin, P. (1995). *The community and the social worker* (2nd ed.). Itasca, IL: F. E. Peacock.

Fellin, P. (2001). Understanding American communities. In J. Rothman, J. L. Erlich, and J. E. Tropman (Eds.), *Strategies of community intervention* (6th ed., pp. 118–132). Itasca, IL: F. E. Peacock.

Florin, P., E. Jones, and A. Wandersman. (1986). Black participation in voluntary associations. *Journal of Voluntary Action Research,* 15(1): 65–86.

Gerloff, R. (1992). Rediscovering the village. *Utne Reader,* 93–100.

Gutierrez, L. M., and E. A. Lewis. (1999). *Empowering women of color.* New York: Columbia University Press.

Hardina, D. (2002). *Analytical skills for community organization practice.* New York: Columbia University Press.

Harrison, W. D. (1995). Community development. In *The Encyclopedia of Social Work* (19th ed., vol. 1, pp. 555–562). Washington, DC: National Association of Social Workers.

Hasenfeld, Y. (1983). *Human service organizations.* Englewood Cliffs, NJ: Prentice-Hall.

Hawley, A. (1950). *A human ecology: A theory of community structure.* New York: Roland Press.

Hawley, A. (1968). *Urban ecology.* Chicago: University of Chicago Press.

Haynes, K., and J. Mickelson. (1999). *Affecting change* (2nd ed.). New York: Longman.

Hillery, G. (1955). Definitions of community: Areas of agreement. *Rural Sociology, 20*: 779–791.

Hoefer, R., R. M. Hoefer, and R. A. Tobias. (1994). Geographic information systems and human services. *Journal of Community Practice, 1*(3): 113–127.

Hunter, A. (1993). National federations: The role of voluntary organizations in linking macro and micro orders in civil society. *Nonprofit and Voluntary Sector Quarterly, 22*(2): 121–136.

Hutcheson, J. D., and L. H. Dominguez. (1986). Ethnic self-help organizations in non-barrio settings: Community identity and voluntary action. *Journal of Voluntary Action Research, 15*(4): 13–22.

Kayal, P. M. (1991). Gay AIDS voluntarism as political activity. *Nonprofit and Voluntary Sector Quarterly, 20*(3): 289–312.

Kettner, P. M., R. M. Moroney, and L. L. Martin. (1999). *Designing and managing programs: An effectiveness-based approach* (2nd ed.). Thousand Oaks, CA: Sage.

Kretzmann, J. P., and J. L. McKnight. (1993). *Building communities from the inside out.* Evanston, IL: Northwestern University, Center for Urban Affairs and Policy Research.

Lohmann, R. A. (1992). *The commons.* San Francisco: Jossey-Bass.

Lynd, R. S., and H. M. Lynd. (1929). *Middletown: A study in contemporary American culture.* New York: Harcourt & Brace.

Lynd, R. S., and H. M. Lynd. (1937). *Middletown in transition: A study in cultural conflicts.* New York: Harcourt & Brace.

Lyon, L. (1987). *The community in urban society.* Philadelphia: Temple University Press.

MacNair, R. H., L. Fowler, and J. Harris. (2000). The diversity functions of organizations that confront oppression: The evolution of three social movements. *Journal of Community Practice, 7*(2): 71–88.

Martin, P. Y., and G. G. O'Connor. (1989). *The social environment: Open systems applications.* New York: Longman.

Martinez-Brawley, E. E. (1995). Community. In *Encyclopedia of Social Work* (19th ed., vol. 1, pp. 539–548). Washington, DC: National Association of Social Workers.

Mayerson, A. (1993). The history of the ADA: A movement perspective. In L. O. Gostin and H. A. Beyer (Eds.), *Implementing the Americans with Disabilities Act: Rights and responsibilities of all Americans* (pp. 17–24). Baltimore: Paul H. Brookes.

McIntyre, E. L. G. (1986). Social networks: Potential for practice. *Social Work, 31*(6): 421–426.

Mondros, J. B., and S. M. Wilson. (1994). *Organizing for power and empowerment.* New York: Columbia University Press.

Mulucci, A. (1995). The process of collective identity. In H. Johnson and B. Klandermans (Eds.), *Social movements and culture* (pp. 41–63). Minneapolis: University of Minnesota Press.

Netting, F. E., and M. K. O'Connor. (2003). *Organization practice.* Boston: Allyn and Bacon.

Norlin, J., and W. Chess. (1997). *Human behavior and the social environment: Social systems theory.* Boston: Allyn and Bacon.

Pantoja, A., and W. Perry. (1992). Community development and restoration: A perspective. In F. G. Rivera and J. L. Erlich (Eds.), *Community organizing in a diverse society* (pp. 223–249). Boston: Allyn and Bacon.

Park, R. E. (1983). Human ecology. In R. L. Warren and L. Lyon (Eds.), *New perspectives on the American community* (pp. 27–36). Homewood, IL: Dorsey.

Parsons, T. (1971). *The system of modern societies.* Englewood Cliffs, NJ: Prentice-Hall.

Rothman, J. (2001). Approaches to community intervention. In J. Rothman, J. L. Erlich, and J. E. Tropman (Eds.), *Strategies for community intervention* (6th ed., pp. 27–64). Itasca, IL: F. E. Peacock.

Saleeby, D. (1997). *The strengths perspective in social work practice* (2nd ed.). New York: Longman.

Smith, D. H. (1991). Four sectors or five? Retaining the member-benefit sector. *Nonprofit and Voluntary Sector Quarterly, 20*(2): 137–150.

Smith, D. H. (2000). *Grassroots associations.* Thousand Oaks, CA: Sage.

Solomon, B. (1976). *Black empowerment.* New York: Columbia University Press.

Solomon, B. (1987). Empowerment: Social work in oppressed communities. *Journal of Social Work Practice, 2*(4): 79–91.

Specht, H. (1986). Social support, social networks, social exchange, and social work practice. *Social Service Review, 60*(2): 218–240.

Specht, H., and M. Courtney. (1994). *Unfaithful angels.* New York: Free Press.

Stanfield, J. H. (1993). African American traditions of civic responsibility. *Nonprofit and Voluntary Sector Quarterly, 22*(2): 137–153.

Tönnies, F. (1887/1957). *Community and society (Gemeinschaft und Gesellschaft).* (C. P. Loomis, trans., ed.). East Lansing: Michigan State University Press. (Original work published 1887).

Van Til, J. (1988). *Mapping the third sector: Voluntarism in a changing social economy.* New York: The Foundation Center.

Warren, R. L. (1978). *The community in America* (3rd ed.). Chicago: Rand McNally.

Weil, M., and D. N. Gamble. (1995). Community practice models. In *The Encyclopedia of Social Work* (19th ed., vol. 1, pp. 577–593). Washington, DC: National Association of Social Workers.

West, J. (1945). *Plainville, U.S.A.* New York: Columbia University Press.

Williams, C., and H. B. Williams. (1984). Contemporary voluntary associations in the urban black church: The development and growth of mutual aid societies. *Journal of Voluntary Action Research, 13*(4): 19–30.

Wineberg, R. J. (1992). Local human services provision by religious congregations. *Nonprofit and Voluntary Sector Quarterly, 21*(2): 107–118.

6 Analyzing Communities

Introduction

Setting out to understand a community is a major undertaking. Long-time residents will often comment, "I've lived here for 40 years and I still don't understand this town!" How, then, can a student or practitioner hope to understand something as complex as a community, much less propose ways to change it? Even more difficult is understanding a nonplace community that does not have geographical boundaries.

First, it should be made clear that there is no one accepted, orderly, systematic method for understanding all the elements that make up a community. Instead, for the macro practitioner, understanding means gathering as much information as possible in a narrowly focused area of interest or concern, within the time frame allotted, and making the best-informed decisions the information will allow.

There are three reasons why macro practitioners need a systematic approach to conceptualizing and analyzing community strengths and social problems. First, the person-in-environment view is critical to professional social work practice. The community in which one lives has a lot to do with who one is, the problems one faces, and the resources available to deal with these problems. Professional social work interventions are not feasible or realistic without an understanding of these community influences. The framework presented here for understanding community is designed to assist in conceptualizing the arena within which clients experience hope and draw strength, as well as face oppression and frustration. Note the word *assist*, which means that this framework does not have to be used in lock-step fashion; it is only a tool to be used in whatever way or order is helpful.

Second, community-level macro change requires an understanding of the history and development of a community as well as an analysis of its current status and subgroups. Without this knowledge, the practitioner has a limited grasp of the breadth and depth of values, attitudes, and traditions, and their significance in either maintaining the status quo or allowing for change.

Third, communities constantly change. Individuals and groups move into power, economic structures change, sources of funding change, and citizens' roles change. A framework for understanding and analyzing community can be helpful in recognizing and interpreting these changes.

Two Community Vignettes

Vignette 1: Canyon City

Located in the western United States, Canyon City had a population of 60,000 people in 1975. Twenty-five years later, it had grown to 250,000 and was continuing to grow when other major cities had long since declined. Because the city was populated by many persons who had moved to the western Sunbelt to follow job opportunities, many of its residents were not native to the area. Census data indicated that 20 percent of Canyon City's population were Latino, 60 percent were European-origin white, 10 percent were Native American, 5 percent were African American, and another 5 percent were Asian American.

Encountering the Community

A recent social work graduate took a position in a multiservice agency in Canyon City. One of her tasks was to develop a program to address the needs of battered women in the community. Data from the police department and various other sources revealed a high incidence of domestic violence within the community relative to other communities of similar size. The social worker was new to Canyon City, having lived in another part of the country most of her life. She viewed this chance to understand and analyze the community with great anticipation.

She began her work by talking with a number of police officers, social workers, and others who had expertise in domestic violence. Through these contacts, she was able to locate a few women who were willing to talk with her confidentially about their situations. She learned that each woman perceived the situation somewhat differently. Based on numerous conversations, she found that there was a general sense of isolation within the community, that neighbors did not always tend to know one another, and that newcomers felt it was hard to become part of the community. Given the transient nature of the community and its rapid growth, this was not surprising. It was soon clear that people tended to focus on the problems and to talk about how awful the situation was. The social worker had to probe for information on community strengths.

The strengths of Canyon City were many. First, community members seemed willing to acknowledge the problem and were anxious to address it. The social worker encountered few people who denied that something needed to be done. Second, there was diversity within the community that made for a rich mix of customs, traditions, and values. Third, there were several women's groups in Canyon City that were willing to volunteer their efforts to whatever program was developed. Fourth, a foundation was willing to fund a well-designed project.

Narrowing the Focus

In the course of collecting data and defining boundaries, the social worker determined that the problem of domestic violence was being addressed in several pockets of the community. There were three battered women's shelters within the city, but they served only a part of the entire community. A counseling service for persons dealing with domestic violence was available, but only to those who could afford the service. It became clear that persons who were not being served by the shelters and the counseling service were primarily Latina. She began to narrow her focus to address their needs.

The social worker had to be careful to recognize the diverse cultural traditions and beliefs of this target population. A number of models were available for developing shelters, safe homes, and services for white middle-class women, but few focused on women of color. The social worker found that Latinas in the community often provided shelter for one another but that this posed an excessive financial burden on these women. She began to talk with the women about how to design a program that would be sensitive and relevant to identified needs.

In the process, the social worker also discovered additional community strengths. There was a strong sense of community among many Latinas who had lived in the area most of their lives. There were associations of women that were not identified in any listings of services or programs because they were not as formalized as other groups. This informal network was a source of pride in the community, yet these relationships were not known or understood in the larger community. Two Latino churches had identified domestic violence as their theme for the coming year and were willing to work with the social worker and her agency. A support group for women of color had been meeting in one of the churches for several years.

Mobilizing Resources

In a period of several weeks, the social worker had realized that there were more resources in the community than she had originally anticipated. However, she had also discovered that there were definite locations of power. Community leaders among the women of color were not visible in the larger community and had often felt invisible in the decision-making process. Within her own agency, she found that members of the board of directors were not certain they wanted to focus on women of color, because the board had originally identified the problems of all women in the community. The foundation was willing to fund a project that would focus on Latinas' needs, but its board members wanted to be assured that the funds would be used to do something "innovative" rather than duplicating an existing model. Also, the foundation was willing to fund the project only if it would be self-sufficient within three years. The women's shelters that were already open were cautious about supporting the new program concept for fear that it might call attention to their failure to serve many women of color in the past. The women's support group in the local church was concerned that the group would lose its focus and become part of a bigger project that would take members away from their feeling of closeness and intimacy.

It was the social worker's job to continue to collect information and to determine the project's feasibility. Although this was time consuming, she continued to hear the perspectives of various women who had been battered and to include them in the development of a community project.

Vignette 2: Lakeside

Lakeside was a planned community developed in the 1930s. The downtown area was built around a small lake, surrounded by weeping willow trees. The Baptist, Methodist, and Presbyterian churches sat side by side along the lake front, forming what was known as "church circle." Each of the Protestant denominations had a children's home, and the Methodist Home for Orphaned Children built in 1902 was a local landmark.

The population in Lakeside during the 1930s was approximately 20,000 people. The majority of employees worked for a major office products manufacturing company, making Lakeside "a company town." There were additional businesses in town that manufactured paper, building supplies, and various other products.

Assessing Major Changes

By the 1970s, Lakeside had grown to a population of 35,000, and the community was going through a number of changes. Many residents had moved to suburbs outside the downtown area and had taken jobs in a larger city nearby, creating problems for the economic base of the town. The various manufacturing companies had experienced occasional layoffs, which made community residents feel uncertain about job security and advancement.

Several public housing developments for elderly and disabled persons had been built downtown. The Methodist Children's Home began targeting services to elders as well as to children, since orphans were few in number but the number of older persons was increasing.

Although Lakeside had been a haven for Protestant families and diversity had been limited, the population was changing. In 1930, only one Catholic church and one Jewish synagogue were located in Lakeside. In 1975, a mosque, two AME Zion churches, and a number of splinter groups had formed from the mainline churches on "church circle." In 1930, 20 percent of the downtown population was African American. By 1975, African Americans comprised 60 percent of the downtown population. The "church circle" remained a centerpiece in the community around the lake, but many of the members commuted to these churches from outside the city limits.

Witnessing the Impact of Change

One social worker at the Methodist Home was assigned to work with older persons and persons with disabilities in Lakeside. Her role was to build community and develop strong support networks for clients. She found that the three public housing developments in Lakeside were home to many of her clients. The target population, however, was very diverse in terms of age, disability, and race. Elderly residents ranged in age from 60 to 105, and persons with disabilities ranged in age from 25 to 95. The public housing community was 55 percent African American, 2 percent Latino, and 43 percent white.

Many of the residents had lived in Lakeside all their lives and knew many of the other residents. Also, there was a large senior citizens' center housed in an old department store that had moved to the mall. The residents often had family in the area and felt "connected" with that part of the country.

The social worker was pleased to learn about these strengths, but she was also aware of the problems that had emerged in Lakeside. There was a definite sense of racial tension in town. There was also tension between the old-old and young persons with disabilities who were living in the same apartment buildings. Older clients complained about loud music and partying at all hours of the night. Younger persons were frustrated at "being forced" to live with old people. The major stores in the downtown area had been vacated, and mobile community members tended to shop at the mall. Persons without transportation walked to the remaining few stores downtown, where prices were high and bargains few. Getting Social Security checks cashed at the one downtown grocery store meant paying a three-dollar fee for cashing privileges.

Amid these tensions and concerns, a tremendous amount of fear had arisen. Two older women who lived alone had been murdered in the last two months, and now a third female victim had just been found. In a small community, this was the "talk of the town," and no one felt safe anymore. Elderly women who lived in the downtown area were being cautioned to keep their doors locked at all times, not to let strangers in, and to call 911 if they had any reason to be suspicious of anyone. A neighborhood crime watch association had been organized, and volunteer escorts were available in the evening hours for anyone having to go out alone. The police department had contacted the social worker in an effort to work together, and the senior center was holding self-defense classes. The social worker heard older residents complain over and over again that Lakeside just wasn't the community they had known.

Implications of Vignettes

Communities change, and it is not unusual for residents to grieve over the loss of what has been. Some changes are planned, such as the deliberate attempts described in Vignette 1 to develop a project to address the needs of Latinas who had been abused. Other changes are unplanned, such as the way in which the "planned" community of Lakeside's downtown area changed. Vignette 1 addresses a substantive problem (violence against Latinas) and Vignette 2 addresses an issue of general community vitality and viability.

The two vignettes offer a glimpse of what social workers experience in many community practice arenas. In Canyon City, the social worker encountered a rapidly growing community with much diversity. In Lakeside, the social worker found a city that was no longer vital and growing. However, both discovered strengths and problems, tensions and frustrations. Both found that the inclusion of multiple perspectives was important but complicated the analysis. For example, in Vignette 1, the social worker had to deal with the power dynamics between a possible funding source, local women's shelters that were already established, and Latinas whose voices were not always heard. In Vignette 2, the social worker encountered racial as well as intergenerational tensions among residents of downtown public housing developments.

Each vignette requires asking many questions in order to know how to intervene. This chapter provides questions with which one might begin to conceptualize communities like Canyon City and Lakeside from the perspective of the target populations served. Keep in mind that some questions in this framework may be useful in some communities and not as useful in others. The identified tasks do not have to be used in the order presented. The point is to find a way to begin to assess a community and to generate questions that will provide further direction.

A Framework for Community Analysis

In any situation in which an assessment is called for—whether for an individual, a family, or an entire community—it is helpful to use a framework that can help guide the analytical process. With respect to assessing communities, the work of Roland Warren (1978) again provides a useful starting point. He proposes that communities can be better understood if selected community variables are analyzed. Of particular interest are variables that represent characteristics that can be used to differentiate one community from another. Some communities are larger than most, some have greater diversity or different kinds of diversity, some are wealthier than others, and so on.

Building on Warren's work, we have identified four tasks that comprise a 12-step framework to be used in understanding and analyzing a community. In subsequent chapters, we will present methods for planning changes based on this approach. The framework is shown in Table 6.1.

Task 1: Focus on Target Population

Many approaches to community analysis contend that the community must be understood in its totality to the greatest extent possible before intervention is planned. We propose, instead, that the definition of community be narrowed by first selecting a target population, and that the community be understood from the perspective of the concerns and needs of that population. The *target population* is defined as those individuals, families, and/or groups who are experiencing a problem or need and for whose benefit some type of community change is being considered.

The choice of a particular target population is a choice of values. In every community there are multiple groups with varying needs. The social worker must realize that in focusing on one target population, he or she is making a choice to examine the community from a specific perspective. It will be important, then, to go back and look at the community again from the perspective of more than one target population so that a richer understanding can develop. For example, existing reports on community issues and populations may predetermine what target group the practitioner will serve, with only limited opportunity to familiarize herself or himself with other community needs and concerns.

We suggest that a community be analyzed and understood from this limited perspective because (1) practically speaking, people who become involved in community change are generally people with full-time jobs, and it is not unusual that macro-level intervention responsibilities are added on top of those jobs; and (2) there is a limit to the amount of information that can be used in macro-level interventions. In short, we do not disagree with those who suggest that, in the

TABLE 6.1   The Community Encounter Framework

Task	Variable	Activity
1. Focus on a Target Population	People	1. To identify the population or subgroup
	Characteristics	2. To understand the characteristics of target population members
	Needs	3. To locate data and information on target population members
2. Determine Community Characteristics	Space	4. To identify geographical boundaries of the community toward which a change effort is to be targeted
	Social Problems	5. To establish a profile of problems affecting the target population within the community
	Values	6. To observe and understand dominant values affecting the target population within the community
3. Recognize Community Differences	Oppression	7. To recognize ways in which the target population has been formally or covertly restricted by powerful persons and/or institutions
	Discrimination	8. To identify examples in which the target population has been subjected to discrimination in the community
4. Identify Community Structure	Power and Resource Availability	9. To recognize stakeholders and where power (and the accompanying resources) are located in addressing target population needs
	Service-Delivery Units	10. To identify informal, mediating, and formal units that deliver services to target population members
	Patterns of Resource Control and Service Delivery	11. To determine who provides and who controls resource delivery to the target population in the community
	Linkages between Units	12. To identify connections between service delivery units or gaps in which connections need to be made in order to serve target population needs

ideal, everything possible should be known and understood about a community in advance. We are simply suggesting that, with limited time and resources, responsible change efforts can be initiated by narrowing the parameters of community analysis.

Identifying a population in need can, in itself, be complex because no one is a part of only one community. Community can be defined in terms of ethnicity (e.g., the Latino community), religion (e.g., the Jewish community), commitment to a position (e.g., the pro-choice community), profession (e.g., the social work community), avocational interest (e.g., recreational and sports enthusiasts), and many other designations. Each individual is part of many different communities at the same time.

It is also important to note that there are critical differences between urban, suburban, and rural communities. This approach may be particularly difficult in a rural community where members of the target population are geographically dispersed. We also caution the reader not to assume that the target population can be disengaged or isolated from the larger community, even though one may focus on the target population in order to manage this complex undertaking. In fact, members of the target population may already feel isolated from the larger community. Certainly, we do not want to reinforce this sense of isolation.

Viewed graphically, a community might appear as a series of overlapping circles representing important elements or reference groups within the community. A given individual could then be represented in a space formed from the overlap of the unique combination of elements relevant to that person, as illustrated in Figure 6.1.

By beginning with a population in need, we are suggesting that a person attempting to understand a community first identify the population of focus. This begins a narrowing-down process. Initial definitions of *population* can be broad, with the understanding that the more precise the definition selected, the more feasible a full understanding of the community context for this population.

For example, issues surrounding alcoholism prompt a concern for macro-level change. The population of focus for a particular community analysis could be "people with alcohol problems who live in Riverdale County" or it could be "ethnic minority women alcoholics who have been convicted of driving while intoxicated within the past two years in Riverdale County." One is more inclusive, the other more focused. It is probably advisable, at this early stage, that a broader definition be adopted, with an understanding that it will become more precise as a clearer understanding of needed change emerges.

Once a population has been identified and the definition appropriately narrowed, all other dimensions of the community are explored and examined from the perspective of that population. For each dimension to be explored, we will identify a task intended to bring focus to the collection of data and information. We will next focus on questions to be asked about the population. Finally, we will propose some questions to be asked about a community that will aid in understanding each dimension and in comparing it to other communities. Although this framework contains a number of tasks, the process of analyzing any community

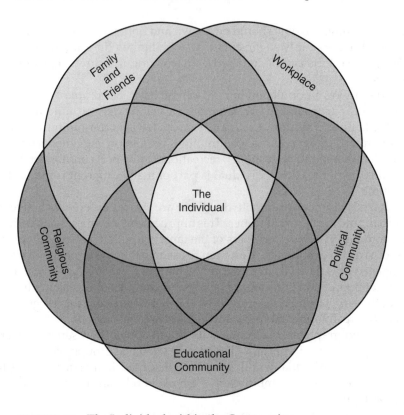

FIGURE 6.1   The Individual within the Community

requires the social worker to go back and forth, returning to refine previous tasks as new information is gathered. The social worker is urged to use the framework as an interactive guide rather than a rigid formula for approaching community.

Identify Target Population.   Questions to be explored for this activity include:

- What target populations have been identified as being in need of services within the community, and how are they categorized?
- What target population will be the focus of this assessment?
- What priority is given to the needs of the target population in this community?
- What percentage of the target population are people of color, ethnic group members, women, gay men or lesbians, older persons, or persons with disabilities?

People who are identified as being in a target population are consumers of services, and ideally the services provided are designed to meet their needs. However, it is important to recognize that people's needs are always changing. This requires a human service system that has flexibility to respond to changing needs. Gonzalez, Gonzalez, Freeman, and Howard-Pitney (1991) remind practitioners that even cultural identity changes. "One can always expect to find both change and diversity within any community. In fact, even a community that appears to represent one culture or cultural group will actually be quite mixed, demonstrating a range of behaviors and beliefs that are common to that culture" (p. 2). Because the characteristics of community residents vary, there may be subgroups that require special attention. For example, if a community has a high proportion of retirees, one can expect that many of the services should be able to address the needs of older people. If services are not available, the delivery system may not be adequately meeting community needs.

For the sake of discussion, consider the following seven target populations. They are frequently used for planning purposes, and funding tends to be clustered around these categories:

- Children
- Youth
- Families
- Older adults
- Adults
- Developmentally disabled persons
- Physically disabled persons

Obviously, these groups are neither exhaustive nor mutually exclusive. In addition, they do not specify the many subgroups that fall within each category. For example, if the target population is children, it is important to recognize that children come from families of all socioeconomic statuses, racial and ethnic groups, and locations within a community.

Although we have identified seven categories of people who may have some common characteristics and needs, individual communities will have their own definitions of target populations. How does the community categorize client groups for planning purposes? Local and regional planning agencies, United Way organizations, community councils, and associations of agencies often produce agreed-upon classification schemes for data collection and planning purposes. Regardless of existing categories, it is ultimately the task of the individual or group doing the community assessment to define the target population.

Understand Characteristics of Target Population Members. Questions to be explored for this activity include:

- What is known about the history of the target population in this community?
- How many persons comprise the target population and what are their relevant characteristics?
- How do persons in the target population perceive their needs?

In their book on community organization, Brager, Specht, and Torczyner (1987) state:

> Demographic differences [do not] exhaust the variations among subgroups of the poor. Although attitudinal differences are more difficult to define and identify, a wide diversity of world views exists even within demographically homogenous populations. Thus, some poor are more alienated than others, some more upwardly aspiring, and some angrier. Where they fall on these dimensions has a bearing on how they will respond to particular efforts to involve them in organizing projects. (p. 60)

It is precisely these differences in the target population that the macro practitioner is attempting to understand. The study usually begins with an examination of available demographic data, and the starting point for this is usually an analysis of socioeconomic status, age, race, and gender by census tract. It is especially important to identify areas of poverty and high need, and to determine whether the target population is heavily concentrated in these areas or is spread across an entire county.

In addition to gathering statistics, it is important to talk with people who understand the community's history, as perceived by the target population. Generally, how do people in this target population (and others close to them) perceive their concerns, problems, issues, and/or needs? Do they tend to see them in terms of a need for empowerment, freedom from oppression, access to opportunity, removal of barriers, need for resources or services, and/or need for protection? Bellah, Madsen, Sullivan, Swidler, and Tipton (1985) explain why this is important:

> A community is a group of people who are socially interdependent, who participate together in discussion and decision-making, and who share certain practices that both define the community and are nurtured by it. Such a community is not quickly formed. It almost always has a history and so is also a community of memory, defined in part by its past and its memory of its past. (p. 313)

Examining the characteristics of the target population and identifying where they are located, together with gathering information from the perspective of people in the target population, completes the second task in the community encounter.

Assess Target Population Needs.   Questions to be explored for this activity include:

- What are feasible and appropriate ways to locate community needs assessment data and other relevant information about the target population?
- How do persons in the target population perceive their community and its responsiveness to their needs?
- How are these needs expressed by the people of this community?

■ What do available data and information indicate about quality of life factors as they affect people of color; women; gay, lesbian, bisexual, and transgendered persons; elderly and disabled persons; and others?

Eight general methods of approaching a needs assessment have been discussed in the literature. They include:

1. Gathering opinions and judgments from key informants through community forums, public hearings, face-to-face interaction, and focus groups;
2. Collecting service statistics such as utilization, waiting lists, and caseload data;
3. Locating epidemiological studies (of the origins of problems);
4. Finding studies of the incidence and prevalence of problems;
5. Using social indicators (e.g., unemployment, crime)
6. Conducting or locating surveys of population group members, providers, and others;
7. Finding secondary analysis of existing studies;
8. Any combination of the above. (Meenaghan & Gibbons, 2000, p. 8)

The preferred approach in assessing need within a particular population is to use existing data. Original data collection is expensive and time consuming, and is usually beyond the scope of the macro practitioner unless a particular change effort has widespread community and financial backing. Table 6.2 summarizes the advantages and disadvantages of using various approaches.

Ideally the macro practitioner would like to know (1) the number of people in the target population who are experiencing each problem and (2) the number of people who can be served using existing resources. The first number minus the second number represents the community's unmet need. Unmet need, inadequately met need, or inappropriately met need are frequently the focus of macro-level change efforts.

With special population groups that require multiple services, classification schemes are often based on the concept of a continuum of care. A continuum of care consists of a broad menu of services from which items can be selected to address the specific needs of certain individuals or groups. Conceivably, each menu will vary based on what is needed for the target population served. Table 6.3 provides one way of classifying continuum of care services for those persons requiring long-term care.

Need is an elusive and complex concept and must be understood from a variety of perspectives. Needs are experienced at the simplest level by individuals who require some type of response. A hungry person needs food; an unemployed person needs a job. If there are resources to meet these needs, the needy person is matched up with the resources and the need is met.

What we have discussed thus far in this chapter is really individual need experienced by many people. When one person is hungry, it is an individual problem. When hundreds of people are hungry and the community is not prepared to feed them, it becomes a social problem. When needs clearly outstrip resources, it

TABLE 6.2 Needs Assessment Methods: Advantages and Disadvantages

Method	Description	Advantages	Disadvantages
Gathering opinions and judgments from key informants	Community forums Public hearings Face-to-face interaction Focus groups	Provides opportunities to hear directly from the target population	Often difficult to locate people who fully understand the issues, also is time consuming
Service statistics	Utilization and rates Waiting lists Caseload data	Provides information from those who serve the target population	Limited by what is collected and how well data are managed
Locating epidemiological studies (of the origins of problems)	Analyzing existing data	Data are already collected and usually accessible	Analysis is restricted by what data were collected
Finding studies of the incidence and prevalence of problems	Reporting what previous studies have found	Studies have already been conducted and findings are available	Generalizability of findings may be limited
Social indicators	Reviews of data such as income, age, occupation, etc.	Data are available and provide broad overview of community	Indicators do not provide detailed information
Conducting and locating surveys	Interviews with community members	Provides broad overview of needs	Requires great time and expense

is a communitywide problem and may require a human service response. More food banks, more homeless shelters, and more employment training services may be needed. It is important to note, however, that just because data collected indicate a particular need, it does not necessarily follow that these data combined with other types of information will translate into widespread support from the community.

There is yet another perspective on need that should be understood by the macro practitioner. It is a need that requires something other than a human service response. It may even require some fundamental redesign of structures and systems. As discussed in the previous chapter, structure and power are important variables for understanding community. When a whole community suffers from inferior housing, transportation, schools, or an inadequate economic base, these

TABLE 6.3 **Continuum of Long-Term Care Services by Category**

In-Home Services	Community-Based Services	Institutional Services
Outreach	Case Management	Alcohol and Drug Treatment
Information and Referral	Transportation	Rehabilitation
Comprehensive Geriatric	Senior Centers	Psychiatric Care
Assessment	Senior Discount Programs	Swing Beds or Step-Down
Emergency Response	Recreational Activities	Units
System	Caregiver Support Groups	Skilled Nursing Care
Companionship/Friendly	Self-Help Groups	Extended Care
Visiting	Counseling	
Telephone Reassurance	Foster Homes	
Caregiver Respite Services	Adult Care Homes	
Homemaker and Chore	Shared Housing	
Services	Congregate Housing	
Household Repair Services	Wellness and Health	
Personal Care	Promotion Clinics	
Home-Delivered Meals	Geriatric Assessment Clinics	
Home Health	Physician Services	
In-Home High Technology	Adult Day Care	
Therapy	Mental Health Clinics	
Hospice	Outpatient Clinics	

problems may be more than simply individual problems on a large scale. They should be understood as collective needs.

It is an assumption among most social scientists that communities need adequately functioning basic systems of service and support to achieve at least a minimally acceptable quality of life for all their citizens. Communities also need an economic base that will produce jobs and income. They need affordable housing, adequate transportation, sound community health practices, protection from disease, good quality and relevant education for their children, protection from harm and violence, and freedom to pursue obligations and interests without fear. When these conditions are absent, a service response (more money, more resources of any kind) may provide temporary relief without dealing with fundamental structural problems.

The long-term need may be for collective empowerment, a collective sense of dignity, full participation in decisions that affect the lives of people in the community, self-direction, and self-control. Assessing collective need requires an understanding of the history and development of the community, an ability to compare economic data and social problem data to other surrounding communities, and a sensitivity to the needs and aspirations of those who live in the community. Collective need may also have to be addressed at another level, such as the state legislature or U.S. Congress. The focus can remain on the local community and actions can be taken locally, but the point of intervention may be outside the community.

When collective need for empowerment, participation, control, and other such factors is identified or expressed, the role of the macro practitioner is different from the role taken when the need is for a human service response. These roles will be discussed in Part Five (Chapters 9 through 11) of this book.

Task 2: Determine Community Characteristics

Size is an important characteristic of a community and it can be assessed in a number of ways. Size can be calculated in terms of the amount of space covered, by the number of people living within its boundaries, or both. It is an important characteristic for the macro practitioner because geographical boundaries established for macro-level interventions can range from neighborhood to county and even larger. Clearly, the size of the community as defined will affect the nature of the macro-level analysis, and ultimately the intervention.

Identify Community Boundaries.   Questions to be explored for this activity include:

- What are the boundaries within which intervention on behalf of the target population will occur?
- Where are members of the target population located within the boundaries? Are they highly concentrated or scattered?
- What physical or social barriers exist for the target population?
- How compatible are jurisdictional boundaries of health and human service programs that serve the target population?
- How accessible are services for the target population?

Space is the area covered by a community. It is one dimension of a community's size. Focusing on space allows the practitioner to establish manageable boundaries. If resources are available to focus on the entire city or county, then these may be appropriate boundaries in that instance. If, however, the effort is to be undertaken by a small committee of volunteers who have limited time and resources available, then one may decide to focus the encounter on a limited part of the city in which there appears to be the greatest need for intervention.

Establishing boundaries for macro-level intervention, therefore, is initially done by focusing on a target population and is then further refined by selecting a geographical boundary. For most macro-level interventions, we recommend beginning one's understanding of community by limiting boundaries to the county or its equivalent, and focusing down from that level to more limited boundaries if appropriate. This is in no way intended to indicate that intervention at state, regional, or national levels is not appropriate. It is simply to recognize that, for the vast majority of interventions, a level of county or smaller will be most relevant.

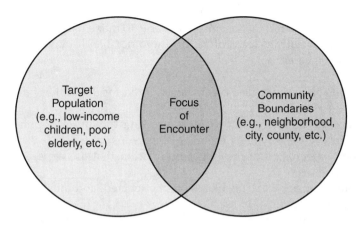

FIGURE 6.2   Setting Parameters for the Community Encounter

Figure 6.2 illustrates the boundary-setting process. Knowing that one cannot address all target population needs within large arenas, the encounter focuses on the target population within a manageable part of the broader community. This becomes the focus of the macro-level intervention.

A community may be a small section of the inner city or a fairly large expanse encompassing scattered farms in a rural area. For example, community as space is applicable to barrios in which groups of Latino people reside within a larger metropolitan area. Spacial concepts of community are also relevant in less population-dense areas but may be more difficult to determine. This was pointed out by a Navajo social worker who explained how difficult it was to determine spatial boundaries on a reservation. There were no street systems, property information and signs indicating county lines, or well-defined human service areas.

Another characteristic important in understanding community as space is jurisdictional units established by various government agencies for planning and service provision purposes (e.g., school districts or mental health catchment areas). Since the macro practitioner's focus is typically limited to a designated geographical area, mapping overlapping jurisdictional units can be important and useful. For example, a change agent may be working with people in a particular county to establish a prenatal health-care campaign for pregnant teens, only to discover that he or she is dealing with representatives from county and multiple city governments. Establishing who is responsible within what geographical domain can be extremely important politically. Similarly, the practitioner hired by a mental health clinic may find that the clinic's geographical boundaries overlap parts of three school districts, requiring letters of agreement with multiple school boards. It pays to know the geographical parameters of various institutional units within the community of focus.

A third characteristic related to space and helpful in understanding target populations is that of service accessibility. If health and human service organizations are scattered across a broad area and there is limited public transportation, consumers may find that they are simply not able to make use of existing services. Centrally located multiservice centers, on the other hand, may make problems much more manageable.

Profile Social Problems.   Questions to be explored for this activity include:

- What are the major social problems affecting the target population in this community as perceived by their spokespersons?
- Are there subgroups of the target population that are experiencing major social problems?
- To what extent are these problems interconnected, and must some be solved before others can be addressed?
- What data sources are available on the identified social problems and how are available data used within the community?
- Who collects the data, and is this an ongoing process?

Macro-level interventions tend to be conceptualized and organized around a selected population and a specific problem they are experiencing. For example, a social worker might discover a lack of child-care options for teen parents who wish to return to school, or an increasing problem of malnutrition among isolated elderly, or a community made up primarily of African Americans and Latinos who believe their requests are not receiving a fair hearing by the city council.

This is not to indicate, however, that any target population experiences only one problem at any one time. If one is to understand a target population, we propose that one must understand as much as possible about the social problems they experience. Do people in this population tend to have limited or adequate financial resources? Are transportation options limited? Is unemployment a problem? What is the condition in the neighborhood?

Understanding social problems helps in two ways: (1) it enables the macro practitioner to appreciate the full range of difficulties experienced by the target population, thereby helping to prioritize needs, and (2) it should help in proposing more realistic solutions. For example, sometimes a transportation need must be addressed before a problem can be solved.

Social problems are negatively labeled conditions recognized by community residents. Identified social problems will vary by community and by target population. Sometimes there are conditions that exist that have not been labeled as a problem. It may be the social worker's task to bring these conditions to the attention of people in power so that they are recognized as social problems. This is not always easy because community residents may have a great deal invested in denying that there is a problem.

The purpose of establishing a profile is to understand conditions affecting the target population. This requires both direct contact and library research. Direct contact with people who can articulate the problems and needs of the target population gives the practitioner a first-person interpretation of issues. Library research adds theoretical knowledge about identified social problems, as well as practice and research findings based on the experiences of others with the same or similar populations and problems.

We cannot emphasize strongly enough the importance of original, authoritative sources in understanding a target population. Populations must be understood in terms of their diversity. In family practice, for example, the meaning of family—of husband-wife relationships, of parent-child relationships, of aging grandparent roles—may differ from one culture to the next. Similarly, the ways in which members of the gay and lesbian community define family may depart radically from traditional community values. A target population will not be adequately understood if these potentially widely divergent views are not taken into consideration.

Once major social problems defined by community members have been identified, one can begin to determine their incidence and prevalence. "Incidence refers to the actual occurrence of a phenomenon during a period." For example, 15 students may have been arrested for drug use in the local high school in the most recent academic year. "Prevalence refers to the number of cases or instances of a phenomenon existing in a community group at a given time" (Kettner, Daley & Nichols, 1985, p. 72). For example, current estimates indicate that drug use among teenagers is as high as 50 percent.

Social indicator data may be helpful in gaining a broad overview of social problems at the national, regional, state and local levels. In this way, the community's social problems can be comparatively assessed. Other professionals in the community, or at the county or state levels, can also be valuable sources of information. They may have firsthand experience with the target population, or their organizations may have conducted surveys or collected statistics of specific social problems. The local public or college/university library may also provide many documents valuable in understanding local problems and needs.

Understand Dominant Values. Questions to be explored for this activity include:

- What cultural values, traditions, and beliefs are important to the target population?
- What are the predominant values that affect the target population within this community?
- What groups and individuals espouse these values, who opposes them, and are there value conflicts surrounding the target population?
- How do people in this community feel about giving and receiving help?
- What are the predominant shared perspectives in this community on inclusion of the target population in decisions that affect them?

Another variable to be considered in attempting to understand a community is values. *Values* are strongly held beliefs, and *community values* are those beliefs that are strongly held by persons who make up the community. These values are often reinforced by the associations and organizations with which community residents affiliate.

The idea of shared values requires refinement in today's changing world. At one time, communities without divisions of labor (e.g., farming communities) were more likely to have shared value systems. As people specialized, community members had limited understanding of what other persons in the community did for a living. In addition, differentiation of interests and associations occurred as society shifted from primary (face-to-face groups such as families and neighbors) to secondary groups (more formalized groups and organizations). Local associations became chapters of national organizations, tying their members into an extra-community network. Technological advances made it possible to maintain contact with others who were geographically dispersed. Given these changes, one must take care not to assume a single, common, shared value system in contemporary communities. Also, the social worker must not assume that members of the target population have equal access to these advances in technology.

Depending on the selected target population, practitioners will find a host of value perspectives. For example, if the target population is people with AIDS, some persons in the community will feel strongly that they deserve the best possible care and comfort, while others will react in fear, not wanting people with AIDS in their local acute and long-term care facilities. Similarly, if the target population is pregnant teens, value conflicts may arise between community residents who believe that teens should be given contraceptive information and those who believe that this information will only encourage sexual activity.

Jansson (1988) states that "value clarification lies at the heart of social welfare" (p. 6). He identifies five moral issues that drive decision making. Applied to the target population within a local community, the following questions arise:

1. Should the target population receive services and on what terms?
2. For what needs and problems is the community responsible and what target population needs should receive priority?
3. What strategies should be used to address specific target population problems?
4. Should the community give preferential assistance or treatment to the target population?
5. Should the community use its resources to address target population needs?

These five value clarification questions may be answered differently depending on the population targeted within the community. This series of questions implies that some populations may be valued more than others, that some may be perceived as "deserving" and others as "undeserving." Whereas there may be an outcry to treat drug-addicted infants, their addicted mothers may be treated with disdain. Whereas homeless families may be perceived as "down on their luck," homeless alcoholics may be seen as "bringing this upon themselves."

Depending on the target population group, there may be subgroups within the larger whole that are viewed differently. Recognition of the importance of diversity will lead the macro practitioner to check carefully the values of each ethnic or racial group affected, the possible different perspectives of women and men in the target population, and the perspectives of representatives of gay and lesbian groups, if they are affected by the change. It is far wiser to take the time to be inclusive of a wide range of values than to find out, too late, that a change effort is not working because differing perspectives were overlooked. Change agents should go into this values-clarification exercise understanding that they may not always like what is discovered about community values, but struggling with value conflicts will give the change agent some understanding of how much the community is committed to addressing the needs of the target population.

As one begins to form an understanding of major community value perspectives, one must take care to recognize the fit (or lack of fit) between target population perspectives and dominant community perspectives. Are target population perspectives taken into consideration when decisions are made that affect them? Recognizing value differences and power discrepancies is an important part of the community-analysis process.

Task 3: Recognize Community Differences

Up to this point we have examined two areas of focus relevant to understanding communities: identifying target populations and determining community characteristics. We turn now to a third area of focus: recognizing differences. No matter what target population one identifies, there will be differences between this population and other groups within the community. There will also be differences within the target population. Potential differences include culture, race, ethnicity, gender, age, and a host of other factors.

The "dynamics of difference" (Cross, Bazron, Dennis, & Isaacs, 1989, p. 20) may involve cross-cultural exchanges where groups with diverse histories and values interact. There is always room for misunderstanding and misinterpretation when this occurs. "Both will bring culturally-prescribed patterns of communication, etiquette, and problem-solving. Both may bring stereotypes or underlying feelings about serving or being served by someone who is 'different' " (Cross et al., 1989, p. 20). For example, professionals who serve the elders may rationalize why they do not serve many Latino clients by stereotyping Latino families as taking care of their own, and therefore needing few formal services. This oversimplification may ignore the fact that one-fourth of the Latino families in a local community are poor, and caring for an older family member is a tremendous financial burden. It also ignores the fact that all Latino elders do not have other family members residing in the community.

Differences may be subtle or taken for granted, yet they may influence the way in which members of the target population communicate with one another and with other groups. Feminist writers encourage the recognition of gender differences in psychological development (Gilligan, 1982), in interpreting the world (Belenky, Clinchy, Goldberger, & Tarule, 1986), and in communication (Tannen, 1990). Tannen's research indicates that men and women speak in "genderlects" that comprise "cross-cultural communication" (p. 18). For example, a male social worker was assessing a community's responsiveness to single mothers with young children. He attended several support groups for the target population and was frustrated that all they did was talk without coming to a consensus on what they wanted from the larger community. He assessed part of the problem as an unwillingness on the part of the target population to face up to their problems and to work on solutions. The women in the support group, however, felt that this was an opportunity to process their thoughts and feelings. They did not view the group as a place to resolve problems for immediate resolution. The group was a place to make connections and to achieve intimacy.

Identify Formal and Covert Mechanisms of Oppression.   Questions to be explored for this activity include:

- What differences are observed among members of the target population?
- What differences are observed between members of the target population and other groups within the community?
- How are target population differences viewed by the larger community?
- Is the target population oppressed because of these differences?
- What target population strengths can be identified and how might these strengths contribute to empowerment?

Oppression is "the social act of placing severe restrictions on a group or institution. Typically, a government or political organization that is in power places these restrictions formally or covertly on oppressed groups so that they may be exploited and less able to compete with other social groups" (Barker, 1995, p. 265). Oppression focuses on differences, the assumption being that some group is lesser than, not as good as, or less worthy than others.

Some people are uncomfortable with differences, and because they assume that one way must be better than another, they look on differences as a problem to be solved. An alternative perspective is that differences reflect a variety of ways to view the world, to believe, and to behave. Social workers can employ differences as potential strengths within a target population, but they must remember that differences often include alternative definitions of a successful outcome. For example, in the women's group just described, the social worker was frustrated because he believed the group members were not solving their problems. For the members, however, the group itself was something of a solution. It provided a forum in which single mothers could share their concerns and find understanding and support. This forum could, in turn, serve as a foundation on which additional solutions might be built.

Areas around which oppression often occurs are gender, race, ethnicity, sexual orientation, age, and ability. Depending on the target population, all or some of the resulting "-isms" may be relevant. In many cases, the target population may be defined as persons affected by one of the "-isms."

Sexism is discrimination based on attitudes and assumptions about gender. Often, these attitudes become barriers to community participation even though they are subtle and difficult to identify. They exist in the values, norms, and traditions of a society to be translated into local community activities. For example, as children are socialized in their educational and familial roles, they are given messages regarding what is considered appropriate for women and men. Bricker-Jenkins and Hooyman (1986) propose that patriarchy within the community be examined. They suggest that the recording of history and the establishment of myths that set direction for succeeding generations are parts of a patriarchal system in which experiences of women tend to be devalued as subordinate to those of their male colleagues.

The devaluation of the homemaker role may also be an important form of sexism. Many women feel compelled to enter the workplace, not so much by economic pressures, but by societal pressures. So much of one's identity is derived from work, yet women's housework, volunteering, childbearing and child rearing are not considered economically productive (Waring, 1988).

Access to employment and services may, in some instances, limit opportunities for women. For example, women may be limited to homemaker roles because work opportunities are not readily available close to home. Lack of services such as day care and transportation may limit access to employment. Inadequate transportation systems within the community may require women to transport children, limiting their abilities to be engaged in some types of employment as well as other pursuits in which they may have an interest (Fellin, 1995). Groups such as the displaced homemakers' network or public offices that deal with equal employment opportunity complaints may be able to help in understanding gender-based practices that affect the target population.

Clearly, the most serious type of oppression against women is violence. Statistics on violence against women and resources to deal with this problem are available from such organizations as women's support groups, women's centers, and shelters for battered women (Kasper & Aponte, 1996).

Racism is stereotyping and generalizing about people based on the physiological characteristics of their racial group. Ethnic groups share a common language, customs, history, culture, race, religion, or origin. *Ethnocentrism* implies that one's ethnic group is superior to others (Barker, 1995).

The terms *ghetto* and *barrio* are important in understanding racial and ethnic communities. Choldin (1985) defines *ghetto* as a "bounded geographical residential area in which a defined racial or ethnic group is forced to live" (p. 236). *Barrio* describes neighborhoods with large proportions of Latino people. Within the ghetto and barrio, residents develop their own culturally driven interactions and ways of looking at the larger society. In many large cities, ethnic communities are named according to the group that occupies that portion of the city—the Polish community, for example (Fellin, 1995).

There are multiple theories that attempt to explain ethnicity, each examining different aspects of the dynamics of ethnic relations. Theories of assimilation focus on the process experienced by ethnic groups in becoming a part of the dominant society, but do not always examine the conflict when differences clash. Therefore, ethnic pluralists react to the concept of assimilation and assumptions about the "melting pot," arguing that maintaining one's ethnicity is a way to cope with discrimination. Biological theories about ethnicity and human genetics have been highly controversial, often viewed as ethnocentric, or even racist. Ecological theories have focused on competition for scarce resources as a critical force in ethnic relations and in leading to subjugation and domination. Stratification theories examine the distribution of power, whereas colonialism theories emphasize exploitation in which one part of society oppresses another (Barrera, Munoz, & Ornelas, 1972). Aguirre and Turner (2001) attempt to take the major principles of each theory, seeing ethnic discrimination in America as stressing several interrelated factors: "ethnic identifiability, the threat that an ethnic population poses, the prejudicial stereotypes that are articulated, the resources possessed by an ethnic population, the size of an ethnic population, and the position of a subpopulation in the stratification system" (p. 41).

The target population may encompass one or more racial or ethnic groups. Information on such factors as rates of employment, educational achievement, and socioeconomic status within these subgroups is important to understanding effects of institutional racism. Involvement of persons from different groups within the target population in decision-making roles is an important indicator of sensitivity to ethnic and cultural issues. Services and other resources available to people from diverse ethnicities in the target population proportionate to their numbers in the community is another.

Homophobia is a term used to describe irrational fears held by people toward others who have a same-gender sexual orientation. Homophobia, in the extreme, has taken the form of "gay bashing," a practice of physically beating gay men. In other forms, homophobia results in job discrimination, ridicule, and ostracizing. Like all prejudices (literally, "pre-judgments"), homophobia blinds those afflicted with it to individual qualities of lesbian women and gay men and causes them to be perceived only in the context of their sexual orientation.

Ageism is stereotyping and generalizing about people because of their age, and *ableism* is discrimination against those who are not considered physically or functionally able to perform as well as others. Although older persons are often perceived as being too physically or mentally limited to engage in ongoing community activities, only 4 percent of those persons over age 65 are living in nursing-home settings (McInnis-Dittrich, 2002, p. 5). Clearly, however, the vast majority are capable of self-sufficiency and productive lives, yet they may be excluded from employment and from playing an important role in the community because of perceptions about their abilities. The same treatment is often experienced by people of any age who have physical or functional limitations.

If age or disability is relevant to understanding the target population, statistics on the numbers and age ranges of those persons in the community should be compiled. How many persons are frail elders (age 85+)? How many persons are physically disabled and what types of disabilities are documented? Is there adequate access to services that engage persons with disabilities in active community roles—transportation and outreach, for example? Are there support services (e.g., nutrition programs, homemaker, respite) that sustain these persons and their caregivers?

Recognize Potential Discrimination.   Questions to be explored for this activity include:

- Are there barriers that inhibit the target population from becoming fully integrated into the community?
- What community groups, organizations, rules, procedures, or policies discriminate for or against the target population?
- To what extent are the perspectives of people of color, women, gay men and lesbians, older persons, and persons with disabilities sought in decisions affecting the target population?

Identifying value conflicts is critical to recognizing oppression and discrimination. Values may be based on prejudices, those pre-judgments that community residents have about the target group that are not grounded in systematic evidence. The issue of systematic evidence is one that needs to be treated with a great deal of care and sensitivity. Many people still believe that each individual essentially controls his or her own destiny, and that hard work and persistence will overcome any barrier or limitation. This belief is reinforced when people who have severe disabilities accomplish incredible physical feats or when people who are severely deprived make it to the top.

These accomplishments become "evidence" for local, state, and national leaders that those who need help are simply not trying hard enough. People who hold this belief look at what they consider to be systematic evidence, and deny that their beliefs are prejudices. What is overlooked here, however, is generations of differential treatment that have made it difficult for people of color, for women, for persons with physical and developmental disabilities, and others to have equal access to economic resources and self-sufficiency. So, for example, when a job is available and a homeless man chooses not to take it, one person will see that as evidence that he is lazy, while another will recognize it as a response to a lifetime of hopeless, discouraging, dead-end jobs. For some, the pain of life on the street is less than the pain of hopelessness in their share of the workplace.

Prejudices are intimately tied to values and may affect how a person feels. *Discrimination* is acting out those prejudices. These actions can be observed in the differences in quality of life between the target population and the rest of the community.

For example, existing data indicate that "most of the elderly poor are female (72%) and either black (40%) or Latina (26%). . . . To be old, female, nonwhite, and living alone is to bear the heaviest burden of all. An astonishing 55% of that multimarked contingent lives *below* the poverty level" (Margolis, 1990, p. 10). This is the type of evidence that points to generations of blocked opportunities, discrimination, and neglect. Serious damage is done to the fabric of the country, and therefore to the fabric of its communities, when any group of people is discriminated against as a whole category, when an individual is treated only as a member of a group, and when individual differences are disregarded. To many who are victims of this attitude, the message is that it doesn't matter how hard they work, how honest and law-abiding they are, how much they play by the rules; they can never escape discrimination and oppression because they are lifetime members of the group. Recognizing discriminatory behavior, then, is important in assessing the community.

Task 4: Identify Community Structure

The fourth task in the pursuit of understanding a community is to identify its structure. Different structural domains will be important, depending on the defined problem and the needs of the target population. For example, one might focus on the city if the problem is homelessness or the school district if the problem is a high dropout rate. The domain may be a mental health catchment area or the planning and service area of an area agency on aging. The goal is to ground the macro practitioner in recognizing the distribution of power, the provision and allocation of resources, and the patterns of service distribution that affect the target population within the domain of the targeted community.

Part of the community's structure is its human service system and the programs it offers those in need. Figure 6.3 identifies the types of units that should be considered when assessing service provision in a community. These units, taken together, comprise the total health and human service delivery system within the community, and they operate interdependently. A given community, depending on availability of resources, may emphasize the provision of services through one set of units more than another. For example, in a resource-poor community, reliance on informal units may be a necessity until publicly funded formal services can be obtained. However, in all communities, elements of informal, mediating, and formal service units will be found. The astute practitioner will carefully assess all avenues of service delivery for the target population.

FIGURE 6.3 Units within the Health and Human Service Delivery System

Informal Units
Household units
Neighborhood groups

Mediating Units
Self-help groups
Grassroots associations
Voluntary associations

Formal Units
Voluntary nonprofit agencies
Public agencies
For-profit agencies

Recognize Locations of Power and Resource Availability. Questions to be explored in this activity include:

- What is the domain or jurisdiction involved, given the target population and problem?
- Who controls the funds?
- Who are the major community leaders within the domain identified who will respond to the concerns of the target population? Who will oppose their concerns?

Originally, primary groups—composed of families, friends, and neighbors—performed the functions necessary for community survival. Gradually, business and government have assumed many of these functions. The most obvious change occurred during the New Deal era in the mid-1930s when government reluctantly responded to the social welfare needs of a post-Depression society. At that time, the balance between public and private service provision shifted, with public dollars taking over an increasing share of human service funding.

Urbanization and industrialization have greatly affected the social, political, and economic structures of this country. One of the major areas of impact, noted by Warren (1978), was the separation of one's working life from where he or she lives. Because of this change, people who hold power change, depending on the way in which a community is defined.

As local and extracommunity ties have expanded, so has bureaucratization and its accompanying impersonalization. Bureaucratic structures are usually adopted by government, business, and voluntary organizations as the size of population increases. Funding patterns can lead to power brokers external to the community. Major sources of funding for local service efforts imply the ability to influence and direct provider decisions in regard to target population needs. For example, the specialized volunteer-run community-based agency that once served the neighborhood may have been transformed into a multiservice agency with many paid staff. This means that there may be a number of leaders within the health and human service system, all representing different sectors (e.g., government, nonprofit, for profit). In addition, the larger multiservice organization may have multiple funding sources, including federal, state, and local government funds; United Way; private contributions; and fees. Each source must be satisfied that its expectations are being met.

Viewing the community from a power perspective requires identifying the formal and informal leaders within a community. It also means examining their effectiveness in getting things done. Assessing the political climate requires reading the local newspaper and talking with local community leaders to determine top-priority issues competing for funding. If a legislative change is needed, it is necessary to identify who may be willing to take the lead on issues affecting the target population.

Community power has been viewed from three perspectives: (1) an elitist structure, (2) a pluralist structure, and (3) an amorphous structure. An elitist approach assumes that a small number of people have disproportionate power in various community sectors. A pluralist perspective implies that as issues change, various interest groups and shifting coalitions arise. This perspective may be increasing as more and more special-interest groups develop within the local community. The amorphous structure implies no persistent pattern of power relationships within the community (Meenaghan & Gibbons, 2000, p. 49). Gaining a growing understanding of the community's power dynamics will enable the practitioner to evaluate the community for this task.

Related to community structure is the issue of available resources. Communities can be described as resource rich or resource poor when it comes to providing for the needs of the target population. Although it is important to consider resources in connection with power, as discussed earlier, it is also important to compile information on resources so that appropriate sources will be targeted in pursuit of community change.

There are many types of resources to consider. Resources may be very tangible, such as a welfare check, or highly symbolic, such as caring or social support. Resources can be grouped into six categories: love, status, information, money, goods, and services (Specht, 1986). Most early community encounters will focus heavily on the more concrete resources that are exchanged (money, goods, and services) because tangible resources are easier to define and observe. However, as the professional becomes more actively engaged in community practice, there will be more and more opportunities to learn about those more symbolic exchanges (love, status, and information) that are equally important to members of the target population.

Resources may be available from a number of different domains. King and Mayers (1984) have developed Guidelines for Community Assessment designed for use in analyzing community resources. They suggest that, in assessing community resources available to a particular population, a number of domains be explored. Within each domain, questions of policy, practice, eligibility, location, and participation must be addressed in order to determine how available each resource is to the target population. Their domains follow:

- Health
- Welfare
- Education
- Housing
- Recreation
- Employment
- Business
- Religion
- Others

For example, if the target population is low-income children, resources to be explored would include Medicaid (health), child welfare services (welfare), school programs (education), public housing, day-care programs provided by their parents' places of employment, corporate community service initiatives (business), and faith-based groups involved in serving their communities (religion). How effective are these systems in meeting the needs of the community's children and satisfying the expectations of the community? How do programs within each of these domains relate to one another?

Having examined the resources available to the target population, those involved in community analysis should then look more specifically to the human service delivery system.

Examine Service-Delivery Units. Questions to be explored in this activity include:

- What informal units (e.g., household, natural, and social networks) are actively engaged in service delivery to the target population within this community?
- What mediating units (e.g., self-help groups, voluntary or grassroots associations) are actively engaged in service delivery to the target population within this community?
- What formal service-delivery units (e.g., nonprofit, public, for-profit) are actively engaged in service delivery in this community?
- Are there differences in service delivery that appear to be based on race or ethnicity, gender, sexual orientation, disability, age, or religion?

In Chapter 5 we discussed the importance of informal and mediating units in understanding communities. Household units consist of persons who reside within a common dwelling, whether they consider themselves families, significant others, friends, partners, or roommates. Natural support systems evolve around mutual support, going beyond purely social networks, and engaging in resource exchange. Assessing these informal and mediating units is somewhat difficult simply because they are "informal," and therefore less accessible. Yet, any information that can be gathered will be helpful, since it is often these less visible activities that make a quality difference for people in need.

Formal vehicles of health and human service delivery are interconnected in numerous ways. We will briefly examine them according to three types of auspice: nonprofit, public (governmental), and for profit (commercial).

Nonprofit Agencies. As voluntary associations become more formalized, they may become incorporated as nonprofit agencies, recognized as publicly chartered tax-free organizations (Van Til, 1988). There are many types of nonprofit agencies, but here we will focus on nonprofit human service agencies, defined by Kramer (1981) as "those [organizations] that are essentially bureaucratic in structure, governed by an elected volunteer board of directors, [and] employing professional or volunteer staff to provide a continuing human service to a clientele in the community" (p. 9).

Nonprofit agencies are formal vehicles of health and human service delivery. They are often viewed traditionally within local communities as the agency of choice—a voluntary initiative that targets a specialized clientele. This traditional view is based on the early welfare system in this country that arose from a profusion of agencies sponsored by various religious and secular groups.

Nonprofit agencies provide many different services within local communities. Although all nonprofit agencies using government funding serve clients without regard to race or gender, a growing number of agencies are specifically designed to serve the special needs of ethnic communities and families, women who are victims of discrimination and/or violence, and other groups underserved by more traditional agencies. The macro practitioner should identify which nonprofit agencies serve the target population and whether they have particular service emphases.

Public Agencies.   The public sector consists of federal, state, regional, county, and city government entities. When the mutual support function is performed by government, it is referred to as *social welfare.* The social welfare system in the United States has been described as a "patchwork quilt," which "does not represent a coordinated, comprehensive, integrated, and nonredundant series of social welfare services; instead, it is a helter-skelter mix of programs and policies that defy a systematic understanding of the welfare state" (Karger & Stoesz, 1990, p. 167).

By the time federal programs are operationalized within the local community, they have usually gone through several levels of bureaucracy. Depending on the structure, which will vary by program type, there may be several extracommunity levels through which dollars have flowed. There may be regional as well as state mandates, rules, regulations, and procedures that instruct local providers regarding what they can and cannot do. Local decision making and autonomy will vary depending on the policies that drive a particular program. In short, extracommunity sources have a definite influence on the local delivery of public services.

In assessing a community's human service system, it is important to gain knowledge about policies and programs that affect the target population (Karger & Stoesz, 2002). For example, working with elders means that one must be familiar with the Older Americans Act. Familiarity with the Older Americans Act reveals that there is a designated state unit on aging in every state and a network of area agencies on aging (AAAs). Every state must have a three- to five-year plan for elder services, and each AAA must have a local plan. Therefore, every community within the United States will be included in a plan that addresses elder needs. Experience suggests that this does not mean that every community *meets* the needs of their older members. Resources will be limited and the actual carrying out of the plan will include the use of Older Americans Act dollars, in partnership with other public and private initiatives. In addition, many communities have waiting lists for services, and state commitments to carrying out the objectives of the federal legislation vary.

If one's target population is single mothers receiving Temporary Aid to Needy Families (TANF), the social worker will need to know that states vary in what income is counted against benefits received. States also establish their own needs standard for families in that state. Therefore, although TANF is a large public assistance program developed at the federal level, state-level decisions influence what benefits families will receive. To be effective, the social worker will need to understand how federal and state governments interact and how community attitudes toward TANF recipients influence clients.

In assessing the distribution of public resources across an entire community, including the funding of social service programs, it is important once again to examine community practices from the perspective of special populations. Voluntary associations often serve as advocates for their members and have had varying degrees of success in influencing the allocation of resources. In many communities, elders have been highly successful in these efforts, but attention to the needs of children varies. Ethnic groups have exercised increasing political power over the last few decades, but still find, in many communities, that their interests and needs are considered a low priority. Lesbian and gay groups have increasingly taken up causes such as funding for AIDS research and have participated in the political arena to influence allocation of resources, but they still face widespread discrimination.

Understanding the political system within the community is a challenge. In the United States, jurisdiction over health and human service programs is distributed across cities, counties, and states. Social workers must contend with multiple federal statutes, regulations, administrative rules, and funding formulae, plus there are state and local laws and funding procedures to identify (Jansson, 2003).

Professional colleagues, however, can provide perspectives on types of services and whether government is truly addressing the needs of the target population. For example, for macro practitioners working in a public housing development, social workers in other developments will be helpful in interpreting how regulations assist as well as constrain their efforts. Locating colleagues in similar settings is important to developing a professional support system to aid in coping with public policies, procedures, and rules.

For-Profit Agencies.   Corporate foundations have played a major role in funding programs that benefit local communities, and many corporations have long provided employee benefits addressing health, human service, and retirement needs. Indeed, a growing number of social workers are involved in the corporate workplace through employee assistance programs (EAPs). These programs have developed as corporations realize that productive employees are those who are supported in all aspects of their lives (Abramovitz & Epstein, 1983). In an aging society, some large corporations have created eldercare support networks for employees caring for aged parents.

In the last decade, the actual delivery of health and human services has been increasingly carried out by for-profit corporations. For example, the majority of nursing homes are now for-profit organizations. These shifting patterns were first noticed in the health-care arena, when proprietary hospitals began competing with traditional nonprofit providers (Marmor, Schlesinger, & Smithey, 1987). Public financing of health care through private mechanisms was only the beginning. As profit-making corporations bid for public contracts, competition with nonprofit organizations increased. Twenty years ago, our discussion of the health and human service systems would have focused almost entirely on the government and nonprofit sectors and their partnership. Today, the term *mixed economy*—including government, nonprofit, and for-profit services—is clearly an accurate description (Karger & Stoesz, 2002).

Given the complexity of the formal service delivery system, the purpose of this assessment is to gain a better understanding of what organizations are providing services to the target population in the community. Having a general idea of what nonprofit, public, and for-profit agencies are available to the community leads to an examination of how they work together, as well as how they relate to the informal units within the service delivery system.

Identify Patterns of Resource Control and Service Delivery.   Questions to be explored for this activity include:

- What groups, associations, and organizations (both within and external to the community) advocate for and provide assistance to the target population?
- How is resource distribution to the target population influenced by interaction within the community?
- What limits are placed on services to the target population, and who establishes these limits?
- What roles do citizens and consumers play in the control of services to the target population?

When assessing patterns and levels of participation, it is important that the macro practitioner distinguish between citizen and consumer-client participation. There are many citizens who, for reasons of altruism and conviction, are committed to fight for the rights of the poor and oppressed. They bring a certain perspective to the discussion, and make a contribution to constructive change in communities. However, it should not be assumed that interested citizen advocates represent the same perspective as those persons directly affected by the problem. Representatives of the target population should, whenever possible, be sought out to represent themselves in their own words; it should not be left to professionals and other concerned citizens to speak for them.

When dealing with the question of control over service availability to a target population, there can be both intracommunity and extracommunity sources of control. In practice, external and internal patterned interactions tend to develop as community units work together. Examples of extracommunity sources of control are state and federal government funding of community-based health clinics. Resources are typically allocated through contracts that include regulations and expectations. Various human service agencies within the local community, then, interact with these extracommunity public entities. Relationships internal to a community have an important part in linking community subsystems together. Organizations with similar interests often form loosely knit federations to accomplish certain functions where there are common interests. For example, several women's groups may form a coalition to establish a battered women's shelter or a political action committee.

Not only are there horizontal relationships that tie one to local informal and formal groups and organizations within the community but there are also numerous vertical ties that transcend geographical boundaries. Local community autonomy may be reduced as extracommunity forces influence what one does and how one thinks. The importance of extracommunity forces on the target population within the local community must be considered in order to understand service distribution patterns. On the other hand, extracommunity forces may actually strengthen communities by providing more options and additional resources.

How powerful the controlling entities become in a community often depends on the extent of citizen participation. Burke (1968) describes five citizen participation roles:

1. Review and comment
2. Consultation
3. Advisory
4. Shared decision making
5. Controlled decision making

One role is to *review proposals* for change within communities. This review process may be carried out in committee meetings, through requests for feedback from selected individuals, or through public hearings. It is a very limited role, and comments may or may not be incorporated. *Consultation* involves giving opinions on the change when asked. An *advisory* role usually involves a formal ongoing mechanism such as a United Way advisory council or planning committee, the purpose of which is to advise decision makers on factors affecting the target population. Although advisory committees do not have the power of policy boards, they can have a strong voice because of their access to decision makers. In addition, their opinions may pro-actively affect proposals rather than simply reacting to programs designed by others. *Shared decision making* is clearly a stronger role than advising, and places citizens and consumers in roles where they can, in collaboration with community leaders and professionals, affect decisions. Finally, *controlled decision making* places citizens and consumers in positions of control over decisions such as policy statements, review boards, or membership on boards of directors. These types of positions allow for the greatest amount of control by citizens and consumers. For example, a consumer who serves on the governing board of a family service agency may convince other board members that quality day-care services for single mothers should be a top agency priority.

One cannot assume that citizen participation automatically goes hand in hand with changes practitioners initiate within the community. The concept of citizen participation is essential to democracy, but it will often involve groups who disagree with one another. Just as citizens may comprise the local board of planned parenthood, there are citizens who believe that some of the services offered by this agency are morally wrong. Whenever interested citizens and consumers participate in community activities, these types of clashes in perspective should be expected.

Knowing what groups and agencies are available does not go far enough. It is important for the macro practitioner to know whether they actually work together so that target groups do not fall through gaps in the service delivery system. Thus, the last task in the assessment process examines the linkages that are evident to the practitioner and require a judgment as to whether these interacting units truly comprise a system that is responsive to multiple needs.

Determine Linkages between Units.   Questions to be explored for this activity include:

- How are the various types of service units generally connected within a community?
- What are the established linkages between units that serve the target population within *this* community?
- Where are linkages between service units obviously needed, but not currently established?
- Are the interests of people of color, women, gay men and lesbians, and other oppressed groups represented in the network established through linkages between units?

If there are multiple agencies with overlapping relationships and numerous types of services, is there a glue that holds the community delivery system together? Certainly there may be competition among units, but there will also be connections. Just as the individual is embedded in a social network, so are the group and organizational units within the community. These relational patterns may change over time.

A number of writers have created typologies of how organizations relate to one another. Tobin, Ellor, and Anderson-Ray (1986) identify five levels of interaction between human service agencies within the community: communication, cooperation, coordination, collaboration, and confederation. Bailey and Koney (2000) identify four levels: affiliation; federation, association, or coalition; consortium, network, or joint venture; and merger, acquisition, or consolidation. Table 6.4 provides an adaptation of these various categories, each of which are discussed below.

Communication.   Communication can be formal or informal. Information and referral exemplify formal communication that happens between units on a daily basis. Communication designed to increase interagency information and understanding may be enhanced through the use of brochures, pamphlets, and media. In this sense, it is an affiliation process. Informal communication occurs between units as groups meet to discuss community issues or staff talk about their programs at conferences. Although communication is assumed to occur, breakdowns in the delivery system often happen because this process of sharing information

TABLE 6.4 Five Levels of Interaction among Service Providers

Level of Interaction	Type of Relationship	Characteristics	Level of Provider Autonomy
Communication	Is friendly, cordial	Sharing of ideas between units, including consultation	High
Cooperation	May be defined as an affiliation	Working together to plan and implement independent programs	High
Coordination	Could be a federation, association, or coalition-type relationship	Working together to avoid duplication and to assist one another in sharing information, advertising for one another, and making referrals	Moderate
Collaboration	Could be a consortium, network, or joint venture	Joining together to provide a single program or service, with shared resources	Moderate
Consolidation		Merging into one entity	Autonomy relinquished

Source: Adapted from the work of Tobin, Ellor, and Anderson-Ray (1986) and Bailey and Koney (2000).

across units is not nurtured. Often, written agreements are developed as a reminder of the importance of constant communication as staff change within organizations and new groups are formed within the community.

Cooperation.   Cooperation occurs when units within the community agree to work toward similar goals. A local private child day-care center may work closely with a public human service agency. Both want to provide supports for single parents with young children, yet these units provide different resources. Social workers at the day-care center meet with staff at the human service agency once a month to discuss common concerns and to maintain a sense of continuity for parents who are clients of both agencies. The practitioner needs to know that these linkages are established and should also be actively involved in establishing them.

Corporate volunteerism represents a cooperative linkage between the for-profit and nonprofit sectors. The Levi Strauss Company provides an example. In communities throughout the United States in which Levi Strauss factories are located, there are community involvement teams. In one southeastern city, the company encouraged its employees to become actively involved with a multicounty nonprofit home aide service for people who are elderly or disabled. Employees donated time to painting and repairing the homes of older shut-ins, as well as provided friendly visits to the agency's clients. If the target population is older widows, the social worker needs to know that the corporate sector is willing to address client needs.

The concept of corporate volunteerism is manifested in a number of ways. A business may subsidize their employees by giving them release time to do community service work. Other companies will loan employees to human service agencies for a specified period of time so that the expertise required for a project can be provided at no cost to the agency. As employees near retirement, the for-profit sector often provides preretirement training in which postretirement volunteer opportunities are presented. In this way, the for-profit sector actually performs a recruitment function for the nonprofit service delivery system.

The interchange between the for-profit and nonprofit sectors also occurs in the form of corporate cash and in-kind contributions. Computer manufacturers may donate hardware to a local service agency, assisting in computerizing its information system. Restaurants donate food to homeless shelters. A local for-profit nursing home may open its doors to older community residents who live alone in a large metropolitan area during a time of anxiety over a crime wave. In a community, what cooperative efforts exist between service units within different sectors that focus on the target population's needs? Are race, ethnicity, gender, or sexual orientation factors that need to be taken into consideration in assessing service system interactions? Are any of these interests left out when they should be included?

Coordination.   Coordination implies a concerted effort to work together. Often, separate units will draft agreements, outlining ways in which coordination will occur. Federations, associations, and coalitions may be formed.

In a continuum of care system that attempts to address the needs of such populations as older persons, those with disabilities, or those with AIDS within the community, coordination is necessary. As consumers exit the acute care hospital, discharge planners work to develop a care plan. This requires knowledge of and close coordination with local service providers. Service plans often include a package to support the client's needs—mobile meals, visiting nurses, and homemaker services. Depending on the level of disability and the length of time expected for recovery, this service plan may make the difference between returning home or convalescing in a long-term care facility. Extensive coordination is required.

The growth of case management within local communities reflects the need for interunit oversight as consumers receive services from multiple units. Case management programs attempt to provide a coordination function so that service delivery flows across informal and formal providers of care. Where there are case managers serving the target population, it is useful to learn how they view the relationships between service units that serve the target population and where they see gaps.

Collaboration.   Collaboration implies the concept of a joint venture. *Joint ventures* are agreements in which two or more units within the community agree to set up a new program or service. This usually occurs when no one separate unit within the community is able or willing to establish the new venture alone. Consortia and networks are typically established for collaborative purposes.

For example, a local senior citizens center identified the need for home repair services for many of its participants. Because older persons tend to own older homes, repairs were often needed. The center did not have the resources to begin this program alone, but by working with a community action agency within the community, a home repair service was sponsored jointly by the center and the agency. Eventually, the home repair service became a separate unit, incorporated as a nonprofit organization.

Coalition building is another form of collaboration. A *coalition* is a loosely developed association of constituent groups and organizations, each of whose primary identification is outside the coalition. For example, state coalitions have been formed as part of the National Health Care Campaign. Community organizations, voluntary associations, public agencies, and interested individuals have joined forces to work toward a common goal—health care for all citizens. In coming together, a new voluntary association is formed. Even though the diverse members of this coalition represent various interests across community units, their collaboration on health-care concerns provides a strong and focused network for change.

In some communities, agencies created to serve the needs of a special population collaborate to assess need, to examine the fit between needs and services, and to present a united front and a stronger voice in pursuing funding for programs. Many federal and state contracts require active collaboration or partnerships, even encouraging the sharing of staff and the hiring of coordinators in order to ensure full participation. Requests for proposals (RFPs) from private foundations typically require grantees to be very specific about how they will collaborate with others.

Consolidation. Units within the community may actually merge, often when one or both units become unable to function autonomously. A horizontal merger occurs, for example, when two mental health centers consolidate into a single organization. A vertical merger occurs when a hospital absorbs a home health provider. A conglomerate merger occurs when units within the community form a confederation of multiple smaller units under a large umbrella agency. These actions are generally limited to nongovernmental agencies.

Agency interaction inevitably involves competition and conflict. Change agents learn to cope with competition and conflict on a regular basis. These types of interactions will be discussed in Part Four of this book.

Overall, the preceding tasks may be approached as a series of general questions to be applied to the task of assessing services in a community. Having looked at the community, consider these overriding concerns:

1. Is the community generally sensitive to the needs of the target population?
2. Are target population needs adequately assessed in this community?

3. Is there a "continuum of care" concept or framework that guides service planning and funding for target population needs?
4. How adequate is funding to meet target population needs in the community?
5. Are services appropriately located for target group accessibility?
6. What is the degree of cooperation, collaboration, and competition in providing services to the target population?
7. What gaps in services and problems affecting the target population have been identified in the process of conducting this assessment?
8. How does the race, ethnicity, gender, or sexual orientation of the target population, or some people in the population, affect the need for and provision of services?

Summary

We began this chapter by discussing three reasons why macro practitioners need a framework for assessing communities. First, social work in general and macro practice in particular require an orientation toward the person-in-environment perspective. In this chapter, the community in which the target population functions comprises the environment. Second, communities change and professionals need a framework for understanding these changes. We discussed 12 tasks that provide insight into how the target population is served within the community. Third, macro-level change requires an understanding of the history and development of a community as well as an analysis of its current status.

The community assessment provides one method of analyzing what has occurred and is occurring within the designated arena. Skilled macro practice requires (1) focused and precise data collection, (2) analysis of historical trends, and (3) a thorough understanding of qualitative elements that reflect human experiences, interactions, and relationships.

The assessment process begins with defining the target population. Following this, the human service response is explored and collective needs are considered. Sources of help are then addressed, including informal sources, such as households and social networks, and mediating sources, such as self-help groups and voluntary associations. Formal sources of services include nonprofit, public, and for-profit providers, and both the nature and orientation of services may differ in important ways across these auspices. Determining the competence of these systems in combining to meet needs in an effective way is the final consideration.

Based on data and information accumulated in the process of assessing a community's human service system, the macro practitioner must finally exercise professional judgment in evaluating the adequacy of resources devoted to the target population within the community. If the assessment has been thorough and productive, the practitioner will have gained enough understanding of what occurs within the community to identify and begin assessing needed change on behalf of the target population.

DISCUSSION QUESTIONS AND EXERCISES

1. *Vignette 1.* Vignette 1 in this chapter is located in Canyon City, population 250,000. Review the details of the vignette, assuming you are the social worker described in this situation. It is your job to collect information and to determine the feasibility of a community project targeting battered women. In narrowing your focus, how might you use the "Framework for Analyzing Community" identified in this chapter? Are there certain activities within this framework that would be particularly important to your community assessment, and how would you use these activities to narrow your focus and then mobilize resources?

2. *Vignette 2.* Vignette 2 is located in Lakeside, a planned community in which major changes have occurred. Review the details of this vignette, assuming you are the social worker who is responsible for community building efforts that will enhance the quality of life of elderly and disabled persons in Lakeside. How would you define the problem(s) in this situation? How might you use the "Framework for Analyzing Community" introduced in this chapter to assist you in your efforts?

3. Select a community with which you are familiar. Apply the questions presented in this chapter. Would this information tell you what you need to know in order to intervene in this community?

4. Although social workers are encouraged to use empowerment and strengths perspectives, it is easy to become overwhelmed with social problems in some communities. What might you do to maintain a strengths perspective even in multiproblem situations?

5. Select a target population with which you are familiar and use the framework in this chapter to understand and analyze the community in which they are located.

6. If you were entering a community for the first time, what factors would you take into consideration in engaging with the target population, community leaders, and other community residents?

7. Assessing needs is a critical task in determining the responsiveness of community service systems. Chapter 6 provides a number of methods for conducting needs assessments. Use an agency with which you are familiar to discuss what combinations of methods could be used to assess needs for a particular target population served by this agency. Would this agency be willing to use these methods? What methods does this agency already use?

8. It is much easier to identify formal agencies in the community than it is to locate the multiple sources of informal support. Yet, recognizing the importance of both is necessary. How might you learn about the informal system in a community? How might the informal system vary by population group?

9. Nonprofit, public, and for-profit agencies are all part of the contemporary service delivery system. What are the major differences between these auspices, from the perspective of the target population? Given the increasing blurred boundaries across sectors, what does auspice really tell you?

10. Connections between units within the service delivery system are essential if clients are not to fall through the cracks. However, developing and nurturing these connections is often easier said than done. Propose an overall strategy to develop linkages between agencies if you were trying to serve a special population group.

11. *Case management* has become a buzzword in the service delivery system. Many sectors employ case managers. Discuss what

case management is and how it relates to communitywide collaboration and cooperation. Do you see alternatives to the case management model to help people in need negotiate the community's social service system?

APPENDIX
Framework for Analyzing Community

Task 1: Focus on Target Population

Identify Target Population
- What target populations have been identified as being in need of services within the community, and how are they categorized?
- What target population will be the focus of this assessment?
- What priority is given to the needs of the target population in this community?
- What percentage of the target population are people of color, ethnic group members, women, gay men or lesbians, older persons, or persons with disabilities?

Understand Characteristics of Target Population Members
- What is known about the history of the target population in this community?
- How many persons comprise the target population and what are their relevant characteristics?
- How do persons in the target population perceive their needs?

Assess Target Population Needs
- What are feasible and appropriate ways to locate community needs assessment data and other relevant information about the target population?
- How do persons in the target population perceive their community and its responsiveness to their needs?
- How are these needs expressed by the people of this community?
- What do available data and information indicate about quality of life factors as they affect people of color; women; gay, lesbian, bisexual, and transgendered persons; elderly and disabled persons; and others?

Task 2: Determine Community Characteristics

Identify Community Boundaries
- What are the boundaries within which intervention on behalf of the target population will occur?
- Where are members of the target population located within the boundaries? Are they highly concentrated or scattered?
- What physical and social barriers exist for the target population?
- How compatible are jurisdictional boundaries of health and human service programs that serve the target population?
- How accessible are services for the target population?

Profile Social Problems
- What are the major social problems affecting the target population in this community as perceived by their spokespersons?
- Are there subgroups of the target population that are experiencing major social problems?
- To what extent are these problems interconnected, and must some be solved before others can be addressed?
- What data sources are available on the identified social problems and how are available data used within the community?
- Who collects the data, and is this an ongoing process?

Understand Dominant Values
- What cultural values, traditions, and beliefs are important to the target population?
- What are the predominant values that affect the target population within this community?
- What groups and individuals espouse these values, who opposes them, and are there value conflicts surrounding the target population?
- How do people in this community feel about giving and receiving help?
- What are the predominant shared perspectives in this community on inclusion of the target population in decisions that affect them?

Task 3: Recognize Community Differences

Identify Formal and Covert Mechanisms of Oppression
- What differences are observed among members of the target population?
- What differences are observed between members of the target population and other groups within the community?
- How are target population differences viewed by the larger community?
- Is the target population oppressed because of these differences?
- What target population strengths can be identified and how might these strengths contribute to empowerment?

Recognize Potential Discrimination
- Are there barriers that inhibit the target population from becoming fully integrated into the community?
- What community groups, organizations, rules, procedures, and policies discriminate for or against the target population?
- To what extent are the perspectives of people of color, women, gay men and lesbians, older persons, and persons with disabilities sought in decisions affecting the target population?

Task 4: Identify Community Structure

Recognize Locations of Power and Resource Availability
- What is the domain or jurisdiction involved, given the target population and problem?

- Who controls the funds?
- Who are the major community leaders within the domain identified who will respond to the concerns of the target population? Who will oppose their concerns?

Examine Service-Delivery Units

- What informal units (e.g., household, natural, and social networks) are actively engaged in service delivery to the target population within this community?
- What mediating units (e.g., self-help groups, voluntary or grassroots associations) are actively engaged in service delivery to the target population within this community?
- What formal service-delivery units (e.g., nonprofit, public, for-profit) are actively engaged in service delivery in this community?
- Are there differences in service delivery that appear to be based on race or ethnicity, gender, sexual orientation, disability, age, or religion?

Identify Patterns of Resource Control and Service Delivery

- What groups, associations, and organizations (both within and external to the community) advocate for and provide assistance to the target population?
- How is resource distribution to the target population influenced by interaction within the community?
- What limits are placed on services to the target population, and who establishes these limits?
- What roles do citizens and consumers play in the control of services to the target population?

Determine Linkages between Units

- How are the various types of service units generally connected within a community?
- What are the established linkages between units that serve the target population within *this* community?
- Where are linkages between service units obviously needed, but not currently established?
- Are the interests of people of color, women, gay men and lesbians, and other oppressed groups represented in the network established through linkages between units?

SUGGESTED READINGS

Appleby, G. A., E. Colon, and J. Hamilton. (2001). *Diversity, oppression, and social functioning.* Boston: Allyn and Bacon.

Figueira-McDonough, J. (1995). Community organization and the underclass: Exploring new prac-

tice directions. *Social Service Review, 69*(1): 57–85.

Hardina, D. (2002). *Analytical skills for community organization practice.* New York: Columbia University Press.

Kirst-Ashman, K. K., and G. H. Hull, Jr. (2001). *Generalist practice with organizations and communities* (2nd ed.). Belmont, CA: Brooks/Cole.

Lazzari, M. M., H. R. Ford, and K. J. Haughey. (1996). Making a difference: Women of action in the community. *Social Work, 41*(2): 197–205.

Lee, J. A. B. (1994). *The empowerment approach to social work practice.* New York: Columbia University Press.

McLaughlin, M., M. Irby, and J. Langman. (1994). *Urban sanctuaries: Neighborhood organizations in the lives and futures of inner city youth.* San Francisco: Jossey-Bass.

Nyden, P., A. Figert, M. Shibley, and D. Burrows. (1997). *Building community.* Thousand Oaks, CA: Pine Forge Press.

Oropesa, S. R. (1995). The ironies of human resource mobilization by neighborhood associations. *Nonprofit and Voluntary Sector Quarterly, 24*(3): 235–252.

Parsons, R. J., and E. O. Cox. (1994). *Empowerment-oriented social work practice with the elderly.* Pacific Grove, CA: Brooks/Cole.

Rivera, F. G., and J. L. Erlich. (1998). *Community organizing in a diverse society.* Boston: Allyn and Bacon.

Rothman, J. (Ed.). (1999). *Reflections on community organization: Enduring themes and critical issues.* Itasca, IL: F. E. Peacock.

Rousseau, M. (1991). *Community: The tie that binds.* New York: University Press of America.

Rubin, H. J., and I. S. Rubin. (2001). *Community organizing and development* (3rd ed.). Boston: Allyn and Bacon.

REFERENCES

Abramovitz, M., and I. Epstein. (1983). The politics of privatization: Industrial social work and private enterprise. *Urban and Social Change Review, 16*(1): 13–19.

Aguirre, A. Jr., and J. H. Turner. (2001). *American ethnicity: The dynamics and consequences of discrimination* (3rd ed.). Boston: McGraw-Hill.

Bailey, D., and K. M. Koney. (2000), *Creating and maintaining strategic alliances: From affiliations to consolidations.* Thousand Oaks, CA: Sage.

Barker, R. L. (1995). *The social work dictionary.* Washington, DC: National Association of Social Workers.

Barrera, M., C. Munoz, and C. Ornelas. (1972). The barrio as an internal colony. *Urban Affairs Annual Review, 6*: 480–498.

Belenky, M. F., B. M. Clinchy, N. R. Goldberger, and J. M. Tarule. (1986). *Women's ways of knowing.* New York: Basic Books.

Bellah, R. N., R. Madsen, W. M. Sullivan, A. Swidler, and S. M. Tipton. (1985). *Habits of the heart: Individualism and commitment in American life.* New York: Harper & Row.

Brager, G., H. Specht, and J. L. Torczyner. (1987). *Community organizing.* New York: Columbia University Press.

Bricker-Jenkins, M., and N. R. Hooyman (Eds.). (1986). *Not for women only.* Silver Spring, MD: National Association of Social Workers.

Burke, E. M. (1968). Citizen participation strategies. *Journal of the American Institute of Planners, 34*(5): 293.

Choldin, H. M. (1985). *Cities and suburbs.* New York: McGraw-Hill.

Cross, T. L., B. J. Bazron, K. W. Dennis, and M. R. Isaacs. (1989). *Towards a culturally competent system of care.* Washington, DC: Georgetown University Child Development Center.

Fellin, P. (1995). *The community and the social worker.* Itasca, IL: F. E. Peacock.

Gilligan, C. (1982). *In a different voice.* Cambridge, MA: Harvard University Press.

Gonzalez, V. M., J. T. Gonzalez, V. Freeman, and B. Howard-Pitney. (1991). *Health promotion in diverse communities.* Palo Alto, CA: Health Promotion Resource Center.

Jansson, B. S. (1988). *The reluctant welfare state: A history of American social welfare policies.* Belmont, CA: Wadsworth.

Jansson, B. S. (2003). *Becoming an effective policy advocate: From policy practice to social justice* (4th ed.). Pacific Grove, CA: Brooks/Cole.

Karger, H. J., and D. Stoesz. (1990). *American social welfare policy.* New York: Longman.

Karger, H. J., and D. Stoesz. (2002). *American social welfare policy: A pluralist approach.* Boston: Allyn and Bacon.

Kasper, B., and C. I. Aponte. (1996). Women, violence and fear: one community's experience. *Affilia, 11*(2): 179–194.

Kettner, P. M., J. M. Daley, and A. W. Nichols. (1985). *Initiating change in organizations and communities.* Monterey, CA: Brooks/Cole.

King, S. W., and R. S. Mayers. (1984). A course syllabus on developing self-help groups among minority elderly. In J. S. McNeil and S. W. King (Eds.), *Guidelines for developing mental health and minority aging curriculum with a focus on self-help groups.* Publication Supported by National Institute Mental Health Grant #MH 15944-04.

Kramer, R. M. (1981). *Voluntary agencies in the welfare state.* Berkeley: University of California Press.

Margolis, R. J. (1990). *Risking old age in America.* Boulder, CO: Westview Press.

Marmor, T. R., M. Schlesinger, and R. W. Smithey. (1987). Nonprofit organizations and health care. In W. W. Powell (Ed.), *The nonprofit sector* (pp. 221–239). New Haven, CT: Yale University Press.

McInnis-Dittrich, K. (2002). *Social work with elders.* Boston: Allyn and Bacon.

Meenaghan, T. M., and W. E. Gibbons. (2000). *Macro practice in the human services.* Chicago: Lyceum.

Specht, H. (1986). Social support, social networks, social exchange, and social work practice. *Social Service Review, 60*(2): 218–240.

Tannen, D. (1990). *You just don't understand.* New York: Williams Morrow.

Tobin, S. S., J. W. Ellor, and S. Anderson-Ray. (1986). *Enabling the elderly: Religious institutions within the community service system.* New York: State University of New York Press.

Van Til, J. (1988). *Mapping the third sector: Voluntarism in a changing social economy.* New York: The Foundation Center.

Waring, M. (1988). *If women counted.* San Francisco: Harper & Row.

Warren, R. L. (1978). *The community in America* (3rd ed.). Chicago: Rand McNally.

PART FOUR

Organizations as Arenas of Change

Part Three addressed communities as the focus of planned change. Communities are important arenas of practice for social workers because they have such a major influence on the lives of clients and establish a context within which human service organizations function. In Part Four, we will discuss organizations as a second critical macro system in which social workers operate. Chapter 7 begins with a review of the considerable body of theoretical literature about organizations. This review is intended to promote an understanding of how and why organizations function as they do. Chapter 8 focuses specifically on human service organizations and identifies the major areas in which organizational problems have been identified and solutions proposed.

OVERVIEW

Introduction

Whether they are large or small, formally or informally structured, it is organizations that carry out the core functions of social order in the United States. As noted in previous chapters, prior to the Industrial Revolution most individuals lived in rural, agrarian settings in which they were personally responsible for meeting their basic needs. People built their own houses, drew their own water, grew their own food, and made their own clothes. In modern times, however, the great majority of the U.S. population lives in large, complex, urban, and suburban communities, where people's needs are met by specialized organizations—supermarkets, restaurants, department stores, municipal utilities, construction companies, schools, social welfare institutions, and many others.

Organizations also comprise the building blocks of larger macro systems, and individuals engage their society through these organizations. Communities are critical societal units, yet individuals tend not to interact directly with their community but with organizations that make up the community. In fact, communities often can be understood not just as masses of individuals but as networks of organizations. Communities provide the superstructure within which organizations interact, but it is organizations that carry out most of the essential community functions we described in Chapter 5. As sociologist Talcott Parsons noted, "The development of organizations is the principal mechanism by which, in a highly differentiated society, it is possible to 'get things done,' to achieve goals beyond the reach of the individual" (1960, p. 41). Macro practice that involves working with communities inevitably requires an understanding of organizations as well.

Of still further importance is the fact that most social workers, as well as most members of society as a whole, carry out their jobs from within organizations. In organizations other than the workplace, social workers usually have a consumer-provider relationship, and they are free to turn to alternative organizations if the relationship is unsatisfactory. The place of work, however, represents a different type of relationship that is not as easily terminated, and the need for a paycheck may force the social worker to maintain a less-than-satisfactory relationship with the organization.

The agency may also be one that does not function well. Over time, an organization can stagnate, lose sight of its mission and goals, and begin to provide services that are unhelpful or even harmful to clients. This can occur because of inadequate resources, poor leadership, poor planning, inappropriate procedures or structures, or a combination of these factors. Social workers in these agencies may have the option to leave, but doing so creates other dilemmas. We believe professional social workers have an obligation to attempt to correct problems in their organizations for the benefit of both their clients and themselves. Just as agencies can lose a sense of mission and direction, so too can they regain it. The path to change begins with an understanding of the organization itself—its history, its underlying theoretical principles and assumptions, and the causes of its current problems. The major focus of this chapter will be on understanding organizations in general, after which the next chapter will address the special case of human service organizations, where most social workers serve.

Defining Organizations

Organizations will be defined here as collectives of individuals gathered together to serve a particular purpose. The key word in this definition is *purpose*. Parsons (1960) contends that *"primacy of orientation to the attainment of a specific goal is the defining characteristic of an organization which distinguishes it from other types of social systems"* (p. 17).

As noted earlier, the kinds of goals that people organize themselves to achieve span the full range of human needs, from obtaining basic necessities to achieving growth of the self. Goals may focus on production and profitability, as is usually the case in profit-making enterprises. In human service agencies, the goal may be to improve the quality of life of persons outside the organization. In each case, the organization exists because, as a collective, it makes possible the accomplishment of tasks that could not be completed as well or at all by a single individual.

As we discussed in Chapter 2, today's society was made possible in large measure by the rise of an "organizationalized" social structure. This point is noted by Etzioni (1964) in the introduction to his classic book on modern organizations:

> We are born in organizations, educated by organizations, and most of us spend much of our lives working for organizations. We spend much of our leisure time paying, playing, and praying in organizations. Most of us will die in an organization, and when the time comes for burial, the largest organization of all—the state—must grant official permission. (p. 1)

The ubiquity of organizations is certainly true in human services as well. The roles within, the interactions with, and the attempts to influence organizations define much of what social workers do.

Clients often seek help because they have been unable to obtain education, employment, assistance, or other resources from organizations in their community. In turn, the services social workers provide often involve interacting with these same organizations on clients' behalf, or helping clients improve their own ability to interact with these organizations. For example, consider the basic social work function of case management that was mentioned in Chapter 6. Barker (1995) defines *case management* as

> [a] procedure to plan, seek, and monitor services from different agencies and staff on behalf of a client. . . . The procedure makes it possible for many social workers in the agency, or different agencies, to coordinate their efforts to serve a given client through professional teamwork, thus expanding the range of needed service offered. Case management may involve monitoring the progress of a client whose needs require the services of several professionals, agencies, health care facilities, and human service programs. (p. 47)

Thus, social work practice, beginning with this fundamental role, requires considerable effort that spans many different agencies and service systems. Social workers with little or no idea of how organizations operate, how they interact, or how they can be influenced and changed from both outside and inside are likely to be severely limited in their effectiveness.

Using Theory

Much of our effort toward the goal of facilitating understanding of organizations will involve a review of the rich and varied theoretical literature that addresses them. *Theories* are conceptual tools that propose a set of general principles to be used for explaining or predicting phenomena such as a thing or event. *Organizational theories* seek to explain how organizations arise, why they take certain forms, and how they operate. As with all theories, they come with a built-in mechanism for judging their value, which is the accuracy with which they describe and predict organizations and organizational behavior. The best theories are those that provide the simplest summary of a phenomenon, cover the widest range of variation within it, and make the most accurate and verifiable predictions about it. This usually involves *identification* of variables that characterize or bring about the phenomenon, and *explanation* of how these variables interact.

As will become apparent, a very large array of theoretical explanations of organizations exists, and each of these emphasizes different variables (e.g., organizational type, managerial style) or explanatory principles (e.g., organizations as open systems, organizations as chaotic or complex systems). By the end of the review, readers may feel overwhelmed by the number of different theories, unsure of how they are applied, or uncertain about which one(s) to choose. To reduce the likelihood of this, it may be helpful to keep in mind a few basic questions that serve as reminders of what the theories are intended to accomplish. Examples of these questions include:

- What variables on which different theories concentrate are of greatest importance in my organization?
- How does my organization resemble or differ from the organizations used as examples in the theories being discussed?
- Does my organization deliberately employ certain design elements or operational guidelines identified in these theories?
- Which theory best describes the structure of my organization? Which seems best able to predict its actions or decisions?

The following is an introduction to organizations as societal units that social workers must work in and work with in order to do their jobs. Our review is by no means complete, as there is such a large body of theory and research that full coverage is well beyond the scope of this book. Instead, we will present a brief review of the most important schools of thought concerning organizations, including a summary of the main tenets of each school and its strengths and weaknesses.

Distinguishing Organizational Theories

In our discussion, we will examine ways of understanding organizations that have been proposed by various theorists, proceeding in a roughly chronological order. An important distinction we will make is between descriptive and prescriptive schools of thought. *Descriptive approaches* are intended to provide a means of analyzing organizations in terms of certain characteristics or procedures. They often reflect a sociological approach to organizations, which has as its goal the understanding of organizations as social phenomena. In contrast, *prescriptive approaches* are designed specifically as "how-to" guides, and their goal is to help build better organizations. Not surprisingly, since managers play important roles in deciding how to build and operate an organization, most prescriptive theories are part of the literature on management and leadership.

Table 7.1 illustrates other distinctions between schools of thought about organizations. These are shown partly in terms of key concepts associated with each

TABLE 7.1 **Comparative Dimensions of Key Organizational Theories**

	Dimension	
Theory (Theorist)	*Key Concepts*	*Conception of Organization in Environment*
Bureaucracy (Weber)	Structure Hierarchy	Closed
Scientific and Universalistic Management (Taylor; Fayol)	Efficiency Measurement	Closed
Human Relations (Mayo)	Social rewards Informal structure	Closed
Theory Y (McGregor)	Higher-order rewards	Closed
Management by Objectives (Drucker)	Setting goals and objectives	Closed
Organizational Goals (Michels; Selznick)	Goal displacement Natural systems	Closed
Decision Making (Simon; March)	Bounded rationality Satisficing	Closed
Open Systems (Katz & Kahn)	Systems theory Inputs/Outputs	Open
Contingency Theory (Burns & Stalker; Morse & Lorsch; Thompson)	Environmental constraints Task environment	(Varies)
Power and Politics (Pfeffer; Wamsley & Zald)	Political economy	Open
Organizational Culture (Schein)	Artifacts, values, beliefs	Open
Theory Z (Ouchi)	Quality circles Team orientation	Open
"In Search of Excellence" (Peters & Waterman)	Worker involvement Consumer focus	Open
Managing Diversity (Thomas)	Empowerment of employees	Open
Total Quality Management (Deming)	Consumer/Quality orientation Process focus	Open
Complex Systems Theory (Marion, Lewin, & Regine)	Order emerging from chaos	Open

school. Also shown are distinctions relating to whether each theory approaches organizations as open systems or closed systems. *Open-system* perspectives are concerned with how organizations are influenced by interactions with their environments, whereas *closed-system* approaches are more concerned with internal structures and processes. The table is likely to be of limited help prior to reading our review of each school of thought. Instead, it is best used as a guide to be referred to periodically while progressing through the reviews. In this way, it can assist in understanding which variables theories address and how they differ.

Bureaucracy and Organizational Structure

Organizational structure refers to the way relationships are constituted among persons within an organization. As we discussed earlier, one of the advantages of organizations is that individuals working in concert can accomplish much more than the same number of individuals working independently. The reason for this is the coordination of organizational members' activities such that the work of each supports or enhances that of the others. Organizational structure is the means by which this coordination is achieved.

Even in informal task groups, all members usually do not attempt to do the same activities. Instead, they divide among themselves the responsibilities for diverse tasks. Members also have varying skills and interests, and the process of dividing up tasks usually takes this into account. Finally, to ensure that each person's activities are both appropriate to reaching the goal and supportive of other members' efforts, at least one individual in the organization usually takes on a management role. These aspects of organizational functioning—including task specialization, matching of person and position, and leadership—are among a group of structural characteristics that are common to virtually all organizations and that provide a means by which they may be analyzed and understood.

The most important conceptual work on organizational structure remains that of German sociologist Max Weber. Weber coined the term *bureaucracy* and applied it to a particular form of organization. The bureaucracy is an *ideal type*, meaning that it is a pure conceptual construct, and it is unlikely that any organization fits perfectly with all the characteristics of a bureaucracy. The bureaucracy typifies descriptive organizational theories in that it provides a model against which organizations can be compared, after which they can be described in terms of the extent to which they fit this model. It is also important to note that Weber did not necessarily intend the bureaucratic model to serve as some sort of goal toward which organizations should strive. Instead, he designed it as a theoretical tool to assist in understanding organizational structure and how organizations vary from one to the next.

Following is a list of characteristics of the bureaucracy adapted from Weber (1947) and subsequent summaries of his work (Rogers, 1975). The characteristics include:

1. Positions in the organization are grouped into a clearly defined hierarchy.
2. Job candidates are selected on the basis of their technical qualifications.
3. Each position has a defined sphere of competence. In a hospital, for example, a physician has exclusive authority to prescribe medications, but a financial officer determines the vendor, quantity of bulk purchases, and so on.
4. Positions reflect a high degree of specialization based on expert training.
5. Positions typically demand the full working capacity (i.e., full-time employment) of their holders.
6. Positions are career oriented. There is a system of promotion according to seniority or achievement, and promotion is dependent on the judgment of superiors.
7. Rules of procedure are outlined for rational coordination of activities.
8. A central system of records is maintained to summarize the activities of the organization.
10. Impersonality governs relationships between organizational members.
11. Distinctions are drawn between private and public lives and positions of members.

Weber was interested in this organizational model because he believed it reflected a change in the values of society as a whole. Indeed, his work began with a more general concern about the way power is legitimized in social relations—why people consent to do the will of others. He used *authority* as the term for power wielded with the consent of those being led, and he identified three major forms of such authority:

1. *Traditional Authority.* The right to govern bestowed by the people on kings, emperors, popes, and other patrimonial leaders. This type of authority rests in the ruler's claim to historic or ancestral rights of control, thus it is associated with long-lasting systems and can be passed from generation to generation of rulers.
2. *Charismatic Authority.* Dominance exercised by an individual through extraordinary personal heroism, piety, fanaticism, martial skill, or other traits. Systems based on this type of authority tend to be unstable and transitional.
3. *Rational/Legal Authority.* Power assigned on the basis of the ability to achieve instrumental goals. This type of authority derives from the legitimacy given to rational rules and processes and from expertise rather than hereditary claims.

Bureaucracies are the embodiment of rational/legal authority, and the fact that they have become a dominant organizational model reflects societal movement away from systems based on traditional or charismatic authority.

Strengths and Weaknesses.   Bureaucratic organization is designed to bring about the accomplishment of specific instrumental tasks, and its focus is on maximizing the *efficiency* with which this is done. Weber argues,

> The decisive reason for the advance of bureaucracy has always been its purely technical superiority over any other form of organization. The fully developed bureaucratic mechanism compares with other organizations exactly as does the machine with the non-mechanical modes of production. (1946, p. 214)

As the bureaucracy evolved, this technical superiority helped bring about the Industrial Revolution and the immense growth in size and complexity of manufacturing, distribution, and other commercial firms. It also furthered the rise of vast governmental institutions, ranging from the military to a broad range of public welfare organizations responsible for income maintenance, child welfare, mental health, corrections, and other services. In particular, bureaucratic organization helped these institutions carry out their tasks in greater quantity than was possible before. Consider the number of people served by governmental organizations providing Social Security payments, Medicare, and other large-scale social programs. These agencies are not simply larger than the social service organizations that preceded them; they are also more bureaucratic in their structure.

In some ways, the practice of social work functions in a manner consistent with specific characteristics of bureaucracies. For example, the profession supports a high degree of specialization based on professional training and practice expertise. Assigning individuals to specific jobs and organizational levels on the basis of this expertise is also considered a part of good practice. Social workers tend to be career oriented, and in most human service organizations the accumulation of experience and expertise is rewarded by favoring more senior persons for promotion. Finally, the profession subscribes to the belief that people's abilities on the job should count for more than who they know or how well liked they are, and fame or fortune outside the organization should not count for more than their competence on the job. In other words, although one does not often think of it in such terms, social workers and the organizations in which they customarily work are like many others in modern society in their adherence to bureaucratic principles.

Still, describing an organization as "bureaucratic" conjures images of a vast, impersonal, monolithic body that is anything but efficient. Organizations often go out of their way to avoid being described as *bureaucracies,* and the term has become one that in everyday usage is almost unfailingly negative. Why is this so? Weber certainly did not believe the bureaucracy was a model for poor organization, and research has shown that bureaucratic organization and structure can indeed contribute to greater productivity and efficiency.

The answer is complex but important. As the bureaucracy has become more prevalent, it has shown both its good and bad sides. For example, the machine-like qualities to which Weber calls attention may be consummately well suited to manufacturing firms but they can be disastrous in organizations (such as human service agencies) in which the goal is to meet unique needs of individuals. Indeed, many theorists subsequent to Weber have explored ways in which characteristics of the bureaucracy actually undermine its presumed strengths.

One example was offered by Merton (1952) in his study of the experiences of individuals working within bureaucracies. He found that over time, workers' concern for completing the key instrumental activities of their jobs was gradually replaced with a concern for meeting the procedural and paperwork requirements of the bureaucracy, regardless of whether the basic job was done. Merton called this the *bureaucratic personality.* He also coined the term *trained incapacity* to describe the ways in which bureaucratic personalities become incapable of meeting the real needs of the people they are supposed to serve. These behaviors are often considered an inevitable consequence of tightly structured chains of command and expectations for unthinking compliance with rules. Most important, Merton believed these behaviors develop from individuals' realizations that their own interests are best served not by doing the job well but by doing it "by the book."

A great deal of contemporary organizational thought has addressed ways such as these in which bureaucracies fall short of their goal of maximal organizational functioning. In particular, writers have addressed elements of complex organizations that go beyond the bureaucracy's emphasis on structural characteristics. As will be seen, many of these elements have been examined specifically from the perspective of how the bureaucratic model fails to account for their importance. Among these are organizational goals, decision-making processes, technology, and the role of the individual within the organization.

BOX 7.1

Weber's Theory of Bureaucracy Structure

- **Purpose.** Descriptive
- **Key Features.** Bureaucracies emphasize efficiency of operation. Decision making is done at the top, and authority to do so is based on expertise rather than inherited authority. Tasks are specialized, organizational relationships are impersonal, and a "by-the-book" orientation restricts individual discretion.
- **Summary.** Organizations with bureaucratic structure are very efficient at repetitive tasks such as mass production of material goods, but they can be dehumanizing. Also, they are less efficient at variable tasks, exist in unpredictable environments, and have staff who must exercise professional judgment.

There is also an argument to be made that ethnic minorities and women have been disadvantaged in bureaucratically structured organizations. "It should be no surprise that feminists have asserted that bureaucracies have a male orientation and a male bias" (Kelly, 1991, p. 97). As employees are promoted through lower and middle levels to upper-level administrative positions, white males have often dominated the highest levels and denied access to others. This phenomenon has been referred to as the *glass ceiling.* Women and minorities can reach a level at which they have a close-up view of functioning at the top, but they cannot get there because those who select persons for top positions often value sameness and fear diversity.

Management Theories

Scientific and Universalistic Management

One of the earliest and most important schools of thought on the management of tasks and functions in the workplace was the work of Frederick Taylor, an American industrialist and educator whose main works appeared in the first two decades of the 1900s. Taylor had experience as both a laborer and a mechanical engineer, and he was primarily concerned with management techniques that would lead to increased productivity. He believed many organizational problems were tied to misunderstandings between managers and workers. Managers thought that workers were lazy and unmotivated, and they also mistakenly believed they understood workers' jobs. Workers thought that managers cared only about exploiting workers, not about productivity.

To solve these problems, Taylor developed what came to be known as *scientific management*, which derives its name from his emphasis on the need for managers to conduct scientific analyses of the workplace (1947). One of the first steps is to complete a careful study of the work itself, commonly by identifying the best worker and studying that person. The goal is to find the optimal way of doing a job—in Taylor's words, the "one best way"—to develop the best possible tools for completing it, fit workers' abilities and interests to particular assignments, and find the level of production the average worker can sustain.

Following this, a next step is to provide incentives to workers to increase productivity. Taylor's favorite tool for this was the piece-rate wage, in which workers are paid for each unit they produce. In this manner, more units are produced, unit cost is reduced, organizational productivity and profitability are enhanced, and workers earn more.

Taylor was seeking, above all, an industrial workplace in which traditional animosity between management and labor could be overcome by a recognition of the mutual aims of each. His points in this regard are summarized by George (1968):

1. The objective of good management is to pay high wages and have low unit production costs;
2. To achieve this objective management has to apply scientific methods of research and experiment . . . in order to formulate principles and standard processes which would allow for control of the manufacturing operations;
3. Employees have to be scientifically placed in jobs where materials and working conditions are scientifically selected so that standards can be met;
4. Employees should be scientifically and precisely trained to improve their skill in performing a job so that the standard of output can be met;
5. An air of close and friendly cooperation has to be cultivated between management and workers in order to ensure the continuance of a psychological environment that would make possible the application of the other principles. (p. 89)

As can be seen from these principles, Taylor's interests were as much in the area of organizational psychology as in traditional management theory. Subsequent to his work, other writers focused more narrowly on Taylor's concern with maximizing organizational productivity and began to ask whether broader principles could be identified that encapsulated the ideals of rational management. They eventually became known as the *universalistic management* theorists. A prominent member of this group was French industrialist Henri Fayol, whose writings focused on specifying the structural attributes of organizations that managers should develop and promote. Scott (1981) condenses Fayol's central ideas into the following six principles:

1. *Scalar Principle.* Calls for a hierarchical structure with a pyramid-shaped chain of command
2. *Unity of Command Principle.* Specifies that each person should have only one immediate supervisor
3. *Span of Control Principle.* Limits a supervisor's number of subordinates to a manageable number, usually no more than six to eight
4. *Exception Principle.* Specifies that subordinates are responsible for routine matters covered by standard rules, leaving the supervisor responsible for exceptional circumstances not covered by these rules
5. *Departmentalization Principle.* Incorporates a strong emphasis on division of labor within the organization, and specifies that similar functions should be grouped together (e.g., functions that are similar in terms of purpose, process, clientele, or location)
6. *Line-Staff Principle.* Distinguishes between line functions, which are those most central to completion of basic organizational activities, and staff functions, which are primarily supportive or advisory

Although somewhat broader in scope, the outcomes intended from the application of these principles were similar to the goals of scientific management. These included stability, predictability (especially with respect to the manufacturing process), and maximum individual productivity. Also, although these writers were prescriptive management theorists whereas Weber was a descriptive sociological observer, it is not difficult to see that a manager adhering to the preceding principles would create an organization that reflected many of the characteristics of the bureaucracy.

Strengths and Weaknesses. The works of both Taylor and Fayol were subsequently criticized for what Mouzelis (1967) termed a *technicist bias*—that is, that both tended to treat workers as little more than cogs in a wheel. No two people, and no two workers, are exactly alike, thus the "one best way" of doing a job may be unique to the person doing it. In fact, forcing a similar approach on a different worker may decrease both productivity and worker satisfaction. Also, because these approaches addressed means for increasing the output of workers, they were subjected to considerable criticism (especially by writers in the labor movement) for facilitating the exploitation of workers by management.

Because both Taylor and Fayol were interested primarily in industrial organizations, their work was generally deemed to have little applicability to human service organizations during the first few decades during which social work began drawing on management theories. For example, the predominant approach to allocating work responsibility followed that of physicians, assigning "cases" or clients to social workers who acted on a very loosely structured mandate to employ their professional skill to meet client needs. As a result, the focus of scientific and universalistic management on precision, measurement, and specialization of function fit poorly with this type of job design.

B O X 7 . 2

Scientific and Universalistic Management Theories

- **Purpose.** Prescriptive
- **Key Features.** Though not influenced by Weber, these theories essentially describe how to create a bureaucracy from the management side. The emphasis is on efficiency, top-down control, and specialized work. Managers are also responsible for studying the work itself and teaching staff the "one best way" of doing each job.
- **Summary.** Organizations managed by these principles can achieve the original goals of stability, predictability, and efficient production, but, as with bureaucracies, the result can also be an oppressive and monotonous workplace.

More recently, though, social work has adopted more "scientific" approaches to practice. In many areas of specialization, procedures and protocols specify parameters for professional activity in certain types of cases. Also, in the interest of improving practice, a great deal of emphasis has been placed on conducting formal research on clients in one's own caseload, often through the use of single-subject designs. Similarly, requirements for outcome evaluation have placed more rigorous demands on the design of interventions and the measurement of success. Although these trends do not necessarily embrace the more mechanistic aspects of Taylor's notions, they echo his concern for organizational operations that are based on the most careful possible analysis of the work itself.

Human Relations

As the field of organizational management and analysis grew, the works of Taylor, Weber, and others were criticized for their focus on rational, structural approaches to understanding organizations. The earliest of these criticisms addressed Taylor's assumptions about factors that motivate organizational actors. In particular, they took issue with the notion that workers are oriented to the instrumental goals of the organization and respond most readily to material rewards (e.g., piece-rate wages) designed to further those goals. One such group of researchers began with the intention of testing Taylor's principles concerning productivity enhancement. Eventually, however, its members concluded that organizations must be viewed as social institutions, and it is social factors—friendship, belongingness, and group solidarity—that are most important in understanding and influencing the behavior of organizational actors.

Often referred to as the *human relations school,* this view had its origins in the so-called Hawthorne studies conducted in the 1920s. Experimenters placed a group of workers in a special room and then varied the intensity of the lighting and other environmental factors to observe the effect on productivity. Initially, the researchers found that the greater the intensity of lighting, the more productivity increased. However, when they reduced the lighting, expecting to find reduced productivity, they found that productivity continued to increase even in very dim lighting. The researchers concluded that the cause of the increase in productivity was *social factors.* Workers appeared not to respond to the lighting but instead to the fact that they were members of a group to which they wanted to contribute their best effort, and it was this sense of social responsibility that prompted improved performance.

Subsequent experiments on the effect of social factors in organizations, including many from the field of industrial psychology, examined more general questions concerning the behavior of groups. Etzioni (1964) summarizes the basic tenets of the human relations approach that developed from these findings:

1. *"The level of production is set by social norms, not by physiological capacities"* (p. 34).
2. *"Non-economic rewards and sanctions significantly affect the behavior of the workers and largely limit the effect of economic incentive plans"* (p. 34). A number of studies found that workers who were capable of producing more would often not do so. The reason seemed to be that they were unwilling to exceed what the group as a whole was able to do, even if this meant a reduction in their earnings.
3. *"Workers do not act or react as individuals but as members of groups"* (p. 35). For example, attempts by management to influence workers' behavior can sometimes be more successful if targeted toward the group as a whole rather than toward individuals who might be unwilling to change unless accompanied by group members.
4. *The role of leadership is important in understanding social forces in organizations, and this leadership may be either formal or informal.* The importance of informal leadership is that it influences behavior in ways that can either amplify or negate formal leadership acting through established organizational structures. In addition, democratic leadership is more effective in eliciting cooperation and willingness to change than more authoritarian forms.

Important elements to be drawn from these tenets include the idea that organizational actors may be equally or more likely to draw satisfaction from social relationships within the organization than from its instrumental activities. Also important is the notion that workers' willingness to follow management comes from willingness to follow members of the work group. As a result, the key to making effective changes in organizational operations lies not in rules and formal structure but in the quality of personal affiliations and the coherence of informal structures. Managers who succeed in increasing productivity are most likely to be those who are responsive to the social needs of workers.

Strengths and Weaknesses.   Criticisms of the human relations school fall into two major categories. First, a number of writers have raised concerns about the methodological soundness of research on which these views are based. For example, the original Hawthorne experiments have earned an infamous place in the history of research methodology. The *Hawthorne effect* refers to the fact that experimental subjects may perform in certain ways simply because of the knowledge that they are being studied. In other words, workers in the Hawthorne plant may have raised production because of neither lighting levels nor a sense of group solidarity but because of self-consciousness about being in an experiment. Other critics have argued that the design of these studies was such that expectations about economic incentives might still have influenced the subjects, further undermining the supposed effect of social factors (Sykes, 1965).

A second line of criticism argues that it is possible to overestimate the importance of social factors in organizations. For example, various research has indicated that informal organizational structures may not be as prevalent or powerful as human relations writers suggest, that democratic leadership is not always associated with greater productivity or worker satisfaction, and that economic benefits *are* important to many employees. Also, Landsberger (1958) argued that this school's emphasis on worker contentedness at the expense of economic rewards could foster an administrative model that is even more manipulative and paternalistic than might be the case with scientific management. This is because human relations theory, like other management approaches of the time, concentrated power and decision making at the top and was never intended to empower employees or assist them in gaining genuine participation in the running of the organization. If people were treated more humanely under human relations management it was because proponents believed this would lead to greater productivity, not because of a desire to create a more democratic workplace. Finally, an emphasis on strengthening personal/social relationships within the workplace may also have disadvantaged some groups of employees over the years. Social relationships within organizations play a role in identifying and securing jobs and promotions for people, but women and ethnic minorities have often been excluded from important networks that control these rewards.

Still, human relations theory has had an important effect on organizational thinking. With respect to management practice, its tenets have provided a counterbalance to the formalized and often rigid approach of other management theories. It has also influenced descriptive approaches by serving as a reminder of how the needs and interests of individual employees can be critical determinants of organizational behavior. Later theories would develop around genuine empowerment for employees, but human relations management eventually died out as an approach to running an organization when it was recognized that a happy workforce was not necessarily a productive workforce, and other variables began to enter the equation. Nevertheless, human relations called attention to factors such as teamwork, cooperation, leadership, and positive attention from management that remain relevant today.

Theory X and Theory Y

Later writers drew on the work of human relations theorists but incorporated them into more general frameworks addressing human motivation. One example is Douglas McGregor (1960), who adopted Maslow's hierarchy of needs as a basis of understanding workers' actions. For McGregor, organizational actors were not just social creatures but *self-actualizing* beings whose ultimate goal in organizations is to meet higher-order needs. To illustrate this point, he identified two contrasting approaches to management, which he labeled "Theory X" and "Theory Y." *Theory X* is a categorization of traditional approaches to management such as that of Taylor, Weber, and others, which, McGregor argued, make the following assumptions about human nature:

1. The average human being has an inherent dislike of work and will avoid it if [he/she] can. (p. 33)
2. Because of this human characteristic of dislike of work, most people must be coerced, controlled, directed, [or] threatened with punishment to get them to put forth adequate effort toward the achievement of organizational objectives.
3. The average human being prefers to be directed, wishes to avoid responsibility, has relatively little ambition, wants security above all. (p. 34)

These assumptions lead to what McGregor sees as the domineering, oppressive aspects of Theory X management.

In contrast, *Theory Y* assumes that the task of management is to recognize workers' higher-order needs and design organizations that allow them to achieve these needs. Its assumptions are:

1. The expenditure of physical and mental effort in work is as natural as play or rest.
2. External control and the threat of punishment are not the only means for bringing about effort toward organizational objectives. [People] will exercise self-direction and self-control in the service of objectives to which [they are] committed.
3. Commitment to objectives is a function of the rewards associated with their achievement.
4. The average human being learns, under proper conditions, not only to accept but to seek responsibility.
5. The capacity to exercise a relatively high degree of imagination, ingenuity, and creativity in the solution of organizational problems is widely, not narrowly, distributed in the population.
6. The intellectual potentialities of the average human being [in modern organization] are only partly utilized. (pp. 47–48)

The critical feature of this approach is its break from the management-dominated approach of previous theories in favor of transferring decision-making power to lower-level actors. Such loosely structured organizations are seen as best for promoting productivity by allowing employees to meet higher-order needs through their work.

Strengths and Weaknesses.   McGregor's analysis was supported by the research of Frederick Herzberg (1966). Herzberg studied motivation among employees, dividing motivational elements into two categories: extrinsic factors and intrinsic factors. Factors *extrinsic* to the job include wages, hours, working conditions, and benefits. *Intrinsic* factors have to do with motivators that lie within the work itself, such as satisfaction with successful task completion. Herzberg discovered that, in the long run, extrinsic factors tend to keep down the levels of dissatisfaction with the job, but they do not motivate workers to work harder. Only intrinsic factors, such as ability to use one's own creativity and problem-solving abilities motivates employees to become more productive.

BOX 7.3

Human Relations and Theory Y

- **Purpose.** Prescriptive
- **Key Features.** These theories assume workers are motivated by factors other than wages. Human relations theories noted that social relations among staff can enhance production, and so they sought to enhance performance by promoting group cohesion and adding social rewards to the range of reinforcements available in the workplace. Others added needs, such as self-actualization, to the list of additional motivating factors.
- **Summary.** Managers are more likely to recognize workers' higher-order needs (beyond merely a paycheck) and expand their awareness of potential motivating factors. Flawed early research overestimated the effect of social influences on production, and the model continued to place discretion and authority solely in the hands of administrators. Later, writers argued that increased worker participation would enhance both productivity and workers' ability to meet their needs.

On the other hand, results of other studies indicated that there were limits to how loosely structured an organization's operations could become and still function effectively. Morse and Lorsch (1970) found that organizations in which tasks were loosely defined and variable appeared to fit well with Theory Y management styles. However, those in which tasks were predictable, repetitive, and required great precision functioned better when organized according to principles McGregor labeled as Theory X. The importance for social work is that its tasks are often loosely defined and seemingly well suited to Theory Y management, yet many human service organizations are still operated with a Theory X mentality. Overall, a key point of McGregor and others is that no single management model applies equally well across all types of organizations.

Management by Objectives (MBO)

Fundamental to the conceptualization and functioning of an organization is *purpose*, a commonly shared understanding of the reason for existence of the organization. In most cases, purpose has to do with productivity and profit. Taylor, Weber, and human relations theorists each stressed a different approach to the achievement of purpose, but all agreed that an understanding of purpose was basic to the construction of a theory of organizational management.

Peter Drucker (1954) proposed a somewhat different approach to organizational management. He suggested that organizational goals and objectives be used in a rational way by making them the central construct around which organizational life would revolve. In other words, instead of focusing on structure, precision, or efficiency and hoping for an increase in productivity and profit, Drucker proposed beginning with the desired outcome and working backward to structure organizational design to achieve that outcome. Termed *management by objectives (MBO)*, this approach involves both short-range and long-range planning, and it is through this planning process that organizational structures and procedures necessary to achieve an outcome are established.

Drucker identifies several elements of MBO's strategic planning process. *Expectations* are the hoped-for outcomes. An example might be the addition of a new service or client population in an agency, or an improvement of some specified amount in the number of clients served or results of their services (e.g., an increase of 25 percent in client satisfaction over current levels). *Objectives* are means of achieving expectations, such as the steps that would be taken to add or improve programs. *Assumptions* reflect what is presumed about how meeting the objectives will achieve expectations (e.g., that the use of better service techniques will improve outcomes).

Other elements in the process include consideration of *alternative courses of action*, such as the costs and benefits of taking no action. Also, the plan must take into account what Drucker terms the *decision structure*, which represents the constraints that exist on how much the plan can do, and the *impact stage*, which addresses costs associated with implementing the plan and limitations it may place on other initiatives or operations. Finally, once implemented, a plan will have *results*, and in essence the result of an MBO process is measured by the extent to which actual outcomes match the original expectations.

Strengths and Weaknesses.   One major advantage of MBO comes in its emphasis on producing clear statements, made available to all employees, about expectations for the coming year. Techniques are also developed for breaking goals and objectives into tasks, and for monitoring progress throughout the year. This type of organization tends to improve collaboration and cooperative activity.

On the other hand, MBO adopts a very particularistic approach to management, which some critics have argued tends to concentrate attention on the trees rather than on the forest. In other words, management requires large-scale strategic thinking in addition to small-scale tactical thinking, yet MBO may tend to focus excessive attention on the latter. Another criticism is that although it is sometimes admirable to be clear and direct about organizational expectations, the concept of building organizational life around goals and objectives has its drawbacks. As we will see in the next section, organizational goals often change, and the stated goals of an organization can be subverted in the interest of promoting unstated goals.

BOX 7.4

Management by Objectives (MBO)

- **Purpose.** Prescriptive
- **Key Features.** MBO argues that management must ensure the continuing presence of clear goals and objectives for the organization. Once these are in place, the task of management becomes one of decision making regarding how to best to achieve each objective. Success is measured by the extent to which objectives were achieved.
- **Summary.** MBO focuses attention on results and reorients management toward the question of how to accomplish desired outcomes. On a day-to-day basis, however, consideration is given mostly to small steps necessary for reaching intermediate objectives, which may lead to a loss of awareness of eventual end goals.

Still, many modern approaches to management include various aspects of MBO in their model. For example, many organizations require the development of an annual plan in which goals and objectives in each programmatic area are made explicit. Also significant has been the growth of attention paid to *outcomes*, both in commercial and human service organizations. Social work as a profession was for many years primarily concerned with *process* in the development of its practice approaches. Management by objectives, together with the accountability movement, establishes program outcomes as the major criteria for determining funding and program continuation.

Organizational Goals and the Natural-System Perspective

One theme made explicit in Drucker's MBO model is the assumption that organizations should be directed by rational actions designed to achieve certain goals. This assumption began to be questioned by writers concerned about whether rational, goal-directed, formalized structures are the best way of serving organizational goals, and whether these goals provide a clear direction. In fact, the idea that the goals of an organization and its members could gradually change had been present in organizational literature for some time.

In the early 1900s, Robert Michels examined political parties as examples of large modern organizations (1949, originally published in 1915). Noting the rise of oligarchies, or small groups of key decision makers, within the parties, he suggested that these and other organizations have identifiable life cycles that proceed through the following steps:

1. The organization develops a formal structure.
2. The original leaders move into positions at the upper levels of the hierarchy.
3. These individuals discover the personal advantages of having such positions.
4. They begin to make more conservative decisions that might not advance their original cause as forcefully as before but that are less likely to jeopardize their own security or that of the organization.
5. The organization's original goals are pushed aside and it becomes mostly a means for achieving the personal goals of upper-level administrators.

Michels called this the Iron Rule of Oligarchy, based on his conclusion that it is an unavoidable fate of large organizations that adopt bureaucratic approaches to structuring themselves.

Philip Selznick (1949) found a related mechanism in his study of the early years of the Tennessee Valley Authority (TVA). The TVA was a creation of the New Deal era, and its goal was to promote economic development in the poverty-stricken Tennessee River valley through an ambitious mix of public works projects and grassroots organizing. With its enormous scope and rather vague goals, it became essential for the organization to delegate decision making to subunits responsible for particular projects in local areas. In this way, its aims became vulnerable to *cooptation* by existing local authorities whose involvement brought needed power and influence but whose own goals began to turn the TVA's subunits in unintended directions. Increasingly, the TVA became a structure for serving goals defined by the interests of local units rather than its original aims. Selznick (1957) refers to this as the process of *institutionalization* of the organization, meaning that the organization takes on a life of its own that may have more to do with the interests of its own participants than with the instrumental goals it is supposedly serving.

Other writers refer to this as the process of *goal displacement*, and mechanisms such as cooptation, growth of oligarchies, and development of the bureaucratic personality are all means by which organizational goals can be displaced. In Selznick's view, the consistency with which these processes appeared in formal organizations argued against theories, such as Weber's, that seek to describe organizations as rational systems. Instead, Selznick believed the better analogy was that of the organization as a *natural system*—an entity that acts much as biological organisms do. The most important parallel is the system's awareness of its own self-interest. Just as the prime motivation of an organism is to protect itself, organizations' principal goals often are to maintain their own functioning. Predicting an organization's behavior on the basis of what it will do to survive may thus be more accurate than predictions based on its expected use of rational approaches to meeting task goals. Etzioni (1964) identifies this in terms of the distinction between organizations' *real* goals and *stated* goals. In situations in which both cannot be served simultaneously, real goals (e.g., self-preservation) almost always determine eventual actions.

Strengths and Weaknesses.   Recognition of the importance of organizational goals, particularly survival goals, has proved to be an important contribution to the development of organizational and management theory. These views have also had considerable influence on the study of human service organizations, such as a well-known study of the March of Dimes (Sills, 1957). Organized originally to unify the efforts of volunteers attempting to raise money for polio research, the March of Dimes became one of the vanguard organizations in the fight against polio nationwide. These efforts were eventually successful, in that funding from the March of Dimes helped lead to Jonas Salk's development of the first polio vaccine. This and subsequent vaccines proved to be so effective that polio quickly became a rare problem, which meant that the activities of the March of Dimes were no longer needed. Having successfully achieved its goal, the organization could thus simply have disbanded, but it did not. Instead, it took on a whole new cause—birth defects—and its efforts shifted toward solving this new problem.

BOX 7.5

Organizational Goals and Goal Displacement

- **Purpose.** Descriptive
- **Key Features.** Organizational goals and goal displacement point out that organizational actors tend to be driven more by personal than organizational goals. Organizations can thus be redirected to serve the self-interests of administrators or others. Also, because organizations are made up of many individuals, they act less like rational systems than organic (natural) ones, seeking to protect themselves just as individuals do.
- **Summary.** Organic systems helped draw theoretical attention away from earlier focus on internal factors, such as structure or management style, and reorient it toward issues of how organizations interact with their environments. Organizational behavior became a new focus of attention.

Sills contends that this is exactly the behavior that would be predicted by the natural-system model. The survival imperative prevails even if it means the system must alter its original reason for existence. The result is not necessarily bad, since in this case an organization with experience in countering public health problems was able to turn itself toward meeting a new challenge. However, as we will review at greater length in the next chapter, organizations with too strong a focus on their own survival can cease to be effective in providing services.

Decision Making

While natural-systems perspectives were gaining prominence, other writers continued the effort to explain organizations as rational systems through an exploration of the limits of rational decision making. One of these was Herbert Simon, whose wide-ranging work would eventually earn him a Nobel Prize in economics. Simon (1957) began by changing the unit of analysis from the organization as a whole to individuals within the organization. More specifically, he was interested in *individual* decisions about organizational matters. He had been influenced by the growing body of psychological research and was drawn to behaviorist views about the importance of stimulus-response connections as explanations for human behavior. He believed organizations can be conceptualized as aggregations of individual decisions within the organization, and organizational decision making can be viewed as a behavior that occurs in response to certain stimuli.

March and Simon (1958) argued that the key to understanding organizational decisions is understanding that there are constraints that limit decision making. They termed this phenomenon *bounded rationality*, and identified three major categories of constraints:

1. Habits, abilities, and other personal characteristics that individuals bring with them into the decision-making process and that influence their actions in certain ways irrespective of the circumstances surrounding a specific decision
2. "Motivations, values, and loyalties [whereby] an individual's strong identification with a certain group whose values diverge from organisational values might limit the individual's rational behavior" (Mouzelis, 1967, p. 124)
3. The inability of the decision maker to know either all the variables that might influence the decision or all possible consequences of the decision

Because all decisions carry some measure of risk, the process of decision making in organizations may be thought of as a risk-management process. The goal of the decision maker is not necessarily to achieve a "perfect" outcome, because this may never be possible. Instead, the decision maker seeks to reduce uncertainty as much as possible in order to make a decision that provides a reasonable likelihood of resulting in an acceptable outcome. March and Simon called this *satisficing*, and they argued that understanding how satisfactory outcomes are pursued via decisions made in the context of bounded rationality is key to understanding organizations.

Subsequent works expanded on these ideas in several directions. For example, Cyert and March (1963) suggest that decision making in aggregate is a process of bargaining between individuals and units having different views and goals. The eventual actions of the organization can be understood as the outcome of these ongoing negotiations among organizational members. Later, March and Olsen (1976) proposed a "garbage can" analogy to describe the rather chaotic process in which decisions emerge from a mixture of people, problems, ideas, and "choice opportunities" that is unique to every organization and situation. This approach assumes that rationality plays a relatively minor role in these situations; instead, the process of interaction among these various elements is the primary determinant of the eventual decisions.

Strengths and Weaknesses.   One aspect of decision-making theory that has had considerable impact on organizational analysis is its concern with the nature and quality of information available to decision makers. This concern generally coincided with the advent of computers, and it has played a part in the rapid growth of interest in information management in organizations. The basic idea is that information systems, augmented by the unique data-processing capabilities of computers, can be used to reduce the uncertainty that decision makers must confront and increase the likelihood that they will make effective decisions.

BOX 7.6

Decision Making

- **Purpose.** Descriptive
- **Key Features.** Much of what organizations are and do is the product of decisions made by individuals throughout the hierarchy, but especially at the administrative level. These decisions are only as good as the information on which they are based, however, and complete information needed to make informed decisions is seldom, if ever, present. Because of this lack of information, organizations can never be fully rational. Decision makers thus learn to *satisfice,* meaning they do not expect optimal outcomes but merely acceptable ones.
- **Summary.** These writers accurately anticipated the computer age, which demonstrated the importance of information as an organizational commodity. The better the quality (though not necessarily quantity) of information available, the better the quality of decision making and, eventually, outcome.

Still, as a means of understanding organizations, the decision-making approach has a number of limitations. For example, in a critique of March and Simon's work, Blau and Scott (1962) argue that the model focuses too narrowly on formal decision making, ignoring the interpersonal aspects of organizations and the influence that informal structures can have on decisions that are made. Champion (1975) also notes that little attention is paid to situations in which a particular individual may not seek overall rationality but personal or local-unit gain. Most important, the decision-making model has been criticized for its focus on internal factors that lead to particular decisions. This emphasis ignores the fact that often it is influences internal to the organization that are most important to eliciting and determining a decision. In fact, growing attention toward the importance of external factors provided the impetus for the next important developments in organizational theory.

Organizations as Open Systems

Understanding Open Systems

In learning about practice with individual clients, most social workers are introduced to systems theory. This approach is based on the work of biologist Ludwig von Bertalanffy (1950), who believed that lessons from fields such as ecology, which concerns organisms' interdependence with their surroundings, provide a basis for conceptualizing other phenomena as systems engaged in environmental interactions. Via this model, individual clients are viewed not merely as isolated entities driven by internal psychological processes. Instead, they are seen as social beings whose personalities and behaviors can be analyzed in terms of their constant interaction with the world around them. As *open systems,* clients both give to and draw from elements external to themselves. Understanding this ongoing process of exchange with critical elements (e.g., culture, community, family, etc.) that comprise their personal environment is the key to understanding clients. Beginning in the 1960s, various writers began to argue that organizations can be understood in similar ways.

One influential example was the work of Katz and Kahn (1966), who noted that previous writers had analyzed organizations as though they were closed systems whose functioning could be understood solely through the study of internal structure and processes. Katz and Kahn considered this naive, arguing that organizations must be understood as open systems that "maintain themselves through constant commerce with the environment, i.e., a continuous inflow and outflow of energy through permeable boundaries" (p. 17). In other words, organizations must be understood as systems that exist within a larger environment, and the design and functioning of the system is shaped by the process of exchange in which it acts on and responds to its environment.

As illustrated in Figure 7.1, systems are comprised of collections of constituent parts (whether cells comprising an organism or people comprising an organization) that receive *inputs,* operate on them through some sort of process called the *throughput,* and produce *outputs.* In human service agencies, inputs include critical resources such as funding, staff, and facilities. Clients who request services are also important inputs, as are the types and severity of the problems for which they seek help. More subtle but also vital are inputs such as values, expectations, and opinions about the agency that are held by community members, funding agencies, regulatory bodies, and other segments of the environment.

Throughput involves the services provided by the agency—often referred to as its *technology*—and the way it is structured to apply this technology to inputs it receives. Output refers to the organization's products. In industrial firms, this is

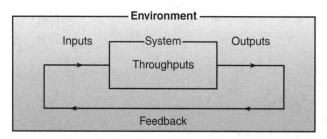

FIGURE 7.1   The Open Systems Model

usually some sort of material object; in social work agencies, it is the completion of a service to a client. As we will discuss, the important aspect of service output is often defined as an *outcome*, which is a measure of a quality-of-life change (improvement, no change, or deterioration) on the part of a client.

BOX 7.7

Organizations as Open Systems

- **Purpose.** Descriptive
- **Key Features.** This theory broadened and extended the natural-systems perspective by showing that all organizations, like all organisms, are open systems. Open systems must acquire resources (*inputs*) from their environments, such as funds, staff, and clients, and they return products or services (*outputs*) to the environment. Understanding organizational actions thus requires viewing them as part of a larger environment in which and with which they carry out these exchanges.
- **Summary.** Organizational behavior can be explained as efforts to make beneficial environmental changes. Also, organizations act in ways that seek to reduce uncertainty and make their environments as predictable as possible. This will lead them to organize themselves in certain ways and to act in certain ways.

A further element of many open systems models is a *feedback* mechanism, which is a defining characteristic of what are called *cybernetic systems*. A cybernetic system is self-correcting, meaning that it is able to garner information from its surroundings, interpret this information, and adjust its functioning accordingly. Biological organisms are examples of cybernetic systems in that they adapt themselves to changing conditions in their environments. Organizations are also cybernetic systems, and it seems impossible to envision one that could survive without gathering information from and taking steps to adjust to environmental conditions. For example, manufacturers must constantly react to changing demand for their goods, and their survival often depends on the ability to adjust quickly by increasing output of fast-selling items and abandoning or altering products that are not selling well. Likewise, human service agencies must provide needed and relevant services or they will go out of business. This process of receiving feedback from the environment and making adaptations to fit external conditions is at the heart of the open-systems approach.

Contingency Theory

Partly in response to the apparent soundness of open-systems thinking and partly because of doubts about management theories that promoted a single model for all organizations, a new outlook began to take shape in the 1960s. The underlying premise was that different organizational styles may be entirely appropriate due to the particular circumstances each organization faces. Known generally as *contingency theory*, this approach can be boiled down to three basic tenets. The first two, proposed by Galbraith (1973), summarize criticisms of earlier management theorists and the decision-making model:

1. There is no one best way to organize.
2. Any way of organizing is not equally effective. (p. 2)

To these, Scott (1981) adds a third principle that incorporates the open-systems perspective:

3. The best way to organize depends on the nature of the environment to which the organization must relate. (p. 114)

The unifying theme across all three principles is that the nature of the organization and its management scheme are contingent on a variety of factors unique to that organization. For example, managing a human service agency in the same way as an auto assembly plant may not help it to achieve maximum productivity.

Morse and Lorsch (1970) took issue with the contention of theorists such as McGregor that a decentralized, humanistic management model should be the preferred approach across most organizations. Their research showed that high organizational effectiveness and a strong sense of personal competence can be found in organizations with relatively rigid rules and structure. Similarly, some organizations having a loose structure and a great deal of individual autonomy were not always effective or satisfying to their workers. The key contingency to which results pointed was the nature of organizational tasks. Organizations with very predictable tasks, such as manufacturing firms, fared best with a tightly controlled structure. Those with less predictable tasks (in this case a research and development role) appeared to be much better suited to a loose structure and management style.

A typology of these differences was proposed by Burns and Stalker (1961), who distinguished between two forms of management that they labeled *mechanistic* and *organic*. Mechanistic management systems, which reflect characteristics of bureaucracies as described by Weber and the managerial techniques laid out by Taylor, are commonly found in organizations having relatively stable environments. Organic forms occur in unstable environments in which the inputs are

TABLE 7.2   Elements of Mechanistic versus Organic Organizations

Variable	Mechanistic Organization	Organic Organization
Focus of work	Completion of discrete tasks	Contribution to overall result
Responsibility for integrating work	Supervisor of each level	Shared within level, across units
Responsibility for problem solving	Limited to precise obligations set out for each position	Owned by affected individual; cannot be shirked as "out of my area"
Structure of control and authority	Hierarchic	Networked
Location of knowledge, information	Concentrated at top	Expertise and need for information assumed to exist at various levels
Character of organizational structure	Rigid; accountability rests with individual	Fluid; accountability is shared by group
Content of communication	Instructions, decisions	Information, advice
Direction of communication	Vertical, between supervisor and subordinate	Lateral and also across ranks
Expected loyalty	To supervisor, unit	To technology, outcome

Source: Adapted from Burns and Stalker (1961).

unpredictable and the organization's viability depends on its capacity to respond in ways that are unconstrained by formal rules and structures. Table 7.2 compares and contrasts characteristics of organic and mechanistic organizations.

Lawrence and Lorsch (1967) also called attention to a stable versus changing environment as the critical contingency on which an analysis of organizational structure and leadership should rest. For example, they noted that "in simplified terms, the classical [e.g., Weberian] theory tends to hold in more stable environments, while the human relations theory is more appropriate to dynamic situations" (p. 183). Incorporating some aspects of the decision-making approach, they also noted the importance of certainty versus uncertainty in determining organizational actions. In this case, however, the unit of analysis was organizational units rather than individual decision makers, and uncertainty applied to the organizational environment rather than individual decisions. Stable environments allow for greater certainty in structuring operations, thus a human service agency that deals mostly with clients having a particular problem (e.g., a food bank) are expected to have fairly routinized operations and formal structure. Conversely, organizations that deal with a wide variety of clients and unpredictable client problems (e.g., a disaster-relief organization) can be expected to be structured loosely and have a much less "by-the-book" approach to operational rules.

James Thompson (1967) agreed that the key issue in organization-environment interactions is the degree of uncertainty in the environment, and he noted that organizations seek predictability in the environment because this allows the ongoing operation of rational (logically planned) structures. However, since environments are never perfectly predictable, an organization that structures itself too rigidly will not long survive. Understanding how an organization has structured itself to respond to environmental uncertainty is thus the key to understanding it as a whole.

Thompson focused considerable attention on the nature of the organization's technology. As illustrated in Figure 7.2, he described three levels of organizational functioning: (1) the technical core, (2) the managerial system, and (3) the institutional system. The *technical core* includes the structures and processes within an organization's boundaries that allow it to carry out the principal functions for which the organization was created (i.e., the manufacture of an object or the delivery of a service). Theoretically, the technical core works best when environmental inputs never vary and it is thus allowed to do the same thing in the same way repeatedly. However, since environments are constantly changing, the rational organization seeks to accommodate to such variations without endangering its most vital elements (the technical core). The *managerial system* includes those structures and processes that manage the work of the technical core. The *institutional system* deals with interactions between the organization and the environment.

The means by which an organization structures itself to respond to environmental change without endangering its viability or basic identity is at the heart of Thompson's analytical model. He hypothesized that adaptive responses fall into a three-part sequence: (1) actions to protect the technical core of the organization, (2) actions to acquire power over the task environment, and (3) actions to absorb important elements of the environment by changing organizational domains. Actions to protect the technical core involve responses that allow the organization to contain necessary changes within itself, such as by increasing or decreasing output, hiring or laying off staff, or shifting resources among different internal units.

The *task environment* is the term Thompson uses to describe external organizations on which an organization depends, either as providers of needed input (money, raw materials, client referrals) or as consumers of its output. If internal

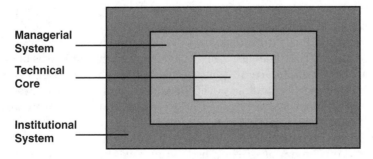

Managerial System

Technical Core

Institutional System

FIGURE 7.2 **Thompson's Organizational Model**

responses are unsuccessful in adjusting to change, Thompson says the next step is for the organization to attempt to alter its relationships with members of the task environment in such a way that it has more control over the change. Examples of this might include negotiating long-term funding agreements or arranging for regular referral of clients (e.g., a residential treatment center may become the exclusive provider of treatment for a particular school district).

Finally, if the organization cannot adapt to change by any of these methods, Thompson predicted that it would seek to incorporate into itself parts of the environment that relate to the change. For example, a human service organization dependent on providing services to substance-abusing clients that are paid for by contracts with a public agency may find itself jeopardized when governmental funding priorities shift toward prevention rather than treatment. If a relatively small and new agency in the area appears to be in line for much of this funding, the older, larger agency may seek to merge with the smaller one in an effort to maintain its funding base by providing these new services. However, because such a move involves changing at least part of the original agency's technical core, this type of response is likely to take place only after other adaptive strategies have been tried and proved inadequate.

Strengths and Weaknesses.   Open-systems models continue to have considerable influence on organizational analysis. The environment has been recognized as a critical variable in the life of every organization. Environmental considerations, such as procurement of funds or other resources, have always been prominent organizational agency concerns, and open-systems theories give proper recognition to that fact. Identification of survival as the primary motivator behind much organization behavior helps one understand and predict that behavior, as do Thompson's postulates about how organizations act to protect their technical core.

Organizations' increasing attention to cultural diversity in the workforce offers an example of how Thompson's ideas can explain organizational actions. As noted earlier, an important input that organizations draw from their environments is employees who have the knowledge and skills to carry out organizational tasks. A report from the U.S. Bureau of Labor Statistics (2002) estimates that between 1998 and 2008, the number of persons in the workforce nationwide will increase by 12 percent overall. The number of white, non-Hispanic workers, however, is projected to increase by only 7 percent, whereas the number of African American, Latino, and Asian American workers is projected to increase by 20, 37, and 40 percent, respectively. If organizations did not constantly monitor their environment and seek to adapt to its changes, it might be expected that little was being done to respond to this trend. In actuality, though, great numbers of organizations have begun adapting their technology, office locations, training procedures, and even rules of interpersonal conduct in an effort to attract, retain, and promote members of an increasingly diverse workforce.

The ideas of the contingency theorists still have certain weaknesses, however. For example, one limitation of Thompson's ideas was his caveat that the processes he described took place under "norms of rationality." By this, he meant that organizations that did not apply rational analytical processes in adapting to environmental change might act in unpredictable ways. The problem is that "rationality" is an elusive notion, particularly when applied to the process of reasoning that different organizations in different circumstances may need to do in order to respond to environmental turbulence. In commercial firms, for example, it may be "rational" to protect the interests of shareholders by maximizing profitability, but it is equally rational to keep profits and dividends modest in order to emphasize long-term investment. Similarly, actions such as stiffening eligibility criteria may be rational for a for-profit human service agency wishing to protect its earning capacity, but irrational for a nonprofit agency wishing to protect its mission of serving people in need, regardless of income.

BOX 7.8

Contingency Theory

- **Purpose.** Varies
- **Key Features.** A one-size-fits-all approach to organizational analysis or management is doomed to fail, since organizations have different purposes and exist in different environments. The question is not how closely an organization adheres to a particular form (e.g., the bureaucratic model) but how well it structures itself to accommodate to its unique environment. Also, contingency theory calls attention to an organization's *technology*, referring to the ways it carries out its tasks. Predictably, environmental input and routine tasks are amenable to more traditional, hierarchical structure, whereas unpredictable environments and nonroutine technology require less rigid structure.
- **Summary.** Organizations cannot be understood in isolation from their environments, and their level of dependence on the environment has much to do with how they operate. In addition, actions taken by organizations in response to environmental variability are not random. Instead, they tend to proceed through a sequence of steps that can be predicted and analyzed.

Similar organizations facing similar circumstances may still choose different courses of action based on differing interpretations of what these circumstances mean. Knowing how an organization perceives and evaluates its environment is useful in predicting how the organization will act, but there are limits to how well environments or organizational decision-making processes can be known. This means that the predictability of organizational actions will also remain limited.

Contemporary Perspectives

The history of organizational and management theory has been, in many ways, the history of a search for insights into the best ways to organize and manage—a search for the theory that will unlock the secrets of productivity. As we have attempted to illustrate in this chapter, the theme was different for each new theory. For Weber, it was structure; for Taylor, it was precision; for human relations theorists, it was attentiveness to social factors; for Drucker, it was a commonly shared sense of direction; for Simon, it was the process of decision making, and for Thompson, it was coping with environmental changes.

A major contribution of contingency theory was the idea that no one theme or set of variables was right for every situation. For contingency theorists, when asked the question, What is the best way to manage an organization? the correct answer was, It depends. Every organization is made up of a unique mix of variables, and contingency theorists argue that there can be no single formula for optimal structure and management style. The direction the organization takes will depend on its environment and on the nature of its core structures and processes.

Whether or not its tenets are always accepted, it is probably fair to state that the contingency approach has been a springboard for contemporary thinking about organizational and management theories. The 1980s and 1990s saw the introduction of a number of alternative perspectives. Although none has dominated the field, each has contributed to the ability to analyze organizations and understand how they are structured and led. Certain terms are prominent in this contemporary literature, including *excellence, quality, culture, vision, empowerment, diversity,* and *values. Leadership* has also become the term of choice over *management,* though both are acknowledged as having their place. The following discussion will briefly introduce the reader to a sampling of themes from organizational literature of the 1980s through today.

Power and Politics

Jeffrey Pfeffer (1981) argued that organizational actions are best understood in terms of power relationships and political forces. He defined *power* as the ability to influence actions and *politics* as the process whereby this influence is used. Asked where power originates, Pfeffer would explain that power is derived from an individual's position within the organization. Therefore, power and organizational structure are closely tied to one another.

To illustrate the relationship of power and organizational structure, Pfeffer compared three models of organizational analysis: (1) the bureaucratic model, (2) the rational-choice model, and (3) the political model. The *bureaucratic model* is based in the classic Weberian approach that assumes an organization is both structured and acts in a manner that maximizes its efficiency in achieving its goals. Pfeffer's criticisms of this model are essentially the same as those detailed earlier in this chapter. The *rational-choice* model derives from the work of decision-making theorists such as Simon. Pfeffer agreed with their points concerning constraints that limit rational decision making, but he noted that these models still assume that decision making is oriented toward a clear organizational goal, thus "they fail to take into account the diversity of interests and goals within organizations" (1981, p. 27). Pfeffer urged the use of a *political model* of structural analysis, which calls attention to the manner in which organizational actions may be either instrumental (serving the presumed goals of the organization as a whole) or parochial (serving the perceived self-interest of a particular individual or organizational unit).

These goals may differ, as does the power of the decision maker to bring to bear his or her choice of action. Pfeffer thus argued that organizational actions must be understood in terms of a complex interplay of forces analogous to that in a political environment.

Furthering this reasoning, Wamsley and Zald (1976) argued that structure and process in organizations is best understood in terms of the interplay of political and economic interests both internal *and* external to the organization. *Political* means the processes by which the organization obtains power and legitimacy. *Economic* means the processes by which the organization gets resources such as clients, staff, and funding.

The goal of the *political economy* perspective was to incorporate much of the work of previous schools into a more general conceptual model. Within this model, elements such as individual interests and goals, the power wielded by the holders of these interests, and environmental resources and the relative influence of those who control them are all seen to interact in a way that creates the unique character of an organization. This character is not static but changes as the political economy of the organization changes.

For an example of how these ideas build on and extend previous work, consider our earlier discussion of the weaknesses of Thompson's model. Pfeffer would argue that Thompson, in assuming that "norms of rationality" govern organizational actions, fails to account for the fact that both instrumental *and* parochial concerns are being addressed. That is, individuals who have the power to choose a particular organizational action will make their decisions based not only on what is best for the organization but also on what is best for themselves. Moreover, the competing self-interest of other powerful individuals within the organization and the interests of powerful organizations in the environment will also be weighed in this person's decisions. This mixing of interests is what Pfeffer as well as Wamsley and Zald refer to as the *political context* of organizations. Their central point is that organizational behavior can be best understood as the outcome of decisions by individuals who have acquired decision-making power, and these decisions will reflect their assessment of what is politically and economically wise for both themselves and the organization.

The topic of power has also been discussed extensively in feminist literature, both in relationship to politics within organizations and within the larger society in general. Gottlieb (1992) calls for a reconceptualization of empowerment and politics in organizations that serve women. She explains, "Women in both corners of the service relationship are affected by the societal definitions and oppression of women, although many members of both groups avoid seeing those effects" (p. 301). Because social work is a profession that has large numbers of women, both as practitioners and clients, Gottlieb encourages an increasing awareness of the political dimensions in the larger society that affect human service organizations.

Organizational Culture

The concept of *organizational culture* has also shaped the development of contemporary theories. Schein (1985) defines *culture* as

> a pattern of basic assumptions—invented, discovered, or developed by a given group as it learns to cope with its problems of external adaptation and internal integration—that has worked well enough to be considered valid and therefore, to be taught to new members as the correct way to perceive, think, and feel in relation to those problems. (p. 9)

Schein explains that an organizational culture develops through shared experiences. Newly formed organizations are heavily influenced by leaders who bring their perspectives to the organization and around which assumptions and beliefs emerge. "Culture, in this sense, is a learned product of group experience and is, therefore, to be found only where there is a definable group with a significant history" (1985, p. 7). Schein argues that leadership and culture are intimately related, and understanding what assumptions leaders bring to organizations is central to analyzing how change occurs within an agency.

The connection of leadership to organizational culture has been explored in numerous ways. Of particular interest is the expanding literature on leadership and gender:

> By 1990 an ongoing debate had developed over whether women want the same type of success as men, whether they are able to demonstrate the behavior and leadership required for modern organizations to compete at high levels, and whether successful female managers need to adopt male behavioral styles in order to lead or compete. (Kelly, 1991, p. 96)

Feminist scholars have begun to analyze the processes of empowerment and collective action within organizations and the effect these processes have on changing cultural assumptions within organizations (Astin & Leland, 1991). Language and communication, values, orientations toward power, perceptions of relationships, and leadership styles are fertile ground for exploration of gender and the development of organizational culture.

Organizational culture is important in understanding any organization; it is highly "visible" and "feelable" (Schein, 1985, p. 24). When entering an organization, one quickly perceives that established patterns occur within that system even if they are not explicitly stated. The social worker who assumes a new place in an organization must be aware that these patterns may be so central to organizational functioning that they are taken for granted by members of that organization. When violated, members may respond emotionally because they are so invested in the "way things have always been done." It is difficult to understand how employees feel about an organization without considering the culture. Organizational culture, then, is much broader than climate, ideology, or philosophy. It is a sense of group identity that permeates decision making and communication within the organization.

Theory Z

In the late 1970s and early 1980s, attention in the United States began to be directed toward growing competition from Japan. Markets long dominated by U.S. firms were being lost to Japanese industries, and there was considerable curiosity about how Japanese companies had overcome their prior reputation for poor products and were now setting worldwide standards of quality.

William Ouchi attempted to capture Japanese-style management in his 1981 book, *Theory Z*. The message of the title was that the philosophical and theoretical principles underlying Japanese management went beyond McGregor's conceptualization of Theory Y. An organization in Japan, said Ouchi, was more than a structural or goal-oriented entity, as it was in America—it was a way of life. It provided lifetime employment; was enmeshed in the social, political, and economic network of the country; and wielded influence that spilled over into other organizations such as universities and public schools, even to the lowest grades.

The basic philosophy of Japanese-style management was that involved workers are the key to increased productivity. This may sound similar to the human relations school, but it was quite different. The Japanese were concerned not simply about having workers feel that their social needs were met in the workplace, but that workers became a demonstrable part of the process through which the organization was run. Ideas and suggestions about how to improve the organization were regularly solicited and, where feasible, implemented. One example was the *quality circle*, where employees set aside time to brainstorm about ways to improve quality and productivity.

In contrast to U.S. organizations, Japanese organizations at the time tended to have neither organizational charts nor written objectives. Most work was done in teams, and consensus was achieved without a designated leader. Cooperation rather than competition was sought between units. Loyalty to the organization was extremely important, and it was rewarded by loyalty to the employee.

Numerous efforts to transplant Japanese-style management to the United States have been tried since the appearance of Ouchi's book, but most have met with limited success. In most cases, it has been concluded that the *Theory Z* philosophy is compatible with a homogenous culture such as Japan's, but it does not fit as well with the more heterogenous and individualistic character of the American workplace. Also, since its height in the 1980s, the Japanese economy has suffered a lengthy downturn. Although the quality of its products remains high, these larger economic woes have diminished interest in Japanese management strategies. Nonetheless, many of the principles described by Ouchi have influenced contemporary management practices and have been incorporated into subsequent thinking.

"In Search of Excellence"

Another important management theme in the 1980s was the "excellence" theme, pioneered by Thomas Peters and Robert Waterman (1982). Both authors were employees at a management consulting firm who became leaders of a project on organizational effectiveness. After creating a definition for what they considered excellent companies, they selected 62 for study. They also immersed themselves in the theory and practices of excellent companies and discovered that the dominant themes were topics such as organizational culture, a family feeling among employees, a preference for smallness, a preference for simplicity rather than com-plexity, and attention to individuals. In effect, they found that management prac-tices in these organizations focused more on personal elements such as those noted by human relations theorists and McGregor and less on elements of organi-zational structure as emphasized by Weber and Fayol.

Peters and Waterman also concluded that, although a rational organizational base built on collection and analysis of data is indispensable, analysis of data must be flexible and take into account a wide range of considerations, including the individual person. Rational approaches, they argued, need to stop considering the human implementer a "necessary nuisance" and instead build on the strengths brought into a system by its employees. Their findings were organized into eight basic principles that have become the focal point of the "excellence approach" to management:

1. *A Bias for Action.* Preferring to do something—anything—rather than send a question through cycles and cycles of analyses and committee reports
2. *Staying Close to the Customer.* Learning preferences and catering to them
3. *Autonomy and Entrepreneurship.* Breaking the corporation into small compa-nies and encouraging them to think independently and competitively
4. *Productivity through People.* Creating in all employees a belief that their best efforts are essential and that they will share the rewards of the company's success
5. *Hands-On, Value Driven.* Insisting that executives keep in touch with the firm's essential mission
6. *Sticking to the Knitting.* Remaining with the business the company knows best
7. *Simple Form, Lean Staff.* Having few administrative layers, few people at the upper levels
8. *Simultaneous Loose/Tight Properties.* Fostering a climate where there is dedi-cation to the central values of the company, combined with tolerance for all employees who accept those values

As the provision of human services has moved closer and closer to a provider-consumer relationship, these principles and the findings of the Peters and Waterman study have grown in importance. Public as well as private agencies have recognized the link between quality of the work environment and quality of the organization's products. In addition, strategies to cope with uncertain envi-ronments have been joined with encouragement for organizations to form flexible and collaborative relationships with others in order to survive and grow.

Managing Diversity

Roosevelt Thomas, Jr. (1991) took a somewhat different approach to managing the workforce of the 1990s. He identified diversity as the key variable affecting pro-ductivity, and saw effective management of diverse populations as a critical skill.

He highlighted three trends that, he believes, will dictate the need for dealing with an increasingly diverse workforce:

1. American corporations must do business in a global market that has become intensely competitive.
2. The makeup of the U.S. workforce is changing dramatically as it becomes more diverse.
3. The "melting pot" concept is becoming less applicable. Instead, individuals have begun to emphasize and take pride in differences.

In order to remain competitive, Thomas believes that U.S. organizations must learn how to draw on the creative resources represented in a workforce made up of Asian Americans, African Americans, Latinos, Anglos, and other races, as well as a more equal mix of males and females. To accomplish this objective, he proposes an analytical framework for understanding organizational culture that breaks diversity down into three phases: (1) affirmative action, (2) valuing differences, and (3) managing diversity.

Affirmative action refers to programs and efforts designed to bring ethnic minorities and women into an organization. The focus is on recruitment, and success is measured by the number and percentage of minorities recruited and retained. Thomas sees affirmative action as a temporary step in moving organizations toward managing diversity.

Valuing differences focuses on enhancing interpersonal relationships among individuals. Much of the responsibility for these efforts falls on staff training and personnel development, with the objective of fostering acceptance and mutual respect across racial and gender lines, enhancing understanding of differences, assisting participants with understanding their own feelings and attitudes toward differences, and enhancing working relationships among people who are different.

Managing diversity, which is Thomas's vision, refers to a complete evaluation of the organization as a system to determine if it is as effective and productive as it must be in a competitive environment. If the system is not effective, and if it is not prepared to deal with a diverse workforce, Thomas suggests it may need to undertake a long-term strategy to modify the core culture. This requires a full understanding of the existing culture and a planned transition to a new culture in which an environment is created that supports full utilization of a diverse workforce. This requires a mindset that recognizes and values differences among all employees, and searches for opportunities to tap the reservoir of talent and strength represented in a diverse staff.

Thomas cites a number of major American corporations that have set out to change their organizational culture and increase productivity and competitiveness by effectively managing diversity. Most human service organizations have had diverse workforces for many years, but a thorough understanding of Thomas's conceptual framework could lead some to conclude that they have not yet moved beyond the phase of affirmative action, and that they have much to learn about valuing differences and managing diversity well.

Total Quality Management (TQM)

As noted earlier in our review of Ouchi's Theory Z, commercial firms in the United States in the 1980s began recognizing that American-made goods were no longer perceived by consumers to be of consistently high quality. This spurred interest in the management practices of foreign firms, such as those in Japan, that had gained a reputation for both competitive price and superior quality. Ironically, the search led to the work of American writers such as W. Edwards Deming, who began in the 1950s to assist the Japanese in developing quality-oriented administrative strategies. Another American, Arnold Feigenbaum, coined the term *total quality* to describe the major thrust of this approach (1991), but its central principles were set out in a summary published by Deming in 1982. The movement quickly became known as total quality management, or TQM.

Total quality management places the quality of organizational outputs, whether goods or services, at the focal point of all operations. Management is charged with creating both structures and procedures within the organization that will continually reinforce this goal. Table 7.3 presents a typology by Martin (1993) that lists principles of TQM in comparison with traditional management approaches.

Some principles in Table 7.3 are unique to TQM; others reflect preceding schools of thought. For example, TQM adopts McGregor's view that workers obtain satisfaction from doing their job productively if they are allowed discretion in determining how the job is to be done. It is also favorable to the use of quality circles and other team-building approaches described by Ouchi and Peters and Waterman. Also, as per Schein's urgings, it encourages promotion of an organizational culture to which staff may become attached. In other cases, though, TQM explicitly rejects prior theoretical views. Among these are bureaucratic (rule-oriented) structure, and models such as those of open-systems theorists that seek to achieve organizational stability and predictability, which TQM principles view as threats to ongoing quality improvement. Saylor (1996) also notes that TQM is incompatible with Drucker's management by objective (MBO) guidelines, because TQM considers customer satisfaction a moving target. This demands a continual *process* orientation to anticipate and adapt to new customer needs, whereas MBO, Saylor argues, focuses on achieving static *outcomes* that may ignore the changing needs of customers and can lead the organization into passivity or outdatedness.

Because TQM has its origins in commercial manufacturing firms, its applicability to human service organizations in the public or private sectors may be questioned. However, interesting historical precursors exist regarding its use in social work agencies, and guidelines have been proposed for applying specific principles of TQM in these organizations. One forerunner of TQM in social work is the effectiveness-driven management movement, which calls for administrative approaches that orient the organization toward meeting client needs (Patti, 1985; Rapp & Poertner, 1992). More recently, Moore and Kelly (1996) argue that "TQM is a useful tool despite the fact that social and public services organizations are not prepared to implement it in its most orthodox form" (p. 33). Among the elements of TQM they believe can be adopted by human service agencies are (1) the use of

TABLE 7.3 Comparison of Traditional American Management Principles with TQM Management Principles

Traditional American Management Principles	Total Quality Management (TQM) Principles
The organization has multiple competing goals.	Quality is the primary organizational goal.
Financial concerns drive the organization.	Customer satisfaction drives the organization.
Management and professionals determine what quality is.	Customers determine what quality is.
The focus is on the status quo—"If it ain't broke, don't fix it."	The focus is on continuous improvement—"Unattended systems tend to run down."
Change is abrupt and is accomplished by champions battling the bureaucracy.	Change is continuous and is accomplished by teamwork.
Employees and departments compete with each other.	Employees and departments cooperate with each other.
Decisions are based on "gut feelings." It is better to do something than to do nothing.	Decisions are based on data analysis. It is better to do nothing than to do something wrong.
Employee training is considered a luxury and a cost.	Employee training is considered essential and an investment.
Organizational communication is primarily top-down.	Organizational communication is top-down, down-up, and sideways.
Contractors are encouraged to compete with each other in the basis of price.	Long-term relationships are developed with contractors who deliver quality products and services.

Source: L. L. Martin, *Total Quality Management in Human Service Organizations,* copyright © 1993 by Sage Publications. Reprinted by Permission of Sage Publications, Inc.

quality circles to improve staff involvement and make services more relevant, (2) the use of careful measurement practices to monitor whether consumer needs are being met, (3) hiring and training staff in ways that ensure front-line staff have both the skills and interests necessary for their jobs, and (4) management staff that can define a quality orientation and move the organization toward that goal.

Organizations as Complex Systems

In 1987, science writer James Gleick described efforts by researchers in several fields who were examining unpredictable or "chaotic" systems. The studies showed that seemingly chaotic behavior was not entirely unpredictable, and the behavior of elements in the systems revealed certain patterns and limits to variability. Weather, because of the difficulty of predicting its behavior, is one representation of such systems. It is impossible, for example, for a forecaster in Chicago to predict on New Year's Day whether the city will have rain on July 4th. Yet, Chicago's weather in July is not wholly random, and though faced with limits, the forecaster can still predict with high confidence that, for example, there will be little chance of snow that day.

Recognizing this, researchers have become less likely to refer to such systems as "chaotic" and more likely to describe them as *complex systems*. Svyantek and Brown (2000) define complex systems as ones "whose behaviors cannot be explained by breaking the system down into its component parts" (p. 69). An engine, for example, is not a complex system, since its function and operation can be deduced from an examination of its mechanical pieces. However, although the previously mentioned weather forecaster may understand the nature of air or water molecules, this does little to assist in prediction. Far too many variables affect the interaction of the vast numbers of molecules throughout the world's atmosphere that, between January 1st and July 4th, could determine Chicago's weather. As we will explain, the same constraints apply when trying to predict how employees in organizations may interact, which is why theorists have begun to conceptualize and analyze them as complex systems.

Interactions among elements of complex systems are termed *nonlinear* because they do not have the same kinds of cause-and-effect relationships as in other systems. As Marion (1999) explains, *nonlinearity*

> means that response is disjointed from cause. That is, a change in a causal agent does not necessarily elicit a proportional response in some variable it affects; rather it may elicit no response, dramatic response, or response only at certain levels of cause. Consider, for example, the behavior of dogs, and assume for the moment that the only emotions these animals experience are fear and anger. As two dogs approach each other, they may express anger at the intrusion of the other and bark furiously. A simple model of causality would predict that the anger of each dog would increase in proportion to the proximity of the other until a fight results. Nonlinear theories argue that a fight is not a foregone conclusion; rather, when the situation reaches a certain level of intensity, the emotional state of one dog may flip to fear, leading it to tuck tail and run. Fight or run: The outcome is sensitively dependent upon the precise state of each dog's emotions, upon subtle nuances of interactions between the dogs, and between each dog and—goodness knows what. (pp. 5–6)

Several points are important in this illustration. First, the units of analysis are elements in the system—in this case just two dogs, but in other systems potentially large numbers of atoms, animals, or people. Second, despite the apparent simplicity of the situation of two dogs meeting, it involves a great many other variables (the physical environment, the prior experiences of each dog, the personality or behavioral tendencies of each) that influence what happens. Third, the course of events can be powerfully affected by small variations in any one of these factors that occurs early in the interaction (e.g., the position of a dog's head or how much its teeth are bared). This *sensitive dependence on initial conditions* is a key element of complex systems. It is also called the *butterfly effect*, referring to how an event as small as a butterfly flapping its wings in one part of the world can be the start of a series of events that result in major changes (a large frontal system, an intense storm, etc.) in some other part of the world. In the social sciences, Lewin and Regine (2000) offer the example of Rosa Park's small but pivotal act of defiance in refusing to move to the back of a Montgomery, Alabama, bus in 1955, which became a trigger for the entire Civil Rights Movement. It illustrates the difficulty of prediction in complex systems, where seemingly minor initial events or circumstances can produce profound effects later on.

A final point to be drawn from Marion's illustration is the idea that, despite the difficulty of predicting what will happen between the two dogs, the final outcome is not similarly complex. Although the interplay of forces seems chaotic, an infinitely large array of outcomes does not arise. In the physical sciences, mathematical models of systems such as the weather have been shown to produce intriguing graphs in which behavior is shown by a moving line that at first takes a random path but eventually begins to loop back on itself and almost, though not quite, repeats. Continued observation shows that, although the line never exactly duplicates a prior path, the general outline of the loop persistently occurs. Scientists dubbed points in such graphs around which behavioral paths tended to loop *strange attractors*, and their significance is in illustrating that hidden order can exist in seemingly chaotic systems, which in turn leads to some degree of predictability.

Returning to the meeting of the two dogs, one sees that the final behavior of the system tends to be relatively constrained—in this case, either a fight will occur or one of the two dogs will back down. Many real-world circumstances are obviously more complex and have more possible outcomes than this, yet the behavior of complex systems rarely slips into true chaos. Lewin and Regine (2000) note,

> Complex adaptive systems often evolve themselves to a critical point poised between chaotic and adaptive states, where their emergent response is measured, richly creative, and adaptive. . . . This poised state has been blessed with the unfortunate term, *the edge of chaos.* Order emerges at the edge of chaos . . . it is not imposed by central design; it derives from distributed influence through the interactions of the system's agents. It is hard—and often impossible—to predict in detail what emergent order will look like, but it is certain order will emerge. (pp. 39–40)

This emergence of order within seemingly chaotic circumstances is why organizational analysts have been attracted to complexity theory. As one example, Wheatley (1999) argues that the repeating patterns reflected in such order may simply be a different name for what others have called organizational culture.

Also relevant is the notion that the behavior of the system ultimately arises from interactions among its elements (e.g., employees) and their interactions with the environment around them. Research suggests that behavior in many complex systems can be explained as decision making on the part of individuals within the system acting on a surprisingly small number of rules. An example is offered by Reynolds (1987), who studied the complex behavior of birds in flocks. He created a computer program that was eventually able to model flocking behavior with great accuracy. The program was based on programming each individual (or "boid" as he whimsically termed them) to follow only three rules: Go the same direction as other birds, try to match their speed, and avoid flying into them or other objects.

BOX 7.9

Contemporary Theories

- **Purpose.** Varies (Some approaches, such as Theory Z and TQM, are strongly prescriptive and offer detailed guidelines for both structure and management; others, such as complexity theory, are more descriptive, offering new ways to understand how organizations work.)
- **Key Features.** Most contemporary theories incorporate ideas from previous works that have been generally accepted. All assume, for example, that environmental circumstances are critical to understanding organizational behavior, that no one structure works equally well for all organizations, and that the personal interests of individuals within organizations powerfully influence how they operate. Where contemporary theories differ is most often in their focus on particular variables that have been ignored or underestimated in prior work. Examples of these include *power* and its exercise through political relationships within organizations (Pfeffer, 1981), *diversity* and the increasing heterogeneity of the workforce (Thomas, 1991), *quality* and the orientation of management toward excellence and consumer satisfaction (Peters & Waterman, 1982; Deming, 1982), and *complexity* and its ramifications for placing limits on the predictability of environmental contingencies that might affect an organization.
- **Summary.** Organizational theory continues to evolve, as new theories either supplant older ones or build on their strong points and extend them in new directions. As in the past, many contemporary ideas arose first in studies of commercial firms, and some are easier to adapt to social work organizations than others. Also of note is the fact that work from fields as diverse as political science, biology, and even meteorology have influenced contemporary organizational theories. Given the increasingly interdisciplinary nature of scientific work, this trend is likely to continue.

Obviously, the actions of humans in complex organizations cannot be reduced to a mere three rules. Nonetheless, this is a further example of how findings from research on complex systems informs organizational analysis. As other theorists have pointed out, individuals in organizations act on predictable motivations to meet certain needs—income, belongingness, self-actualization, and others. If by these means analysts can understand actions taken and decisions made by individual elements, then within limits set by the complexity of the environment and the natural presence of a certain level of randomness in the system, complexity theory holds out the promise of making useful predictions about how organizations behave.

Summary and Analysis of Contemporary Theories

The perspectives we've discussed come together in interesting ways. Clearly, one trend coming out of the 1980s was the move toward a better, more thorough understanding of organizational culture. Often, this begins with an identification of the locus of power and an understanding of the effectiveness of various individuals or groups in exercising political and leadership skills. These factors, together with others identified by Schein, make up what has come to be understood as *organizational culture,* a powerful and sometimes seemingly intractable force for continuation of "business as usual."

An increasingly important factor in the development and evolution of organizational culture will be the diversity of the workforce. Despite the current debate over affirmative action and methods by which opportunities can be equalized across gender and racial groups, it is manifestly clear that both workers and administrators of the future will be much more diverse than in the past. This means that organizations will need to continuously address the question of whether their structures and procedures are compatible with the diversity of their workforce, and whether they are positioned to use this diversity in ways that benefit both the organization and its individual members.

The notion of quality has become a criterion for designing structures and processes as well as for evaluating organizational success. Whether this will bring about genuine change, however, may be largely dependent on how *quality* is defined. In his discussion of goal displacement in organizations, Selznick (1949) argued that one starting point for the process is "unanalyzed abstractions," which are touted by management as being noble goals but which may have little real meaning in practice. (References by politicians to powerful but often vague symbols such as "freedom" or "patriotism" are examples of such abstractions.) If "quality" becomes merely another unanalyzed abstraction, it is likely to have little long-term effect on organizations.

Still, advocates of the approaches suggested by Ouchi, Peters and Waterman, and Deming all argue that they represent truly new ideas due to their emphasis on *process* rather than exclusively on outcomes. Through this process orientation, they argue, fundamental changes can occur in the way organizations work. Such changes might include increased involvement by line staff in the design of procedures and services. They might also include a definition of quality operations that effectively incorporates workforce diversity as an organizational resource.

Or, finally, it may be seen that no "one-size-fits-all" approach to organizing will be found. In Burns and Stalker's language, one might find that some organizations must indeed move away from a mechanistic structure and design toward a more organic approach. For others, however, it may be found preferable to avoid entrepreneurial, laissez-faire styles of management in favor of more circumscribed, even mechanistic, approaches. Still more pointedly, theories of complex systems suggest that there may be fundamental limits to how well the almost infinitely subtle interactions among organizational members can be understood, hence there are corresponding limits to how much can be said about actions administrators should take and what effects those actions are likely to have.

As contingency theorists are fond of saying, "It depends." The most useful organizational and management theories and approaches for today's human service agencies will depend on such factors as mission, objectives, target population served, personal, family and social problems addressed, types of persons employed, the state of the art of treatment or intervention, the clarity of outcome expectations, and the nature of the delicate dance between rationality and randomness performed by organizations and other complex systems at the "edge of chaos." All things considered, what faces the nation is a compelling challenge for the application of new knowledge and the discovery of new approaches to understanding and managing organizations, particularly those in which social workers operate.

Summary

The goal of this chapter has been to introduce theoretical approaches to organizations and to begin tying these ideas to the task of understanding organizations in which most social workers practice. These theories and perspectives can be understood partly in terms of the way they differ among themselves (Table 7.1). Some theories (such as scientific management and the human relations school) are prescriptive models, meaning that they provide guidelines on how to organize. In contrast, descriptive theories (such as the bureaucracy model and the decision-making model) offer conceptual strategies for analyzing organizations and their operations.

These theories can be distinguished according to their approach to explaining organizational behavior. Some theories assume a rational model in which behavior is seen as the result of logical decision making oriented toward the instrumental goals of the organization. Other theories employ a natural systems approach, in which the organization is seen as being analogous to a biological organism and its behavior as responding to basic concerns for survival and self-maintenance.

Organizational theories also differ as to whether they adopt a closed- or open-systems perspective on the role of the organization's environment. Closed-systems approaches implicitly focus on internal structure and process in organizations and tend to direct little or no attention to the role of the environment. Open-systems models emphasize organizations' dependence on their environment and adopt analytical strategies that view internal structure and process as the product of interactions with the environment.

Each theory we have reviewed can also be understood in terms of one or a small group of organizational variables toward which it direct attentions. These variables include structure (the bureaucracy), productivity and the role of management (scientific and universalistic management), social interactions and self-actualization (human relations and Theory Y), organizational goals (the institutional school and management by objectives), strategic choice (the decision-making model), environmental interactions (contingency theory), the exercise of power and political influence (the political economy model), organizational culture and quality (Theory Z and TQM), and finding predictability within seeming randomness (complexity theory). As is often the case with theory building in many different arenas, many of the models have developed out of criticisms of earlier works that have directed attention in new and fruitful directions. Nonetheless, even the earliest of these theories still has some validity, and the critical task in organizational analysis is to glean from these various models the ideas that best explain the particular organization being addressed.

Organizational analysis in human service organizations has already produced a substantial body of literature that can be very helpful to macro practice. Chapter 8 will review this literature and discuss means for applying it to specific problems that may arise in human service organizations.

DISCUSSION QUESTIONS AND EXERCISES

1. We define *formal organizations* as "collectives of individuals gathered together to serve a particular purpose." Discuss how formal organizations differ from other types of groups. Make a list of the formal organizations and other types of groups with which you come in contact during a typical day.

2. Think of an organization with which you are familiar. Which of the theories reviewed in Chapter 7 seemed the most interesting or useful in explaining dynamics of this organization? How is this theory useful in helping you understand this organization?

3. Most theories reviewed in Chapter 7 originally addressed commercial firms and industrial organizations. Do you believe that theories created to explain these types of organizations apply equally well to those in which most social workers are involved? Discuss why or why not.

4. One definition for *bureaucracy* in the dictionary is "rigid adherence to administrative routine." This sums up many of the negative aspects of bureaucratic organization, yet in first describing the characteristics of bureaucracies, Weber clearly thought they had many advantages over other organizational types. Do you believe bureaucratic organization has positive as well as negative points? If so, identify both and propose how an organization might take advantage of the positives while minimizing the negatives.

5. Taylor's scientific management is grounded on the principle of the "one best way." Do you believe there is indeed one best way of helping individuals with a common need, such as, for example, homeless single men in need of work and a place to live? Discuss the pros and cons of standardizing versus individualizing the helping process.

6. Describe the process of goal displacement in organizations. Have you ever seen the process or results of goal displacement in an organization? If so, describe what happened or its consequences.

7. Give a practical example of the process of "satisficing" in an organization. Then describe how different or better information, if it were available to the decision maker in your example, might result in a better decision.

8. Contingency theory posits that some organizations perform best when structured in a relatively rigid, hierarchical fashion, whereas others are best organized loosely, with few rules and flexible individual roles. Does this thinking apply to organizations in which social workers serve? If not, explain why not. If so, compare and contrast a social work organization that may be better suited to a more rigid structure with one that is better suited for a loose structure. Discuss the differences between the two that favor one model over another, paying special attention to how their technologies differ.

9. Total quality management (TQM) is perhaps the most influential organizational theory at present. Assume you are a mid-level manager in the social work department of a large hospital in an urban area. Your department serves patients who receive medical services from the hospital, but it also provides general counseling services to clients who are referred by other health-care providers affiliated with the hospital. You have been assigned to a task force whose job is to apply TQM prin-

ciples to develop a plan for reorganizing your department in ways that will improve its management and maximize service quality. Assume that in the early stages of the work of the task force, you have been directed to address the following questions:

- How would you define *quality* in this situation?

- What are two examples of ways that quality could be measured?

- How would you organize services in such a way as to make quality a process orientation rather than an outcome?

- Give an example of how you would apply at least one other principle of TQM listed in Table 7.3 to your department's redesign.

10. Complexity theorists describe organizations as resting constantly on the "edge of chaos," yet their behavior is neither random or apparently irrational. Explain what is meant by *chaos* in organizations, and give an example of how responses of individual elements (i.e., employees) to this chaos can nonetheless lead to seemingly rational outcomes. Also, give an example of an organization's "sensitive dependence on initial conditions" by describing how small events can produce much larger subsequent effects.

SUGGESTED READINGS

Ashkanasy, N. M., C. Wilderom, and M. F. Peterson. (2000). *Handbook of organizational culture and climate*. Thousand Oaks, CA: Sage.

Banner, D. K., and T. E. Gagne. (1995). *Designing effective organizations: Traditional and transformational views*. Thousand Oaks, CA: Sage.

Connor, D. R. (1998). *Leading at the edge of chaos: How to create the nimble organization*. New York: John Wiley & Sons.

Cooper, C. L. (2001). *Classics in management thought*. Northampton, MA: E. Elgar Publications.

Golembiewski, R. T. (1995). *Managing diversity in organizations*. Tuscaloosa: University of Alabama Press.

Kanter, R. B. (2001). *Evolve! Succeeding in the digital culture of tomorrow*. Boston: Harvard Business School Press.

March, J. S., H. A. Simon, and H. S. Guetzkow.

(1993). *Organizations* (2nd ed.). Cambridge, MA: Blackwell.

Matteson, M. T., and J. M. Ivancevich. (1999). *Management and organizational behavior classics* (7th ed.). Boston: Irwin/McGraw Hill.

Powell, G. N. (1999). *Handbook of gender and work.* Thousand Oaks, CA: Sage.

Prasad, P. (1997). *Managing the organizational melting pot: Dilemmas of workplace diversity.* Thousand Oaks, CA: Sage.

Roberts, K. H. (1993). *New challenges to understanding organizations.* New York: Macmillan.

Sanchez, R. (2001). *Knowledge management and organizational competence.* New York: Oxford University Press.

Shafritz, J. M., and J. S. Ott. (2001). *Classics of organizational theory* (5th ed.). Fort Worth, TX: Harcourt College Publishers.

REFERENCES

Astin, H. S., and C. Leland. (1991). *Women of influence, women of vision: A cross-generational study of leaders and social change.* San Francisco: Jossey-Bass.

Barker, R. L. (1995). *The social work dictionary* (3rd ed.). Washington, DC: National Association of Social Workers.

Blau, P. M., and W. R. Scott. (1962). *Formal organizations.* San Francisco: Chandler.

Burns, T., and G. M. Stalker. (1961). *The management of innovation.* London: Tavistock.

Champion, D. J. (1975). *The sociology of organizations.* New York: McGraw-Hill.

Cyert, R. M., and J. G. March. (1963). *A behavioral theory of the firm.* Englewood Cliffs, NJ: Prentice-Hall.

Deming, W. E. (1982). *Out of the crisis.* Cambridge, MA: Massachusetts Institute of Technology, Center for Advanced Engineering Study.

Drucker, P. F. (1954). *The practice of management.* New York: Harper.

Etzioni, A. (1964). *Modern organizations.* Englewood Cliffs, NJ: Prentice-Hall.

Feigenbaum, A. V. (1991). *Total quality control.* New York: McGraw-Hill.

Galbraith, J. R. (1973). *Designing complex organizations.* Reading, MA: Addison-Wesley.

George, C. S., Jr. (1968). *The history of management thought.* Englewood Cliffs, NJ: Prentice-Hall.

Gleick, J. (1987). *Chaos: Making a new science.* New York: Viking-Penguin.

Gottlieb, N. (1992). Empowerment, political analyses, and services for women. In Y. Hasenfeld (Ed.), *Human services as complex organizations* (pp. 301–319) Newbury Park, CA: Sage.

Herzberg, F. (1966). *Work and the nature of man.* Cleveland: World.

Katz, D., and R. L. Kahn. (1966). *The social psychology of organizations.* New York: Wiley.

Kelly, R. M. (1991). *The gendered economy: Work, careers, and success.* Newbury Park, CA: Sage.

Landsberger, H. A. (1958). *Hawthorne revisited.* Ithaca, NY: Cornell University Press.

Lawrence, P. R., and J. W. Lorsch. (1967). *Organization and environment: Managing differentiation and integration.* Boston: Graduate School of Business Administration, Harvard University.

Lewin, R., and B. Regine. (2000). *The soul at work: Embracing complexity science for business success.* New York: Simon & Schuster.

March, J. G., and J. P. Olsen. (1976). *Ambiguity and choice in organizations.* Bergen, Norway: Universitetsforlaget.

March, J. G., and H. A. Simon. (1958). *Organizations.* New York: Wiley.

Marion, R. (1999). *The edge of organization: Chaos and complexity theories of formal social systems.* Thousand Oaks, CA: Sage.

Martin, L. L. (1993). *Total quality management in human service organizations.* Thousand Oaks, CA: Sage.

McGregor, D. (1960). *The human side of enterprise.* New York: McGraw-Hill.

Merton, R. K. (1952). Bureaucratic structure and personality. In R. K. Merton, A. P. Gray, B. Hockey, and H. C. Selvin. (Eds.), *Reader in bureaucracy* (pp. 261–372) Glencoe, IL: Free Press.

Michels, R. (1949). *Political parties* (E. Paul and C. Paul, trans.) Glencoe, IL: Free Press. (First published in 1915).

Moore, S. T., and M. J. Kelly. (1996). Quality now: Moving human services organizations toward a consumer orientation to service quality. *Social Work, 41*(1): 33–40.

Morse, J. J., and J. W. Lorsch. (1970). Beyond Theory Y. *Harvard Business Review, 45,* 61–68.

Mouzelis, N. P. (1967). *Organization and bureaucracy.* London: Routledge & Kegan Paul.

Ouchi, W. (1981). *Theory Z: How American business can meet the Japanese challenge.* Reading, MA: Addison-Wesley.

Parsons, T. (1960). *Structure and process in modern societies.* Glencoe, IL: Free Press.

Patti, R. (1985). In search of purpose for social welfare administration. *Administration in Social Work, 9*(3): 1–14.

Peters, T. J., and R. H. Waterman. (1982). *In search of excellence: Lessons from America's best-run companies.* New York: Harper & Row.

Pfeffer, J. (1981). *Power in organizations.* Marshfield, MA: Pitman.

Rapp, C. A., and J. Poertner. (1992). *Social administration: A client-centered approach.* New York: Longman.

Reynolds, C. W. (1987). Flocks, herds, and schools: A distributed behavioral model, in computer graphics. *Proceedings of the 1987 SIGGRAPH Conference, 21*(4): 25–34.

Rogers, R. E. (1975). *Organizational theory.* Boston: Allyn and Bacon.

Saylor, J. H. (1996). *TQM simplified: A practical guide* (2nd ed.). New York: McGraw-Hill.

Schein, E. H. (1985). *Organizational culture and leadership.* San Francisco: Jossey-Bass.

Scott, W. R. (1981). *Organizations: Rational, natural, and open Systems.* Englewood Cliffs, NJ: Prentice-Hall.

Selznick, P. (1949). *TVA and the grass roots.* Berkeley: University of California Press.

Selznick, P. (1957). *Leadership in administration.* New York: Harper & Row.

Sills, D. L. (1957). *The volunteers.* New York: Free Press.

Simon, H. A. (1957). *Administrative behavior* (2nd ed.). New York: Macmillan.

Svyantek, D. J., and L. L. Brown. (2000). A complex-systems approach to organizations. *Current Directions in Psychological Science, 9,* 74.

Sykes, A. J. M. (1965). Economic interests and the Hawthorne researchers: A comment. *Human Relations, 18,* 253–263.

Taylor, F. W. (1947). *Scientific management.* New York: Harper & Row.

Thomas, R. R., Jr. (1991). *Beyond race and gender: Unleashing the power of your total work force by managing diversity.* New York: AMACOM.

Thompson, J. D. (1967). *Organizations in action.* New York: McGraw-Hill.

U.S. Bureau of Labor Statistics. (2002). *Working in the 21st century.* Retrieved on September 3, 2002, from www.bls.gov/opub/working/home.htm.

von Bertalanffy, L. (1950). An outline of general system theory. *British Journal for the Philosophy of Science, 1*(2): 493–512.

Wamsley, G. L., and M. N. Zald. (1976). *The political economy of public organizations.* Bloomington: Indiana University Press.

Weber, M. (1946). *From Max Weber: Essays in sociology.* (H. H. Gerth and C. W. Mills, trans.) New York: Oxford University Press.

Weber, M. (1947). *The theory of social and economic organization.* (A. M. Henderson and T. Parsons, trans.) New York: Macmillan. (First published in 1924).

Wheatley, M. J. (1999). *Leadership and the new science: Discovering order in a chaotic world.* San Francisco: Berrett-Koehler.

8 Analyzing Human Service Organizations

OVERVIEW

Introduction

Having reviewed in the previous chapter a large variety of approaches to understanding organizations in general, we now focus our attention on human service organizations (HSOs), where most social workers are employed. These organizations have unique characteristics that distinguish them from other types, and social workers must understand these characteristics in order to employ their macro-practice skills effectively. The distinguishing features of HSOs are not always clear-cut, however, so we begin with a discussion of the ways in which these organizations are defined.

Brager and Holloway (1978) define *HSOs* as "the vast array of formal organizations that have as their stated purpose enhancement of the social, emotional, physical, and/or intellectual well-being of some component of the population" (p. 2). This definition provides a starting point, but it is not fully satisfactory in differentiating human service organizations from others. For example, manufacturing firms increase the well-being of the population by producing useful goods, but does this make them HSOs? Also, groups ranging from political lobbying firms to the Ku Klux Klan seek to promote what they perceive as the well-being of some component of the population, so does this make them HSOs? Hasenfeld (1983) addresses this question in part by noting that HSOs "work directly with and on people whose attributes they attempt to shape. People are, in a sense, their 'raw material' " (p. 1). In other words, HSOs operate in some way on the people they serve, and although they may distribute or even produce certain goods (as in a food bank or housing cooperative) their focus is on improving the quality of life of their constituents, consumers, or clients.

Still, many kinds of organizations work with or on people, and service providers from boutiques to barber shops to bistros are carefully designed to enhance at least the perceived well-being of their clients. So are these HSOs? Hasenfeld (1983) addresses this point in the second part of his definition, which specifies that HSOs "are mandated . . . to protect and to promote the welfare of the people they serve" (p. 1). In other words, these organizations are expected to conform to societal expectations (both implicit and explicit) that services are provided to clients in ways that also promote the overall welfare of the public. Agencies whose activities cannot be legitimized in the context of these expectations cannot be considered HSOs.

A great many organizations may still be encompassed within this definition, and to make sense of such variety, the most important consideration is the auspice, or sectoral location, of the organization. Human service organizations may be classified as one of three types, corresponding to the three major sectors of the economy: public, nonprofit, and for-profit. These are important distinctions because the mission, service orientation, and nature of practice within an organization vary greatly across these types. Although for-profit agencies are growing in importance as employers of social workers, public and nonprofit agencies remain the most common practice venues.

Two Vignettes of Human Service Organizations

The following vignettes illustrate the issues and problems encountered by social workers in governmental and nonprofit settings. Vignette 1 focuses on a large public agency and its development. The issues described include growth of bureaucracy, hierarchical structure, the role of elected officials, frustrations concerning slow change processes, limited creative application, and barriers to client services.

The second vignette describes a medium-sized nonprofit agency established in the early 1900s. As times change, the organization grows through the receipt of government grants and contracts. Issues related to working with boards of directors and sponsoring groups, attempts to address the needs of multiple constituencies in an increasingly regulated environment, and the use of volunteers are presented.

We hope these vignettes will show how social workers can begin to analyze circumstances in their own agencies or others with which they interact. Immediately following the vignettes we will discuss some of the issues raised and present a framework for analyzing HSOs.

Vignette 1: Canyon County Department of Child Welfare

Creating a Dynamic Organization

Canyon County Department of Child Welfare had long considered itself a unique and innovative organization. Created in the early 1960s, its initial years of development came during a time when national attention was focused on the creation of high-quality human service programs designed to address both client needs and community problems. The department's director was hired after an extensive national search. She had built a strong reputation as a person who ran successful programs and was well liked by the community, her staff, and clients.

The director took the job at Canyon County because she was excited by the challenge of building a department from scratch with more-than-adequate resources made available from federal, state, and county governments. She hired staff members who, like she, were committed to teamwork, collaboration, and problem solving. Middle managers and supervisors were professionals with many years of experience, most of whom had M.S.W. degrees, and line workers tended to be recent graduates of M.S.W. programs. In hiring interviews, the director stressed high energy, enthusiasm, collective effort, mutual support, *esprit de corps*, and competence.

From the 1960s through the 1980s, Canyon County built a reputation for high-quality services, a high rate of success, and a positive work environment. It was an organization other counties looked to for leadership in dealing with prominent problems of the time—not only child abuse and neglect but domestic violence, drug and alcohol abuse, and other family-related problems.

Dismantling a Dynamic Organization

Toward the end of the 1980s, two things happened to change the direction of the department. First, as a county in a state with one of the fastest-growing populations in the country, Canyon County doubled its population during the 1980s. Increasing fiscal and political conservatism influenced decisions of the county board of supervisors, and the child welfare budget became the focus of a major budget reduction effort. Second, the original director reached retirement age.

The board of supervisors used this opportunity to appoint a person who had spent his career in the insurance industry. The board saw this as an opportunity to introduce "hard-nosed business practices" into the running of human service programs. Because of its strong national reputation, employment at Canyon County served as a solid reference and made staff members highly marketable in other counties and states. Many managers and supervisors took advantage of this to accept other employment offers, and their positions were filled by individuals who had political connections to the board or to the director. The team approach that had dominated for two decades was replaced by a more rigid bureaucratic structure, and collegial practices were replaced by strictly enforced administrative policies.

By the end of the 1990s, the department bore little resemblance to the one that had built such a strong reputation in prior years. The most noticeable change was in the structure of the agency. Its organizational chart reflected clearly defined work units, with reporting lines from entry level all the way to the director. Standardized workloads were assigned regardless of the difficulty or complexity of cases, and standardized performance criteria were used to judge success. Individual discretion in decision making was severely limited, and employee-oriented efforts such as job rotation, job sharing, and flex-time had been eliminated.

Involvement of the County Board

Members of the county board of supervisors began to experience mounting complaints about Canyon County. Although most child maltreatment reports were investigated, many children for whom an initial report was judged invalid were later re-reported as victims of recurring abuse or neglect. Also, annual reports revealed a steady decline in the successful resolution of problems for families served by the department. Eventually, a consultant was hired to do an organizational analysis and to make recommendations to the board of supervisors.

The consultant found that the staff expressed little personal commitment to organizational objectives. Line workers felt their opinions did not matter, so most either kept comments to themselves or complained to colleagues. When problems were identified, little effort was expended to analyze them or to propose solutions. Most staff members believed that success was defined in terms of adherence to policies and procedures. Ambitious staff members who hoped for successful careers in the department became experts on internal policies, not on family problems or service provision.

Among those in management positions, the consultant found that most emphasized control. Virtually all decisions about cases had to pass through and be signed by a supervisor and administrator. Managers felt that the staff ignored their efforts to adhere to policies and procedures, especially when it came to keeping paperwork up to date. Compliance with rules and completion of required reports and forms were the main criteria by which staff members' performances were judged, and little attention was paid to the question of whether case plans were followed or successful client outcomes achieved. An ability to "do things by the book" and "not rock the boat" was viewed as being more important in assuring positive evaluations than skill in helping clients achieve case objectives.

Vignette 2: Lakeside Family Services

Historical Development

Lakeside Family Services Agency was originally incorporated as the Methodist Home for Orphaned Children in 1902. Begun by the Methodist Church, the home served children with no living relatives. Situated on a large parcel of donated land on the outskirts of a metropolitan area, the home was the site of many church gatherings as well as fund-raising events over the years. Volunteers from the church and community were part of almost every activity at the home.

During the 1920s, the home was the recipient of generous contributions from wealthy church and civic leaders, and in the 1930s, it became a Red Feather Agency. The Red Feather fund-raising campaign was the forerunner of what was now the local United Way. As campaign contributions increased, so did the scope of the home. By the mid-1940s, the home had expanded to include family counseling and services for unwed mothers, and it had hired several professionally trained social workers.

Originally, the 15-member voluntary board of directors was elected by the Annual Conference of the Methodist Church. The bylaws specified that the executive director and at least 75 percent of board members had to be members of the church. Although it was not required, most staff were also church members, and there was an active volunteer auxiliary of over 100 persons.

Major Changes Occur

During the 1970s, the board engaged in a number of controversial meetings to determine the future of the home. In addition to changing service needs, fewer and fewer orphans were present and in need of placement. The United Way was putting pressure on the home to merge with two other family service agencies in the same city, and the percentage of the home's budget that came from the Methodist Church dwindled each year, even though actual dollar amounts increased. Several board members were encouraging the home to rethink its mission and to actively seek state and federal funding. By 1980, after a decade of controversy, the home changed its name to Lakeside Family Services Agency, disaffiliated with the Methodist Church, and became a nonprofit provider of government contract services to children, families, and the aged. The agency relocated, and the property on which the home stood reverted to the church, which owned the land. Lakeside remained a United Way agency, and its funding allocations increased yearly. By the mid-1990s, however, a majority of the agency's budget (70 percent) came from government contracts and grants.

The remaining board members who had supported these changes in the agency's mission, funding, and structure were joined by persons carefully selected for their expertise in fund raising and politics. They chose an executive director with an M.S.W. and hired a director of development to search for new funds.

The agency was structured into three program components: (1) children's services, (2) family services, and (3) aging services. Each program component received funds from government contracts, along with United Way funds and private contributions, and within each component there was service diversification. For example, aging services included homemaker/chore services, home health, and adult day care.

Program directors began complaining that contract dollars never truly covered the full cost of services and that state and federal regulations were restricting their ability to provide adequate care to their respective clientele. The executive director searched for strategies to deal with these complaints and spent considerable time conferring with directors of other nonprofit organizations.

The Search for Strategies

As the recession of the early 2000s hit, Lakeside witnessed a period of government retrenchment, and the result was major cutbacks in two of its program areas. In talking with other providers, the executive director detected a new sense of competitiveness that she had not noticed before. When staff suggested using volunteers to help keep services in place, the executive director realized that the active volunteer pool of earlier days had not been nurtured and maintained. In fact, only the aging services program was using volunteers—in this case to do home visits to frail elders. Even this use was limited, because the volunteers' activities were carefully structured and greatly restricted by state regulations. At the executive director's request, the board approved a fee-for-service schedule and instructed the director of development to create a plan for recruiting fee-paying clients. Staff were angered by the agency's new focus on private fee payers, fearing this meant that the poorest clients, who were often those in greatest need, would go unserved. By 2003, the agency was in serious financial difficulty, and in desperation the executive director approached United Methodist Church officials about the possibility of taking the agency back under the Church's wing.

It is not unusual for organizations, over time, to display inconsistent or counterproductive behavior such as described in the vignettes. When this happens, it is tempting to opt for seemingly simple solutions, such as changing directors (Vignette 1) or competing for high-paying clients (Vignette 2). Changes in organizational culture do not occur rapidly, however, as prevailing attitudes and behaviors tend to permeate all levels of staff. Efforts to solve problems through sudden and dramatic change are thus seldom successful, especially if the changes conflict with the mission (perceived or actual) of the agency.

The two vignettes differ in that one organization is public and exists because of a government mandate, whereas the other evolved in the private, nonprofit sector. There are also many parallels, however. Both organizations developed in growth climates, only to face severe financial and political constraints in recent years. Whereas Canyon County became more bureaucratic, Lakeside became more professionalized. Just as rigid rules developed within Canyon County, Lakeside experienced the constraints of state and federal regulations when it began receiving more and more governmental funds. Both organizations searched for answers to complex problems that could not be easily solved. In this chapter, we propose a method of conducting organizational analyses that will enable practitioners to understand more fully what is happening in agencies such as Canyon County and Lakeside.

A Framework for Organizational Analysis

The framework we propose for analyzing organizations is presented in the form of tasks to be completed and questions to be asked within each task. Certainly no listing of tasks can be comprehensive for every type of organization, but we will attempt to cover the major elements and considerations as they relate to HSOs. Hasenfeld (1995) identifies a framework for analyzing these types of agencies that examines (1) the agency and interorganizational relationships and (2) the functioning of the organization itself. The framework recommended here uses a similar "road map" in directing the organizational analysis.

Completion of tasks associated with assessing agency-environment relationships and identifying selected elements of the organization is intended to lead to a more complete and accurate understanding of the organization as a whole. It is expected that this, in turn, will facilitate change efforts. Table 8.1 provides an overview of the framework.

The process of using the framework in Table 8.1 may be thought of as collecting information in relation to organizational boundaries (see Figure 8.1). The framework proposes (1) *identification* of the significant elements of an organization's environment and *assessment* of organization-environment relationships and (2) *understanding* the internal workings of the organization.

Task 1: Analyze the Task Environment

To describe critical elements external to the organization, we will utilize the concept of an organization's *task environment*. As noted in our review of the work of James Thompson (1967) in Chapter 7, the task environment consists of elements outside an organization that enable it to operate and that set the basic context for these operations. Thompson notes that, as originally defined by Dill (1958), the task environment includes four key components: "(1) customers (both distributors and users); (2) suppliers of materials, labor, capital, equipment, and work space;

TABLE 8.1 Framework for Assessing Organizations

Activity	Variable	Rationale
1. Identify and assess relationships with revenue sources.	Cash revenues	1. To identify sources of cash funding in an agency's task environment.
	Noncash revenues	2. To identify sources and types of revenue other than cash.
	Resource dependence	3. To assess relationships with other organizations in the agency's task environment on which it is dependent for cash and noncash revenues.
2. Identify and assess relationships with clients and referral sources.	Client characteristics	4. To profile the problems, needs, demographic characteristics, and sources to which clients are referred.
	Client funding	5. To determine how services to clients are funded and whether the full cost of services is paid.
	Domain	6. To determine whether claimed and de facto domains differ and whether boundary control is high or low.
3. Identify and assess relationships with other elements in the task environment.	Environmental demand	7. To understand how the agency responds to demands from regulatory agencies, professional organizations, and the general public.
	Competition/ Cooperation	8. To assess the agency's cooperation and competition with other agencies.
4. Identify corporate authority and mission.	Corporate authority	9. To identify the agency's legal basis and reason for existence.
5. Understand program structure and management style.	Structure	10. To assess formal organization, patterns of informal authority, and job design in the agency.
	Managerial style	11. To determine what theoretical model best describes the management style in the agency.
6. Assess the organization's programs and services.	Accountability	12. To assess how service efficiency, quality, and effectiveness are measured and used in decision making.
7. Assess personnel policies, procedures, and practices.	Employee relations	13. To identify how staff are recruited, trained, evaluated, and retained or terminated.

(continued)

TABLE 8.1 (Continued)

Activity	Variable	Rationale
8. Assess adequacy of technical resources and systems.	Budget management	14. To determine the budgeting method in the agency and its means of calculating and assessing unit costs.
	Technical resources	15. To assess facilities, equipment, and computer/information technology.

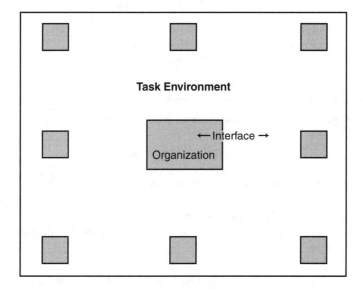

FIGURE 8.1 Organization, Task Environment, and Interface

(3) competitors for both markets and resources; and (4) regulatory groups, including governmental agencies, unions, and inter-firm associations" (pp. 27–28). These are illustrated in Figure 8.2.

Hasenfeld (1995) proposes a slightly different model that includes three components: (1) a generalized agency environment (organizations, entities, and systems important to the agency); (2) market relations with entities that receive an agency's outputs and with those offering complementary or competing services; and (3) regulatory groups. Martin (1980) also identifies environmental entities important to HSOs. In his model, the most critical of these elements are (1) funding sources, (2) sources of noncash revenues, (3) clients and client sources, and (4) other constituents.

We will draw on the preceding works and will distill Martin's four elements into two key variables to be used in analyzing an organization's task environment: (1) cash and noncash revenues and (2) clients and other constituents, including regulatory groups.

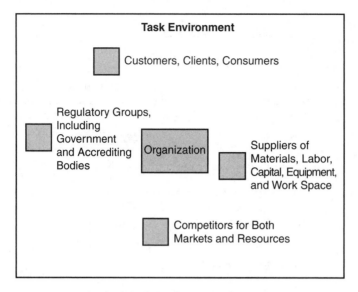

FIGURE 8.2   Typical Task Environment for an Organization

Identify and Assess Relationships with Revenue Sources

Cash Revenues.   Questions to be explored for this activity include:

- What are the agency's funding sources?
- How much and what percentage of the agency's total funds are received from each source?

A cynical variation on the Golden Rule states that "those who have the gold make the rules." There is a certain element of truth to this, especially in the operation of most organizations. Understanding how an agency is financed is often essential to understanding the agency itself. However, this process can be difficult in light of the fact that modern HSOs typically obtain funds from a multitude of sources. Moreover, most organizations do not make detailed funding information readily available except in cases where public funds are used and budget documents are, by law, a matter of public record.

The first step in analyzing organizational funding is to determine the sources from which funds are acquired. The following list details those sources for HSOs.

Major Revenue Sources for Human Service Organizations
1. Government funds
   - Direct government appropriation
   - Government purchase-of-service contracts
   - Government grants
   - Matching funds
   - Tax benefits

2. Donated funds
   - Direct charitable contributions (from individuals, groups, and associations such as religious groups)
   - Indirect contributions (e.g., via United Way)
   - Private grants (e.g., foundation funds)
   - Endowments
3. Fees for service
   - Direct payments from clients
   - Payments from third parties (e.g., private or public insurers)
4. Other agency income
   - Investments (e.g., interest, dividends, royalties)
   - Profit-making subsidiaries
   - Fund-raising events and appeals

As might be expected, the sources of its funds greatly influence an organization's flexibility in how it responds to proposed change. Governmental agencies that depend totally on direct appropriations are likely to have most of their activities rigidly specified by public policy. Nonprofit agencies tend to receive funds from a greater variety of sources and thus may have greater flexibility, but even donated funds usually come with strings attached. For-profit agencies that depend on paying clients also have greater flexibility than public agencies, but their decision making is guided foremost by the requirement that they return profits for their investors.

Direct appropriations are virtually the exclusive source of revenues for organizations at the federal level. This source is also primary for many state, county, and local agencies, but these organizations also make use of a mixture of funds from higher levels of government. In general, the lower the level of government, the larger the number of funding sources from which organizations at that level are likely to draw revenues. Among the most important mechanisms for dissemination are *block grants* (lump-sum appropriations in which specific allocations are left to local governments), *matching funds* (which, for example, provide a certain amount of federal funds for each dollar expended by state-level agencies), and *grant programs* in which funds are targeted for a specific use and are restricted to that program. In the vignette regarding Canyon County earlier in this chapter, the Child Welfare Department was funded solely by government funds, although from a combination of direct appropriations, block grants, and matching funds.

Nonprofit agencies, such as Lakeside Family Services in Vignette 2, tend to have a greater range of funding sources. Moreover, although by definition these are the agencies toward which most charitable contributions are targeted, such contributions usually make up only a small portion of the annual budget of most nonprofit agencies. The most recent figures available show that in 1997, nonprofit organizations garnered an average of 20 percent of their funds from charitable contributions (down from 26 percent in 1977); 38 percent from dues, fees, and charges; 31 percent from government sources (up from 27 percent in 1977); and 11 percent from other sources (Independent Sector, 2001).

In a study that focused specifically on nonprofit HSOs, we found the average distribution across funding sources to be 34 percent from government contracts, 33 percent from charitable donations, 13 percent from client fees, 10 percent from public grants, 5 percent from private grants, and 5 percent from other sources (McMurtry, Netting, & Kettner 1991). *Government contract funds* are those in which a nonprofit or for-profit agency contracts with a public agency to provide specific services to specific clients. When these funds were combined with those acquired from public grants, it meant that the average agency in our study drew almost half its funds (44 percent) from the government, and some reported receiving all funds from these sources. This suggests that many human service agencies, although nominally part of the nonprofit sector, can more accurately be viewed as quasi-public agencies.

More recently, Boris (1998) examined revenue sources of nonprofit organizations and found they received 19 percent from private contributions, 32 percent from government sources, 10 percent from other sources, and a surprising 39 percent—the largest single share—from commercial activities (ranging from client fees for services to revenues from sales of various merchandise). This represents an important change from the earlier data indicating that governmental funds were the most important revenue source for nonprofit agencies, and it raises questions as to whether some of them should be viewed not as quasi-public but quasi-for-profit organizations. For some observers (Froelich, 1999; Gronbjerg, 2001), it also poses concerns about the long-term viability of the traditional role of the nonprofit sector. As Weisbrod (1998) asks, "Can nonprofits simultaneous mimic private enterprise and perform their social missions?" (p. 167).

For-profit firms are a growing arena for social work practice, and among such organizations as hospitals and nursing homes they are major service providers. Stoesz (1988) notes that in the middle 1980s two hospital corporations each had revenues exceeding all charitable contributions collected nationwide by the United Way that year. By 2002, 35 health-care companies were on the *Fortune 500* list of the largest commercial firms in the United States (*Fortune Magazine*, 2002), and all but two of these 35 had annual revenues exceeding the $3.95 billion in charitable donations raised by United Way nationally in its 2001–2002 campaign (United Way of America, 2002). Other areas in which large human service corporations have developed include child care, home-based nursing care, and corrections. Also, private counseling firms, although traditionally small in scale, are a part of this sector. All these organizations share a principal reliance on fee-for-service revenues.

Sometimes these fees are paid directly by the agency's clients, but most client fees are paid by other organizations. This can mean that consumers themselves are a less important part of the task environment of private agencies than their insurance companies and other third-party payers who establish criteria and rates for reimbursement. For example, a for-profit counseling agency may draw most of its clients from the employee assistance program of a nearby manufacturing plant, thus relationships with the manufacturer are likely to be the key environmental consideration for the counseling agency.

In general, a critical point in understanding funding sources is that most funds come with strings attached, and decisions on how to spend them may rest much more with the funding agency than with the recipient. This means, using governmental organizations as an example, that a county agency that appears to be subject to local decision-making processes may in fact be more accurately viewed as a local extension of the state agency that provides the bulk of its funds. A change episode that attempted to influence the use of these funds would be unlikely to succeed unless the persons seeking change recognized that decision-making power over the funds rested with organizations in the agency's task environment rather than inside its own boundaries.

The number of sources from which an agency's funds are drawn is also a key consideration. Somewhat paradoxically, an agency with many funding sources often has greater autonomy and flexibility than one with few, because the loss of any single source is less likely to jeopardize the overall viability of the organization. On the other hand, the greater the number of funding sources, the more complex the agency's operations become. With each new source comes another layer of regulatory constraints, program diversity, and accountability expectations. The agency with a single funding source may risk becoming rigid and highly specialized, but the agency with many sources may have difficulty defining or focusing on its mission.

Noncash Revenues.   Questions to be explored for this activity include:

- Does the organization use volunteers? If yes, how many and for what purposes?
- Are appropriate efforts made to match volunteers' skills and abilities to the tasks assigned?
- What materials and in-kind resources (e.g., food, clothing, physical facilities, etc.) does the organization receive?
- What tax benefits does the organization receive?

In considering resources, it should be noted that actual dollars coming into an HSO are not its only form of resources. Many other assets on which agencies rely are less obvious than cash revenues but sometimes equally important. Three such assets are volunteers, in-kind contributions, and tax benefits.

Volunteers have traditionally been a mainstay of human service organizations. As noted in Chapter 2, the entire nonprofit human service sector originated with the activities of individual volunteers who began to work together in order to make their efforts more productive. In the Lakeside vignette presented earlier in this chapter, volunteers were critical to the organization's early development. Today, the contribution of these individuals to HSOs is enormous. In the year 1998 (the most recent for which figures are available), 109 million adult Americans, accounting for 55.5 percent of the adult population (up from 48 percent in 1994) volunteered an average of 3.5 hours per week of their time. This represents the equivalent of 9.3 million full-time employees and equates to a monetary value of

$225.9 billion. Roughly 11 percent of all volunteer time was devoted to health-related organizations, and just under 16 percent was given to human services (Independent Sector, 2001).

Volunteers span almost all age ranges and perform a vast array of tasks, from serving meals in senior centers to sitting on boards of directors of counseling agencies, to staffing crisis hotlines. Some agencies rely on volunteers to provide supplementary services that undergird or enhance the work of professional staff, as in hospitals, whereas in other agencies most services are provided directly by volunteers themselves, as in Big Brothers or Big Sisters programs. Volunteers also bring with them a wide range of knowledge and skills, and many organizations that rely heavily on the work of volunteers employ part-time or full-time volunteer coordinators. In addition to supervising activities, coordinators also seek to match volunteers' skills to the tasks needing to be done. Their success in achieving this can have a dramatic effect on the productivity, satisfaction, and service longevity of each volunteer.

A second type of resource is *in-kind contributions* of material goods. Examples include food, clothing, physical facilities, real estate, vehicles, and a wide variety of household and office materials. In some cases, these goods are provided for use directly by the agency; in others, they are donated for the purpose of resale in order to generate cash revenues, or they are simply passed through the agency for distribution directly to clients. In each circumstance, the total value of these resources to organizations is substantial. Specific figures are difficult to obtain, but one clue to the magnitude of this source of income is offered by deductions on individual income taxes claimed for noncash charitable contributions. In 1999, more than 18 million individual filers claimed noncash charitable contributions, the monetary value of which exceeded $37.4 billion dollars (Internal Revenue Service, 1999).

Tax benefits are particularly important for private, nonprofit HSOs. Indeed, one defining characteristic of nonprofit agencies is an official designation as a charitable organization under section 501(c)(3) of federal Internal Revenue Service regulations. Meeting the requirements of this section allows nonprofit agencies to avoid income taxes that for-profit firms must pay, and this can be a critical benefit in service arenas such as health care, where nonprofit and for-profit hospitals often engage in intense competition for patients and physicians. Tax laws are also important in terms of their effects on other revenue sources, especially charitable contributions. For example, Karger and Stoesz (2002) note that the Tax Reform Act of 1986 may have reduced contributions to nonprofit agencies by limiting tax breaks for contributors to those who itemize deductions on their tax returns. Tax deductions claimed for cash contributions (including prior-year carryover amounts) totaled just under $100 billion in 1999 (Internal Revenue Service, 1999), and it is likely that this source of funds for HSOs would drop precipitously if changes in tax laws were to make charitable contributions no longer deductible. Karger and Stoesz also note that contributions would likely be higher if taxpayers who do not itemize were allowed to deduct the value of their charitable contributions, as was the case before the 1986 tax revisions.

Noncash resources are important considerations in an organizational analysis because an agency's behaviors may be understood as efforts to acquire and maximize these assets. For example, an organization that relies heavily on volunteers may seek to protect this resource even if in doing so it comes into conflict with the interests of professional staff. Similarly, the structure of an agency may be altered to take advantage of one of these resources, as with the large number of nonprofit agencies that have begun raising funds by collecting donated material goods and reselling them through thrift stores. Attention to noncash resources may also be important in initiating change efforts. For example, some organizational problems are often left unaddressed due to pessimism about the ability to obtain revenues to add or augment services, and a change agent's awareness of the possibilities offered by the use of noncash resources may be key to overcoming this barrier. Using a tool such as the one depicted in Table 8.2 can be helpful in assessing the status of cash and noncash resources for an organization.

Relationships with Revenue Sources. The question to be explored for this activity is:

- What is the quality of the relationship between funding sources and the agency?

The concept of *resource dependence* refers to the fact that, because organizations are open systems, they must rely on elements in their environment from

TABLE 8.2 Tool for Assessing Cash and Noncash Resources

Sources of Cash Revenues	% of Revenue	Flexibility in Using Resources
Contract with state department of social services	26	Low
Client fees	22	High
Charitable donations	14	High
Government grant	8	Low
Other	30	Depends

Sources of Noncash Revenues	Description
Volunteers	9 board of directors 33 respite care for foster parents 12 transportation providers
In-kind	1 van 1 branch office
Tax benefits	$120,000 annually in savings from nonprofit status

which they can obtain resources needed for survival. Being dependent on these elements, organizations seek to establish relationships that minimize uncertainty concerning the availability of resources. Relationships with elements in the task environment involve exchanges of funds, clients, or services, and exchanges are always reciprocal to some degree (Thompson, 1967). Exchanges may be relatively equal ones that benefit both organizations and in which each member holds similar power, but they may still occur even if inequality exists and one organization holds more power and benefits more than the other.

Elements of the resource dependence model can also be used to describe some of the dynamics of client selection. The model posits that external bodies upon which an organization depends for vital resources are often more powerful determinants of organizational actions than internal factors (Pfeffer & Salancik, 1978). Within this model, clients can be seen as one of a variety of resources (funds, qualified staff, favorable locations) for which agencies compete.

Still, cash funding, for better or worse, is central to the consideration of resources. The extent and consequences of external control are affected both by the source of funds and the circumstances of the agency acquiring them. For example, Hardina (1990) studied the funding base of 53 organizations to determine the relationship between clients' access to service and agencies' relative reliance on various funding sources. Results showed that agencies restricted to grassroots funding (primarily local donations) were less able than those who drew funds from outside the community to establish and maintain reliable service availability. In general, the greater the variety of funding, the greater the fiscal health and service flexibility of the organization. The exception was government funds, which were found to limit service flexibility and client self-help, stiffen eligibility requirements, and reduce citizen participation.

Wardell (1988), in a study of youth programs, developed four propositions embodying the dynamics resource dependence:

1. An organization's survival is a function of its ability to learn and adapt to changing environmental contingencies.
2. The degree of an organization's dependence on some element of its task environment is (a) directly related to the organization's need for resources which that element can provide, and (b) inversely related to the ability of other elements to provide the same resource.
3. Organizations which are perceived as threatening to an existing organizational configuration will evoke defensive reactions by established local organizations.
4. The persistence (or survival) of an organization over time is directly related to the degree of formalization it attains in exchange agreements with other organizations constituting its task environment. (pp. 92–93)

Lewis and Crook (2001) illustrate some of these principles in their description of states' responses to increased costs of drugs to AIDS patients. In responding to a combination of increased demand and caps on federal funding, many states acted by limiting new client enrollment, capping funds made available for drugs, restricting the quantity of drugs allowed to be prescribed, increasing client co-

TABLE 8.3 Assessing the Relationship to Funding Sources

Relevant Funding Sources	Nature of Communication, Length of Relationship, Changes in Funding
Contract with state department of social services	Quarterly site visits; have contracted for 12 years; funding has always stayed steady or increased
Client fees	Most clients are seen on a weekly basis; they either pay directly or through their insurance plan; client fees have declined 2 percent in the past three years.
Charitable donations	Largest donations come from church groups; agency staff visit church representatives once a year; donations have increased 3.5 percent in the past year.

payments, and other measures. The tool depicted in Table 8.3 summarizes these and other points and can be helpful in assessing agencies' relationships with revenue sources.

Identify and Assess Relationships with Clients and Referral Sources. Questions to be explored for this activity include:

- What client groups does this organization serve?
- What are the demographic characteristics of clients?
- What percentages of clients pay full fees, partial fees, no fees, or are covered by contract revenues?
- What are the major sources of client referrals?

Understanding a client population begins with identifying the problems and needs they are experiencing and the services that are being provided. Programs and services provided by an HSO should be seen as responses to a community need. When a community suffers from a problem of dependent, abused, and neglected children, for example, child welfare agencies respond by providing both in-home and out-of-home services.

In attempting to understand a client population as a part of the task environment, it is important to understand (1) what problems are being addressed (e.g., family violence, depression, economic stress); (2) clients' beliefs about the etiology (cause-and-effect relationships) of the problem; (3) community perspectives on the etiology of the problem; and (4) how well client and community needs and expectations are being addressed.

This assessment requires background research and data collection, often through interviews with key informants. Results can provide the change agent with a sense of how relevant, important, and valued an agency's services are to both the client population and the community.

Another useful step toward understanding the client population is to produce a demographic profile. This profile typically includes factors such as age, gender, cultural/ethnic group, marital status, educational background, and other important variables. It is important to understand the degree of demographic homogeneity or diversity among clients, and to compare client demographics with those of the population in need. This comparison will provide a basis for understanding the quality of agency-community relationships. For example, how an agency is perceived by the African American community or by the gay, lesbian, and bisexual community in terms of its ability to meet their needs can be critical to future agency appeals for funding or other types of support.

Also of importance in understanding the client population is the financial relationship between client and agency. In commercial firms, customers are those who purchase goods or services, and these organizations carefully design their outputs to meet the needs of this group. In HSOs, however, those who pay for services often are not the same as those who receive them. This is an important distinction, and for our purposes, we will define the *clients of HSOs* as those who are direct recipients of services.

Within this definition, clients can be divided into two groups. The first group, *full-pay clients,* are those who are able to pay the agency (either personally or through third-party reimbursement) an amount equal to or greater than the cost of their services. Full-pay clients are important resources that agencies seek to attract and are most likely to serve. Revenues from full-pay clients are typically used to offset the cost of serving other clients in a nonprofit agency.

The second group, *non-full-pay clients,* consists of those who are able to pay less than the cost of their services—whether in part or not at all (Netting, McMurtry, Kettner, & Jones-McClintic, 1990). Because revenues for serving these clients must be generated from other sources (e.g., charitable funds, profits earned from serving full-pay clients, and other means), agencies often tend not to seek these clients and/or to erect eligibility barriers to restrict their numbers.

Still, agencies must have clients in order to fulfill their mission and function, so sources of client referrals are important elements in the task environments of HSOs. Formal and informal referral arrangements among agencies for exchange of clients are often viewed as being of equal importance as relationships with funding sources. As an example, residential treatment centers for youth are dependent on client referrals from family counseling centers, juvenile courts, school districts, and other agencies. Table 8.4 depicts a tool that may be helpful in identifying client populations and referral sources.

Relationships with Referral Sources.   Questions to be explored for this activity include:

- What is the organization's domain (specifically, for what types of expertise is the agency recognized?)

- Does the agency claim a larger domain than it serves?
- Does demand for services outstrip supply or is there unused capacity?
- What types of clients does the organization refuse (e.g., are there disproportionate numbers of poor, elderly, persons of color, women, persons with disabilities, gays/lesbians, or other groups that are typically underserved?)?

A useful concept for understanding agency-client-community relationships,
taken from the systems framework, is the notion of organizational domain (Levine
& White, 1961). A *domain* refers to what the organization does and whom it serves,
and it is the means by which the organization establishes its role or niche within
the environment.

Domain setting refers to the process by which organizations establish themselves and their roles among others within their task environment. One part of the
process is domain legitimation, in which the organization wins acknowledgment

TABLE 8.4 **Identifying Client Populations and Referral Sources**

Client Groups Served

1. Couples/individuals relinquishing children
2. Couples wanting to adopt
3. Foster parent applications
4. Foster parents
5. Individuals in need of personal counseling
6. Families in need of counseling
7. Drug abusers

Demographic Makeup of Client Population

Age	%	Ethnicity	%	Gender	%	Fees	%
Under 20	5	American Indian	3	Female	64	Full pay	26
20–29	15	African American	14	Male	36	Some pay	38
30–39	22	Asian American	4			No pay	15
40–49	29	Hispanic	19			Contract	21
50–59	19	White	60				
60–69	8						
70+	2						

Referral Sources	%
School counselors/teachers	31
Clergy	22
Social service agencies	19
Physicians and clinics	15
Attorneys	13

of claims it makes as to its sphere of activities and expertise. Legitimation is not always immediately forthcoming, and there is usually a disparity between what an organization says are its boundaries (the *claimed domain*) and what these boundaries actually are (the *de facto domain*) (Greenley & Kirk, 1973).

Claims regarding domains tend to evolve along with circumstances in the environment. Agencies seek to take advantage of available resources, and most are constantly adjusting their domains as a means of doing so. Funding trends from charitable or governmental sources are usually closely watched, and in order to ensure resource flow, agencies may attempt to compete for funds in areas where they have little experience or expertise.

As noted earlier, clients are also resources, though an individual client may be viewed as either an asset or a liability, depending on whether the client fits within the agency's domain and whether he or she can pay for services. Recognizing this dynamic, a long-standing concern relative to agencies' relationships with clients is whether certain groups of clients, especially the most needy, are deliberately excluded from access to services (Cloward & Epstein, 1965). Research results have suggested that this may indeed be the case.

In one early study, Kirk and Greenley (1974) examined clients' efforts to obtain services. Their results showed that only 47 of every 100 clients were served by the first two agencies they visited; the rest were either rejected or referred elsewhere. In a companion piece, Greenley and Kirk (1973) analyzed the dynamics of these outcomes and identified domain selection as a key factor. Because most agencies had larger claimed domains than de facto domains, they attracted clients that they were unable to serve. This disparity was apparently seen as desirable by many agencies, since it provided a sort of cushion and afforded the opportunity to select only the best-fitting, full-pay clients. This process is known as *creaming*.

In addition, important distinctions appeared between organizations with respect to *boundary control*, which refers to the ability of the agency to reject clients it does not wish to serve. Agencies with high boundary control (usually for-profit and high-prestige nonprofit organizations) were those most likely to engage in creaming, leaving clients who were rejected with the task of finding agencies that had low boundary control. This resulted in clients with the greatest difficulties and the least ability to pay having as their only option those agencies that were already the most overcrowded and had the fewest available resources (Greenley & Kirk, 1973). In a study of services to homeless clients, Sosin (2001) also documented the presence of these dynamics.

Boundary control is generally highest in for-profit organizations, where the primary goal is making money, and lowest in governmental organizations, which are intended to provide a safety net for clients who cannot obtain services elsewhere. However, since the early 1980s, governmental policies have favored *privatization*—the shifting of more services to the private sector. A guiding assumption has been that private-sector organizations can provide services more efficiently and effectively than large governmental bureaucracies, and that, in the case of nonprofit organizations, they can also draw on their traditional commitments to the poor to ensure that these clients are served.

Unfortunately, a number of studies suggest that this trend has often led to service reductions or restrictions, particularly on the part of nonprofit agencies. Among the reasons for these cutbacks have been changes in governmental rules (Berg & Wright, 1981) and delays in reimbursement for contract services (Kramer & Grossman, 1987). Gronbjerg (1990) studied the effects of changing governmental policies on nonprofit agencies in the Chicago area. She found that services often diminished because these policies misunderstood the nature of the private sector, noting,

> These [policies] were unrealistic because only a few nonprofit organizations focus on the poor and their problems, and relatively few made significant efforts to move in that direction during the early to mid-1980s. Nonprofit organizations are not as responsive to the poor as public stereotypes might suggest, probably because they have enough to do without focusing on the poor and their difficult problems. [The policies] falsely assumed that nonprofit organizations have a strong commitment to the poor that is independent of the incentives provided by government funding. (pp. 228–229)

Human service agencies adjust their boundaries according to a wide range of factors, and a misunderstanding of these may lead to critical service gaps. One key criterion in boundary setting is the nature of the clients themselves, and being poor or having complex, long-standing problems are characteristics that simultaneously increase the level of need yet decrease the likelihood of being served. Table 8.5 provides a tool that may be helpful in assessing an agency's relationship to client populations and referral sources.

Identify and Assess Relationships with Other Elements in the Task Environment. Questions to be explored for this activity include:

- What state and federal regulatory bodies oversee programs provided by this organization?

TABLE 8.5   Assessing Relationships with Clients and Referral Sources

Client Population	Supply vs. Demand	Unserved/Underserved
Adoptive couples/ children available	5 couples for every child available	Special needs children
Foster homes/ children in need	1.5 children in need for every home available	Special needs children
Families in need of counseling	2- to 3-week waiting list	Non-English-speaking families
Drug abusers	3-month waiting list	Poor, no pay, low pay, uninsured

- With what government agencies does this organization contract for service provision?
- What professional associations, labor unions, or accrediting bodies influence agency operations?
- What are the perceptions of the "general public" in terms of the relevance, value, and quality of agency services?

Within an organization's task environment are groups that do not necessarily provide resources but set the context in which the agency operates. One example is regulatory bodies that are responsible for establishing the boundaries of acceptable service practices. Many of these are governmental licensing agencies that inspect and certify both the physical environment and services of organizations such as nursing homes, child-care institutions, and residential treatment facilities. Others are government contracting agencies that often require provider agencies to conform to detailed procedural guidelines in order to be reimbursed for the services they deliver. Still others are local, state, and federal revenue departments that levy taxes and monitor financial accounting procedures. Extensive accounting and funding-usage requirements are imposed as well by nongovernmental funding sources such as the United Way.

Organizations such as professional associations, labor unions, and accrediting bodies further help to establish the regulatory boundaries of practice. Unlike those just mentioned, however, the influence of these organizations is often exerted through individuals within the agency rather than on the organization as a whole. Standards established in the National Association of Social Workers (NASW) Code of Ethics and for members of the Academy of Certified Social Workers (ACSW), for example, govern the activities of staff who are members of these bodies. State licensing agencies impose similar constraints, and organizations with a high proportion of employees who meet these requirements may function differently than those with relatively few. Accrediting bodies such as the Joint Commission on Accreditation of Health Care Organizations (JCAHO) have the power to determine whether organizations will be allowed to continue in an accredited status. Loss of this status can adversely affect funding, referrals, and continued viability as an organization.

The "general public" is another part of this set of constituents. By their nature, HSOs are dependent on some form of social sanction for their activities, and loss of public support may jeopardize their existence. Unfortunately, views of members of the general public are not always apparent. Moreover, public opinion is seldom unanimous, so organizations must often determine which of a wide variety of expressed views represents the predominant attitude. Finally, agencies may also be forced at times to stand against public opinion, as in the case of advocacy organizations that must confront ignorance or discrimination against particular clients or client groups.

Within the task environment, public opinion is often conveyed through a bewildering diversity of elements. These include elected representatives, interest groups, civic organizations, and others. In addition, funding sources are indirect but nonetheless important indicators of public views. Patterns in the ebb and flow of charitable donations, for example, suggest both general levels of public concern and particular problems toward which this concern is directed (as do the priorities of private foundations). Finally, mass media outlets are critical purveyors of public attitudes, although by their nature they often emphasize the most extreme rather than the most typical opinions.

Child protective services offer an example of the relationship between agencies, public opinion, and mass media (as both a carrier and shaper of public opinion). Deciding whether to remove an at-risk child from his or her home involves a delicate balancing act between concern for the child's well-being and concern for parental rights. In one well-publicized case in Washington state, for example, the fatal abuse of a child led to public outcry, which resulted in legislative changes that instructed protective service workers to favor the safety of the child in such decisions. However, publicity about cases in other locations has featured allegations of "child snatching" by protective service workers, which led to legislative imposition of stricter guidelines governing the removal of children.

Cordes and Henig (2001) call attention to how shifts in public opinion affect where and how funds are allocated. In particular, they make note of new methods of giving that allow contributors to more actively select the agencies and causes they wish to support. This provides greater freedom on the part of the giver, but it may also diminish the effectiveness of umbrella organizations, such as the United Way, in assessing community needs broadly and distributing funds based on those assessments.

The key point is that public opinion is dynamic rather than static, and similar agencies at different times or in different places may encounter widely divergent attitudes and expectations. Identifying the task environment is thus an ongoing process as public attitudes change and funding methods evolve. A tool such as the one depicted in Table 8.6 can be used to help identify important elements in the agency's task environment.

Assessing Relationships with Other Elements. Questions to be explored for this activity include:

- What other agencies provide the same services to the same clientele as this organization?
- With whom does the organization compete?
- With whom does the organization cooperate? Is the organization part of a coalition or an alliance?
- How is the organization perceived by regulatory bodies, government contracting agencies, professional organizations, accrediting bodies, and the general public in relation to its peers and competitors?

One further critical element in an organization's environment is other service providers. Relationships among agencies that occupy each others' task environments can be competitive, cooperative, or a mixture of the two, depending on the circumstances.

TABLE 8.6 **Identifying Other Important Organizations**

Other Important Organizations	Programs Affected
Regulatory	
State Department of Child Welfare	Day care
County Health Department	Day care
Contracts	
State Department of	Respite Care
Developmental Disabilities	Vocational training
Professional associations	
National Association of Social Workers	Individual and family counseling
American Psychological Association	
Accreditation	
Council on Accreditation	Individual and family counseling
General public	
Media accounts (past 3 years)	Drug and alcohol programs
Advocacy groups	

In Chapter 6, Table 6.4 delineated five levels of interaction leading to improved programming. These levels were communication, cooperation, coordination, collaboration, and consolidation. The levels can be used to assess how an HSO relates to other members of its task environment.

Competitive relationships characterize circumstances in which two or more agencies seek the same resources (clients, funds, volunteers, etc.) from the same sources. Nonprofit agencies compete among themselves for charitable donations as well as government and private foundation grants. McMurtry and colleagues (1991) found that nonprofit agencies reported that their greatest competition for both funds and clients came from other nonprofits rather than from for-profit organizations. However, substantial and still-evolving competition is also taking place between nonprofit and for-profit agencies in areas such as welfare-to-work transitions (Alexander, Nank, & Stivers, 1999; Frumkin & Andre-Clark, 2000). In this case, the competition targets mostly contract-eligible clients, but in other settings, the focus is on fee-for-service clients.

Direct competition for funds is not inevitable, however. Cooperative arrangements are also common, as in the case of referral agreements between agencies, which are used as a means of exchanging clients that do not fit the referring agency but are considered resources by the agency to whom they are referred. Agencies have also developed large-scale coalition-building efforts designed to improve their ability to meet client needs (Mizrahi & Rosenthal, 2001). Others have developed community-oriented cooperative arrangements to ensure more complete service coverage within particular areas (Dunlop & Angell, 2001). Factors contributing to this behavior include community awareness of service needs, resource scarcity, the capacity of local governments to coordinate these arrangements, and the fact that many contracts now mandate collaboration and interagency coordination.

The final assessment of agency-community relationships, then, has to do with how the agency is perceived relative to its peers and competitors. In what light do regulatory agencies, accrediting bodies, government contracting agencies, professional associations, the media, and the general public view this organization? Is it seen as a valued part of a community service network? Is it seen as self-serving and unconcerned about its community? Or do community members see it as too controversial, or, in contrast, too timid in responding to emerging needs? Assessing these perceptions assumes that the agency has some sort of a track record in the community, and that key informants are willing to share perceptions of how the agency fits into the overall community service network. A tool such as the one depicted in Table 8.7 can assist in assessing an organization's relationships to others in its task environment.

Task 2: Analyze the Organization Internally

Analysis of organizations, like analysis of communities, requires a breakdown of a large, complex entity into elements. The objective is to identify the points or locations within the organization that help to explain organizational strengths and to understand its weaknesses or problem areas. Each element should be approached in terms of how it relates or does not relate to identified problems, with the goal of understanding how interactions among elements support or fail to support the continuation of problems.

For an illustration of organizational analysis, let us return to the examples of the Canyon County Department of Child Welfare and the Lakeside Family Services Agency presented at the beginning of this chapter. When public organizations such as Canyon County experience problems in productivity, in quality of client service, in morale, or in worker-management relationships, it would not be unusual for an oversight body such as the county board of supervisors to hire a management consultant to do an analysis of the department. Similarly, in a non-

TABLE 8.7   Relationships with Other Service Providers

Other Agencies Providing Service

State Department of Child Welfare	Collaborative
Central City Family Services	Competitive
Counseling Advocates, Inc.	Competitive
New Foundations	Collaborative
Baptist Family Services	Collaborative
Etc. . . .	

profit organization such as Lakeside that has become more professional, that has become dependent on government funds, whose mission has evolved, and which is now experiencing cutbacks in funding, a consultant is often engaged by the board of directors to study the organization and recommend strategies needed for it to regain economic self-sufficiency.

A plausible scenario is that consultants—after interviewing representative staff, consumers, board members, and others—would be able to document the problems identified in the vignettes, pose reasons for the presence of the problems (working hypotheses), and recommend solutions or remedies. Using such an approach, consultants are often misled into recommending short-term solutions such as staff development and training, employee incentive programs, morale-building activities such as social events, relationship-building activities between management and staff, attempts to humanize the chief executive officer, or other such actions. These steps rarely solve the kinds of fundamental problems that brought about the use of a management consultant in the first place.

An alternative approach to organizational analysis is to conduct a systematic examination of a number of organizational elements. These elements might include (1) organizational mission; (2) organizational structure, including location, management, staffing of programs and services, and workload; (3) goals and objectives of programs; (4) adequacy of funding; (5) personnel policies and practices; (6) management style; and (7) problem-solving and communication patterns, along with other such characteristics of the agency. Within each element one could examine ideal models or optimal levels of functioning as illustrated in current theoretical or research literature. From the ideal, the review can then proceed to an examination of data and documentation that depict the actual situation, and finally to an examination of the gaps between ideal and real. The goal is to find underlying causes as definitively as possible in the interest of solving long-term problems and avoiding merely treating symptoms.

In this section we propose a framework for analysis that identifies elements to be examined within an organization, explores relevant theoretical frameworks, identifies the questions to be answered, and proposes data and documentation to be collected or examined. The elements addressed include:

1. Corporate authority and mission
2. Administrative, management, and leadership style
3. Organizational and program structure
4. Planning, delivery, and evaluation of programs and services
5. Personnel policies and practices
6. Adequacy of technology and resources

Identify Corporate Authority and Mission.   Questions to be explored for this activity include:

- What is the basis for and extent of the organization's corporate authority?
- What is its mission?

- Is the organization operating in a manner that is consistent with its authority and mission?
- To what extent is the mission supported by staff who perform different roles within the organization?
- Are policies and procedures consistent with mission and authority?

As described earlier in this chapter, a basic step toward understanding any organization is understanding its domain. An agency's corporate authority forms the legal basis for its operations, which constitutes one of the boundaries that define its domain. If the organization is public (governmental), its legal basis is established in statute or executive order. If it is private, its legal basis rests in articles of incorporation. In some situations it can be important to examine these documents firsthand rather than accept secondary reports. Cases occur in which organizations are incorporated for one purpose (and perhaps even funded through a trust that specifies that purpose, such as the running of an orphanage as in the example of Lakeside Family Services), but over the years new populations and services, such as help for pregnant teens, are added to the mission. This expansion can reach a point where the agency begins operating outside its legally authorized area.

A statement of mission specifies the problems or needs to be addressed, populations to be served, and, in general terms, client outcomes to be expected. Mission statements are relatively permanent expressions of the reasons for existence of an agency, and they are not expected to change unless the organization's fundamental reason for existence also changes. Lack of clarity in a mission statement or differences between mission and activities can be indicators of a problem. For example, Lakeside Family Services is a prime candidate for reexamining its original mission, which was established in the early 1900s when orphanages and the need for them were common. If Lakeside has not revised this mission, it seems safe to say that its stated reason for existence no longer reflects what it actually does. Rethinking the mission and what the organization wants to be can begin the process of redirecting operations.

Peters and Waterman (1982) are unequivocal in their commitment to the notion of shared vision as integral to the success of an organization. Without some common understanding of mission and direction, individuals and groups will inevitably begin to work at cross-purposes. With a shared vision there may still be differences about strategies, but a commitment to the same ends or outcomes will remain. Results from a study by Yeatts, Pillai, and Stanley-Stevens (2001) in for-profit organizations illustrates the importance of goal clarity at the team level, and this applies to the full organization as well.

Some of the more important documentation and data sources to be examined in understanding corporate authority and mission include:

1. Articles of incorporation, statutes, or executive orders
2. Mission statement
3. Bylaws of the organization

4. Minutes of selected board meetings
5. Interviews with selected administrators, managers, and staff

Table 8.8 depicts a tool that can help in assessing agencies' corporate authority and mission.

Understand Program Structure and Management Style.   Questions to be explored for this activity include:

■ What are the major departmental or program units on the organizational chart?
■ What is the rationale for the existing organizational structure?
■ Is this the most logical structure? Is it consistent with and supportive of the mission?
■ Is supervision logical and capable of performing expected functions? Are staff capable of performing expected functions?
■ Is there an informal structure (people who carry authority because they are respected by staff, and thus exert influence) that is different from those in formally designated positions of authority?

When people think of organizational structure, they tend to think of a pyramid-shaped chart with boxes and lines indicating a hierarchy that extends from the top administrator's position level down to many entry-level positions. These charts help individuals visualize the organization in terms of who reports to whom, who is responsible for which divisions of the organization, and how the chain of command proceeds from bottom to top.

This system is patterned after the bureaucratic model described by Weber (1946) that we reviewed in Chapter 7. It is a widely used structure because it is easy to understand and apply, it ensures that everyone has one and only one supervi-

TABLE 8.8   **Assessing Corporate Authority and Mission**

Checklist	Yes	No
1. Are articles of incorporation on file?	——	——
2. Is there a written set of bylaws?	——	——
3. Are board members and agency directory familiar with bylaws?	——	——
4. Is there a mission statement?	——	——
5. Is it one page or less?	——	——
6. Does it make a statement about expected client outcomes?	——	——
7. Are staff aware of, and do they practice in accordance with the mission statement?	——	——

sor, and it provides for lines of communication, exercise of authority, performance evaluation, discipline, and the many other functions necessary to the running of an organization.

As we also noted in Chapter 7, however, there are many critics of bureaucratic structure who believe it is not the best design for human service agencies. Their central point is that bureaucratic structure fails to work effectively in HSOs because it was designed for organizations in which both inputs and operations are predictable and repetitive, whereas individual clients and their problems are quite unique. Rules that govern the production process in manufacturing enterprises, for example, may be helpful in ensuring consistent quality of the goods produced, but in a HSO these rules may serve only to constrain workers' ability to exercise professional judgment.

A number of terms have been used to describe the dysfunctions of bureaucracies. Merton (1952) warns of *learned incompetence* that develops among employees in bureaucracies who rely so heavily on a policy manual to make their decisions that they are unable to think logically or creatively about the problems clients bring to the agency. Lipsky (1984) uses the term *bureaucratic disentitlement* to describe situations in which clients fail to receive benefits or services to which they are entitled due to decisions that are based on internal organizational considerations rather than service needs. Hasenfeld (1983) calls attention to *goal displacement,* which describes the tendency of organizations to lose sight of organizational mission and goals and to focus on the concerns of units and subunits within the organization.

Contingency theorists, in addressing the question of what organizational structure is best, contend that it depends on what it is that the organization is expected to produce. Morse and Lorsch (1970) demonstrated that higher productivity in one type of organization (a container-manufacturing plant) was achieved through a traditional structure with clearly defined roles, responsibilities, and lines of supervision. Another type of organization (a research lab) achieved higher productivity through a very loose structure, which allowed researchers maximum flexibility to carry out their own work unfettered by rules, regulations, and supervision. Alternative structures are depicted in Figure 8.3.

Miles (1975) proposes several alternatives to bureaucratic structure. One option, adapted from the work of Likert (1961), is called a *linking-pin structure.* In this type of organization, rigid lines of reporting and one-on-one relationships are abandoned in favor of placing an emphasis on work units. One or more persons within a work unit are then selected to play a linking role to other work units, in which collaboration is important. By serving as a fully functioning participant in both units, persons in the linking role are able to facilitate better communication and working relationships than are possible through the traditional structure.

Another option is *matrix structure,* where supervision is assigned to a function rather than to a person. Under this type of structure, staff are likely to have more than one supervisor, and constant communication is a necessity. A matrix management structure might be used in a ward of a mental hospital, where supervision of a social worker with an M.S.W. degree for the activities of the ward falls

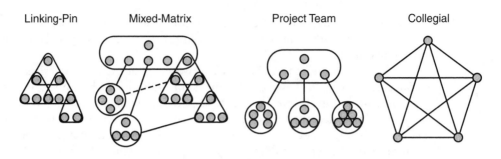

Stable	ENVIRONMENT	Turbulent
Fixed	GOALS	Ambiguous
Standardized	TECHNOLOGY	Unprogrammed

FIGURE 8.3   Human Resources Structures and Environmental Conditions

Note: This figure is based on a diagram developed by Robert Biller.
Source: R. Miles, *Theories of Management: Implications for Organizational Behavior and Development* (New York: McGraw-Hill, 1978), p. 91. Reprinted with permission of The McGraw-Hill Companies.

to the designated ward supervisor who may be a registered nurse, whereas supervision of professional functioning and performance evaluation falls to a senior-level M.S.W. social worker.

Still another structure is the *project team structure,* in which teams working on the same effort take responsibility for different functions and work relatively independently. For example, in starting up a community project, one team might conduct a needs assessment, another explore funding, another handle incorporation responsibilities, and another secure a facility. Work is coordinated by a committee of team leaders to ensure that the project teams are heading in the same direction and that their efforts are oriented toward a common end.

A final structural option proposed by Miles is the *collegial structure.* In this type of organization, individual professionals operate relatively independently and come together only in circumstances in which their work overlaps. A private counseling clinic would be a good example. Five psychologists and social workers may form a partnership to purchase a building and equipment and hire receptionists and other support staff. No single partner has more authority than any other. Each generates her or his own income and otherwise operates as an entrepreneur, except in situations in which the functioning of the organization requires overlap.

It is likely that no single organizational structure can be said to be superior to all others as applied to the field of human services. For large public agencies, some type of bureaucratic structure may be useful because of size, predictability of operations, and accountability considerations. For a small, community-based agency, a collegial model may work very effectively. Much will depend on the mission, purpose, and goals of the organization, the services provided, and the expectations for accountability.

A related issue has to do with staff competence and preparation for the roles they fill and the responsibilities they hold. The field of human services encompasses a wide range of specializations, including, but not limited to, health, mental health, substance use, developmental disabilities, child welfare, services to elderly persons, residential treatment for a variety of populations, adult and juvenile corrections, and many others.

Each organization that provides direct service within these fields may also employ staff from a wide variety of disciplines. These include social work, counseling, psychology, child care, medicine, nursing, rehabilitation, education, and others. Support services may be provided by people from diverse fields such as accounting, management, public relations, and finance.

The important consideration in examining professional competence is the standards of the organization that govern job expectations, hiring, supervision, and evaluation of performance. What, for example, are the educational requirements for each position? Does the organization adhere to these requirements? What experience is required? What licenses or certifications are necessary?

In their early work on job performance, both Taylor (1947) and Weber (1946) emphasized the importance of clearly defined job expectations, workers who were well prepared to perform expected functions, supervision, evaluation, and feedback to improve performance. Taylor, of course, focused his efforts on what would be considered assembly-line technologies. Weber's work is more applicable to the definition, supervision, and evaluation of professional functions.

Miles (1975) refers to this issue as *job design.* He notes that in organizations where the prevailing management philosophy comes from the traditional model, jobs are designed in a manner that permits only the carrying out of routine physical and mental tasks. This type of job design is appropriate when the work is something such as forms completion or data processing. Conflicts will eventually emerge, however, when the staff member has professional training and complex professional responsibilities but is allowed to perform only routine tasks.

Operating under a human relations philosophy, although it sounds more employee oriented, can be deceptive. Constraints are often the same as those under the traditional model. The only difference is that a concern is expressed for the human needs of the employee, such as the desire for self-esteem. Teamwork may be emphasized in order to support employee needs for belonging, but the fundamental assumption is that managers can predict and routinize staff activities and should maintain relatively tight control of decision making.

Job design under the human resources model is more complex. In this type of organization, employees are involved with management in both goal setting and decision making. Work is performed under conditions of self-direction and self-control. Data and information generated about individual performance and program performance are shared with the employee in the interest of promoting professional growth and development. This type of job design is ideal for the experienced employee with professional education, but it may be inappropriate for positions in which the job requires more task definition and supervision.

Documentation and data to be examined in order to understand organizational structure might include:

1. Organizational chart
2. Job descriptions
3. Relevant policy and procedure manuals
4. Interviews with selected administrators, managers, staff, and representatives of each discipline

A tool such as the one depicted in Table 8.9 can be used to assess the appropriateness of organization and program structure.

Management and Leadership Style.   Questions to be explored for this activity include:

- How is the workplace organized and work allocated?
- Is appropriate authority and information passed on along with responsibility?
- How close is supervision, and what, exactly, is supervised? Is it tasks, is it functions, or is it the employee?
- How are decisions made? Is information solicited from those affected?
- Do employees feel valued at every level? Do they believe they are making a contribution to the success of the organization?
- How is conflict handled?

TABLE 8.9   Assessing Organizational and Program Structure

	Total Organization	Program A	Program B	Program C
1. Would you describe the structure as rigid or flexible?	____	____	____	____
2. Is the structure appropriate to the needs of the organization or program?	____	____	____	____
3. Is communication primarily top down, or in all directions?	____	____	____	____
4. Are staff competent to do the jobs expected of them?	____	____	____	____
5. Is supervision appropriate to the need?	____	____	____	____

A wealth of theoretical literature exists concerning approaches to administration, management, and leadership. Miles (1975) classifies managerial theories or models into one of three categories: (1) the traditional model, (2) the human relations model, and (3) the human resources model.

The *traditional model* is characterized by very close supervision of work, control of subordinates, breaking work down into simple tasks that are easily learned, and establishing detailed work routines. Similar to McGregor's characterization of Theory X, the assumptions of this model are that people inherently dislike work, that they are not self-motivated or self-directed, and that they do it only because they need the money. The traditional model would include such theorists as Weber, Taylor, and others committed to the basic tenets of bureaucracy or scientific management (as discussed in Chapter 7).

The *human relations model* is characterized by efforts on the part of management to make each worker feel useful and important. Management is open to feedback, and subordinates are allowed to exercise some self-direction on routine matters. Assumptions are that people want to feel useful and important, that they have a need to belong, and that these needs are more important than money in motivating people to work. Theories that support the human relations model would include Mayo's human relations theory, as well as many of the theorists who expanded on Mayo's work and focused on employee motivation.

The *human resources model* is characterized by a focus on the use of untapped resources that exist within employees. The manager is expected to create an environment in which all members may contribute to the limits of their abilities. Full participation is encouraged on all matters, and self-direction and self-control are supported and promoted. Assumptions are that work means more than merely earning a paycheck. It is an important part of people's lives, and they want to contribute to the success of the total work effort. Furthermore, people are assumed to be creative, resourceful, and capable of contributing more when they are unrestricted by the constraints of the traditional or the human relations models. The theories that support the human resources model are drawn essentially from the work on contingency theory (Burns & Stalker, 1961) and supported by a number of contemporary authors (Peters & Waterman, 1982).

This philosophy of management is important to understand because it influences so many facets of organizational life. It can affect, for example, whether adult protective service workers are allowed merely to collect facts from a battered elderly person and then turn to a supervisor who will direct the next steps, or whether they are allowed to use professional judgment to intervene as they see fit. Recent research supports the efficacy of these principles in different types of human service organizations. Pine, Warsh, and Maluccio (1998) report increases in worker satisfaction and productivity following the introduction of participatory management techniques in a child welfare agency, and Van Beinum (2000) finds similar effects in a rehabilitation services organization.

Some of the more important documents and data sources to be examined in understanding organizational administration, management, and leadership style include:

1. Job description of the chief executive officer (CEO) and other staff in positions of leadership
2. Interviews with board members (if the agency is private) or the person to whom the CEO is accountable (if the agency is public) to determine their expectations of the CEO
3. Criteria used for performance evaluation of the CEO and other staff in positions of leadership
4. An interview with the CEO to determine expectations for other staff in positions of leadership
5. Organizational chart
6. Interviews with staff in various roles to determine perceptions about the job, the workplace, supervision, and administration

A tool such as the one depicted in Table 8.10 can be useful in assessing the agency's management and leadership style.

Assess the Organization's Programs and Services.   Questions to be explored for this activity include:

- What programs and services are offered?
- Are the services consistent with the goals and objectives of the program?

TABLE 8.10   Assessing Leadership and Management Style

	Carried Out by Management Only	Input Allowed but Ignored	Input Solicited and Used	Group Consensus, Full Participation
1. How are organizational goals established?	____	____	____	____
2. What is the climate for supporting the achievement of goals?	____	____	____	____
3. Where are program-level decisions made?	____	____	____	____
4. How does information flow throughout the organization?	____	____	____	____
5. Who has involvement in providing feedback about performance?	____	____	____	____

- Are staffing patterns appropriate to the services to be provided? Are workload expectations reasonable given expectations for achievement with each client and within each service and program?
- Is there a common understanding among management and line staff within each program about problems to be addressed, populations to be served, services to be provided, and client outcomes to be achieved?
- Are there established standards for quality of services?

Central to understanding every HSO is assessing indicators of efficiency, effectiveness, and quality that reflect a commitment to providing the best services possible at the lowest cost. Government initiatives continue to emphasize the establishment of standards and implementation of performance monitoring for all organizations using government funding (Martin & Kettner, 1996). These standards encompass efficiency accountability, quality accountability, and effectiveness accountability.

Efficiency accountability focuses on the ratio of outputs to inputs or, more specifically, the ratio of volume of service provided to dollars expended. If Agency ABC provides 1,000 hours of counseling at a cost of $75,000 and Agency XYZ provides 1,000 hours of counseling at a cost of $100,000, Agency ABC is determined to be more efficient. Greater efficiency offers clear productivity benefits to agencies, and it presumably positions them better to seek funds from revenue sources. Somewhat surprisingly, research evidence does not consistently support this, as in the findings of Frumkin and Kim (2001), who showed that providers of charitable funds do not necessarily reward more efficient agencies over less efficient ones. Nonetheless, most organizations that seek donated funds attempt to demonstrate efficiency by paying attention to measures such as the ratio of administrative costs to total expenditures.

Quality accountability focuses on the provision of services and differentiates between organizations that meet a quality standard and those that do not. For example, using "timeliness" as a quality standard, an organization would be required to monitor whether services were provided within a certain time frame (such as no more than 10 minutes following the scheduled time of appointment).

Assessing quality can make an important contribution to understanding HSOs. Most people have experienced the uncertainty of entering an unfamiliar organization and immediately sensing dynamics that are not easily interpreted. For example, a social work intern described her feelings about entering a particular nursing home for the first time. She stated that she "did not feel good about it," but when questioned about what that meant, she was at a loss for words to describe why she felt that way.

Several weeks later, the young intern was able to identify reasons for her concern. The nursing home's unpleasant odor, disturbing interactions observed between staff and residents, the receptionist's lack of interest in greeting visitors, the arrangement of furniture in the lobby in a way that was not conducive to conversations, the fact that some residents were lined up in wheelchairs in hallways, and the staff's discouragement of residents who wanted to bring personal possessions into the home were all problematic for her. These elements began to paint a picture of an organization that did not fully value its residents, staff, or visitors.

These types of concerns do not always surface when evaluating efficiency, productivity, or effectiveness. However, identifying quality standards and using them as a basis for evaluating the service quality directly addresses these concerns. Some of the quality indicators used by organizations to evaluate quality include accessibility, assurance, communication, competence, conformity, courtesy, deficiency, durability, empathy, humaneness, performance, reliability, responsiveness, security, and tangibles (Martin, 1993).

Effectiveness accountability focuses on the results, effects, and accomplishments of human service programs. Two central questions for HSOs in the 2000s are (1) Are clients better off after coming to this organization than they were before they came? and (2) Do programs and services offered resolve the client problems they are funded to address?

These questions need to be dealt with in the context of understanding what goes into the planning, delivery, and evaluation of programs. A complete program should include a problem analysis, goals and objectives, program and service design, a data-collection and management-information system, and a plan for evaluation (Kettner, Moroney, & Martin, 1999). Written plans provide the blueprints for programs and services and also serve as standards against which programs, when implemented, can be evaluated.

Each program should be based on a clear understanding of the problems it is intended to address and the populations it is intended to serve. It is not unusual to find that in some long-standing programs there has been a shift in emphasis over the years. For example, a program that was designed to deal with heroin use may have begun with an emphasis on detoxification and long-term intensive therapy, later shifting to provision of methadone, and finally to intensive self-help groups. Each of these emphases stems from a different understanding of the etiology of the problem and requires a different working hypothesis. These changes, in turn, may lead to alterations in the population served, resources, patterns of staffing, and methods of evaluating effectiveness. Such changes should be made consciously, not through "drift," and written program plans should reflect the revisions.

Some of the more important documents and data sources to be examined to understand the planning, delivery, and evaluation of programs and services might include:

1. Program plans
2. Organizational charts
3. Roster of staff and job descriptions
4. Annual reports of programs and services
5. Needs assessment surveys
6. Evaluation findings, including client satisfaction surveys
7. Case records

TABLE 8.11 Assessing Efficiency, Quality, and Effectiveness

	Program A	Program B	Program C
1. Does each program specify and monitor measures for efficiency (e.g., productivity per worker)?	____	____	____
2. Does each program specify and monitor quality measures (e.g., reliability/ consistency of services)?	____	____	____
3. Does each program specify and monitor client outcomes (e.g., standardized scales that measure severity of problems before and after treatment)?	____	____	____

A tool such as the one depicted in Table 8.11 can be useful in assessing an agency's programs and services.

Assess Personnel Policies, Procedures, and Practices. Questions to be explored for this activity include:

- Is there a written human resources plan?
- Is there a job analysis for each position?
- Is there a plan for recruitment and selection?
- Is there a plan for enhancing agency diversity?
- Is there a plan for staff development and training?
- Is there a performance evaluation system in place?
- Are there written procedures for employee termination?

Most organizations go to great lengths to ensure that their equipment will be in good working order, such as by purchasing maintenance contracts for their photocopy machines, computers, printers, vehicles, and other essential items. Ironically, not all agencies invest the same level of concern or resources in their employees, even though employees also have a variety of needs to be met if they are to function at optimal levels of productivity. Perhaps one way to understand how effectively an organization is addressing its personnel needs is to understand how an "ideal" personnel system might function.

One approach recommended in the literature to ensure that personnel needs and issues are properly addressed is to develop a human resources plan (Schmidt,

Riggar, Crimando, & Bordieri, 1992). Overall agency planning is referred to as *strategic planning;* it focuses on establishing goals, processes, and actions that determine future agency directions. Once future directions are established, they form the basis for human resource planning—the forecasting of personnel needs to implement the mission. The significance of a human resources plan is that it is critical to the success of an organization that new employees be brought on board in an orderly, systematic manner that maximizes the likelihood that they will be successful and productive during their tenure at the agency.

Basic to a human resources plan is a job analysis. "Job analysis identifies those tasks a job entails and determines the relationships between and among positions. It also specifies the qualifications of positions" (Schmidt et al., 1992, p. 31). A job analysis becomes the basis for writing a job description, which in turn establishes the organizing theme for the components of the human resources plan: recruitment, selection, orientation, supervision, training and development, performance appraisal, and, if necessary, termination.

The process of job analysis involves the gathering, evaluating, and recording of accurate, objective, and complete information about a given position from a variety of sources (Malinowski, 1981). It begins with an itemization of tasks carried out by those who hold a particular job. For each task or group of tasks, the job analyst must identify methods or techniques for carrying out the task(s), knowledge and skills needed, and the results expected. The finished product should provide a complete review of the requirements and expectations associated with a particular job. From this document, a briefer, more concise job description is developed.

After job qualifications and expectations are understood, the next step is to design a recruitment and selection plan. Effective recruitment requires a strategy, including selection of the recruitment territory (local, statewide, or national), consideration of labor market conditions, and determination of recruitment audience and the intensity of search and recruiting efforts. These decisions are crucial to successful staffing, since employee selection can be made only from the pool of applicants generated by the recruitment strategy. This is a critical point at which the agency needs to assess the diversity of its staff and give special attention to recruitment of persons from diverse racial/ethnic groups as well as women, gays and lesbians, and older and/or disabled employees, to ensure a heterogeneous and representative staff.

Selection involves a three-stage process. Recruitment typically produces applications, including résumés. In the first stage, résumés and letters of reference are reviewed to eliminate applicants who are not qualified or not a good fit for organizational needs. In the second stage, those with the highest qualifications are further narrowed down to a short list, usually a maximum of three to five applicants. In the third stage, those on the short list are interviewed. A job offer is then made to one of those interviewed. Screening criteria and interview questions are developed ahead of time so that they match the qualifications and job expectations established in the job analysis.

Upon being hired, the new employee is provided a complete orientation to the job, the workplace, and the community. After completion of the orientation, a plan for supervision, training and development is initiated. This is intended to ensure a smooth entry into the job and to provide the information, knowledge, and resources necessary for successful and productive employment.

In order to ensure that employee performance is appropriately monitored and evaluated, a well-designed personnel or human resources system will have a performance-appraisal system based, again, on the job analysis. Tasks identified in the job analysis should be used as a basis for designing the performance-appraisal instrument. This will ensure that the job, as described at the point of recruitment and hiring, is the same job for which orientation and training have been provided, and is the same job on which the employee is evaluated. Criteria and procedures for performance evaluation should always be specified in writing and given to employees at the time of hiring. In a well-designed performance-appraisal system, it should be a rare occurrence for employees to be surprised by the written evaluation.

Policies and procedures for termination should also be clearly defined and distributed in writing at the time of hiring. At a minimum, these statements should include a description of grounds for termination. These may relate to unsatisfactory job performance or to unacceptable behavior, such as sexual harassment. In either case, criteria for determining what constitutes unsatisfactory performance or unacceptable behavior should be specified in objective, measurable terms and as clearly and unambiguously as possible. Procedures and time frames for notifying employees of poor performance well before reaching the stage of termination should also be delineated. Doing so is part of sound human resource management, but it is also a practical matter in that agencies that follow such guidelines are much more likely to avoid extended grievances or litigation.

In assessing an agency's effectiveness in the area of personnel policies and procedures, these are the types of elements one would want to examine. Helpful and informative documents for conducting the assessment include:

1. Manual of personnel policies and procedures
2. Copy of a human resource plan, including affirmative action/equal employment opportunity plans
3. Job analysis and job descriptions
4. Recruitment and selection procedures
5. Staff development and training plan
6. Performance evaluation forms
7. Statistics on absenteeism, turnover, usage of sick leave
8. Grievances and complaints filed with the human resource department
9. Interviews with representative staff who perform different roles

Figure 8.4 may be useful in assessing the quality of an organization's personnel or human resources system.

Assess Adequacy of Technical Resources and Systems. Questions to be explored for this activity include:

FIGURE 8.4   **Assessing an Organization's Human Resources System**

A. Does the organization have a job analysis for each position within the agency that includes the following?

Responsibilities and Tasks	Methods	Knowledge and Skill	Results
Counseling			
1. Counsel individuals	One-on-one	Human behavior;	Client
2. Counsel families	Family treatment	group and family	develops
3. Lead groups	Group treatment	dynamics; under-	independent
4. Consult with self-	Occasional	stand professional	living and
help groups	group meetings	role	social skills

B. Is this job analysis consistent with the following?
  1. The job description
  2. The recruitment and selection plan (or procedures)
  3. The plan or practices relative to hiring a diverse workforce.
  4. Staff development and training plans or activities.
  5. Performance evaluation criteria
  6. Plans for involuntary termination

- Are program staff involved in a meaningful way in providing budgetary input? Do they get useful feedback about expenditures and unit costs during the year?
- Do program staff use budget data as a measure by which they attempt to improve efficiency?
- Do resources appear to be adequate to achieve stated program goals and objectives?

This task encompasses (1) budgetary management and (2) assessment of facilities, equipment, computer technology, and information management. Additional questions arise that are specific to these two categories.

Budget Management.   Relevant questions to be asked include:

- What type of budgeting system is used by the agency?
- How are unit costs calculated? Do staff understand the meaning of unit costs? How are they used?

Budgeting and budget management is often an activity left to upper administration and treated as though line staff, first-line supervisors, and other persons involved in service delivery need not be involved. To the contrary, good financial management practices involve all levels of staff. Fiscal soundness and budgeting practices affect programs and services in a profound way. To put it simply, organizations cannot run without money, but good financial management practices suggest that programs and services drive the budget, not the other way around.

For many years, human service agencies were limited to a very simplified type of budgeting called *line-item budgeting*. This involved identifying expenditure categories and estimating the number of dollars that would be needed to cover all expenses in each category for one year. Categories typically included personnel; operating expenses such as rent, utilities, supplies, and travel; and other items.

Since the 1970s, increasingly sophisticated budgeting techniques have been developed for application to human service agencies (Lohmann, 1980; Kettner et al., 1999). These techniques, referred to as *functional budgeting* and *program budgeting*, are based on program planning and budgeting systems (PPBS) (Lee & Johnson, 1973). Both approaches to budgeting operate within the conceptual framework of programs. Both produce cost and expenditure data in relation to programs rather than in relation to the entire agency. Functional and program budgeting techniques produce data such as total program costs, cost per unit of service, cost per output (client completion of program or service), and cost per outcome (the cost of producing measurable change in a client's quality of life). Martin (2000) calls this last approach *outcome budgeting* and describes its use in state-level human service agencies. It can be useful in facilitating cost-benefit and cost-effectiveness assessments, and also in helping agencies maintain a focus on measurement of outcomes.

Budget data become increasingly important in an environment of intense competition for scarce and diminishing resources. In the same manner that individuals shop for the best buy with their own personal purchases, government contracting agencies—in competitive environments—shop for the lowest unit cost. Organizations that do not have the type of budgeting system or database that permits calculation of unit costs increasingly find themselves at a distinct disadvantage in a competitive market.

Some of the more important documentation and data sources to be examined in order to understand the agency's approach to financial management and accountability include:

1. Annual reports
2. Audit reports
3. A cost allocation plan
4. Program goals and objectives
5. Communitywide comparative studies of unit costs
6. Interviews with all levels of program staff

Facilities, Equipment, Computer Technology, and Information Management. Questions to be asked are:

■ Is the physical work environment attractive and conducive to high productivity? Do employees feel they have enough space and space of an appropriate type?

- Have problems been identified with current facilities and equipment? If so, is there a plan to address the problems and to fund solutions?
- Are there conditions related to facilities or equipment (especially computers) that appear to act as barriers to productivity or work flow?
- Does the agency have a computerized management information system (MIS)? Is there also a client data system (separate from or as part of the MIS) that line staff can use?
- Do all line staff have a computer at their desk? Do they have access to the Internet, word-processing software, email, and other applications? Is this technology up to date?

Considerations in the area of facilities include quantity of space, physical condition and maintenance of facilities, and geographical location of the agency and its branches. Offices and work space allotted to personnel should be suited to the needs and resources of the agency and provide as pleasant a work environment as possible for staff. Plans for renovation and expansion, if necessary, should be in place and appropriate to reasonable expectations for growth.

Equipment analysis should include an assessment of computer availability to staff. Advances in computer technology have made possible many of the substantial gains in productivity enjoyed by both commercial and human service organizations during the past few decades. Most human service workers now have access to desktop or notebook computers in their workplace, and most agencies have network systems that provide for entry and retrieval of client data, Internet access, and messaging capabilities for staff. Most also have or are developing websites that are not merely informational but also allow online completion of forms, provide links to resources, enable communications with staff, and offer other features. As a result of these developments, HSOs are following the lead of commercial firms by creating positions for specialized information technology (IT) staff and information officers.

As computers become ever more sophisticated, they are able to serve an increasing variety of needs. One role of IT staff is to anticipate both capabilities and needs and to plan accordingly. They should also have in place a plan for regular upgrades of software and hardware, and plans for ongoing staff training. Many organizations seek to maintain a three-year schedule for replacing staff members' computer equipment, both hardware and software, and some that are more technology intensive require still briefer time frames. Tools such as the one depicted in Table 8.12 can be useful in assessing the adequacy of technical resources and systems.

Summary

In order to really understand an organization, with all its strengths and weaknesses, one would have to spend years analyzing documents and talking to people familiar with it. However, an overview of selected elements of the organization

TABLE 8.12 **Assessing Adequacy of Technical Systems and Resources**

	Staff Involved in Design and/or Given Access to Resource?	Up-to-Date Technology?
1. Budgeting process	____	____
2. Location of office	____	____
3. Design/decor of office space	____	____
4. Management information system	____	____
5. Client data system	____	____
6. Computer hardware for line staff	____	____
7. Computer software for line staff	____	____

and its relationships to its environment can provide a basis for understanding why certain problems may exist, as well as possible clues as to how they may be resolved.

In this chapter we have proposed that understanding an organization involves two activities: (1) identifying the task environment and understanding the relationship of the organization to the significant elements of the task environment and (2) understanding the inner workings of the organization itself.

Significant elements of the task environment include funding sources and those who contribute noncash resources, clients and referral sources, and other important organizations such as regulating and accrediting bodies. Strong and positive relationships with these entities make an important contribution to the overall strength and stability of the agency.

Assessing the internal functioning of the organization includes understanding components such as corporate authority and mission; management and leadership style; organizational and program structure; agency measures of efficiency, quality, and effectiveness; personnel policies and practices; and adequacy of resources.

Using the tools provided in this chapter should enable a student or beginning practitioner to better understand the organizational context within which problems are identified and changes are proposed.

DISCUSSION QUESTIONS AND EXERCISES

1. Why are human service agencies typically so dependent on their environment? What are some of the elements of the task environment that affect agency functioning?

2. Identify as many potential funding sources for a human service agency as you can. Speculate about what types of restrictions may come with each type of funding.

3. Use selected agencies in the community to explore the concepts of organizational domain and boundary control. What do they claim as their areas of expertise? How do they exercise control over their boundaries?

4. Explain the concept of accreditation by using CSWE as an example. Ask students to identify elements they might look at if they were part of an accrediting body. What standards would they establish? How does this apply to agency accreditation?

5. Discuss student perceptions of management and leadership style in field agencies (especially in terms of staff participation in decision making). What impact do they perceive management and leadership style to have on agency functioning and staff morale?

6. Discuss some of the criteria that might be used to determine whether a particular type of service (e.g., counseling) is effective in helping clients deal with their prob-lems. What is currently being done in field agencies to measure effectiveness?

7. In a group of four or five students, select a community agency with which some group members are familiar. Using the diagrams in Chapter 8 as a guide, diagram the task environment for this agency. When this is completed:

■ Put the diagrams on the board or over-head transparency, describe them to the class, and explain the significance of the task environment to the agency.

■ List some of the factors the group members think they might use to determine the type and quality of relationships between this agency and others in the task environment. Aspects of these rela-tionships include type (e.g., funding source, referral source) length of rela-tionship, trends in resource exchange in the past five years (e.g., increasing or decreasing), how these trends compare to those of competitors, and so on.

A P P E N D I X
Framework for Analyzing a Human Service Organization

Task 1: Analyze the Task Environment

Identify and Assess Relationships with Revenue Sources

Cash Revenues
■ What are the agency's funding sources?
■ How much and what percentage of the agency's total funds are received from each source?

Noncash Revenues
■ Does the organization use volunteers? If yes, how many and for what purposes?
■ Are appropriate efforts made to match volunteers' skills and abilities to the tasks assigned?
■ What materials and in-kind resources (e.g., food, clothing, physical facilities, etc.) does the organization receive?
■ What tax benefits does the organization receive?

Relationships with Revenue Sources
- What is the quality of the relationship between funding sources and the agency?

Identify and Assess Relationships with Clients and Referral Sources
- What client groups does this organization serve?
- What are the demographic characteristics of clients?
- What percentages of clients pay full fees, partial fees, no fees, or are covered by contract revenues?
- What are the major sources of client referrals?

Relationships with Referral Sources
- What is the organization's domain (specifically, for what types of expertise is the agency recognized)?
- Does the agency claim a larger domain than it serves?
- Does demand for services outstrip supply or is there unused capacity?
- What types of clients does the organization refuse (e.g., are there disproportionate numbers of poor, elderly, persons of color, women, persons with disabilities, gays/lesbians, or other groups that are typically underserved?)?

Identify and Assess Relationships with Other Elements in the Task Environment
- What state and federal regulatory bodies oversee programs provided by this organization?
- With what government agencies does this organization contract for service provision?
- What professional associations, labor unions, or accrediting bodies influence agency operations?
- What are the perceptions of the "general public" in terms of the relevance, value, and quality of agency services?

Assessing Relationships with Other Elements
- What other agencies provide the same services to the same clientele as this organization?
- With whom does the organization compete?
- With whom does the organization cooperate? Is the organization part of a coalition or an alliance?
- How is the organization perceived by regulatory bodies, government contracting agencies, professional organizations, accrediting bodies, and the general public in relation to its peers and competitors?

Task 2: Analyze the Organization Internally

Identify Corporate Authority and Mission
- What is the basis for and extent of the organization's corporate authority?
- What is its mission?

- Is the organization operating in a manner that is consistent with its authority and mission?
- To what extent is the mission supported by staff who perform different roles within the organization?
- Are policies and procedures consistent with mission and authority?

Understand Program Structure and Management Style

- What are the major departmental or program units on the organizational chart?
- What is the rationale for the existing organizational structure?
- Is this the most logical structure? Is it consistent with and supportive of the mission?
- Is supervision logical and capable of performing expected functions? Are staff capable of performing expected functions?
- Is there an informal structure (people who carry authority because they are respected by staff, and thus exert influence) that is different from those in formally designated positions of authority?

Management and Leadership Style

- How is the workplace organized and work allocated?
- Is appropriate authority and information passed on along with responsibility?
- How close is supervision, and what, exactly, is supervised? Is it tasks, is it functions, or is it the employee?
- How are decisions made? Is information solicited from those affected?
- Do employees feel valued at every level? Do they believe they are making a contribution to the success of the organization?
- How is conflict handled?

Assess the Organization's Programs and Services

- What programs and services are offered?
- Are the services consistent with the goals and objectives of the program?
- Are staffing patterns appropriate to the services to be provided? Are workload expectations reasonable given expectations for achievement with each client and within each service and program?
- Is there a common understanding among management and line staff within each program about problems to be addressed, populations to be served, services to be provided, and client outcomes to be achieved?
- Are there established standards for quality of services?

Assess Personnel Policies, Procedures, and Practices

- Is there a written human resources plan?
- Is there a job analysis for each position?
- Is there a plan for recruitment and selection?
- Is there a plan for enhancing agency diversity?
- Is there a plan for staff development and training?

- Is there a performance evaluation system in place?
- Are there written procedures for employee termination?

Assess Adequacy of Technical Resources and Systems
- Are program staff involved in a meaningful way in providing budgetary input? Do they get useful feedback about expenditures and unit costs during the year?
- Do program staff use budget data as a measure by which they attempt to improve efficiency?
- Do resources appear to be adequate to achieve stated program goals and objectives?

Budget Management
- What type of budgeting system is used by the agency?
- How are unit costs calculated? Do staff understand the meaning of unit costs? How are they used?

Facilities, Equipment, Computer Technology, and Information Management
- Is the physical work environment attractive and conducive to high productivity? Do employees feel they have enough space and space of an appropriate type?
- Have problems been identified with current facilities and equipment? If so, is there a plan to address the problems and to fund solutions?
- Are there conditions related to facilities or equipment (especially computers) that appear to act as barriers to productivity or work flow?
- Does the agency have a computerized management information system (MIS)? Is there also a client data system (separate from or as part of the MIS) that line staff can use?
- Do all line staff have a computer at their desk? Do they have access to the Internet, word-processing software, email, and other applications? Is this technology up to date?

SUGGESTED READINGS

Alle-Corliss, L., and R. Alle-Corliss. (1998). *Human service agencies: An orientation to fieldwork.* Pacific Grove, CA: Brooks/Cole.

Alle-Corliss, L., and R. Alle-Corliss. (1999). *Advanced practice in human service agencies: Issues, trends, and treatment perspectives.* Pacific Grove, CA: Brooks/Cole.

Brody, R. (2000). *Effectively managing human service organizations* (2nd ed.). Thousand Oaks, CA: Sage.

Bryce, H. J. (2000). *Financial and strategic management for nonprofit organizations: A comprehensive reference to legal, financial, management, and operations rules and guidelines for nonprofits* (3rd ed.). San Francisco: Jossey-Bass.

Finn, J., and G. Holden. (2000). *Human services online: A new arena for service delivery.* New York: Haworth.

Galaskiewicz, J., and B. Wolfgang. (1998). *Nonprofit organizations in an age of uncertainty: A study of organizational change.* New York: Aldine de Gruyter.

Gilbertsen, B., and V. Ramchandani. (1999). *The Wilder nonprofit field guide to developing effective teams.* Saint Paul, MN: Amherst H. Wilder Foundation.

Herron, D. B. (1997). *Marketing nonprofit programs and services: Proven and practical strategies to get more customers, members, and donors.* San Francisco: Jossey-Bass.

Jinkins, M., and D. B. Jinkins. (1998). *The character of leadership: Political realism and public virtue in nonprofit organizations.* San Francisco: Jossey-Bass.

Kettner, P. M. (2002). *Achieving excellence in the management of human service organizations.* Boston: Allyn and Bacon.

Letts, C., W. P. Ryan, and A. Grossman. (1999). *High performance nonprofit organizations: Managing upstream for greater impact.* New York: John Wiley & Sons.

Mengerink, W. C. (1992) *Hand in hand: Funding strategies for human service agencies.* Rockville, MD: Fund Raising Institute

Nanus, B., and S. M. Dobbs. (1999). *Leaders who make a difference: Essential strategies for meeting the nonprofit challenge.* San Francisco: Jossey-Bass.

Nash, K. A. (1999). *Cultural competence: A guide for human service agencies.* Washington, DC: Child Welfare League of America Press.

Packard, T. (1993). Managers' and workers' views of the dimensions of participation in organizational decision-making. *Administration in Social Work, 17:* 53–65.

Simon, J. S. (1999). *The Wilder nonprofit field guide to conducting successful focus groups.* Saint Paul, MN: Amherst H. Wilder Foundation.

Stone, M. M., M. A. Hager, and J. J. Griffin. (2001). Organizational characteristics and funding environments: A study of a population of United Way-affiliated nonprofits. *Public Administration Review, 61:* 276–289.

Zunz, S. J. (1991). Gender-related issues in the career development of social work managers. *Affilia: Journal of Women and Social Work, 6:* 39–52.

REFERENCES

Alexander, J., R. Nank, and C. Stivers. (1999). Implications of welfare reform: Do nonprofit survival strategies threaten civil society? *Nonprofit and Voluntary Sector Quarterly, 28:* 452–475.

Berg, W. E., and R. Wright. (1981). Goal displacement in social work programs. *Administration in Social Work, 20:* 25–39.

Boris, E. T. (1998). Myths about the nonprofit sector. In E. T. Boris (Ed.), *Charting Civil Society* (pp. 1–14). Washington, DC: The Urban Institute.

Brager, G., and S. Holloway. (1978). *Changing human service organizations: Politics and practice.* New York: Free Press.

Burns, T., and G. M. Stalker. (1961). *The management of innovation.* London: Tavistock.

Cloward, R. A., and I. Epstein. (1965). Private social welfare's disengagement from the poor. In M. N. Zald (Ed.), *Social welfare institutions* (pp. 623–644). New York: John Wiley.

Cordes, J., and J. R. Henig. (2001). Nonprofit human service providers in an era of privatization: Toward a theory of economic and political response. *Policy Studies Review, 18:* 91–110.

Dill, W. R. (1958). Environment as an influence on managerial autonomy. *Administrative Science Quarterly, 2(1):* 409–443.

Dunlop, J. M., and G. B. Angell. (2001). Inside-outside: Boundary-spanning challenges in building rural health coalitions. *Professional Development: The International Journal of Continuing Social Work Education, 4:* 40–48.

Fortune Magazine. (2002). The Fortune 500—2002. Retrieved on November 22, 2002, from www.fortune.com/fortune/fortune500.

Froelich, K. A. (1999). Diversification of revenue strategies: Evolving resource dependence in nonprofit organizations. *Nonprofit and Voluntary Sector Quarterly, 28:* 246–268.

Frumkin, P., and A. Andre-Clark. (2000). When missions, markets, and politics collide: Values and strategy in the nonprofit human services. *Nonprofit and Voluntary Sector Quarterly, 29:* 141–163.

Frumkin, P., and M. T. Kim. (2001). Strategic positioning and the financing of nonprofit organizations: Is efficiency rewarded in the contributions marketplace? *Public Administration Review, 61:* 266–275.

Greenley, J. R., and S. A. Kirk. (1973). Organizational characteristics of agencies and the distribution of services to applicants. *Journal of Health and Social Behavior, 14:* 70–79.

Gronbjerg, K. A. (1990). Poverty and nonprofit organizations. *Social Services Review, 64(2):* 208–243.

Gronbjerg, K. A. (2001). The U.S. nonprofit human service sector: A creeping revolution. *Nonprofit and Voluntary Sector Quarterly, 30:* 276–297.

Hardina, D. (1990). The effect of funding sources on client access to services. *Administration in Social Work, 14*(3): 33–46.

Hasenfeld, Y. (1983). *Human service organizations.* Englewood Cliffs, NJ: Prentice-Hall.

Hasenfeld, Y. (1995). Analyzing the human service agency. In J. Tropman, J. L. Erlich, and J. Rothman (Eds.), *Tactics and techniques of community intervention.* Itasca, IL: F. E. Peacock.

Independent Sector. (2001). *The Nonprofit Almanac in Brief.* Washington, DC: Author. (Available online at www.independentsector.org/PDFs/inbrief.pdf)

Internal Revenue Service, Statistics of Income Division. (1999). *Statistics of Income—1999, Individual Income Tax Returns* (Publication no. 1304). Washington, DC: Author.

Karger, H. J., and D. Stoesz. (2002). *American social welfare policy: A structural approach* (4th ed.). Boston: Allyn and Bacon.

Kettner, P. M., R. M. Moroney, and L. L. Martin. (1999). *Designing and managing programs: An effectiveness-based approach* (2nd ed.). Thousand Oaks, CA: Sage.

Kirk, S. A., and J. R. Greenley. (1974). Denying or delivering services? *Social Work, 19*(4): 439–447.

Kramer, R., and B. Grossman. (1987). Contracting for social services. *Social Service Review, 61*(1): 32–55.

Lee, R. D., and R. W. Johnson. (1973). *Public budgeting systems.* Baltimore: University Park Press.

Levine, S., and P. E. White. (1961). Exchange as a conceptual framework for the study of interorganizational relationships. *Administrative Science Quarterly, 5*: 583–601.

Lewis, S., and W. P. Crook. (2001). Shifting sands: An AIDS service organization adapts to a changing environment. *Administration in Social Work, 25:* 1–20.

Likert, R. (1961). *New patterns of management.* New York: McGraw-Hill.

Lipsky, M. (1984). Bureaucratic disentitlement in social welfare programs. *Social Service Review, 58*(1): 3–27.

Lohmann, R. (1980). Financial management and social administration. In F. D. Perlmutter and S. Slavin (Eds.), *Leadership in social administration.* Philadelphia: Temple University Press.

Malinowski, F. A. (1981). Job selection using task analysis. *Personnel Journal, 60*(4): 288–291.

Martin, L. L. (1993). *Total quality management in human service organizations.* Newbury Park, CA: Sage.

Martin, L. L. (2000). Budgeting for outcomes in state human agencies. *Administration in Social Work, 24:* 71–88.

Martin, L. L., and P. M. Kettner. (1996). *Measuring the performance of human service programs.* Newbury Park, CA: Sage.

Martin, P. Y. (1980). Multiple constituencies, dominant societal values, and the human service administrator. *Administration in Social Work, 4*(2): 15–27.

McMurtry, S. L., F. E. Netting, and P. M. Kettner. (1991). How nonprofits adapt to a stringent environment. *Nonprofit Management and Leadership, 1*(3): 235–252.

Merton, R. K. (1952). Bureaucratic structure and personality. In R. K. Merton, A. P. Gray, B. Hockey, and H. C. Selvin (Eds.), *Reader in bureaucracy* (pp. 261–372). Glencoe, IL: Free Press.

Miles, R. E. (1975). *Theories of management: Implications for organizational behavior and development.* New York: McGraw-Hill.

Mizrahi, T., and B. B. Rosenthal. (2001). Complexities of coalition building: Leaders' successes, strategies, struggles, and solutions. *Social Work, 46:* 63–78.

Morse, J. J., and J. W. Lorsch. (1970). Beyond theory Y. *Harvard Business Review, 48:* 61–68.

Netting, F. E., S. L. McMurtry, P. M. Kettner, and S. Jones-McClintic. (1990). Privatization and its impact on nonprofit service providers. *Nonprofit and Voluntary Sector Quarterly, 19*(1): 33–46.

Peters, T. J., and R. H. Waterman. (1982). *In search of excellence: Lessons from America's best-run companies.* New York: Harper & Row.

Pfeffer, J., and G. R. Salancik. (1978). *The external control of organizations: A resource dependent perspective.* New York: Harper & Row.

Pine, B. A., R. Warsh, and A. N. Maluccio. (1998). Participatory management in a public child welfare agency: A key to effective change. *Administration in Social Work, 22:* 19–32.

Schmidt, M. J., T. F. Riggar, W. Crimando, and J. E. Bordieri. (1992). *Staffing for success.* Newbury Park, CA: Sage.

Sosin, M. R. (2001). Service intensity and organizational attributes: A preliminary inquiry. *Administration and Policy in Mental Health, 28:* 371–392.

Stoesz, D. (1988). Human service corporations and the welfare state. *Society, 25*(5), 53–58.

Taylor, F. W. (1947). *Scientific management.* New York: Harper & Row.

Thomas, R. R. (1991). *Beyond race and gender.* New York: AMACOM.

Thompson, J. D. (1967). *Organizations in action.* New York: McGraw-Hill.

United Way of America. (2002). *2001–2002 United Way Resources Backgrounder.* Retrieved November 22, 2002, from http://national. unitedway .org/aboutuwa/2001results.cfm.

Van Beinum, I. L. (2000). Organizational rehabilitation through rehabilitating people: Transcending the original structure of a project. *Concepts and Transformation, 5:* 97–120.

Wardell, P. J. (1988). The implications of changing interorganizational relationships and resource constraints for human services survival: A case study. *Administration in Social Work, 12*(1): 89–105.

Weber, M. (1946). *From Max Weber: Essays in sociology.* (H. H. Gerth and C. W. Mills, trans.) Oxford, England: Oxford University Press.

Weisbrod, B. A. (1998). The nonprofit sector and its financing. *Journal of Policy Analysis and Management, 17:* 165–174.

Yeatts, D. E., V. Pillai, and L. Stanley-Stevens. (2001). Factors affecting self-managed work team performance: An empirical assessment. *Journal of Applied Sociology, 18:* 79–111.

Changing Macro Systems

In the previous four parts of this book we have attempted to provide an historical context for macro practice, to promote the kind of research and interaction with key informants that leads to understanding of the problem and population, and to provide a framework for understanding and analyzing two major macro systems—communities and organizations. This type of preparation, although sometimes tedious, is a necessary prerequisite for planned intervention at the macro level.

In Part Five, the final part of the book, we will present a model for acting within and on these systems. Specifically, we will detail means for bringing about change in communities and organizations that will lead to improvements in these systems' abilities to facilitate empowerment and serve those in need.

Building on the framework for understanding problems, target populations, and arenas that was presented in Chapters 3 through 8, the three chapters in Part Five address the planned change process in sequential order. Chapter 9 provides a framework for distilling information compiled to date, and for identifying key participants in the change. Chapter 10 helps raise a number of appropriate questions related to the planned intervention, and explores a range of strategies and a number of tactics. Chapter 11 provides guidelines for laying out an intervention plan as well as for implementing, monitoring, and evaluating the plan's effectiveness.

9 Building Support for the Proposed Change

Macro practice in social work can be viewed as having four major parts: (1) understanding the important components to be affected by the change—problem, population, and arena; (2) preparing an overall plan designed to get the change accepted; (3) preparing a detailed plan for intervention; and (4) implementing the intervention and following up to assess its effectiveness. Chapters 3 through 8 focused on understanding. Chapters 9 and 10 concentrate on distilling the information gathered into a clearly thought-out plan to get the change accepted, and making decisions about strategy and tactics. Chapter 11 looks at developing and implementing an intervention plan, and then following up to insure its success.

Writers who deal with macro practice in social work sometimes use the terms *strategy* and *tactics* in different ways. Brager, Specht, and Torczyner (1987) link strategy to long-range goals and tactics to the short-range and specific behaviors of groups: "Groups having widely different long range goals (strategies) may engage in the same kinds of behaviors (tactics). And a specific group may utilize a wide range of tactics in pursuit of their goals" (p. 177). Morales (1992) identifies several types of strategies and tactics used in macro practice:

> All have stressed coalition building, consciousness raising, educating client systems to their own oppression and the oppression of others, political awareness, and empowerment. The importance of cultural sensitivity, knowledge of specific communities, good research skills, and alternative explanation of history and political power have been highlighted. (pp. 108–109)

When we use the term *strategy* in this text, we will be referring to the *overall efforts* designed to ensure that the proposed change is accepted. The term *tactics* will refer to the *specific techniques* and behaviors employed in relation to the target system designed to maximize the probability that the strategy will be successful and the proposed change adopted. Strategies and associated tactics will be discussed in greater detail in Chapter 10.

The development of strategies and tactics involves some critical decisions and requires careful thought. The approach(es) taken can have far-reaching effects on the success of the change effort and its impact on the problem and the target population. Before developing a change strategy, however, it is first necessary to be clear on the nature of the proposed intervention. Strategy and tactics planning would be premature in the absence of a substantive understanding of what the change entails. This understanding can be achieved by developing a working intervention hypothesis.

Designing the Intervention

A number of tasks need to be accomplished in the process of developing an appropriate intervention. First, in order to ensure that there are some common themes in the way participants are framing the problem and the proposed interventions, it is important to refine the *hypothesis of etiology* (developed in Chapter 4) and to develop a *working intervention hypothesis.* When the change agent and other participants are able to reach agreement on these statements, the second task is to identify some of the major participants who will be critical to the success of the proposed change. After identifying key participants, the next task is to examine organizational and/or community readiness for change. Finally, when these tasks have been accomplished, the change agent and participants are ready to select a change approach. Table 9.1 summarizes the major tasks and activities involved in reaching consensus on an intervention.

TABLE 9.1 **Framework for Developing an Intervention Strategy**

Tasks	Activities
1. Develop the Intervention Hypothesis	1.1. Refine the Working Hypothesis of Etiology 1.2. Develop a Working Intervention Hypothesis
2. Define Participants	2.1. Identify the Initiator System 2.2. Identify the Change Agent System 2.3. Identify the Client System 2.4. Identify the Support System 2.5. Identify the Controlling System 2.6. Identify the Host and Implementing Systems 2.7. Identify the Target System 2.8. Identify the Action System
3. Examine System Readiness for Change	3.1. Assess General Openness to Change 3.2. Identify Anticipated or Actual Response 3.3. Determine Availability of Resources 3.4. Examine Outside Opposition to Change
4. Select a Change Approach	4.1. Select a Policy, Program, Project, Personnel, or Practice Approach

Task 1: Develop the Intervention Hypothesis

During the early phases of problem identification, numerous people involved in change efforts, both professionals and volunteers, are eager to propose a specific intervention. Many have experienced the frustration of working in what they perceive to be flawed programs, under what they perceive to be oppressive community or organizational policies, or as participants or members of communities that seem powerless to bring about meaningful change. Understandably, they are eager to propose immediate change, and may be resistant to the idea of carefully thinking through the alternatives.

A professional, scholarly approach to macro-level change requires that the foregoing tasks associated with problem identification and analysis in Chapters 3 through 8 be addressed first. However, it is the unusual change agent who is not constantly mindful of a preferred intervention and who is not continually molding and shaping it as the analysis unfolds.

Decisions about the nature, shape, and design of the intervention should wait until the analytical work has been completed. When an acceptable degree of consensus has been achieved about the nature of the problem and its etiology, an intervention hypothesis is proposed.

Refine the Working Hypothesis of Etiology.   Questions to be explored include:

- What factors gleaned from the problem analysis, the population analysis, and the arena analysis help in understanding cause-and-effect relationships?
- What themes seem to fit best with the current situation?
- How should the working hypothesis of etiology be framed?

Study and analysis of the problem, the population, and the arena invariably produce a wide variety of quantitative data and other types of information. It is the nature of this type of study that not all findings are relevant to the immediate situation. They must be sorted out, and only those that are useful and relevant to the change effort should be retained.

Take, for example, a situation where the problem identified is that there has been an increase in gang violence in a community, leading to a rapidly increasing population of young men and women who have become physically disabled due to gunshot wounds. A study of the problem may reveal the incidence of disabling gunshot wounds over the last five years, the demographic makeup of the community, poverty rates, high school dropout rates, comparison to similar communities, a history of the development of gang activity in the community, as well as an understanding of the nature and causes of violence.

A study of the population may reveal that violent youth in this community tend to cluster within a lower socioeconomic status, that many are from families that have not been able to meet basic needs, that parental neglect is common, that they have generally not had positive experiences with education, that they are in a stage at which they are struggling to develop an identity, that peer relationships are critical to their social development, and generally that they find few incentives to conform to societal expectations.

A study of the community may reveal that there is a sense of hopelessness among adults in the community, that many are unemployed, that there are low skill levels among community members, that education is not highly valued, that parents rarely support the efforts of the teachers, that there are clearly defined groups of teens, and that associations are almost exclusively along ethnic lines. It may be further discovered that patterns of participation in extracurricular activities tend to favor white students, and that Hispanic and African American students are left to develop their own activities.

Not everything discovered can be used. To be useful, the data and information produced in the analysis phase must be distilled into a working hypothesis about etiology (cause-and-effect relationships). In short, the change agent must ask: Having studied problem, population, and arena as well as their areas of overlap, what do I now believe to be the *most significant* contributing factors that have led to the need for change? A working hypothesis of etiology can be expressed in a statement (or series of statements) similar to this example:

Example of a Working Hypothesis of Etiology

Because of the following factors (drawn from analysis of the problem, population, and/or arena):

1. A trauma that led to a disabling physical condition,
2. Limited basic education and marketable skills,
3. Limited job opportunities, and
4. The need, during the teen years, to develop a positive, socially accept-able identity while, at the same time, being denied opportunities

The results have been:

1. Very limited physical activity and declining health,
2. Little to offer the job marketplace,
3. Discouragement and hopelessness relative to developing a sense of independence, and
4. Development of a negative, anti-social identity and behavior pattern.

This example is, of course, oversimplified for the sake of illustration. Completion of this task should result in a working statement that expresses at least some degree of consensus of what participants currently see as the cause-and-effect relationships as applied to the need for change.

Develop a Working Intervention Hypothesis.   Questions to be explored include:

- What interventions are implied by the hypothesis of etiology?
- Does it appear that these interventions are most likely to reduce or eliminate the problem?
- What results can be expected from these interventions?

Based on a distillation of the information gathered in the problem analysis phase as expressed in the working hypothesis of etiology, a working intervention hypothesis is developed. The *hypothesis* is a declarative statement (or series of statements) that proposes a relationship between a specific intervention and a result or outcome. The statement identifies the following: (1) a target population (or specific subgroup) and problem, (2) the change or intervention proposed, and (3) the results expected from the intervention. These elements combine to form a complete package that makes clear the expected relationship between problem, intervention, and result. A working intervention hypothesis to deal with rehabilitation of phys-ically disabled teens might read something like this example:

Example of a Working Intervention Hypothesis

If the following interventions are implemented for physically disabled teens:

1. Increase physical activity and exercise;
2. Provide opportunities for education and development of marketable skills;
3. Pair with a mentor who has overcome a physical disability;
4. Work with local employers to identify job slots,

Then the following results can be expected:

1. Improved physical health and self esteem;
2. Increased incidence of acquiring a GED or equivalent;
3. Development of a positive identity as demonstrated by articulation of life and career goals; and
4. At least a 50 percent increase in successful employment.

This would be considered a testable hypothesis. The strength of this model is that it encourages change agents to focus on a specified set of contributing or causal factors, and develop a set of cause → effect relationships. Then, based on these understandings, the intervention framework is developed. If the model is followed correctly, the fit within hypotheses and between hypotheses should be readily recognized. There should be clearly understood relationships between causal factors and results in the hypothesis of etiology, and between proposed intervention and expected results in the working intervention hypothesis. Furthermore, the relationships between causal or contributing factors in the working hypothesis of etiology and proposed interventions should be clear, as should the relationships between results specified in etiology and expected results expected of the intervention. These relationships are diagramed in Figure 9.1.

It is not necessary that each factor match up precisely as illustrated. In formulating the intervention in this manner, the point in developing these hypotheses is that the intervention be designed to address the problems or needs specified, and that the results be clearly defined so that they can be tracked. Using this format, the relationship between intervention and results can be established.

An important issue in relation to developing working hypotheses of etiology and intervention is that they be developed based on findings from the problem, population, and arena analysis. It is not unusual for people involved in change to

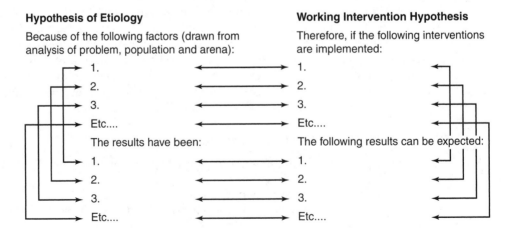

FIGURE 9.1 Relationship of Factors and Results in Working Hypotheses

attempt to impose their own perceptions and agendas on change efforts. A principal or school board member may have had a successful experience imposing strict discipline on an individual student, for example, and firmly believe that this approach is the answer for all teens who pose disciplinary problems, regardless of findings. Every effort must be expended to resist having these pat solutions imposed. Solutions should come from well-researched analysis.

It is not necessary at this point to flesh out the intervention in detail (that will be addressed in Chapter 11). However, for the change effort to proceed, it is necessary to make at least a preliminary decision about the nature and form of the intervention so that building support for a strategy to introduce the change may proceed.

Summary of Steps in Developing the Intervention Hypothesis. The following is a summary checklist reviewing all the important points made so far about developing an intervention hypothesis:

1. A representative group should reexamine all relevant findings from analyses of problem, population, and arena.
2. Relevant quantitative data and other types of information should be distilled into a clear working hypothesis of etiology, establishing an understanding about cause → effect relationships.
3. Based on the working hypothesis of etiology, creative ideas should be generated about interventions that appear to be relevant to the need as it is currently understood.
4. Using these proposed interventions, a working intervention hypothesis should be developed. A series of statements should lay out a clear set of understandings about the nature of the intervention and the expected results or outcomes.

Building Support

A broad base of support is often critical to successful change. Building support requires planning and effort, and begins with an understanding of those who should be considered as the major participants or stakeholders, given the proposed change. A systematic effort to identify the major participants begins with an understanding of each of the systems to be considered. These are discussed in the following sections.

Task 2: Define Participants

Up to this point in the change process it is not unusual for the people involved to be a small core of committed individuals, possibly even close friends or colleagues, who recognize a condition or problem and are concerned enough to take action. It is perfectly appropriate for this small group to undertake some of the early activities of problem identification and analysis, as long as they do not prematurely become totally committed to a particular perspective on the problem.

In order for effective macro change to occur, it is necessary to have allies. A good deal of strategy development involves the building of coalitions. People willing to commit themselves to change rarely accept someone else's definitions and perspectives on problems and solutions without some revision. Full participation should be a goal right from the outset, even if the initiating group is small. It is often true that the greater the level of participation in the problem identification and analysis phases, the greater the likelihood of achievement of consensus on the problem and proposed solution.

It is important that participants critical to the success of the change effort be identified in a systematic manner. Haphazard brainstorming risks overlooking some potentially important systems and overrepresenting others. If participation is to be representative of a wide variety of groups and interests, change agents need to understand all of the systems involved. A number of systems will play critical roles in determining success or failure of the proposed change. Representatives of these systems should be selected carefully and asked to participate in designing the change or intervention.

We will use the term *system* to describe these critical participants. This term is used in the context of systems theory, implying that participants should be viewed as more than simply a collection of individuals who happen to have some common interests and characteristics. As a system or subsystem critical to the success of the change effort, they represent a complex set of interrelationships having systemlike attributes that must be recognized and attended to by the core planning group. One of these attributes, for example, is entropy, which refers to the natural tendency of systems to expire without input and regeneration from outside the system. The concept is directly applicable to the types of systems involved in planned change. (For further discussion of systems theory, see Katz and Kahn, 1966.)

The systems to be considered include (1) an initiator system, (2) a change agent system, (3) a client system, (4) a support system, (5) a controlling system, (6) host and implementing systems, (7) a target system, and (8) an action system. It is worth noting here that these terms are used strictly for conceptual purposes to assist in understanding who should be involved and why. They are not terms commonly used among people involved in change efforts. It is more likely that terms such as *agency, office-holder, position, committee,* or *task force* will be used to designate individuals and groups, but the professional person who coordinates the effort should be aware, conceptually, of what systems need to be represented and why.

Identify the Initiator System.   Questions to be explored include:

- Who first recognized the problem and brought attention to it?
- How should/can the initiators be involved in the change effort?

The *initiator system* is made up of those individuals who first recognize the existence of a problem and bring attention to it. This could be a group of parents raising concerns with a school board about the lack of resources for children who are developmentally disabled, or a group of staff members concerned about a lengthening waiting list for service in the counseling program.

Individuals who first raise the issue may or may not become a part of the initial planning process. If possible, key roles in the change effort should be assigned to initiators. Having already demonstrated an interest in the issue, they may be in a position to bring other supporters along. This becomes especially important if initiators are indigenous to the community. People who have lived with the problem or need are likely to be knowledgeable about the problem, but may see themselves as powerless to affect the system. Empowerment strategies such as teaching, training, group counseling, and consciousness-raising efforts at this point can pay rich dividends in the long run, and can place appropriate spokespersons in leadership positions. In any case, it is important for change agents to be aware of who first raised the issue, and to keep in close contact as the problem or need is framed for public consumption.

Identify the Change Agent System.   The key question to be explored for this activity is:

■ Who will be responsible for leadership and coordination in the early stages of the change effort?

For a professionally assisted change effort to be successful, there must be one or more individuals designated as coordinator(s) of the change effort. We will refer to this person or these persons as the *change agent.* The change agent, together with an initial core planning committee or task force, comprises the change agent system. If the change activity will require drawing on the resources of an organization, it is essential that the organization sanction the change and also be identified as part of the change agent system. This may involve getting formal approval from the executive board, and may require release time from other duties, secretarial support, and other allocation of resources.

The makeup of this system is critical to the change effort because much of what is accomplished will be framed in the perspectives of these individuals. Ideally, this system will include representation from the initiator system—people who have experienced the identified problem, people who have had experience in trying to solve the problem, and people who can be influential in getting the change accepted.

The function of the change agent system is to act as an initial coordinating or steering committee until a wider range of participants can be incorporated into the change effort. Many participants in the change effort will be taking on different activities at the same time. It is the job of the change agent system to ensure that the change effort is properly organized and carried out from its early conceptualization to the point at which it is turned over to others for implementation. As the major systems and perspectives are identified and the action system (discussed in a later section in this chapter) is formed, the coordinating functions are shifted to the action system.

The work of the change agent system begins with coordinating and carrying out the problem, population, and arena analyses as described in Chapters 3 through 8. As new participants are added, responsibilities are assigned until a point is reached where the analytical work is complete and a strategy is developed for getting the change accepted and implemented.

Identify the Client System.   Questions to be explored include:

- Who will be the primary beneficiaries of change?
- Who will be the secondary beneficiaries of change?

The client system is made up of individuals who are asking for and will become either direct or indirect beneficiaries of the change if it is implemented. In Chapter 3, we pointed out that macro change efforts begin with identification of a target population and a problem. The client system is always in some way linked to the target population for whom the specific change effort is being undertaken. In some cases, it is possible that the target population and the client system could even be synonymous. For example, if the target population is all homeless people in the town of Liberty, and they organize for the purpose of requesting housing and services for all homeless people in Liberty, then the target population and the client system are the same. However, if drugs are being sold out of a house in a neighborhood, and if the neighborhood residents ask for help in organizing to get rid of the drug dealers, then the neighbors represent the client system and the drug dealers become the target system.

Different terms are used for conceptual purposes. A *target population* brings focus to the population analysis and usually represents a broader spectrum of people. A *client system* refers to the people who are intended to benefit from the change effort. Sometimes they are the same, sometimes they are not.

In defining the client system, the change agent should resist the temptation to jump to the easy and obvious definition of the primary beneficiaries, and should patiently and carefully analyze details. For example, if the identified problem is increasing vandalism in an elementary school, several potential beneficiaries could be considered as the client system. A partial list of people who would benefit from eliminating vandalism from the school would include students, teachers, administrators, parents, local police, campus security, neighbors, the school board, and the community as a whole. The question, then, becomes one of establishing priorities for direct benefits and distinguishing between primary and secondary beneficiaries. The decision will have an important impact on the change effort. If "students who want a good education in a vandalism-free environment" are identified as primary beneficiaries, then the intervention may well be directed toward tighter security and stricter discipline. If, on the other hand, primary beneficiaries are described as "students who commit acts of vandalism and are unable to maximize their educational opportunities due to antisocial attitudes," then the intervention may be directed toward treatment.

The boundaries for macro-level changes tend to be defined in a way that the primary focus is on a segment of a community or organization. Total communities as defined by political boundaries (entire towns, cities, counties) or total organizations are rarely the focus of a professionally directed change effort led by a social worker, but it is certainly not out of the question that they could be.

However the primary beneficiaries are defined, the remaining groups should be identified and listed as secondary beneficiaries. It may be important to call on secondary beneficiaries when the change effort needs public support. We will refer to secondary beneficiaries as the *support system*. Remember that systems frequently overlap, and it is possible for individuals or groups to be part of more than one system.

Identify the Support System. The key question to be explored for this activity is:

- What other individuals and groups (in addition to the primary and secondary beneficiaries) will support the change effort?

The *support system* is a catch-all system that refers to everyone in the community or organization who has an interest in the success of the proposed change. Some may receive secondary benefits. This group is expected to be positively inclined toward change, and may be willing to be involved in supporting and advocating for the change if they are needed.

The support system is defined largely by who is in the target population or client system and by the nature of the problem. People have an interest in certain populations and problems for a variety of reasons: a loved one is afflicted with the problem, their employment brings them into close contact, their church or service organization has selected this population for assistance. They are sometimes described by the related concern or issue, such as the "mental health community" or the "foster care community." These are the people the change agent will count on to become involved if decision makers need to be persuaded that the change is necessary. Figure 9.2 illustrates the relationship between initiator, change agent, client, and support systems.

Initiator, change agent, and client systems can be seen as incorporated within the boundaries of the support system in that they all have an interest in addressing the need for change. They may overlap or may represent separate and distinct constituencies.

Identify the Controlling System. The key question to be explored for this activity is:

- Who has the formally delegated authority and the power to approve and order implementation of the proposed change?

The *controlling system* is defined as that person or group of individuals with the formally delegated authority and the power to approve and order the imple-

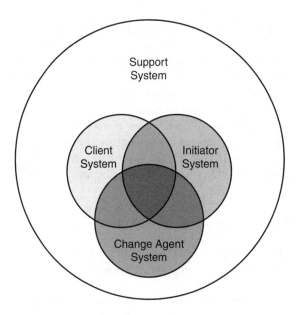

FIGURE 9.2   Relationship of Systems

mentation of the proposed change. Macro-level change invariably involves approval by some formally designated authority. If the change involves a public agency or publicly funded or regulated services, control may rest with a body of elected officials. If the change involves a private agency, control may rest with a board of directors. The question that must be answered in defining the controlling system is: What is the highest level to which one must appeal in order to receive sanction and approval for the proposed change? These individuals or bodies are significant to acceptance and implementation of the change effort, and their position(s) on the proposed change(s) must be known and considered.

   The controlling system in a given episode of change is not necessarily always the individual or group at the highest level of authority. It is common for authority to be vested in individuals who are expected to make decisions at lower levels so that not every proposed change elevates to the top. For example, if staff in a domestic violence shelter find that it is necessary to add legal consultation to the shelter's counseling program, it is possible that the controlling system may be the program manager of the counseling program, it may be the CEO of the shelter, or it may be the board of directors. Much depends on the pattern of delegation adopted within the organization and on the extent to which additional resources will be required. Some probing will be necessary to determine who has authority to approve and order implementation of the proposed change, since each situation is unique.

Identify the Host and Implementing Systems. Questions to be explored include:

- What organization or organizational unit will be responsible for sponsoring and delivering the activities of the change effort?
- What individuals will be involved in direct delivery of services or other activities necessary to implement the change effort?

The *host system* is the organization or unit with formally designated responsibility for the area to be addressed by the proposed change. The organizational chart should provide some guidance in identifying the host system. Typically, the host is located below the controlling system on the organizational chart. Within the host system is one or more employees and/or volunteers who will have day-to-day responsibility for carrying out the change. We refer to these employees or volunteers as the *implementing system.* In most instances of macro-level change, the host system will be a subunit of an organization that will be expected to implement a policy change, a new program, or a project. The listing of systems in Table 9.2 identifies controlling, host, and implementing systems in a school system and in a law-enforcement system.

The change agent should be careful not to assume that the positions and perspectives of the controlling system, host system, and implementing system about the proposed change are identical. It is not unusual for those involved in the execution of policy to disagree with the policymakers and vice versa. Each system should be assessed separately. Figure 9.3 depicts the typical relationships of the controlling, host, and implementing systems.

Identify the Target System. Questions to be explored include:

- What is it that needs to be changed (e.g., individual, group, structure, policy, practice, etc.) in order for the effort to be successful?
- Where (within the organization or community) is the target system located?

The *target system* is the individual, group, structure, policy, or practice that needs to be changed for the primary beneficiaries to achieve the desired benefits.

TABLE 9.2 Examples of Controlling, Host, and Implementing Systems

	Controlling	Host	Implementing
School System	School Board	A particular school and its principle	Teachers in the school involved in the change
Law-Enforcement System	City Council	Police Chief and Department	Police officers involved in the change

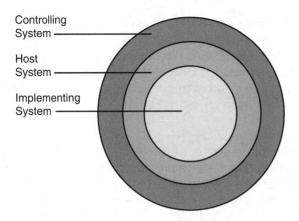

Controlling
System

Host
System

Implementing
System

FIGURE 9.3   Relationships between Controlling, Host, and Implementing Systems

The target system (not to be confused with our earlier use of the term *target population*) is a complex concept that cannot always be defined in clear and simple
terms. Often, what needs to be changed may include philosophy, values, attitudes,
practices, and policies as well as the provision of services. Another complicating
factor is that many change efforts must address multiple targets. For example, in
addressing the issue of "deadbeat dads," it may be necessary to educate the state
legislature about the costs to the state of failure to pay child support before the legislators are willing to support proposed legislation. The expected beneficiary is single mothers who are not receiving court-ordered child support, and the remedy is
to pass legislation that allows officials to pursue delinquent parents across state
lines and to seize assets until delinquent payments are made. But some reluctant
legislators may resist government involvement in what they perceive as private
matters, and may need to be persuaded that the proposed legislation is appropriate. In this case, reluctant legislators become the first target system and, if the effort
with them is successful, passage of the legislation becomes the second target system. Finally, when the proposed legislation is passed, efforts can be focused on the
third target system, delinquent parents, so that the client system, single mothers,
can finally receive the child support payments due them.

      Two questions need to be answered in defining the target system: (1) What
change (or series of changes) needs to take place in order for the primary beneficiaries to achieve the desired benefits? and (2) What individuals or groups need to
agree to the change (or series of changes)? We have defined these individuals or
groups as controlling, host, and implementing systems. The target system may lie
within the boundaries of any or all of these systems, or it may lie entirely outside
any of them. The target system in a school experience may include selected school
board members, a principal and assistant principals, or a subgroup of teachers, or
the target system may be a selected group of students. The decision will be made
based on what change is proposed and who needs to be convinced to support it.

Identify the Action System.   The key question to be explored for this activity is:

■ Who should be represented on an expanded "steering committee" or deci-sion-making group that will see the change effort through to completion?

As all other systems are being defined and participants selected, an action sys-tem is being formed. The *action system* is made up of individuals from other systems who have an active role in planning the change and moving it toward implementa-tion. Clearly, there is a good deal of overlap here with the change agent system, ear-lier defined as the professional change agent, sanctioning organization, and sometimes a core planning group. Although the change agent system forms the core of the action system, other actors also have important roles in providing input into decision making and should be added as the change effort proceeds. The action sys-tem should include representatives from as many other systems as possible, includ-ing those systems in need of change, if the relationship is not excessively adversarial.

For example, if the social problem under consideration is the unmet needs of the homeless, the concern might first be raised by a person who passes by a few old men sleeping in doorways every day on her way from the bus to her place of work *(initiator).* She finds that several other employees at her place of work have the same concern, and she raises the issue to the city council *(controlling system),* where it is assigned to the City Department of Human Services *(change agent system and host sys-tem).* The social worker from the department *(change agent and possibly implementer)* forms a task force that includes those who brought the issue to the council. As the condition is researched and analyzed, more people are added to the task force. Pro-fessionals who work with the homeless *(support system)* would be asked to join, as would some current or former homeless people *(client system)* and someone from the city's political or administrative structure who understands the potentialities and limitations of the city's participation *(controlling system).* When all the significant par-ticipants have been identified, this group would become the central decision-making body in the change effort and would be defined as the *action system.*

Systems in Interaction.   In examining these systems in interaction, it is important to remember that we distinguish among them and define them separately for conceptual purposes only. In actual practice, all systems could be within one orga-nization, and it is highly probable that many systems will overlap. The interrela-tionships of all systems is depicted in Figure 9.4.

One side of the diagram includes the systems proposing and favoring change. The larger system is the support system, and includes all systems presumably favoring change. Contained within the support system are the initiator, client, and change agent systems, all with possibly varying degrees of overlap. On the other side of the diagram we find the systems identified as in need of change. The con-trolling, host, and implementing systems are represented by concentric circles in that each subsystem is typically contained within the span of control of the next larger system. The target system may lie within any of these systems or even out-side all three. The action system may overlap any or all of these systems.

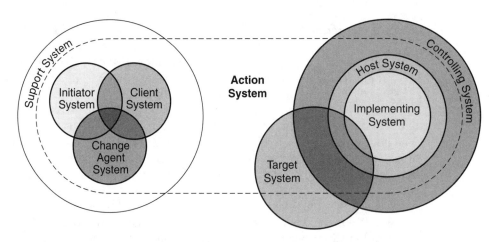

FIGURE 9.4   Systems in Interaction

An example illustrating all systems within one organization would be a situation in which an organizational change is proposed. For example, a human service agency may have a special program for "crack babies" (babies born addicted to drugs) and their mothers *(client system)* that includes detoxification, rehabilitation, counseling, and parent training. After six months, a community child welfare advocate *(initiator system)* notices that the case managers *(implementing system)* have been practicing "creaming," providing the bulk of services to the most highly motivated clients and ignoring the needs of the least motivated. In this example, this practice of "creaming" would be the target—that which is to be changed *(target system)*. The child welfare advocate calls the problem to the attention of the executive director (representing the *controlling system*) and the executive director directs the program supervisor *(change agent)* to form a small task group to study the problem and propose several alternative solutions. The task force *(action system)* is made up of the supervisor, a case manager, a board member, an administrator, a representative of the child welfare advocacy group, and a former client now volunteering for the agency. They explore the problems and possibilities of directing more service to unmotivated clients.

All this has taken place within the boundaries of a single organization with some input from extraorganizational sources. Because of the shifting nature of boundaries of systems, the eventual target could become some entity completely outside the agency as well. The reason for retaining conceptual clarity in defining the systems is that the change agent can ensure that each important perspective is represented, even if the focus of the change effort shifts over time.

Even though the terms *controlling, host,* and *implementing* may never be used, it is important that the change agent understand the domain, authority, and power of each, and keep roles, responsibilities, and expectations for each clear and distinct. A roster such as the one illustrated in Table 9.3 may be useful in keeping track of systems and their representatives.

TABLE 9.3   A Roster of Systems and System Representatives

System	Definition	System Representative
Initiator	Those who first brought the problem to attention	Two women who struggled through the experience of coming to this community from another country with no help available to make the adjustment
Change Agent	The professional social worker, agency, and others coordinating the change effort	The social worker employed by the local community center, where the new program will be housed and sponsored
Client	Primary and secondary beneficiaries	Immigrant families (both adults and children); local schools; employers; neighborhood residents
Support	Others who may be expected to support the change effort	Churches in the neighborhood; community organizations that deal with immigrants; city officials; selected politicians; people from other, similar neighborhoods
Controlling	The person or persons who have the power and authority to approve the change and direct that it be implemented	The mayor, city manager, and city council, who are being asked to extend some city services, provide bilingual staff, and provide some funding
Host	The part of the organization or community that will provide auspices for administration of the intervention	The City Department of Human Services, Neighborhood Services Division (NSD)
Implementing	The staff and/or volunteers who will carry out the intervention	One staff member from the NSD (a community organizer, and 10 volunteers who were once newly arrived immigrants)
Target	That which must be changed for the intervention to be successful	Members of the City Council, most of whom oppose this effort because of the precedent they believe will be established and the number of neighborhoods that will subsequently ask for funding for special needs
Action	The expanded planning and coordinating committee responsible for seeing the change effort through to completion	The Coordinating Committee will be made up of the initiator system representatives, the change agent, two representatives of the client system, one City Council member, one teacher, one employer, the community organizer from NSD, and two volunteers

Task 3: Examine System Readiness for Change

As the change process unfolds, each of the systems just defined should be assessed for its readiness to support the proposed change. An assessment of readiness should include consideration of an openness to change in general, commitment to the proposed change, availability of resources to implement the proposed change, and the degree of outside resistance to the proposed change. These considerations should be assessed for each system.

Assess General Openness to Change.   The key question for this activity is:

- What has been the past experience with each of the systems with regard to organizational or community change?

General openness to change involves an informal assessment, based on experience, of how people in decision-making positions have dealt with earlier proposals. This is not likely to be a consideration for those systems promoting change, since these systems are clearly in support of (and therefore open to) change in this instance. However, when examining the systems to be changed, it can be a very different story.

Much has been written, for example, about the difficulties of getting organizations (especially bureaucracies) to change (see, for example, Gortner, Mahler, & Nicholson, 1987; Kalleberg, Knoke, Marsden, & Spaeth, 1996; Perrow, 1979). Analyzing past experiences and general openness to change may be helpful in finding the subsystems or individuals that are most likely to be responsive to the proposed change. Discovering openness is not a simple matter of asking people in decision-making positions if they are open to change. Background research on positions taken in response to earlier proposed changes is also needed. Have there been communitywide issues or initiatives that included (or could have included) this agency? Did the agency participate? What was its position? Have agency leaders been willing to take stands on public issues? Or is it seen as an agency that prefers to keep to itself and continue business-as-usual? Answers to these questions will be helpful in assessing the agency's general openness to change.

Identify Anticipated or Actual Response.   The key question to be explored for this activity is:

- What level of commitment to the proposed change is anticipated from each of the systems?

Commitment to the proposed change should be examined in terms of each system's enthusiasm in endorsing the change in its existing form (as identified in the intervention hypothesis). It is characteristic of community and organizational change that there will be differences in perspective on what form changes should take, even when there is enthusiastic agreement that change is needed. Low levels of commitment to the change as proposed can have a negative effect on its acceptance and eventual implementation. Assessment of commitment should involve examination of degree of enthusiasm as well as degree of internal consensus about the design of the proposed change. Open meetings with parties affected by the proposed change are useful for gaining a sense of support and degree of consensus.

Determine Availability of Resources. Questions to be explored include:

- From what sources will resources be solicited?
- What resources will be requested?

Availability of resources, for many change efforts, will be the key issue. Although openness to change and commitment to the proposed change are helpful, availability of resources is a *sine qua non. Resources for the systems to be changed* usually refers to budgeted dollars, but should also be understood to include reassigning staff, use of volunteers, and in-kind resources such as computer time, supplies, space, and so on. *Resources for the systems promoting change* usually refers to number of people, time available, and the willingness to persist if opposed. An inventory of resources available to promote the change, as well as resources needed to implement the change, will help guide the change effort.

Examine Outside Opposition to Change. The key question to be explored in this activity is:

- What individuals or groups outside the systems identified can be expected to oppose the change effort?

The final factor to be explored with each system is the degree of external resistance or opposition experienced. There may be instances in which a controlling system—elected local officials, for example—supports a proposed change but the constituency it represents—certain local neighborhood groups, for example—is opposed. Almost any proposed change that requires public funds will find external resistance from groups that are competing for the funds. If pressure tactics are to be used, the change agent should ascertain whether the pressures that can be brought about through this change effort will be able to offset pressures brought by those resisting the change. For the systems promoting change, it is important to identify possible vulnerable points in its overall strategic considerations. Weaknesses in supporting data or other information, illogical arguments, or people who can be pressured to back down may represent liabilities, and those promoting change should be aware of them. A summary of considerations is illustrated in Table 9.4.

TABLE 9.4   Assessing System Readiness for Change

	Systems Promoting Change	Systems to Be Changed
	Initiator, Client Change Agent, Support, Action	Controlling, Host, Implementing, Target
General Openness to Change	Probably not an issue, since these groups are promoting change.	If these systems have shown tendencies in the past to resist changes of this type, this should serve as an early warning.
Anticipated or Actual Response to Proposed Change	How committed are those promoting change to the type change being proposed? What are the differences, if any? Are some committed only to a highly specific solution?	Is there consensus or disagreement about the type of change being proposed? How strong are feelings for and/or against it?
Availability of Resources	Do the systems promoting change have the skills and human resources to see the change effort through to completion, even if there is resistance?	Do the systems to be changed have the funding, staff, facilities, equipment, or other resources needed to implement the proposed change?
Opposition to Change	What forces outside these systems are opposing change? How strong is the opposition?	What is the source of outside opposition? How strong are the pressures to reject the proposed change? What significant actors are most vulnerable to pressures?

Selecting an Approach to Change

Task 4: Select a Change Approach

As the change agent moves toward completion of all of the problem, population, and arena identification and analysis tasks covered in Chapters 3 through 8, the nature of the problem and significant supporting information should be coming into focus. This makes clear *what* needs to be changed. An important question yet to be answered is *how* the change should come about. For example, an agency's funding may be in jeopardy because its drug-treatment program has been unable to demonstrate effectiveness for the past three years. Changing the ways in which these services are provided may require a policy change (e.g., redefining eligibility). This same situation could also require a program change (e.g., changing the type of treatment provided), or a project change (e.g., testing a new treatment approach with a limited number of clients). Changes in personnel and practices are also options, but we recommend that their use be limited to situations in which policy, program, or project approaches are determined not to be either effective or feasible. These five change approaches will be discussed below.

Select a Policy, Program, Project, Personnel, or Practice Approach. The key question to be explored for this activity is:

- What approach (or combination of approaches) is most likely to achieve the desired change?

The professionally assisted change efforts discussed in these chapters are intended to fall into two very general categories: (1) those that lead to an improved quality of life for the clients or communities served or (2) those that lead to an improved quality of work life for employees so that their energies can be devoted toward providing the best possible services to clients and/or communities. In order to address these two categories, we propose five approaches to change. The approach selected determines the focus of the target system.

Policy. Policy is represented by a formally adopted statement that reflects goals and strategies or agreements on a settled course of action. Policies may be established by elected representatives, boards, or administrators, or by a vote of the people affected. In some instances, a policy may be needed in order to change a situation. For example, a new policy that outlines a grievance process for staff may be empowering to employees who feel they have no recourse when they disagree with agency practices. In other situations, existing policy may be unnecessarily restrictive and need to be amended. For example, a family member may be the best and most appropriate caregiver for an elderly or disabled person, but agency policy may prevent provision of respite care services to family members.

Program. Programs are prearranged sets of activities designed to achieve a set of goals and objectives. In macro practice, programs are usually intended to provide services directly to clients or communities. Sometimes they are of a supportive nature, such as fund-raising or public relations programs.

Program change will vary. Some change efforts will result in the establishment of new programs to serve a special population group. Other change efforts may focus on altering existing programs so that they are designed to be more responsive to client or community needs.

Project. Projects are much like programs but have a time-limited existence and are more flexible so that they can be adapted to the needs of a changing environment. Projects, if deemed successful and worthwhile, are often permanently installed as programs. The term *pilot project* came into use to illustrate this type of small-scale experimentation.

Often, change agents will find that creating a project that demonstrates a new or untested intervention is more palatable to decision makers than making a long-term program commitment. For this reason, it is common to select a demonstration or pilot project as a first approach, and then to attempt a more expansive program change if the project is successful.

Personnel.   Communities and organizations are made up of people *(personnel)* who find themselves in interaction with each other. Sometimes people experience seemingly insurmountable differences and engage in ongoing conflict. Employees occasionally get involved in an attempt to depose an unpopular administrator. The professional change agent should proceed very carefully before getting involved in personnel-related issues. Several factors should be considered. First is the proposed personnel-related change effort being considered because of the reasons stated earlier: improvement of the quality of life of clients or communities or improvement of work life so that clients or communities can be better served. Second, will the proposed change be dealt with through regularly established channels? When the target of a change effort is an individual, there is often a temptation to proceed "underground."

Brager and Holloway (1978) suggest that, under certain circumstances, covert tactics may be appropriate. First, one must determine if agency officials are ignoring client or community needs in favor of their own interests. Second, the change agent must decide if the use of formal, overt sources may jeopardize self, clients, or colleagues. Third, if overt means have failed or are clearly not feasible, one may consider covert tactics. In any case, the professional change agent should recognize the potential risks (including loss of job), should be convinced that the change is worth the consequences, and should be prepared to accept them if necessary. Ethical practice is basic to social work, and ethical dilemmas often emerge in situations in which one has a conflict over who is right, with competing perspectives possibly coming from employer, colleagues, community interests, client advocates, and others. Ethical dilemmas were discussed in Chapter 1 and will be reexamined in the next chapter.

Practice.   The fifth focus of change, *practice,* refers to the way organizations or individuals within them go about doing business. Practices are less formal than policies. They may even be specific to individuals or groups, and are therefore more elusive than policies. Well-designed policy, together with monitoring and evaluation capability, is usually a stronger and more permanent remedy for ineffective or offensive practices. For example, if at a homeless shelter it has become common practice to have residents participate in the decision making, running, and maintenance of the shelter, and if some residents choose not to participate, several options are available. The staff can ignore the nonparticipants, they can make participation a condition of remaining in the shelter, or they can make participation voluntary. Addressed in this way, the practice is often left to the discretion of the staff member who happens to be involved.

Rethinking these practices may lead to a conclusion that participation should be part of the treatment plan, including job training and preparation. If this is elevated to the level of a policy change, the practice becomes more uniformly enforced, and becomes integrated into an overall plan for self-sufficiency. If it remains at the level of a practice, it invariably is treated as discretionary. Some practice issues can be resolved by consensus among the staff, and some need to be addressed at higher levels in the organization.

Approaches in Interaction.   A decision about the change approach is obviously intimately connected to a decision about the nature of the problem, the target system, and the arena. The important issues to be resolved in defining the change approach are (1) Who or what needs to be changed in order for the problem or need to be resolved? (2) What is the appropriate point of entry to address the problem or need? and (3) What approaches, or combinations of approaches, are most likely to yield the desired results?

Many changes can be handled in a very simple and straightforward manner. More day-care slots are needed for single mothers in employment training programs; the change agent calls this to the attention of the appropriate administrator and budget director. Resources may be allocated and more day-care slots added. Parents want drug and alcohol education in the high schools; the school board agrees to provide it.

Other changes may require multiple approaches in order to be successful. For example, a community center in a poor, Latino community is committed to improving the quality of life for residents. The center provides many services to the community, including a health clinic, back-to-school clothing, a food bank, after-school programs, and other community services. The social worker and several interns have completed a needs assessment to determine what the community sees as priority needs. The workers have also completed an assets assessment to determine what talents and interests community members can contribute toward strengthening the community. At an informational meeting, center staff inform community members about grants that have been applied for and about negotiations with the city to become a neighborhood targeted for specialized services. The residents express dissatisfaction that they have not been involved in these decisions, and accuse the staff of having elitist attitudes about participation in decision making. Community leaders threaten to appeal to funding sources if they are not more actively involved by the center in decision making.

This issue can be approached in a number of ways. A *policy* approach would focus on creating a policy, to be passed by the board of directors, designed to ensure that community residents are involved in program and budget decisions. A policy, if monitored and enforced, would be the strongest assurance that the participation issue would be addressed, but it could become cumbersome and lead to micro management of even small decisions within the center.

Another alternative would be to create a formal volunteer *program*, directed to continue ongoing assets assessments and to actively pursue community mem-

bers to encourage and facilitate involvement in the various programs and decisions of the center. This approach may increase the number of residents involved
in the center, but may not ensure that community members are at the appropriate
table when decisions are made.

A *project* might also be undertaken designed to survey participants periodically
to determine whether they support pursuit of various special grant and contract
funded efforts. Results of surveys could be compiled and disseminated through the
community newsletter. This may satisfy some of the concern about participation, but
may eliminate some projects that require short time frames for response.

Another option may focus on *personnel*. The social worker and other staff
could be sent for training to ensure that they understand how to work with community members and how to involve them at critical points in the decision-making
process. Involvement of community members could be made a part of their
job descriptions, and could be incorporated into their annual performance
evaluations.

Finally, the focus could be on the specific *practices* identified in the community meeting—grant writing and collaboration with the city. Community representatives could be identified to work with staff on an ongoing basis to ensure that
appropriate local input was a part of each decision on funding or collaboration.

An innovative change agent could probably come up with many more
options, and may even find ways to use a bit of each approach, if that is what it
would take to bring about greater empowerment and participation. Deciding on
who or what needs to be changed and what systems need to be involved are
important components of successful change. When agreement has been reached on
these decisions, the change process is ready to move on to selection of tactics, to be
discussed in the next chapter.

Summary

As we have discussed in earlier chapters, planned change requires careful study
and analysis before action is taken. We propose in this chapter that the information
compiled during the study and analysis phases be summarized into a working
hypothesis of etiology and a working intervention hypothesis. This exercise
ensures that the intervention will logically flow from an understanding of all the
factors that contribute to the problem, need, issue, or opportunity.

Once a clearly conceptualized intervention has been proposed, it is necessary
to begin a systematic process of enlisting support of critical participants. We have
used the term *systems* and have identified eight systems that will have roles of
varying importance to the success of the intervention. Change agents need to know
what individuals and groups make up each of these systems, who speaks for these
groups, and what their positions are on the proposed change. Without this knowledge, a change agent will be severely limited in getting the change accepted. A
series of assessments will help the change agent to understand the positions of
each of the systems on the proposed change.

Finally, before selecting a strategy, as discussed in the next chapter, the change agent selects a change approach. We suggest choosing a policy, program, project, personnel, or practice approach, or some combination. When these tasks have been accomplished, the change effort is ready to move toward selection of strategy and tactics.

DISCUSSION QUESTIONS AND EXERCISES

1. *Developing an Intervention Strategy.* In order to complete this exercise, you will need to select a case example with which you are familiar. You may want to use material you developed in an earlier chapter, or you may want to create your own example. First, you will need to summarize the analytical work required for understanding problem, population, and arena by identifying major factors associated with each. Next, develop a working hypothesis of etiology and a working intervention hypothesis, using the following format:

Because of the following factors drawn from analysis of problem, population, and arena:

a.

b.

c.

Etc. . . .

The result (or response) has been:

a.

b.

c.

Etc. . . .

Therefore if the following interventions are provided:

a.

b.

c.

Etc. . . .

We would expect to see the following results:

a.

b.

c.

Etc. . . .

■ Identify persons or groups affected by this proposed intervention and complete the following chart:

Persons Affected	How Affected	Approximate Numbers within the Boundaries of this Change Episode
_____	_____	_____
_____	_____	_____
_____	_____	_____
_____	_____	_____
_____	_____	_____
_____	_____	_____

- Identify the domain within which this problem or opportunity resides (e.g., education, social services, corrections, city government, tribal government, county government, etc.).

- Through what organizational structure would one work to resolve this problem?

2. Identify by title a representative of each of the following systems:

System	Description	Representative(s)
Example: Controlling System	School Board	School Board President
Initiator System		
Change Agent System		
Client System		
Support System		
Controlling System		
Host System		
Implementing System		
Target System		
Action System		

3. How do different systems view participation in problem identification and resolution (e.g., do they see themselves as active participants or as shut out from the process?)?

4. Select a policy, program, project, personnel, or practice approach to change. Briefly explain why you would select this approach.

APPENDIX
Framework for Developing an Intervention

Task 1: Develop the Intervention Hypothesis

Refine the Working Hypothesis of Etiology
- What factors gleaned from the problem analysis, the population analysis, and the arena analysis help in understanding cause-and-effect relationships?

- What themes seem to fit best with the current situation?
- How should the working hypothesis of etiology be framed?

Develop a Working Intervention Hypothesis
- What interventions are implied by the hypothesis of etiology?
- Does it appear that these interventions are most likely to reduce or eliminate the problem?
- What results can be expected from these interventions?

Task 2: Define Participants

Identify the Initiator System
- Who first recognized the problem and brought attention to it?
- How should/can the initiators be involved in the change effort?

Identify the Change Agent System
- Who will be responsible for leadership and coordination in the early stages of the change effort?

Identify the Client System
- Who will be the primary beneficiaries of change?
- Who will be the secondary beneficiaries of change?

Identify the Support System
- What other individuals and groups (in addition to the primary and secondary beneficiaries) will support the change effort?

Identify the Controlling System
- Who has the formally delegated authority and the power to approve and order implementation of the proposed change?

Identify the Host and Implementing Systems
- What organization or organizational unit will be responsible for sponsoring and delivering the activities of the change effort?
- What individuals will be involved in direct delivery of services or other activities necessary to implement the change effort?

Identify the Target System
- What is it that needs to be changed (e.g., individual, group, structure, policy, practice, etc.) in order for the effort to be successful?
- Where (within the organization or community) is the target system located?

Identify the Action System
- Who should be represented on an expanded "steering committee" or decision-making group that will see the change effort through to completion?

Task 3: Examine System Readiness for Change

Assess General Openness to Change
- What has been the past experience with each of the systems with regard to organizational or community change?

Identify Anticipated or Actual Response
- What level of commitment to the proposed change is anticipated from each of the systems?

Determine Availability of Resources
- From what sources will resources be solicited?
- What resources will be requested?

Examine Outside Opposition to Change
- What individuals or groups outside the systems identified can be expected to oppose the change effort?

Task 4: Select a Change Approach

Select a Policy, Program, Project, Personnel, or Practice Approach
- What approach (or combination of approaches) is most likely to achieve the desired change?

SUGGESTED READINGS

Arches, J. (2001). Powerful partnerships. *Journal of Community Practice, 9*(2): 15–30.

Bargal, D., and H. Schmid (Guest Eds.). (1992). Organizational change and development in human service organizations. *Administration in Social Work, 16*(3/4): entire issue.

Brueggemann, W. G. (2002). *The practice of macro social work* (2nd ed.). Belmont, CA: Brooks/Cole.

Castelloe, P., and J. Prokopy. (2002). Recruiting participants for community practice interventions: Merging community practice theory with social movement theory. *Journal of Community Practice, 9*(2): 31–48

Delgado, M. (2000). *Community social work practice in an urban context.* New York: Oxford University Press.

Edelman, I. (2000). Participation and service integration in community-based initiatives. *Journal of Community Practice, 9*(1): 57–76.

Fatout, M., and S. R. Rose. (1995). *Task groups in the social services.* Thousand Oaks, CA: Sage.

Haynes, K. S., and J. S. Mickelson. (1997). *Affecting change* (3rd ed.). New York: Longman.

Kretzmann, J. P., and J. L. McKnight. (1993). *Building communities from the inside out.* Chicago: Author.

Meenaghan, T. M., and W. E. Gibbons. (2000). *Generalist practice in larger settings.* Chicago: Lyceum Books.

Rosenthal, J. M., and B. Taudieu. (2000). *Artisans of democracy: How ordinary people, families of extreme poverty, and social institutions become allies to overcome social exclusion.* Lanham, VA: University Press of America.

Rubin, H. J., and I. S. Rubin. (2001). *Community organizing and development* (3rd ed.). Boston: Allyn and Bacon.

Salipante, P. F., and K. Golden-Biddle. (1995). Managing traditionality and strategic change in nonprofit organizations. *Nonprofit Management and Leadership, 6*(1): 3–20.

Snavely, K., and M. B. Tracy. (2002). Developing of trust in rural nonprofit collaborations. *Nonprofit and Voluntary Sector Quarterly, 31*(1): 62–83.

REFERENCES

Brager, G., and S. Holloway. (1978). *Changing human service organizations: Politics and practice.* New York: Free Press.

Brager, G., H. Specht, and J. L. Torczyner. (1987). *Community organizing.* New York: Columbia University Press.

Gortner, H., J. Mahler, and J. Nicholson. (1987). *Organization theory: A public perspective.* Chicago: Dorsey Press.

Kalleberg, A., D. Knoke, P. Marsden, and J. Spaeth. (1996). *Organizations in America: Analyzing their* structures and human resource practices. Thousand Oaks, CA: Sage.

Katz, D., and R. L. Kahn. (1966). *The social psychology of organizations.* New York: Wiley.

Morales, J. (1992). Community social work with Puerto Rican communities in the United States: One organizer's perspective. In F. Rivera and J. Erlich (Eds.), *Community organizing in a diverse society.* Boston: Allyn and Bacon.

Perrow, C. (1979). *Complex organizations. A critical Essay* (2nd ed.). Glenview, IL: Scott, Foresman.

10 Selecting Appropriate Strategies and Tactics

OVERVIEW

In Chapter 9, we emphasized that deciding on a strategy can be a time-consuming and detailed process. Although many people may agree that a problem exists, getting agreement on just how the situation should be changed is seldom easy. Therefore, social workers should be open to the possibility that practices in many of the arenas in which they operate are well entrenched and there will be a natural tendency to resist change.

The fact that agency missions are stated in inspiring words does not mean that all agencies carry out those missions. Practitioners must be aware that they are a part of legitimized systems that often contribute to the oppression experienced by the client group they are trying to serve. Selecting appropriate tactics requires one to think critically about the politics of the situation and to analyze the target system carefully. As pointed out in Chapter 9, there may even be sequential or multiple targets.

Guidelines for Assessing the Political and Economic Context

Analyzing the target system means thinking systematically. Recall in earlier chapters that we introduced five analogies used by social scientists to view social systems: (1) mechanical, (2) organismic, (3) morphogenic, (4) factional, and (5) catastrophic (Martin & O'Connor, 1989, p. 54). Whereas mechanical analogies see social systems as machines, organismic approaches are grounded in the fields of ecology and biology in which social systems are compared to biological organisms. Both mechanical and organismic analogies are fairly conservative in that systems are seen as working toward stability, seeking to reestablish equilibrium, preserving the status quo, and focusing on order over conflict. However, morphogenic, factional, and catastrophic analogies to social systems assume that conflict is not only inevitable but is to be expected. Morphogenic perspectives view social systems as always changing. A factional analogy views social systems as comprised of competing subgroups that are not cooperative, characterized by contentiousness. And last, a catastrophic analogy sees systems as in continual flux, changing so much that they appear chaotic.

In attempting to understand the political and economic environment within which the proposed change will take place, consider what analogy might apply. Having identified the various systems (initiator, change agent, client, support, controlling, host and implementing, target, and action) and their readiness for change in Chapter 9, one will have an increased awareness of the politics of the organization or community within which the change intervention will occur. Also, consider that even if a change agent thinks that this is a situation in which there is little contentiousness or conflict, this perspective may not be held by others. For example, if a community is viewed as highly factional, then attention to creating linkages among groups may be necessary before any planned change can occur. However, if one's organization is fairly closed and machine-like, then attention will be focused on internal operations and the environment may be seen as a threat. This requires a different approach to change because change may not be welcomed. Some groups, organizations, and communities will be more amenable to change than others, some will be more closed, and others more open to conflict. Being able to assess these arenas and their openness to change is central to the planned change process.

No matter how one defines the problem or how one views conflict, we assure you that conflict is inevitable. Anytime that change is proposed, no matter how simple it may seem, there will be resistance. Even with willing target systems that agree to collaborate, there will be points of disagreement—even contentiousness—over details or specifics of the proposed change. In any change effort, one cannot and should not avoid conflict. Instead, it is the degree or level of conflict and the possibility of overcoming disagreements that will vary in each situation. Be prepared to encounter resistance, but be equally prepared to assess the consequences of this resistance for the proposed change opportunity.

Task 1: Assess Political and Interpersonal Considerations

Earlier we discussed the importance of politics in bringing about change. We address these considerations more directly in this section. *Politics* is used here in a broad sense of having to do with the different ways individuals important to a change effort may respond when asked to support the change. For example, a community leader may personally support a change but may publicly withhold support as a favor to someone who opposes it. These kinds of actions may be taken for partisan reasons or simply as a way of trading favors among decision makers. This includes consideration of partisan politics, but it is not limited to that arena.

Address Public Image and Relationships.   Questions to be explored include:

- Who is involved in promoting the proposed change, and how are they perceived by decision makers?
- Who can serve as effective spokespersons for the proposed change?
- Who should keep a low profile when the proposed change is presented to decision makers?

Preparing a list of participants in each system and assessing the political and interpersonal strengths and liabilities of each participant can assist the change agent and action system in making the best use of each participant. Some people with valuable technical expertise may be seen as highly controversial and a liability when viewed from the interpersonal/political perspective. Previous negative experiences with decision makers should serve as a "red flag" but should not necessarily rule out someone from assuming a high-profile role. Regardless of who is designated as the public spokesperson, careful consideration should be given to how well and by whom this person is perceived and respected. This principle applies to both community and organizational change efforts, but may be even more important in organizational change because of the closeness of working relationships and the greater likelihood of people knowing more about each other than they would in the community arena.

Identify Alternative Perspectives.   Questions to be explored include:

- Has anyone key to the success of the change effort been left out?
- How will opponents of the change effort frame their opposition?
- How much conflict or contentiousness is expected?

The first question is particularly important from a political perspective. Failure to involve people who can help can be as damaging as involving people who may harm the effort.

Another consideration is perspective. People involved in change in the field of human services are often amazed to learn that there is almost no concern raised that does not have an opposing view. For every advocate of a woman's right to have control over her own body, there is one who will support a fetus's right to survive. For every person concerned about child abuse, there is one who is equally concerned about perceived abuses of parental prerogatives by child welfare workers. It is tempting to dismiss opponents' views as uninformed and unenlightened, but in undertaking macro-level change, it is unwise to do so. Alternative perspectives should be carefully analyzed for their merit and their potential or actual political appeal. Even plotting a spectrum of opinions, together with some educated estimates of levels of public support of each, can be an informative exercise for action system participants.

Each perspective should also be weighed for the intensity of its support. The likelihood is that the closer to the extremes, the more intense the feelings. Figure 10.1 illustrates a continuum of possible perspectives on services to AIDS patients. Recognize that as one moves along the continuum, strong feelings may be accompanied by greater conflict and contentiousness.

Assess Duration and Urgency.   Questions to be explored include:

- How long has the problem existed?
- Is the problem considered an emergency?

An area of consideration that affects perception of a problem is the length of time a problem has existed and the extent to which it is considered threatening to individual, organizational, or community survival. We refer to these as *duration and urgency,* and deal with them together because in many ways they are interrelated.

Long-standing problems are hard to change. People become desensitized, and community and organizational leaders are not easily persuaded that there is really a problem that needs attention. For example, it took a class action suit on behalf of the chronically mentally ill citizens of Arizona to force the state legislature to address their needs. Recently emerging problems such as homelessness among young families tend to have more popular support for change. Occasionally, long-standing problems can be presented in a new way, as has been done with alcohol abuse in the campaign against drunk driving over the past decades.

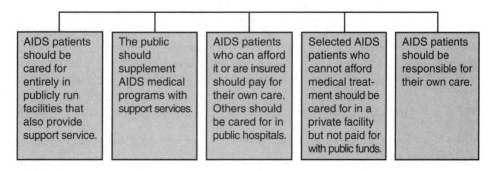

FIGURE 10.1   A Continuum of Perspectives

For newly emerging or newly defined problems, the change agent should examine the issue of urgency. The closer the problem is to threatening survival needs such as food, clothing, shelter, safety, and medical care, the more likely those in a position to make changes will attend to it. Within organizations, problems that directly or indirectly affect the budget, and therefore the capacity of the organization to survive, tend to receive a relatively higher priority than nonbudget-related problems. The proposed change should be weighed in terms of its duration and urgency, and these factors used appropriately in selecting tactics for promoting the proposed change.

Task 2: Assess Resource Considerations

A major concern of decision makers about proposed change in most cases comes down to how much it will cost. Whether or not social workers agree with this value perspective, we operate within a money-oriented system. Decision makers often look at the cost before they even consider the rationale for implementing the change. Improved quality of life is not, in itself, enough of a rationale for persons responsible for managing limited resources to agree to support a particular change effort.

Determine the Cost of Change.   Questions to be explored include:

- What anticipated costs related to the proposed change can be itemized? What must be estimated?
- What sources of financial support or in-kind donations should be approached?

The change agent must make some estimates of what the proposed change will cost. This can be difficult because in many cases the details of the intervention design are not even worked out until there are some assurances that the change will be accepted. Take, for example, a situation in which the parents in a community want the school board to sponsor more organized and supervised after-school activities. Some may want arts and crafts, some athletic activities, some drama and music options. When the school board is approached, these details have probably not been addressed. The change agent must be prepared for a response that "the proposed change will cost too much and resources are not available." To counter this, some preliminary calculations must be prepared, at least to the point of estimating the number of staff persons, approximate salaries required, estimated square feet of space needed, cost per square foot, and other rough calculations. Technical expertise may have to be consulted to arrive at realistic cost estimates. Most decision makers will want to conduct their own analysis of costs, but estimates by the proposers of change can at least serve as standards for comparison.

Determine the Cost of Doing Nothing.   Questions to be explored include:

- What will this problem cost the organization or community if nothing is done?

- How can this cost be framed so that it will impress decision makers as a good investment to support the proposed change?

A very valuable statistic for comparative purposes, if it can be calculated, is the cost of nonresolution of this problem or nonimplementation of the proposed change. It is important to impress on decision makers that there are also long-term costs associated with doing nothing. For example, costs for in-patient or residential services can run as high as $6,000 to $7,000 a month. At first blush, an intensive vocational training program for high-risk adolescents costing $12,000 per client per year may appear outrageously expensive. However, if presented side by side with data demonstrating that 90 percent of the clients who complete this program become self-sufficient and do not need residential treatment, decision makers may be persuaded that it really represents a long-term cost savings.

Task 3: Weigh the Likelihood of Success

When the major participants, the proposed change, and the political and economic issues have been identified, the time has come to weigh the relative strength of supporting and opposing forces and to decide if the change effort is to be a "go" or a "no-go." This can be done in an orderly fashion by adapting Kurt Lewin's techniques of force-field analysis (1951). The issue for consideration here is whether to invest additional time, energy, and resources. The experienced change agent recognizes that there is little value in moral victories. If a change effort is to be undertaken, there should be some chance of succeeding. Force-field analysis can enable the change agent to make an informed decision about the likelihood of success.

We propose a modification of Lewin's framework that examines two areas: (1) support from individuals, groups, and organizations, and (2) support from facts and perspectives.

Assess Support from Individuals, Groups, and Organizations. Questions to be explored include:

- Who supports the proposed change?
- Who opposes the proposed change?
- Who is neutral about the proposed change?

Applying the force-field analysis model, support from individuals, groups, and organizations can be laid out in three columns. Column one represents the driving or supporting forces. Column two represents neutral forces, and column three represents the restraining or opposing forces. Identifying each of the systems involved, together with their key individuals or groups, will provide a graphic depiction of supporting and opposing forces and will help in determining the possibility of success if the change effort goes forward. Figure 10.2 illustrates a force-field analysis.

SUPPORT FROM INDIVIDUALS, GROUPS, AND ORGANIZATIONS			
System	**Driving/Supporting Forces** ⟶	**Neutral Entities** ⟵	**Restraining/Opposing Forces**

Initiator System	• Homeless Advocates
	   T. Johnson
	   L. Stearns		

Change Agent System	• St. Catharine's
	  Parish youth worker
	   J. Foster		

Client System	• Homeless teens in Douglas County		
Support System	• Homeless Advocates • Parents of Runaway, Inc. • Existing homeless programs		

Controlling System	• City Council
	  Members supporting
	  change
		• City Council
		  Members not yet
		  taking position
			• City Council
			  Members opposed
			  to teen shelter

Host System		• City Department of Human Services	
Implementing System	• Potential contract agencies		

Target System		• City Council member
		  votes in favor of
		  funding proposed
		  teen shelter	

Action System	• Advocates
	  (T. Johnson and L.Stearns),
	  youth worker (J. Foster),
	  two homeless teens,
	  two social workers
	  from existing shelters		

Others		• A large percentage
		  of the general public
			• Taxpayers Against
			  Increased Public
			  Social Services
			  (TAPS)
			• City Newspaper
			• Task Force on
			  CMI Homeless
			  (who are competing
			  for funding)

FIGURE 10.2 Force-Field Analysis of Individuals, Groups, and Organizations Supporting and Opposing a Proposed Project to Serve Homeless Teens

Assess Level of Support. Questions to be explored include:

- What facts and perspectives gleaned from the problem, population, and arena analysis support the proposed change?
- What facts and perspectives oppose the proposed change?

Following the identification of individuals, groups, and organizations supporting and opposing the change effort, we propose that facts and perspectives be identified in the same way. It is unlikely that any new research or analysis is necessary at this point. Identifying supporting and opposing facts and perspectives involves drawing on everything now known and available in terms of statistics, history, theory, research, etiology, interpersonal and political factors, and resource considerations. Each should be examined for its potential driving or restraining effects on the change effort. Figure 10.3 illustrates examples of support from facts and perspectives.

Schneider and Lester (2001) identify three groups of persons who may oppose a change effort, illustrating just how diverse opposition can be. These are (1) individuals or groups who need more knowledge about an issue, and who with adequate information might even support it; (2) individuals and groups who are indifferent or neutral and would have to be convinced; and (3) those persons who are certain about their disagreement and may even be hostile (p. 125). These categories underscore the necessity of recognizing intensity of feeling, rather than just recognizing who opposes the change.

Using this format, action system participants next initiate a discussion session focused on making the "go/no-go" decision. An option, of course, is to gather more facts or to postpone the decision to a more opportune time. Additional fact gathering, if absolutely necessary, is considered advisable only if it is highly focused and time limited. If, however, fact gathering is proposed as a delaying tactic or intended simply to avoid making a difficult decision, it should be recognized

Driving/Supporting Forces --➤|◀--	Restraining/Opposing Forces
1. Teen homelessness is increasing by 20% per year.	1. Resources are already inadequate to meet existing needs of homeless families.
2. Homeless teens have been drawn into drug trafficking, prostitution, and many property crimes.	2. No federal or state funding is available; homelessness is considered a local problem.
3. Media have increased coverage of the problem; the public increasingly favors some action.	3. Suburban cities are not willing to contribute needed support; major urban city council feels it should be considered a regional problem.
Etc....	Etc....

FIGURE 10.3 Support from Facts and Perspectives on the Problems of Homeless Teens

for what it is and rejected. It should also be recognized that this may be the point at which some participants will believe the proposed change to be unattainable and will decide to drop out, whereas others may choose to pursue the effort. Here again, it should be emphasized that the professional person acting as change agent must make as sound a decision as possible in the interest of achieving the change objectives. Necessary changes that have a good chance of success should be supported. Causes that are likely to be defeated as currently conceptualized should be tabled until they are more fully developed or the timing is better.

Guidelines for Selecting Tactics

If one decides to pursue the change, with knowledge of the political and economic context, an array of actions can be used. Certain actions can raise ethical dilemmas. Selecting strategies and their accompanying tactics calls for mature, professional judgment in community and organizational change.

Task 4: Select Strategies and Tactics

In Chapter 9, we provided guidelines for how to develop an intervention strategy based on what is known about the identified opportunity or problem. Strategies involve a long-range linking of activities to achieve the desired goal and are composed of tactics.

Consider Strategies.   Questions to be explored include:

- With which strategy will the change effort begin?
- Will it be necessary to consider sequential strategies, if one isn't working?
- If there are multiple, sequential targets, which strategies will be used with each target?

Change almost always involves influencing the allocation of scarce resources—authority, status, power, goods, services, or money. Decisions about strategies must therefore take into consideration whether the resources are being allocated willingly or whether someone must be persuaded to make the allocation. If there is agreement on the part of the action and target systems that the proposed change is acceptable and that resources will be allocated, a collaborative strategy can be adopted. If there is agreement that the proposed change is acceptable but a reluctance or refusal to allocate resources, or if there is disagreement about the need for the proposed change, then a more conflictual strategy may be necessary if the change effort is to proceed.

For example, a change effort may focus on the inability of persons with physical disabilities to get around the city and to travel to needed service providers. A thorough study documents the problem, and a dial-a-ride transportation service is proposed. The planning commission and city council graciously accept the report, agree on the need, and thank the Transportation Task Force for Disabled Persons.

Three city council members favor funding, three are opposed, and one is unde-cided. If the undecided council member can be persuaded to favor funding, then collaboration is possible. If, however, she decides to oppose funding or if a com-promise would undermine the change effort, then a different strategy may be used to aggressively push for her support. For a collaborative strategy to be adopted, there must be agreement on both the proposed change and the allocation of needed resources.

In the social work literature, strategies have been categorized under three broad headings: collaboration, campaign, and contest (Brager, Specht, & Tor-czyner, 1987; Schneider & Lester, 2001). In this chapter, we use these strategies to describe the relationship between the action and target systems. *Collaboration* implies a working relationship where the two systems agree that change must occur. *Campaign* is used when the target must be convinced of the importance of the change, but when communication is still possible between the two systems. The effectiveness of the "campaign" may determine whether collaboration or con-test follows. *Contest* is used when neither of the other two are possible any longer. Change efforts that begin with one strategy may progress to other sets, depending on the evolving relationship between the action and target systems. The contin-uum along which these strategies fall is as follows:

Collaboration ◄————————► Campaign ◄————————► Contest

Although we categorize these relationships, success may hinge on the change agent's ability to keep the action and target systems in a state of continual interac-tion. It is possible that what begins as a collaborative relationship will move to con-flict when new issues arise during the change process. It is equally likely that the relationship will vacillate between various gradations of communication, with both systems uncertain about the other, even when compromise can be reached. In short, these relationships ebb and flow, sometimes unpredictably given the politi-cal situation and sometimes all too predictably given the change agent's prior experience with the target system.

Our concern is that the social worker never take the relationship between the action and target systems for granted. To assume that the target is immovable before communication has been attempted demonstrates poor use of professional judgment. To assume that the target will embrace the cause once the facts are known is naive. Assumptions about how others think have little place in assessing the relationship between the action and the target system. We believe that regard-less of which strategy is used, communication should be maintained with the tar-get system if at all possible. If communication ceases, it should be because the target system refuses to continue interaction.

Identify Tactics. Questions to be explored include:

■ Given the strategy most likely to succeed, what tactic (or combination of tactics) is needed first?

■ As the change progresses, is it anticipated that changing strategies may lead to the use of different tactics?

Within each of the three strategic categories are tactics that are typically used. The choice of tactics is a critical decision point in planned change. "Tactics are the day-to-day decisions that practitioners make and which, they hope, will steer them toward the accomplishment of their goal" (Tropman, Erlich, & Rothman, 2001, p. 3). As the change agent engages in tactical behavior, it is important not to lose sight of the intervention toward which these behaviors are directed as well as the overriding strategies that guide the change process.

Brager and colleagues (1987) identify four essential properties of tactics used by professional change agents: "1) they are planned . . . 2) they are used to evoke specific responses . . . 3) they involve interaction with others . . . and 4) they are goal-oriented" (p. 288). In addition, it is our contention that a fifth property must be in place in professional social work change efforts: 5) the tactic will do no harm to members of the client system and whenever possible members of that system will be involved in tactical decision making.

The framework in Table 10.1 guides our discussion. Some of the following conceptualization is drawn from previous literature (Brager & Holloway 1978; Brager et al. 1987; Schneider & Lester, 2001). In some areas we offer slightly differ-

TABLE 10.1   **Strategies and Tactical Behaviors**

Relationship of Action and Target Systems	Tactics

Collaboration
Target system agrees (or is easily convinced to agree) with action system that change is needed and supports allocation of resources
	1. Implementation
	2. Capacity building
	   a. Participation
	   b. Empowerment

Campaign
Target system is willing to communicate with action system, but there is little consensus that change is needed; or target system supports change but not allocation of resources
	3. Education
	4. Persuasion
	   a. Cooptation
	   b. Lobbying
	5. Mass media appeal

Contest
Target system opposes change and/or allocation of resources and is not open to further communication about opposition
	6. Bargaining and negotiation
	7. Large-group or community action
	   a. Legal (e.g., demonstrations)
	   b. Illegal (e.g., civil disobedience)
	8. Class action lawsuit

ent perspectives or add new tactics. Throughout the following discussion, we attempt to provide an analytical framework to guide an action system in selecting the most appropriate mix of tactics.

Consider the Pros and Cons of Collaboration. Questions to be explored include:

- Is it certain that there is little opposition?
- Can the desired change be achieved by identifying appropriate roles for participants and implementing the change?

Collaborative strategies include instances in which the target and action systems agree that change is needed. Recall in Chapter 6 that five categories of linkages between community units were identified: communication, cooperation, coordination, collaboration, and consolidation (see Table 10.2). *Communication* can be informal or formal, and is simply the sharing of information across boundaries. *Cooperation* occurs when two or more units agree to work toward similar goals. *Coordination* implies a concerted effort to work together. Often separate units will draft agreements, outlining ways in which coordination will occur. *Collaboration* implies a joint venture in which two or more units agree to move toward a change

TABLE 10.2 Five Levels of Interaction among Participants

Level of Interaction	Type of Relationship	Characteristics	Level of Provider Autonomy
Communication	Is friendly, cordial	Sharing of ideas between units, including consultation	High
Cooperation	May be defined as an affiliation	Working together to plan and implement independent programs	High
Coordination	Could be a federation, association, or coalition-type relationship	Working together to avoid duplication and to assist one another in sharing information, advertising for one another, and making referrals	Moderate
Collaboration	Could be a consortium, network, or joint venture	Joining together to provide a single program or service, with shared resources	Moderate
Consolidation		Merging into one entity	Autonomy relinquished

Source: Adapted from the work of Tobin, Ellor, and Anderson-Ray (1986) and Bailey and Koney (2000).

that could not be accomplished alone. *Confederation* occurs when separate units actually merge.

Collaboration, then, implies a partnership of some sort that goes beyond what one person, group, or unit could achieve alone. This process involves communication, cooperation, and coordination, but it goes farther. Collaboration requires commitment among members of an action system to move toward a joint effort that will create change in a community or organization. The collaboration could take a policy, program, project, personnel, or practice approach but it requires a commitment to the approach by all members of the action system.

Collaboration is likely one of the most used and misused terms in the social science literature. Its definition will vary and it is often used loosely to mean communication, cooperation, or coordination. For the purposes of planned change, however, collaboration must be more than just a loose affiliation. This planned change strategy requires a committed partnership among action system members to see the change process through, including the evaluation of those efforts.

A substantial body of literature on collaboration and partnerships attests to its effectiveness in enhancing service delivery and capacity building within organizations and communities (see, for example, Clegg & Hardy, 1999; Cropper, 1996; Harrison & Weiss, 1998; Weiner & Alexander, 1998). Interest in collaboration as a strategy has led to a great deal of research on partnering, which attests to the challenges of maintaining the long-term effects of collaborative strategies (Israel, Schulz, Parker, & Becker, 1998). Studies have also raised a number of challenges inherent in collaboration,

> including overcoming turf and territoriality issues, identifying and addressing differences in organizational norms and procedures, expanding communication both within and across organizations, coping with tensions concerning organizational accountability, and identifying appropriate community representatives, and managing logistical issues such as program monitoring and the time-consuming nature of establishing and maintaining multi-organizational partnerships. (Takahashi & Smutny, 2002, pp. 166–167)

Therefore, this suggests that communication between the action and target system is only a beginning in collaboration. It is important to recognize the challenges raised in the literature regarding the sustainability of collaborative efforts. However, collaborative strategies can be ideal when they are possible because the energies and resources of the participants can focus on the agreed upon change as opposed to resolving their disagreements over what should happen.

Under a collaboration strategy, we place implementation and capacity-building tactics.

Implementation.   Implementation tactics are used when the action and target systems are willing to work together. When these systems agree that change is needed and allocation of resources is supported by critical decision makers, the change can move toward implementation. Implementation will most likely involve some problem solving, but it is not expected that highly adversarial relationships will be a concern in these types of collaborative efforts.

Schneider and Lester (2001) include tactics such as conducting research and studying the issue, developing fact sheets and alternative proposals, creating task forces or subcommittees, conducting workshops, and communicating regularly with the opposition (p. 129). These types of activities are typically used in an implementation process.

Although implementation may move along with communication, cooperation, and coordination occurring among systems, it is important to recognize that implementation does not guarantee that the change will be sustained. Therefore, ongoing monitoring will be needed.

Capacity Building. Capacity building includes the tactics of participation and empowerment. *Participation* refers to those activities that involve members of the client system in the change effort. An "empowerment perspective is grounded in an understanding that separate groups exist within our societies, each possessing different levels of power and control over resources . . . [arising] from the failure of society to meet the needs of all people. It holds that the potential for positive change exists within every individual, family, or group" (Gutierrez & Lewis, 1999, p. 4). *Empowerment* can be viewed as both a process and an outcome in which people actually gain a psychological view that it is possible to make change happen.

For example, a problem may be defined as exclusion of a neighborhood from decisions that affect it. The focus of the intervention is on building a capacity for greater self-direction and self-control—that is, actually teaching people how to get involved in the decision-making processes in their communities and taking greater control over the decisions that affect their lives. This approach often emerges in situations where disenfranchised communities become targets for development, freeways, airport expansion, and other such encroachments, or when a neighborhood is neglected and allowed to deteriorate by an apathetic and unconcerned city council.

Through professionally assisted change efforts, perhaps led by a neighborhood social service organization (change agent system), neighborhood resident (client system), and city council (controlling system and perhaps target system), all agree that community citizens should have a greater voice in developments that affect their community. The focus of the change or intervention, however, is not on the target system (city council/planning commission) but on educating, training, and preparing community citizens for a fuller participation in decisions that affect their communities. Tactics would include education, training, and actual participation in civic organizations and activities.

Empowerment involves enabling people to become aware of their rights, and teaching them how to exercise those rights so that they become better able to take control over factors that affect their lives. Mobilizing the efforts of self-help groups and voluntary associations identified in Chapter 5, as well as the client system's informal support structure, may be used to assist in guiding the target system toward consensus with the change effort.

Consider the Pros and Cons of Campaign.   Questions to be explored include:

■ Who needs to be convinced that the proposed change is needed?
■ What persuasive techniques are most likely to be effective?

A campaign strategy implies a group effort to convince members of the target system that a cause is just or a change is needed, and that resources should be allocated. Campaign tactics require a good deal of skill on the part of the change agent and action system. Lack of consensus rules out collaboration, yet it is not certain that a clear disagreement exists. Under this heading, we include the use of education, persuasion, and mass media appeals designed to influence public opinion.

Education.   *Educational tactics* are interactions in which the action system presents perceptions, attitudes, opinions, data, and information about the proposed change with the intent of convincing the target system to think or to act differently. The objective is to inform. The assumption is that more and better information will lead to a change in behavior. It is a difficult tactic to use because opponents of the change can also be expected to inform decision makers armed with different sets of data and information, and there is no absolute "truth" in dealing with complex organizational and community problems. In many cases, where education fails to produce the desired result or falls short of having the desired impact, the change agent turns to persuasion.

Persuasion.   *Persuasion* refers to the art of convincing others to accept and support one's point of view or perspective on an issue. Social workers must frequently use persuasive tactics in addition to collaborative tactics because their causes are not always embraced by decision makers, who often must be convinced through persuasion that the change is worth pursuing. This means that the change agent must understand the motives and reasoning of the target system in order to identify what incentives or information might be considered persuasive by members of the target system.

Skillful communication requires that the action system must carefully select its leadership from persons who have the ability to persuade. Persons who are seen as nonthreatening to the target system and who can articulate the reasoning behind the planned change are particularly useful. For example, in a change effort, particular actors may be perceived as unreasonable, as troublemakers, or as chronic complainers by members of the controlling system. It is not in the best interest of the client system for those persons to be the only spokespersons for the change. Credibility with representatives is an important consideration in selecting a spokesperson. Clients themselves can sometimes be powerful spokespersons, providing information and a viewpoint that persuades people of the need for change.

Framing the problem statement to make it more palatable to members of the target system is a persuasive technique. This requires the ability to think as the target thinks. For example, a social worker is hired as a long-term care ombudsperson and works closely with a coalition of advocates for nursing home reform to end abuse in long-term care facilities. Nursing home administrators are very upset over the nursing home reform coalition and perceive the group as not understanding the difficulties with which administrators cope on a daily basis. They sincerely want to provide quality care, but are frustrated by staff who are not properly trained to work with geriatric populations. By framing the problem as a training problem designed to better prepare employees and reduce turnover, the ombudsperson is able to persuade administrators to cooperate with the action system. When the ombudsperson meets with the local nursing home association, she acknowledges that she is aware that the administrators want to operate high-quality facilities. She also notes that recent studies reveal that high staff turnover rates often contribute to lack of continuity and lower-quality patient care, sometimes leading to abuse. She explains that she and her colleagues are willing to develop training for nurses aides because they interact most intimately with patients, yet are most vulnerable to high turnover. Essentially, one of the contributing factors leading to abuse is being addressed, but it is framed as reducing an administrative nightmare—high staff turnover.

Cooptation is defined as minimizing anticipated opposition by absorbing or including members of the target system in the action system. Once target-system members are part of the planned change effort, it is likely that they will assume some ownership of the change process. Persuasion is used to coopt new persons into the action system. This is valuable to the success of the change effort because it is important to include persons who are viewed as powerful by the target system. These persons may be relatively neutral and may have little interest in obstructing the change effort. However, if they can be convinced to support the change effort (or even to allow their names to be used in publicity), their participation may sway others who respect their opinions. Cooptation is most effective as a tactic when opponents or neutral parties can be helped to recognize a self-interest in the proposed change.

Cooptation can be formal or informal. Coopting individuals is called *informal cooptation,* whereas coopting organized groups is referred to as *formal cooptation.* Formal cooptation means that an entire group agrees to support a cause. Because their governing structure agrees that the change effort is worthwhile, the group may issue a statement to that effect. This formalizes the commitment, even though there are always members of any group who may, as individuals, disagree with the proposed change.

Formal cooptation of a number of groups leads to *coalition building.* A coalition is a loosely woven, ad hoc association of constituent groups, each of whose primary identification is outside the coalition (Haynes & Mickelson, 2000). For example, the purpose of the National Health Care Campaign was to provide health-care coverage to all U.S. citizens. This change effort brought together hundreds of organizations, such as the National Association of Social Workers and the American Public Health Association. On a state-by-state basis, health-care campaign chapters were forming. Interested change agents encouraged local groups to join in the efforts—forming a coalition dedicated to the stated goal. The diversity of the coalition contributed to a powerful alliance of individuals and groups that vacillated between collaboration and campaign tactics as they attempted to address health care needs.

Lobbying is a form of persuasion that addresses policy change under the domain of the controlling system. The action system will have to determine if it is necessary to change agency policy, to amend current legislation, or to develop new legislation in order to achieve their goal. Haynes and Mickelson (2000, pp. 96–97) delineate three essential concepts for social work/lobbyists to consider. First, one should always be factual and honest. Trying to second-guess or stretch the facts to support one's position is devastating to one's professional reputation as well as to the change effort's credibility. Second, any presentation should be straightforward and supported by the available data. The problem identification and analysis process discussed in Chapter 3 will assist the change agent in organizing the rationale for change. Third, any discussion should include the two critical concerns of decision makers—cost and social impact of what is proposed. If the cost is high, the social worker is advised to calculate the costs of allowing the identified problem to remain unresolved.

Mass Media Appeal.   *Mass media appeal* refers to the development and release of newsworthy stories to the print and electronic media for the purpose of influencing public opinion. This tactic is used to pressure decision makers into a favorable resolution to the identified problem. The expectation is that if the proposed change can be presented to the public in a positive way and decision makers' refusal to support the proposed change can be presented as obstructionist or somehow negative, then decision makers will feel pressured to change their position. Since decision makers are often high-profile people, such as elected representatives who depend on a positive public perception, this can be an effective tactic. Use of mass media depends on news reporters' agreements that the proposed change is a newsworthy story, and assurance that one's cause will be presented accurately. Use of any media must always include consideration of clients' rights to privacy.

Electronic advocacy is being used more and more to rapidly reach large numbers of people. For example, Menon (2000) reports how one online discussion group developed a campaign to educate others about the issues of persons with severe mental illnesses. In the process of being transformed from a discussion group to a virtual community, participants experienced how important it is to deal with issues while they are hot. They also recognized the importance of having a campaign plan when numerous messages are posted in a short time frame.

Consider the Pros and Cons of Contest.   Questions to be explored include:

- Is opposition to the proposed change so strong that it can only be successful by imposing the change on an unwilling target system?

- Can the proposed change be effective if it is forced?
- What are the anticipated consequences of conflict?

Under the heading of *contest* strategies, we categorize the tactics of bargaining and negotiating, the use of large group or community action, and class action lawsuits. Large groups in community action can be further divided into legal and illegal tactics. Similarly, Schneider and Lester (2001) include the following contest tactics: seeking a negotiator or mediator; organizing large demonstrations; coordinating boycotts, picketing, strikes, and petition drives; initiating legal action; organizing civil disobedience and passive resistance; and arranging a media expose (p. 129).

Contest tactics are used in situations where (1) the target system cannot be persuaded by the action system, (2) the target system refuses to communicate with the action system, or (3) it is perceived that only lip service is being given to the proposed change. *Contest tactics* mean that the change effort becomes an open, public conflict as attempts are made to draw broad support and/or to pressure or even force the target system into supporting or at least accepting the change. Once this occurs, the action system must be prepared to face open confrontation and to escalate its coercive techniques.

Conflict is inevitable in social work practice. There will be times in the experience of every practitioner when formidable resistance is encountered in addressing the needs of oppressed population groups. At these times, it may be helpful to remember the tradition of social work as a profession that developed in response to a basic societal conflict—the persistent antagonism over individualism and the common good. For example, when a local neighborhood protests having a group home for people with mental illnesses in their community, this is a conflict over the needs of the mentally ill to dwell within the larger community and the fears and concerns of neighbors who have a sense of their common good that does not include individuals with mental illness. Conflicts over the rights of various population groups have spawned violent confrontations rooted in basic value systems and beliefs. We believe that physical violence and terrorism cannot be condoned in any change efforts in a civilized society. Nonviolent confrontation, however, including civil disobedience, is an option when there is a communication stalemate between the target and action systems and when other possible avenues have been exhausted.

Contest tactics will require widespread commitment and possible participation from members of the support system. Rubin and Rubin (2001) refer to these tactics as *confrontational approaches* (p. 286). It is critical to the success of these tactics that the support system and its subsystems—initiator, client, and change agent—are comfortable with contest tactics because there are risks that are not present when using collaboration and campaign tactics. It is likely that the time and energy necessary for effective change will increase and relationships can become disrupted. When collaborative and campaign tactics are employed, tactics can move toward contest. However, once contest tactics are employed, it is not likely that one can return to collaborative or campaign tactics. Without a clear understanding of what contest tactics involve and without full commitment from the support system, contest tactics are not advised.

Bargaining and Negotiation. *Bargaining and negotiation* refer to those situations in which the action and target system confront one another with the reasons for their support and/or opposition to a proposal or an issue. Bargaining and negotiation occur when there is a recognized power differential between parties and a compromise needs to be made. These tactics are more formalized than persuasion, sometimes involving a third-party mediator. Members of the target system will typically agree to negotiate when the following factors are in place: (1) there is some understanding of the intentions and preferred outcomes of the action system, (2) there is a degree of urgency, (3) the relative importance and scope of the proposed change is known, (4) there are resources that facilitate the exercise of power, and (5) the members perceive the action system as having some legitimacy. In order to negotiate, both the action and the target systems must perceive that each has something the other wants; otherwise, there is no reason to come together. Schneider and Lester (2001) suggest that when alienation between the action and target systems occurs, it may be helpful to use the skills of a third-party mediator or negotiator. For example, a coalition advocating for the disabled may want improved transportation opportunities, whereas the city council wants a letter of support for a federal grant.

Bargaining and negotiation can result in a win/win situation, where both target and action systems are pleased with and fully support the outcome. The result can also be a win/lose, where one system is clearly the victor, or a lose/lose, where both systems give something up, are disappointed in the results, and are possibly worse off than before the change.

Large Group or Community Action. *Large group or community action* refers to the preparing, training, and organizing of large numbers of people who are willing to form a pressure group and advocate for change through various forms of collective action such as picketing, disruption of meetings, sit-ins, boycotting, and other such pressure tactics. Peaceful demonstrations are legal activities, often used by both groups at either extreme of an issue to express their views.

Civil disobedience activities intentionally break the law. For example, Rosa Parks deliberately broke the law when she did not sit in the back of the bus. Similarly, environmental advocates have blocked access to construction sites when endangered species or entire forests were at risk. Animal rights groups have sprayed paint on fur coats, destroying property in protest. Persons who strongly believe in the right to life have harassed physicians who work in abortion clinics. When action-system members deliberately engage in illegal activities, they must be ready to pay the consequences of their actions. The change agent is responsible for making potential participants fully aware of these risks before the decision is made to proceed.

Class Action Lawsuits. *Class action lawsuits* refer to those instances where an entity is sued for a perceived violation of the law and it is expected that the finding of the court will apply to an entire class of people. These tactics are often used with highly vulnerable populations, such as people with chronic mental illnesses, the homeless, or children, who are unlikely to have the capacity or the resources to protect their own rights. Public interest law organizations may be resources for the action system in developing class action tactics.

Weigh Relevant Considerations in Selecting Tactics. Questions to be explored include:

- What is the purpose of the change effort and has it been changed in the process?
- What is the perception (by those promoting change) of the controlling and host systems?
- What is the perception (by those promoting change) of the role of the client system?
- What resources are needed and available for each tactic?
- What are the ethical dilemmas inherent in the range of tactical choices?

Following is a brief discussion of a few salient considerations that need to be weighed in selecting the best tactic or mix of tactics.

Purpose. Change goals often tend to evolve as the change process moves along. When this occurs, a reexamination prior to selection of tactics is in order. For example, with the problem of domestic violence, the condition may have been brought to public awareness by the perceived need for additional emergency shelter space for battered women. However, as the problem is analyzed and better understood, the purpose may shift toward consciousness raising for all women in the community who are perceived to be at risk of violence. Thus, strategy and tactics would move from advocating for service provision to educating for empowerment. Since tactics can change as purpose and goals change, it is worthwhile to make one last check to ensure that all are clear and in agreement on what the change is about. Action system members may have concerns about the intent of the change effort that require further dialogue. A range of goals and likely accompanying tactics are indicated in Table 10.3.

Controlling and Host Systems. The controlling and host systems can be perceived in a variety of ways. If they are seen as employers or sponsors of the change, then collaboration is likely. If they are seen as supporters of, but not participants in, the change, then capacity building (through participation and empowerment) may be the tactic of choice. If they are seen as neutral or indifferent, a campaign strategy might be in order. If, however, they are seen as oppressive or unresponsive to their primary clientele, then some type of contest approach will likely be selected.

Assessing the relationship with the controlling and host system is critical to the change effort. Action system members may have differing perceptions about relationships. If there are dissimilar perceptions, it will be important to talk about

TABLE 10.3   Relationship of Goals to Tactics

Current Objective	Relationship of Target and Action System	Possible Tactics
1. Solving a substantive problem; providing a needed service	Collaborative	Implementation through joint action
2. Self-direction; self-control	Collaborative	Capacity building through participation and empowerment
3. Influencing decision makers	In disagreement but with open communication	Education, and persuasion through cooptation, lobbying, etc.
4. Changing public opinion	In disagreement but with open communication/Adversarial	Education, persuasion, mass media appeal; large-group or community action
5. Shifting power	Adversarial	Large-group community action
6. Mandating action	Adversarial	Class action lawsuit

the implications of this divergence of opinion for the change effort. Table 10.4 illustrates the various perceptions of roles that might be assigned to the controlling and host systems, and the logical tactic for each.

Primary Client.   The role of the primary client can vary, and the way in which this role is perceived can affect selection of change tactics. Sometimes it may be difficult to determine who the primary client really is. For example, in addressing the needs of elderly persons, the change agent may discover that caregivers are suffering from stress and fatigue, and are unable to provide quality care to the elderly persons for whom they are responsible. In this situation, one must ask, Will the primary beneficiaries of a change effort be the older persons themselves or their caregivers?

   If the primary client is seen as a consumer or recipient of service, then a collaborative change approach is the most likely tactic. If the primary role is as a resident of a community or potential participant in an effort to achieve self-direction and control, then a capacity building approach is perhaps more appropriate. If the primary client is seen as a person who needs a service (but this need is not acknowledged by the controlling system), as a victim, or as a voter or constituent with potential power to influence decision makers, then some type of contest approach is likely to be employed.

TABLE 10.4 Relationship of Controlling and Host System Roles to Tactics

Perception of Role of Controlling and Host Systems	Relationship of Controlling, Host, and Action Systems	Possible Tactics
1. Sponsors; supporters; coparticipants; colleagues	Collaborative	Implementation through joint action
2. Neutrality or indifference	Collaborative	Capacity building through participation and empowerment
3. Uninformed barriers/ not sure about change	In disagreement but with open communication	Education and persuasion
4. Informed barriers/opponents to successful change	Adversarial	Bargaining; large-group or community action
5. Oppressors	Adversarial	Large-group community action
6. Violators of rights	Adversarial	Class action lawsuit

It will be important to know how members of the action system describe the primary client and if they agree or disagree in their descriptions. It is equally important to know how clients perceive their roles and if their perceptions are congruent with other members of the action system. Having clients as action-system members becomes vitally important (overlapping the client and action system) so that there is a logical mechanism for information exchange between clients and change agents. Table 10.5 displays client roles, approaches, and tactics.

Resources A key consideration in choosing tactics is the amount and types of resources available to the action system, since different tactics require more or different types of resources than others. If collaboration is the tactic of choice, for example, one necessary resource will be technical expertise capable of understanding whether the change is being properly implemented, monitored, and evaluated. In order for a capacity-building tactic to be used, grassroots organizing ability, together with some teaching and training expertise, must be available to the action system. If there is conflict, either skilled persuaders, media support, large numbers of people willing to do what is necessary to bring about change, or legal expertise must be available.

Tactics require resources and it will be important to figure in advance what resources (e.g., expertise, training, time, funding, equipment, etc.) are needed. Action-system members may be called on to provide resources or to assist in accessing what is needed. If additional resources are needed, it may become nec-

TABLE 10.5   Relationship of Client-System Role to Tactics

Perception of Role of Client System	Relationship of Client and Target Systems	Possible Tactics
1. Consumer; recipient of service	Collaborative	Implementation through joint action
2. Resident of the community in need of greater self-direction and self-control	Collaborative	Capacity building through participation and empowerment
3. Citizen/taxpayer not permitted full participation	In disagreement but with open communication	Education and persuasion
4. Victim; underserved needy person	Adversarial	Mass media appeal
5. Victim; exploited person	Adversarial	Large-group community action
6. Person denied civil rights	Adversarial	Class action lawsuit

essary to expand the boundaries of the action system to include persons or groups who have access to additional resources. Resource considerations are illustrated in Table 10.6.

Professional Ethics.   In Chapter 1, we discussed the importance of values in social work practice. *Ethics* are the behaviors that bring values into action. An *ethical dilemma* is defined as a situation in which a choice has to be made between equally important values. Tactical choices are no exception. Decisions regarding what tactics to use are based on the values held by action-system members. It is often the clash of action- and target-system values that leads to the selection of contest tactics.

   Three ethical principles were highlighted in Chapter 1: autonomy, beneficence, and social justice. These principles are deeply enmeshed in macro-practice change. A clash between autonomy and beneficence occurs when the client system is not willing to risk the little it has, yet the action system wants to push for a quality-of-life change. Members of the client system may have limited control over their lives, but their right to decide (self-determination) that they do not want to risk the little control they have must be respected by action-system members if it is clear that client-system opinion is being fairly represented. Alternately, the action system may be heavily composed of professionals who are acting on the principle of beneficence. They may sincerely believe that they know what is best for the client system. Rights of clients take precedence over the wishes of the action system when such a conflict emerges.

TABLE 10.6 Resources Needed by Action System for Each Tactic

Tactic	Resources Needed
1. Collaboration—joint action or problem solving	Technical expertise; monitoring and evaluation capability
2. Capacity building	Grass-roots organizing ability; teaching/ training expertise; opportunities for participation; some indigenous leadership; willing participants
3. Persuasion	Informed people; data/information; skilled persuaders/lobbyists
4. Mass media appeal	Data/information; newsworthy issue or slant; access to news reporters; technical expertise to write news releases
5. Large-group or community action	Large numbers of committed people (support system); training and organization expertise; informed leadership; bargaining and negotiating skills
6. Class action lawsuits	Legal expertise; victims willing to bring action and provide information; at least enough money for court costs

This clash is illustrated in a social work intern's first field experience. Working for a small community center in the southwest, she discovered that many of her Hispanic clients lived in a crowded apartment complex with faulty wiring and inadequate plumbing. With the backing of her agency, she began talking with clients to see if they would be willing to engage in a change process directed toward their living conditions. As she analyzed the situation, she realized that any change process would involve housing and public health personnel in the action system. Her clients begged her not to bring these concerns to the attention of local authorities. Many members of the client system were illegal immigrants and they feared that their exposure to public authorities would assure their deportation. The client system was willing to accept poor housing conditions rather than risk the consequences of exposure. The client system's autonomy was in conflict with the change agent system's beneficence.

The clash between social justice and autonomy is exemplified when the action system demands redistribution of resources and the target system believes that in giving up their control over valued resources they have less freedom. Macro change frequently appeals to the principle of justice, for it is usually through the redistribution of valued resources (e.g., power, money, status, etc.) that change occurs. Because social justice is a basic ethical principle that raises emotions when it is violated, change agents can become so obsessed with injustice that any means is viewed as an appropriate tactic if it leads to a successful end. It is our contention that this type of thinking can lead to professional anarchy whereby tactics are perceived as weapons to punish the target system rather than as actions to enrich the client system. In these situations, it may be too easy for the change to take on a life of its own and for the professional to assume a beneficent role. Righteous indignation may overtake sound judgment. The foregoing points should not be interpreted to mean that factors such as horrible living conditions or basic needs should be ignored if a client is fearful. The issue is *client system rights.* If clients can be persuaded that conditions can be improved without risk, then it is acceptable to proceed. If they cannot be persuaded, then activities must be discontinued.

Use of Covert Tactics.   In the previous chapter, we discussed the use of covert tactics in certain situations where legitimate channels of communication have been tried and where clients agree that covert means may be their only chance for success. The concept of transparency is becoming increasingly important in transactions that take place in the public domain. *Transparency* refers to keeping actions and decision-making processes in the open and available to the public and the media, and is intended to protect the public against self-serving actions or ethical lapses. However, when change is being considered that may require a more powerful segment of the community to give up some of its power to a less powerful segment, there may be a fear that openness or transparency will result in failure of the change effort. In situations like these, the need for secrecy must be carefully weighed because the use of covert tactics can raise suspicions and sometimes raise ethical concerns. To guide the action system in discussing professional ethics, see Figure 10.4.

Selecting the Correct Tactics.   Very few situations involve clearly a "right" or "wrong" tactic. Berlin (1990) explains,

> We are all vulnerable to oversimplified bipolarizations. We search for order, find meaning in contrasts, and learn by maintaining an "essential tension" between divergent experiences, events, and possibilities. It is this allowance of contrasts that differentiates either-or, narrowing and excluding bipolarizations from those that are encompassing or transforming. (p. 54)

It is common to think dichotomously (e.g., win-lose, right-wrong, good-bad, consensus-conflict). In conflict situations, dichotomous thinking may assist the radical change agent in believing that the target system represents evil, whereas the action system represents good. This fuels the fire of confrontation and is appropriate in some situations. However, we believe that the professional social worker has a responsibility to analyze carefully what is happening before making assumptions that lead directly to the use of contest tactics. This means that the majority of change efforts will utilize collaboration and campaign tactics as the action and target systems attempt to communicate with one another. Although consensus-con-

FIGURE 10.4   Questions to Guide Consideration of Professional Ethics

1. What are the value conflicts between the target and action systems?
2. What ethical principle(s) appear to be guiding the activities of the action system?
3. Is there the potential for a clash of ethical principles between the client and action systems?
4. If covert tactics are being considered, what conditions have led to this decision?
   a. The mission of the target agency or the community mandate is being ignored.
   b. The mission of the target agency or the community mandate is being denied for personal gain.
   c. Change efforts have been tried through legitimate channels, but the target system will not listen.
   d. Client system members are fully aware of the risks involved, but are willing to take the risks.
   e. Other.

flict is a dichotomy, we believe that the majority of interactions happen in the various gradations in between—where varying degrees of communication occur.

If the action system attempts to collaborate or is willing to compromise but the target system remains unmoved, then contest tactics may have to be employed. What one wants to guard against, however, is action-system members making assumptions about target-system members without attempting to communicate with one another. In short, decisions about what tactics to use depends on the situation, the proposed change, and the relationships among actors in the action, client, and target systems.

When all the foregoing tasks have been completed, the proposed change should be written up in the form of a short, concise plan. Chapter 11 is devoted to this process.

Summary

In this chapter, we proposed a systematic approach designed to identify strategies and accompanying tactics that offer the potential for successful change. The approach includes a carefully thought-out series of tasks intended to maximize participation, to think through all possible types of change, and to select the options that will most likely achieve the desired results. Planners of change consider a number of political, interpersonal, and economic factors in order to be able to assess strengths and weaknesses of the proposed change. Itemizing the supporting and opposing people and factors allows the planners of change visually and cognitively to assess the likelihood of success. If it appears that the chances for success are good, the change effort moves to the stage of selecting appropriate tactics.

As with all professional practice, the approach is modified by the practitioner to fit the situation. If conditions dictate immediate action, some procedures will be shortened or streamlined. If time allows and the significance of the proposed change dictates, each task will be carried out with careful attention to detail.

In any case, it is our position that some changes will always be needed in the field of human services, both in organizations and in communities. These changes, we believe, require the professional assistance and consultation of social workers knowledgeable about macro-level change. They require informed and sometimes scholarly participation and guidance in order to ensure that what is achieved is what is most needed to address the social problem in the best interest of the target population. Social workers are well qualified to lead or coordinate the planning stages of such change efforts and to bring them to the point of action, and Chapter 11 is intended to assist in that process.

DISCUSSION QUESTIONS AND EXERCISES

1. In this chapter, we argue that collaboration, campaign, and context strategies are not separate categories but points along a continuum. What does this mean? Give an example of each of the major types of tactics that are linked with these strategies. Explain how the differences between them represent changes in location on the continuum.

2. Assume you are involved in a change episode and you have decided that a collaborative tactic will be appropriate, but you are unsure which type of collaborative tactic to use. Discuss the considerations you believe should go into determining whether to move forward with an implementation approach as opposed to a capacity-building approach.

3. Mass media appeals involve getting one or more type of media interested in the problem you are addressing and using their ability to arouse public concern as leverage for proceeding with the change episode. Are there hazards as well as benefits associated with attempts to use mass media? Identify and discuss the pros and cons of mass media appeals in the context of such hazards.

4. Electronic advocacy is being used more and more as people join lists and participate in virtual communities. If you were using a campaign strategy to get the word out about a problem you have identified, what protocols would you put in place to avoid being overloaded with rapid responses and information? How might you organize the flow of information?

5. Within the realm of contest tactics, we discuss large-group actions that might include acts of civil disobedience such as sit-ins or unauthorized processions and demonstrations. Is there an ethical basis for professional social workers to knowingly violate the law? Is it defensible for them to explicitly or implicitly encourage clients to violate the law?

6. In discussing the ethics of choosing a particular tactic, we refer to the importance of avoiding "dichotomous thinking." What

does this mean? Give an example of a situation where dichotomous thinking may lead to one choice of tactics, whereas a more open, multifaceted review of the situation might produce a different choice.

APPENDIX
Framework for Selecting Appropriate Tactics

Task 1: Assess Political and Interpersonal Considerations

Address Public Image and Relationships
- Who is involved in promoting the proposed change, and how are they perceived by decision makers?
- Who can serve as effective spokespersons for the proposed change?
- Who should keep a low profile when the proposed change is presented to decision makers?

Identify Alternative Perspectives
- Has anyone key to the success of the change effort been left out?
- How will opponents of the change effort frame their opposition?
- How much conflict or contentiousness is expected?

Assess Duration and Urgency
- How long has the problem existed?
- Is the problem considered an emergency?

Task 2: Assess Resource Considerations

Determine the Cost of Change
- What anticipated costs related to the proposed change can be itemized? What must be estimated?
- What sources of financial support or in-kind donations should be approached?

Determine the Cost of Doing Nothing
- What will this problem cost the organization or community if nothing is done?
- How can this cost be framed so that it will impress decision makers as a good investment to support the proposed change?

Task 3: Weigh the Likelihood of Success

Assess Support from Individuals, Groups, and Organizations
- Who supports the proposed change?

- Who opposes the proposed change?
- Who is neutral about the proposed change?

Assess Level of Support
- What facts and perspectives gleaned from the problem, population, and arena analysis support the proposed change?
- What facts and perspectives oppose the proposed change?

Task 4: Selecting Strategies and Tactics

Consider Strategies
- With which strategy will the change effort begin?
- Will it be necessary to consider sequential strategies, if one isn't working?
- If there are multiple, sequential targets, which strategies will be used with each target?

Identify Tactics
- Given the strategy most likely to succeed, what tactic (or combination of tactics) is needed first?
- As the change progresses, is it anticipated that changing strategies may lead to the use of different tactics?

Consider the Pros and Cons of Collaboration
- Is it certain that there is little opposition?
- Can the desired change be achieved by identifying appropriate roles for participants and implementing the change?

Consider the Pros and Cons of Campaign
- Who needs to be convinced that the proposed change is needed?
- What persuasive techniques are most likely to be effective?

Consider the Pros and Cons of Contest
- Is opposition to the proposed change so strong that it can only be successful by imposing the change on an unwilling target system?
- Can the proposed change be effective if it is forced?
- What are the anticipated consequences of conflict?

Weigh Relevant Considerations in Selecting Tactics
- What is the purpose of the change effort and has it changed in the process?
- What is the perception (by those promoting change) of the controlling and host systems?
- What is the perception (by those promoting change) of the role of the client system?
- What resources are needed and available for each tactic?
- What are the ethical dilemmas inherent in the range of tactical choices?

SUGGESTED READINGS

Blundo, R. G., C. Mele, R. Hairston, and J. Watson. (1999). The Internet and demystifying power differentials: A few women on-line and the housing authority. *Journal of Community Practice, 6*(2), 11–26.

Cohen, D., R. De la Vega, and G. Watson. (2001). *Advocacy for social justice.* Bloomfield, CT: Kumarian Press.

Delgado, M. (2000). *Community social work practice in an urban context: The potential of a capacity-enhancement perspective.* New York: Oxford.

Kaufman, R. (2001). Coalition activity of social change organizations in a public campaign: The influence of motives, resources and processes on levels of activity. *Journal of Community Practice, 9*(2): 21–42.

Lakey, B., G. Lakey, R. Napier, and J. Robinson. (1995). *Grassroots and nonprofit leadership: A guide for organizations in changing times.* Philadelphia: New Society Publishers.

Lee, J. A. B. (1994). *The empowerment approach to social work practice.* New York: Columbia University Press.

McInnis-Dittrich, K. (1994). *Integrating social welfare policy and social work practice.* Pacific Grove, CA: Brooks/Cole.

Mondros, J. B., and S. M. Wilson. (1994). *Organizing for power and empowerment.* New York: Columbia University Press.

Richan, W. C. (1996). *Lobbying for social change* (2nd ed.). Binghamton, NY: Haworth.

Rothman, J. (2000). Collaborative self-help community development: When is the strategy warranted? *Journal of Community Practice, 7*(2): 89–105.

Soifer, S., and J. Singer. (1999). The campaign to restore the disability assistance and loan program in the state of Maryland. *Journal of Community Practice, 6*(2): 1–10,

REFERENCES

Bailey, D., and K. M. Koney. (2000). *Creating and maintaining strategic alliances: From affiliations to consolidations.* Thousand Oaks, CA: Sage.

Barker, R. L. (1995). *The social work dictionary.* Washington, DC: National Association of Social Workers.

Berlin, S. B. (1990). Dichotomous and complex thinking. *Social Service Review, 64*(1): 46–59.

Brager, G., and S. Holloway. (1978). *Changing human service organizations: Politics and practice.* New York: Free Press.

Brager, G., H. Specht, and J. L. Torczyner. (1987). *Community organizing.* New York: Columbia University Press.

Clegg, S. R., and C. Hardy. (1999). *Studying organizations: Theory and method.* London: Sage.

Cropper, S. (1996). Collaborative working and the issue of sustainability. In C. Huxham (Ed.), *Creating collaborative advantage* (pp. 80–100). London: Sage.

Gutierrez, L. M., and E. A. Lewis. (1999). *Empowering women of color.* New York: Columbia University Press.

Harrison, B., and M. Weiss. (1998). *Workforce development networks: Community-based organizations and regional alliances.* Thousand Oaks, CA: Sage.

Haynes, K. S., and J. S. Mickelson. (2001). *Effecting change: Social workers in the political arena* (4th ed.). Boston: Allyn and Bacon.

Israel, B. A., A. J. Schultz, E. A. Parker, and A. B. Becker. (1998). Review of community-based research: Assessing partnership approaches to improve public health. *Annual Review of Public Health, 19:* 173–202.

Lewin, K. (1951). *Field theory in social science.* New York: Harper & Row.

Martin, P. Y., and G. G. O'Connor. (1989). *The social environment: Open systems applications.* New York: Longman.

Menon, G. M. (2000). The 79-cent campaign: The use of on-line mailing lists for electronic advocacy. *Journal of Community Practice, 8*(3): 73–81.

Rubin, H. J., and I. S. Rubin. (2001). *Community organizing and development* (3rd ed.). Boston: Allyn and Bacon.

Schneider, R. L., and L. Lester. (2001). *Social work advocacy.* Belmont, CA: Brooks/Cole.

Takahashi, L. M., and G. Smutny. (2002). Collaborative windows and organizational governance: Exploring the formation and demise of social service partnerships. *Nonprofit and Voluntary Sector Quarterly, 31*(2): 165–185.

Tobin, S. S., J. W. Ellor, and S. Anderson-Ray. (1986). *Enabling the elderly: Religious institutions within the community service system.* New York: State University of New York Press.

Tropman, J. E., J. L. Erlich, and J. Rothman. (2001). *Tactics and techniques of community intervention* (4th ed.). Itasca, IL: F. E. Peacock.

Weiner, B. J., and J. A. Alexander. (1998). The challenges of governing public-private community health partnerships. *Health Care Management Review,* 23(2): 39–55.

Planning, Implementing, Monitoring and Evaluating the Intervention

OVERVIEW

Throughout the analytical phases of the change episode we have encouraged the development of a hypothesis of etiology and a working intervention hypothesis. Their purpose is to make clear the thought processes that go into the decision to select a particular intervention. By now it should be clear that selecting an intervention is not a simple matter of brainstorming or choosing the most popular suggestion. Macro-level intervention is a carefully researched and thoroughly planned effort. The working intervention hypothesis provides an opportunity to ensure that all participants understand the logic behind the proposed intervention, and that an acceptable level of consensus has been achieved around its design. Following these activities, strategy(ies) and tactics are chosen, depending on the levels of acceptance and/or resistance to the proposed change.

A brief written document may be prepared that includes (1) a statement that clearly explains the problem or need, (2) a description of the proposed change and its expected results, and (3) a description of strategies and tactics planned to get the change accepted. This document can be circulated among participants to provide an opportunity for review and comment as a way of achieving consensus. However, participation throughout this process should not be assumed to mean support for the final design. A final check on disagreements is appropriate and necessary before developing the details of the intervention, and certainly prior to implementation.

Planning the Details of the Intervention

It is tempting to assume that, with all the planning and consensus building that has gone into the change effort, nothing can go wrong. But even carefully planned change can fail because of lack of attention to detail during the implementation phase. Consider the following examples:

Example 1: A Program Approach

A group of single mothers in the small town of Crestview has been meeting to discuss their common concerns and to provide mutual support. Their concerns center on quality child care for their preschool children, constructive after-school activities for their school-aged children, and finding a way out of dead-end jobs. A core planning group, with the help of a local social worker, puts together a plan to initiate programs in child care, after school-activities, and career development. The group plans to ask a local church to help establish a child-care center, ask the school district to sponsor the after-school program, and work with the local community college to develop a flexible program for a certificate in computer skills. The group's working intervention hypothesis reads as follows:

- If the following interventions are implemented for single mothers in Crestview:
  1. Provision of child care within the local community;
  2. Provision of after-school activities; and
  3. Provision of opportunities for education and career improvement.

- Then the following results can be expected:

    1. Improved healthy growth and development of the preschool children who receive care;
    2. Improved school and extracurricular performance for school-aged children;
    3. Increased incidence of program participants acquiring a certificate in computer skills; and
    4. At least 75 percent of the participants having a successful career change.

The town council agreed to provide some funding for the child-care center, and facilities were already in place and ready to go. Two of the single mothers agreed to staff it. Several teachers agreed to design an after-school program that would include tutoring, group discussion, and recreation, staffed by volunteers. The college was able to direct some of its resources to a career advancement program for single mothers. The participants were ready to celebrate! All that was left now was to implement the program.

The change effort had been initiated by Marie, a single mother of boundless energy who worked in a local video store. Of course, the participants reasoned, Marie would see it through to completion. Unfortunately, Marie's administrative skills did not match her community organizing skills. There was little or no follow-up on any of the new initiatives. By the time volunteers learned that the project was at a standstill, significant damage had been done. Church and school volunteers had lost interest and moved on to other activities. The town was ready to reclaim the money allocated, and the college returned its resources to traditional programs.

Example 2: A Policy Approach

The Department on Aging had just completed a statewide needs assessment survey. Findings revealed that an increasing number of older gay men and lesbians were caregivers for chronically ill, same-sex partners in local communities throughout the state. Advocates who were sensitive to the fact that same-sex partners were not always "out" wanted to learn as much as possible about the issues confronting the caregivers but knew that confidentiality had to be assured. They created a temporary hotline for caregivers to talk with a social worker who was trusted in the gay/lesbian community and who had connections throughout the state. The hotline was advertised in diverse publications targeted to the gay/lesbian population. Calls came in slowly in the beginning, but as word spread that someone was genuinely interested in the issues faced by caregivers of same-sex partners, more and more calls were received.

A major problem identified by caregivers throughout the state, and supported in the limited literature available on the topic (Hash, 2001), was that health-care professionals were often insensitive to the relationship of the caregiver and patient. Caregivers were told that because they were not blood relatives that they could not sign medical forms pertinent to their loved one's care and treatment. Thus, they were not allowed to be active participants in the decision-making process. Also, in trying to explain their relationships to health-care providers, they were often forced to disclose the nature of their relationship under insensitive circumstances, with no assurance that it would assist in their being accepted as the responsible party for the patient.

Given what the social worker heard on hotline calls, combined with what advocates had learned from the survey, the following intervention hypothesis emerged:

- If the following interventions are implemented for gay men and lesbian caregivers of partners in the state:
  1. Introduction of legislation allowing hospitals to let partners who are not blood-related to sign medical forms and to serve as the responsible party;
  2. Provision of sensitivity training for health-care workers; and
  3. Establishment of support groups for caregivers of same-sex partners.

- Then the following results can be expected:
  1. Increased opportunities for gay men and lesbian caregivers to participate in decision-making processes concerning their loved ones' care;
  2. Improved attitudes of health care professionals toward caregivers of same-sex partners; and
  3. Increased social support for caregivers of same-sex partners.

The social worker and advocates from around the state worked with the legal services unit at the State Department on Aging to draft legislative language to submit to the Legislative Drafting Office in the state capital. A bill was introduced at the next session to amend existing legislation. The advocates' hope was to raise the consciousness of legislators and the general public, knowing that the possibility of getting any change passed the first year was unlikely. In the meantime, they began work on designing a series of sensitivity training sessions that could be introduced into the continuing education programs of hospitals around the state. A local foundation agreed to provide funding for the training intervention within Region I of the state, and volunteer trainers were recruited through the area agency on aging network. Volunteers were also recruited as potential support group leaders.

As momentum spread, the bill was assigned to a committee in the Senate and a similar bill introduced into the House. On news and talk shows throughout the state, pros and cons of the "gay/lesbian caregiver bill" were debated. Amid this heated dialogue and after much work on the part of advocates, the bill passed. As advocates celebrated their victory, local hospital administrators showed reluctance to have their staff engage in sensitivity training sessions. They explained that the bill mandated who could sign forms, but that sensitivity training was not mandated. For busy health-care professionals, time off for continuing education was limited, and although sensitivity training was "nice," it would not replace CEUs (continuing education units) needed to keep up-to-date on medical knowledge. Volunteers became disillusioned when support groups were developed and few people attended.

The lesson here is that the work of the action system is not complete at the point of implementation. Implementation is a process, and needs to be carefully monitored and evaluated. Example 1 focuses on single mothers and children in a small town. A program approach is taken. Example 2 is much broader, initially focusing on a statewide change effort using a policy approach. Yet, in both examples, the celebration of success comes too soon. In this chapter, we will discuss what goes into the detailed planning, implementation, monitoring, and evaluation of a change effort.

Intervention Planning

Whether one is taking a policy, program, project, personnel or practice approach (as discussed in Chapter 9), it is necessary to engage in an intentional planning process. Weinbach (1998) observes that "planning is necessary because managers cannot afford to leave too much to chance," because "activities tend to get side-tracked within organizations unless someone puts into place certain vehicles designed to keep them on track" (pp. 77–78). Weinbach's observation is evident in Example 1 when Marie does not attend to the required details. Similarly, Hardina (2002) focuses on the community arena in which planning occurs among organizations as well as with multiple constituency groups. "Planners need political and administrative skills to ensure that plans are actually implemented. They must use all the steps in the problem-solving model—problem identification, assessment, goal setting, implementation, and evaluation—to create appropriate plans" (Hardina, 2002, p. 272). Hardina's reminder that political skills must be combined with administrative skills is important in both cases, but particularly in the broader context of Example 2. Regardless of the approach taken, attention to planning details is critical to the change effort

Planning the details of the intervention includes establishing goals, writing objectives, listing all the activities that will need to be carried out, and setting time frames, due dates, and responsibilities. This is a plan that absolutely must be in writing, with copies distributed to all participants who will be involved in implementation. These documents are then used to orient and train the implementers, and later as a basis for monitoring and evaluating the effectiveness of the intervention.

Task 1: Set a Goal for the Intervention

The key question to be explored is:

- What is the overall outcome that is expected if the intervention is successful?

Goals provide a beacon or focal point for the change effort that serve as reminders of the real purpose of the change effort. They also provide a tool around which people with diverse views can begin the process of building consensus. Goals are stated in outcome terms, and should include a target population, a boundary, and an expected result or outcome (Brody, 1993; Montana and Charnov, 1993). The processes or methods intended to achieve goals should never be included in the goal statement itself. For example, the Single Moms' Program hopes to achieve the following goal:

- To enhance growth and development of participating children while improving the career options of single mothers in Crestview.

The goal of the caregiver policy change might be stated as follows:

- To protect the rights of gay and lesbian caregivers with regard to medical authorization, and to strengthen the network of caregiver support within the state.

Other illustrations of goal statements might include:

- The goal of this project is to increase the number of Latino students who remain in high school and achieve their diplomas in the Jackson School District.
- The goal of this program is to reduce the number of isolated elderly in the town of Elwood.
- The goal of this change effort is to pass and implement a policy that will ensure a positive and productive lifestyle for first-time offenders in Washington County.

Note that these statements are not measurable as they are stated. Building in measurement criteria is the function of objectives.

Developing Objectives for the Intervention

If the decision is made to proceed with the change effort, designated members of the action system should develop an intervention plan that includes goals, objectives, and activities. Objectives serve as an elaboration of goals. They spell out the details of the planned intervention in measurable terms, including expected out-comes and the processes to achieve them. Activities are lists of tasks that must be undertaken and completed in order to achieve each objective.

Setting goals and objectives requires that the concepts and ideas generated during the analytical phase be translated into concrete terms. The purpose of this approach to planning is to take what can be a very large and complex undertaking and to break it up into manageable subsets.

The process begins with reexamining the working intervention hypothesis and translating the proposed interventions into objectives. In order to illustrate this process, we will continue with the examples of a working intervention hypothesis used in the Single Moms' Program, which focused on (1) child care, (2) after-school activities, and (3) career advancement; and with Gay/Lesbian Care-givers, which focused on (1) legislative changes, (2) sensitivity training, and (3) social support.

Objectives can be developed around each of the proposed interventions. *Objectives* are intended to move the change effort toward the goal; they are highly specific and measurable. There are two types: outcome objectives and process objectives. One *outcome objective* is generally written for each intervention, and specifies the result or outcome to be achieved with and for the target population. One or more *process objectives* is written for each outcome objective. Process objec-tives specify the process to be followed in order to achieve the result. When the outcome objective and all its related process objectives are completed and written out, it should be evident that (1) the process objectives, when completed, will lead to achievement of the outcome objective; and (2) the outcome objective, when accomplished, will move the effort toward the goal. (For a more complete discus-sion of goals and objectives, see Kettner, Moroney, and Martin, 1999 [Chapter 6], or Hardina, 2002 [Chapter 11].)

Task 2: Write Outcome Objectives

Writing objectives in outcome terms is often a tricky and elusive process for begin-ners. Practitioners are so conditioned to think in terms of what it is that they will be providing that it is tempting to try to use objectives to describe the services. Writing outcome objectives requires thinking in terms of what is expected to hap-pen to program participants as a result of the intervention. An outcome must be stated as a quality-of-life change for the client or consumer of services. For exam-ple, it is not the objective of a counseling program that clients participate in coun-seling, but rather that they strengthen and improve their relationships, or that they avoid an impending divorce. The time will come to deal with the process, but first the expected outcome must be addressed.

A complete objective, whether outcome or process, has four parts: (1) a time frame, (2) a target, (3) a result, and (4) a criterion for measuring or documenting the result (Kettner, Daley, & Nichols, 1985). The following sections will explain how each of these parts is applied to outcome objectives.

Establish a Time Frame for the Objective.   Questions to be explored for this activity include:

- At what point in the future is it reasonable to expect to see measurable results from this intervention?
- Is it possible to establish a day, month, and year when the first results should be evident?

The time frame ideally should be stated in terms of the month, day, and year by which the result will be achieved, because this information will later be needed for monitoring purposes. When a start date is unknown, the time frame may be specified in terms of time elapsed from the beginning of the change effort (e.g., "within three months of the beginning of the project" or "by the end of the first year"). Once a start date is known, it is wise to go back and fill in actual dates, since objectives are often also used as monitoring tools.

Funding and sponsoring sources usually expect at least annual reporting on progress and results. In situations where it is expected to take more than a year to achieve results, thought should be given to what kind of annual milestones can be established that will indicate that the project is on track (e.g., at least six mothers will achieve a certificate in computer skills; at least three mothers will have new jobs; at least six hospital staff will demonstrate sensitivity to gay/lesbian caregiver relationships). These milestones should be stated as outcomes. Technically, they are referred to as *intermediate outcomes* (Kettner, Moroney, & Martin, 1999).

Define the Target Population.   The key question to be explored for this activity is:

- Who are the expected primary beneficiaries of the intervention?

The second part of an objective, the target, specifies the individuals or focal point for which the objective is written. Outcome objectives are focused on a quality-of-life change and identify the individuals for whom the change is intended. By the time the change agent reaches this point, there should be no doubt about the makeup of the target system. Even so, there can be complexities is writing this part of the objective.

Statements should be as precise as current knowledge will allow. An outpatient drug treatment program, for example, might specify "24 cocaine addicts at least 18 years of age and currently employed" as its target. In Example 1, the Single Moms' Program, a decision would have to be made about the target system. Two of the three initiatives (child care and after-school activities) are for the children of single mothers. The third is for the mothers. Objectives could be written focusing on the children, the mothers, or the family unit as the target. For example, the target might be defined as "12 family units headed by a single mother," or there might be three different target populations (in three different outcome objectives)—one for child care, one for after-school programs, and one for career enhancement. The more precise the target, the greater the likelihood of a successful intervention.

Specify a Result or Outcome.   The key question to be explored for this activity is:

■ What quality-of-life changes are expected for the target population from this intervention?

The third part of an objective is a phrase that specifies the expected result or outcome to be achieved when all activities are completed. An outcome objective focuses on a quality-of-life change for the target population; that is, something must happen to make their lives better or more stable. *Outcome objectives* refer to such factors as improved knowledge and skill, improved relationships with spouse, reduction of alcohol abuse, more control over community decision making, and other such changes. The process designed to achieve the result is not the focal point at this time, and is not included in the statement. That will be dealt with later. Results or outcomes for the Single Moms' Program might be stated as follows: "Improvement in computer knowledge and skills, achievement of a certificate, upgrade in job and career path, increased stability and healthy development of children, and/or improved performance in school and extracurricular activities." Much will depend here on how the outcome objective(s) is/are written. This project can be handled with one overall objective that focuses on strengthening the family, with multiple indicators used to demonstrate strength, or it may make sense to write three different outcome objectives. Either approach is acceptable.

Results or outcomes for the Gay/Lesbian Caregiver change might be stated as follows: (1) increased caregiver participation in health-care decision making, (2) improved interaction with health-care professionals, and (3) increased social support. Note that in changes that involve policy approaches, the approval or enactment of the policy is actually a process to get to an outcome. It is assumed in this situation, for example, that the policy will facilitate the participation of gay men and lesbian caregivers in hospital settings. It is also assumed that this participation would be a quality-of-life change for them. Similarly, the intervention targets health professionals who must be more sensitive to the caregivers before their participation is accepted and affirmed. Just having a mandate that allows nonblood-related kin to sign forms does not assure that professionals' attitudes will be respectful. Change efforts such as these actually target legislators *and* health-care employees, even though the primary beneficiaries are caregivers as clients whose quality of life is improved.

Define a Criterion for Measuring Success.   Questions to be explored for this activity include:

■ How will the result as stated in the objective be measured?
■ Are there observable criteria readily available for measurement, or will criteria need to be designed?

The final part of an objective is the criterion that will be used to determine whether the objective has been achieved. Objectives must be precise and measurable, yet sometimes the result to be achieved seems vague and elusive. Some programs, for example, are designed to improve self-esteem. The question is, How does one know whether or not self-esteem has been improved? The criterion specified in the objective ensures that only one standard will be used. If improving self-esteem is the result, then it must be measured by a standardized test designed to measure self-esteem. The criterion for an outcome objective usually begins with, "as measured by . . . ." Increased self-esteem, for example, might be measured by the Index of Self-Esteem (Hudson, 1982), a paper-and-pencil test that is taken by participants before and after the project.

In Example 1, child development may be measured by using a standardized scale of indicators for age-appropriate development and behavior for each of the participating children. Improved school performance is usually measured in terms of grades. Extracurricular participation can be measured in terms of hours devoted to newly acquired interests. Achievement of a certificate can be used as a measure of the single mothers' successful completion of the educational program, and a job change that presents more opportunities for career enhancement and advancement is evidence of success in the area of employment.

In Example 2, decision-making participation requires that a policy change occur. An enacted policy could certainly facilitate participation, but actual participation by caregivers in treatment decision making becomes the ultimate measure of success. Health-care professionals' attitudes could be measured by tests focusing on how one views sexual orientation and work with gay and lesbian clients. However, to fully evaluate the success of the intervention, observational data would be helpful. In addition, a survey that asks caregivers to assess how they were treated by health professionals may be key to knowing their perceptions that attitudes have changed. Last, increased social support can be measured by continued participation in caregiver groups in addition to documented feedback from individual caregivers attesting to feeling more supported.

Examples of Complete Outcome Objectives. Example 1, the program to strengthen families that are headed by single mothers, includes three major components: (1) provision of child care, (2) after-school activities, and (3) career development. Using the first of these, child care, an outcome objective would include the following parts:

Time Frame: By June 30, 20XX
Target: At least 10 preschool children of single mothers who are part of the program and have received child-care services
Result: Will demonstrate ability to perform 10 age-appropriate tasks at minimum standards or better
Criterion: As measured by a standardized performance test for preschool children.

In Example 2, designed to address the needs of gay men and lesbian caregivers, there are also three components: (1) participation in decision making, (2) better attitudes toward caregivers, and (3) social support. Using the first of these components, participation, an outcome objective could include the following parts:

Time Frame:	By October 1, 20XX
Target:	At least 30 caregivers of nonblood-related patients admitted for treatment within hospitals in Region I of the state
Result:	Will have participated to their satisfaction in the patient care decision-making process
Criterion:	As measured by a confidential follow-up caregiver survey.

Task 3: Develop Process Objectives

Each outcome objective is followed by a number of process objectives designed to spell out the ways in which the outcome objective will be achieved. Process objectives should identify the major components of a planned intervention, not the specific details. Brody (1993) points out that process objectives usually involve the interaction of people and organizations (p. 62). For example, if one were to plan a community garden project for an inner-city community, process objectives would be written for such project components as recruiting and training participants, finding land, securing resources, and assigning responsibilities. Details, such as purchasing seeds, shovels, rakes, and hoes, or watering responsibilities become part of the activities to be discussed in a following section. A complete process objective includes the same four parts: time, target, result, and criterion.

Establish a Time Frame for the Process Objective.   The key question to be explored is:

- When will the actions specified in this objective begin and end?

Time frames are specified in the same way for both outcome and process objectives. Ideally, due dates or milestones are established in terms of specific dates—day, month, and year. When this information is not known, it is permissible to express a time frame in terms of the number of weeks, months, or years from the time the intervention begins. The actual date selected for a process objective should be the date when the process is expected to be completed, such as: "By December 31, 20XX, at least 24 participants will complete . . . ." Time frames for process objectives must, of course, be coordinated with the time frame for the related outcome objective.

Define the Target.   The key question to be explored is:

- Who will be the participants in the process named in this objective?

Process objectives are used to specify the various components of an intervention. Each process objective may very well have a different target. For some process objectives, the target may be the same individuals as specified in the outcome objective. For others, it may be that the target of a process objective is not people at all, but rather an object, such as a training curriculum or a policy.

The logic behind a process objective is that everything that needs to be changed or accomplished in order to achieve the outcome objective should be laid out in sequence. As described by Montana and Charnov (1993):

> The manager [or organizer] breaks down the objective into pieces and hands out responsibility for those pieces to various units or individuals. When all the assigned responsibilities are fulfilled, they should equal the successful accomplishment of the objective. (p. 90)

Each major component of the intervention is translated into a process objective. For example, if the outcome specified is "self-sufficiency," then the process might include (1) completion of a GED, (2) a skills training course, (3) job counseling, (4) job placement, and (5) follow-up. Individuals intended to receive each of these services would be defined as the target for each process objective.

Specify a Result for the Process Objective.   The key question to be explored for this activity is:

- What result will provide evidence that the objective has been achieved?

Process objectives focus on the result expected that indicates that the process has been completed. The result must be stated in a way that is concrete and observable. If the process involves services to people, the result might be something like completion of a course, completion of at least six counseling sessions, or attendance of at least six training sessions on the political process. If the process involves changing some part of an organization or community, the result might be described as a completed report, a new strategic plan, or the design of a new data-collection form.

Define a Criterion to Be Used for Documentation Purposes.   The key question to be explored for this activity is:

- What observable or measurable factor(s) can be used to determine whether the process objective has been achieved?

Process objectives may be directed either to the completion of a part of the process by participants or to the production of products or achievement of milestones. A wide variety of criteria can be used to measure the result of a process objective. The focus in writing process objectives is on record-keeping or documentation that clearly demonstrates that the result has been achieved. In most cases, process objectives will use the phrases, "as documented by . . ." or "as demonstrated by . . . ." Completion of a course, for example, can be documented by receipt of a certificate of completion, by attendance records, or by a formal transcript. Creation of a new form or writing of a new policy can be documented by submission of these items in writing to a specified person by a due date.

Examples of Process Objectives. In Example 1, the first outcome specified for preschool children of single mothers was that they would be able to demonstrate ability to successfully perform 10 age-appropriate tasks at minimum standards or better, as measured by a standardized performance test. The question then becomes: How can we get this group of preschool children to the point where they can complete the necessary sets of exercises? Let's assume that their performance in 10 areas (such as recognition of shapes, colors, letters, etc.; ability to listen, understand, get along, etc.) would be tested at their point of entry into the program. The program would then be designed to give the children an opportunity to learn more about appropriate performance and to practice and improve their performances in each of the 10 areas over a one-year program. The process objective would include the following parts:

Time Frame:	By June 1, 20XX
Target:	The 10 preschool children who have been accepted into the preschool program
Result:	Will complete a one-year curriculum designed to teach 10 basic competency skills
Criterion:	As documented by a Certificate of Completion signed by the director of the child-care program.

In Example 2, the first outcome specified for caregivers is satisfactory participation in health-care decision making. This requires that they be allowed to sign the appropriate forms that had previously been the domain of blood-related kin. The question then becomes: How does one get caregivers to the point at which they have the legal standing necessary to be able to participate in medical decisions for nonblood-related kin? Since the practice currently has no protection in law, a policy approach would focus on creating a new law that would allow caregivers to sign the forms that dictate what medical treatment can be provided. When such a policy has been passed and implemented, the actual signing of medical forms can serve as documentation that the policy is working. A process objective, then, might include the following parts:

Time Frame:	By July 1, 20XX
Target:	At least 80 percent of hospitals in Region I within the state
Result:	Will demonstrate that they have implemented the policy that allows nonblood-related kin to sign medical forms for same-sex partners' health care
Criterion:	As documented by signed and witnessed forms.

When all four parts—time frame, target, result, and criterion—have been written, the objective is complete. The foregoing examples are reproduced in Figure 11.1 to reinforce the understanding of the differences between outcome and process objectives.

Typically, a set of goals and objectives will include one goal, a number of outcome objectives, and several process objectives for each outcome objective. In Example 1, the goal involved strengthening families by improving the performance of children while enhancing the career opportunities for single mothers. Outcome objectives would be written for (1) the preschool program, (2) the after-school program, and (3) the career development program.

In Example 2, the goal involved protecting the rights of gay and lesbian caregivers with regard to medical authorization, and strengthening the network of caregiver support within the state. Outcome objectives would be written for (1)

FIGURE 11.1   Illustration of Relationship between Goal, Outcome Objective, and Process Objectives

Goal
To enhance growth and development of participating children while improving the career options of single mothers in Crestview

Outcome Objective
Time Frame: By June 30, 20XX
Target: At least 10 preschool children of single mothers who are part of the program and have received child-care services
Result: Will demonstrate ability to perform 10 age-appropriate tasks at minimum standards or better
Criterion: As measured by a standardized performance test for preschool children.

Process Objective 1
Time Frame: By June 1, 20XX
Target: The 10 preschool children who have been accepted into the preschool program
Result: Will complete a one-year curriculum designed to teach 10 basic competency skills
Criterion: As documented by a Certificate of Completion signed by the director of the child-care program.

(Two additional outcomes and their accompanying process objectives would be written to cover the after-school program and the career development program.)

medical decision making by nonblood-related caregivers, (2) sensitivity training for hospital staff, and (3) social support.

Each of these objectives would require a series of process objectives. It is important that each of these phases of the implementation process become clear and visible parts of the plan, so that the implementers will know precisely what was intended, and will implement the plan as designed without skipping important elements.

Task 4: List Activities for Process Objectives

The final step in developing the intervention plan is to itemize activities. Activities represent the highest level of detail incorporated into the plan. Each activity represents a step that, when accomplished, moves the change effort closer to achievement of a process objective. Activities should specify the work to be done, the person responsible, and a time frame.

Format Activities for Easy Monitoring.   Questions to be explored for this activity include:

- What activities or tasks must be successfully completed in order to achieve the process objective?
- When should each activity begin and end?
- Who should be assigned responsibility for completion of the activity?

The Gantt chart, developed by management pioneer Henry L. Gantt, has proved to be a useful format for setting up activities (Gantt, 1919). The chart is made up of columns and rows. Each row represents an activity, and columns are used to identify activity number, person responsible, and the beginning and ending dates. Brody (1993) points out that Gantt charts are valuable because they

> illustrate how various tasks should be subsumed under major activities in a comprehensible, easy-to-construct format. The chart clarifies the beginning and ending points projected for each task and shows at a glance what efforts must be made within a specific time period. (p. 76)

An example of a Gantt chart is illustrated in Figure 11.2. The process objective is identified, activities are listed, time frames are specified, and responsibilities are assigned.

In preparing an action plan for a macro-level change, each subsection of the intervention should include a set of outcome objectives, process objectives, and activities. When these are developed at an acceptable level of precision, with responsibilities and time frames clearly specified, the action plan is complete. The last steps in macro-level change involve the implementation and monitoring of the plan, and evaluation of its effectiveness.

Activity Number Activity	Person Responsible	Time Frame											
		Jun	Jul	Aug	Sep	Oct	Nov	Dec	Jan	Feb	Mar	Apr	May
1. Recruit an advisory committee of six child-development experts.	M. Green	■											
2. Have committee identify 10 basic competency skills for preschoolers.	M. Green		▬										
3. Have committee design a curriculum to teach the 10 skills.	M. Green			▬									
4. Recruit and select a director for the program.	B. Turner				▬								
5. Recruit and select child-care staff volunteers.	B. Turner					▬							
6. Train child-care staff volunteers.	T. Banks						▬						
7. Set up the child-care center.	J. Johns						▬						
8. Recruit and select 10 preschool children for the program.	B. Turner							▬					
9. Set a start date and implement the program.									▬▬▬▬				
10. Evaluate performance of 10 preschool participants.												▬	
11. Issue certificates of completion to all who meet attendance criteria.													■

FIGURE 11.2   Gantt Chart of Activities

Implementing and Monitoring the Plan

Based on his research, Bardach (1979) states that in either simple or complex situations, there is still a fundamental implementation question: Can the change effort be carried out, keeping in mind the underlying intent of what was decided? His classic study of implementation revealed that the answer is often "no" when well-intentioned people are trying to address complex social problems (p. 36). Example 2 is particularly relevant here. When a statewide policy approach is needed in order to benefit individual caregivers at the local level, there is often premature jubilation when a policy is enacted. Enactment of the policy only assures that hospitals are allowed to let caregivers sign medical forms that dictate treatment. It does not mean that persons responsible for getting those forms signed will fully explain what the forms mean, will treat gay and lesbian caregivers with the respect they deserve, or will even recognize the significance of their being able to participate. Implementation *begins* when the policy is enacted, and attending to whether it is consonant with the original intent of the change effort requires constant vigilance.

In many ways, the types of changes that are often initiated in organizations and communities are unique or special in some way. Inherent in the change effort is a recognition that the standardized approaches that have been used have not been effective in getting the job done, so something new needs to be tried. At the same time, it is not unusual for at least part of the implementing system to be made up of people who have been using standardized approaches for many years. The situation described sets up the potential for conflict. "Traditionalists" may feel threatened by new approaches or feel that their previous work is being discredited; "Innovators" may have reservations about long-time employees in terms of their ability to take a fresh approach. The key to addressing these potential problems is to plan for overlap between the planners and the implementers. Ideally, implementers should be involved in the planning process, but if this is not possible, it is important to work with the implementing system to make certain that all facets and complexities of the change are properly understood and enthusiastically supported.

Task 5: Initiate the Action Plan

Putting the plan into action usually requires a number of tasks that need to be completed in advance, prior to involving clients, consumers, or participants. For change efforts such as the ones described in this book to be successful, it is critical that they be well organized at the point of implementation, and that they have a clearly defined lead person or coordinator. The primary focus of this person is to get others to get the job done, to maintain morale, and to motivate participants (Dessler, 1997).

Up to this point, the major phases of the change effort (researching the change, creating the design, soliciting support, developing strategy and tactics, and planning the details of implementation) have been carried out by many groups of interacting and overlapping individuals and systems. In preparation for implementation, it is necessary that the intervention become more formalized. Logistical considerations such as facilities and equipment need to be addressed. Depending on the approach to change, some type of lead person or point person must be appointed. Some of the earlier participants may now form a policy-making board or an advisory board to provide consultation and guidance. In the case of project or program approaches, personnel issues—including hiring, orienting, and training—must be planned. Coordination and communication among new and old participants will help ensure successful implementation.

Manage Logistics.   Questions to be explored for this activity include:

- What facilities, equipment, and other resources will need to be made available prior to implementation?
- If needed, where will new personnel, including volunteers, be housed?
- How can the steps or phases be depicted in flowchart form?

The planned change will involve either existing staff and volunteers, new services, new staff, and perhaps new clients, consumers, or participants, or some combination. If new personnel are to be involved, appropriate accommodations will have to be identified. If existing staff and volunteers are to be used, decisions need to be made about sharing space and equipment between the old and new programs. It may be necessary to sketch out a floor plan to make clear where all personnel will be located. Appropriate resources need to be made available, including computers, if needed, copying equipment, desk, telephone, and other necessities. It may also be helpful to prepare a flowchart that depicts client flow through the system, if the change involves services to clients. Figure 11.3 illustrates a simple flowchart that can be used to clarify the steps in the service process. If a policy change is involved, a similar flowchart could be constructed to depict the steps or phases of the change process.

Select and Train Participants.   Questions to be explored for this activity include:

- Who will have overall leadership and management responsibilities for the intervention?
- Will existing or new staff and/or volunteers be used in the intervention?
- What preparations need to be made to bring new participants on board?
- What type of orientation and training will be needed?

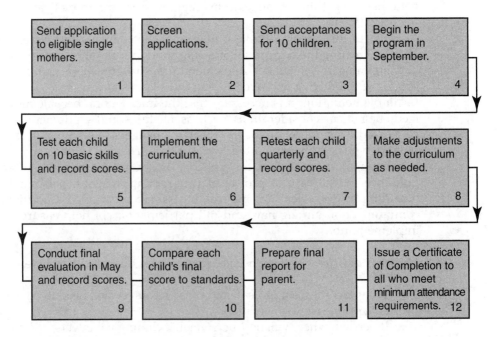

FIGURE 11.3   Flowchart for Processing Children through the Preschool Program

One of the first steps in getting the intervention underway is the selection of a lead person or point person. This person will be critical to the success of the intervention, and therefore should be screened with great care. If the intervention is designed as a new initiative, with its own funding and other resources, then formal job descriptions and job announcements will need to be written. In large-scale changes, where time permits, it is desirable first to go through the recruitment, selection, and hiring process for the lead person, and then to have the person selected take a leading role in selecting other staff. Whether additional staff and volunteers will be new or drawn from current employees or from community groups, it is advisable to have a job description for each position, and to go through a selection process, including interviews. (For a more complete discussion of recruitment, selection, and hiring issues, see Dessler, 1997; Kettner, 2002; Weinbach, 1998).

Once personnel have been selected, an orientation is in order. It is advisable to involve as many of the early participants in the change effort in orientation in order to maintain continuity. Once orientation has been completed, plans for ongoing training should be addressed, based on findings from early implementation experiences and training needs expressed by staff and volunteers.

Task 6: Monitor and Evaluate the Intervention

What happens during the monitoring and evaluation phases will depend heavily on the size and scope of the intervention. Monitoring and evaluation systems require data collection and the building of a management information system. For a very large-scale intervention designed, for example, to recruit and train 25 people to take on various roles in the decision-making process in a community, a substantial database would have to be developed, designed to track efforts and accomplishments. This would very likely require computer capacity and people skilled in data entry and aggregation.

At the other extreme, a change effort within a high school might be designed to provide a support group for six students identified as at-risk of dropping out. In this case, some fairly simple data collection to track attendance at support group meetings and progress in the classroom might suffice. At either extreme, certain principles should be followed to ensure adequate collection of quantitative data and other types of information for monitoring and evaluation purposes.

Monitor Technical Activities.   Questions to be explored for this activity include:

- What is the appropriate sequencing for the activities that must be completed in order to achieve the process objective?
- Who will be assigned responsibility for completion of each activity?
- When must each activity be completed in order for the process objective to be achieved on time?

In order to achieve a process objective, it is necessary to complete a number of activities. If activities have been carefully itemized (preferably in Gantt chart form), monitoring technical activities is greatly simplified. For example, in constructing the preschool component as a part of the Single Moms' Program, we identified the following process objective and activities:

Process Objective 1

By June 1, 20XX, the 10 preschool children who have been accepted into the preschool program will complete a one-year curriculum designed to teach 10 basic competency skills as documented by a Certificate of Completion signed by the director of the child care program.

1. Recruit an advisory committee of six child development experts.
2. Have the committee identify 10 basic competency skills for preschoolers.
3. Have the committee design a curriculum to teach the 10 skills.
4. Recruit and select a director for the program.
5. Recruit and select child-care staff volunteers.
6. Train child-care staff.
7. Set up the child-care center.
8. Recruit and select 10 preschool children for the program.
9. Set a start date and implement the program.
10. Evaluate performance of 10 preschool participants.
11. Issue certificates of completion to all who meet attendance criteria.

These activities are designed to happen in sequence. In most cases, one activity is a prerequisite for the next and subsequent activities. For example, the work of the Child Development Advisory Committee mentioned in activities 2 and 3 cannot meet to do its work until the six participants have been recruited, as specified in activity 1.

When start and completion dates, together with a person responsible, have been established for each activity, monitoring simply requires confirming with the person responsible that the activity has been started/completed as of the date specified. Where these activities have not met deadlines, or where problems emerge, the lead person becomes involved in problem solving and decision making. Brody (1993) points out that problem solving involves formulating a problem statement and examining potential alternatives, whereas decision making requires choosing from among alternatives and implementing an approach to deal with the problem.

The critical issue in managing change efforts is keeping on schedule. If the due date for designing the curriculum slips, then each subsequent date may slip, delaying implementation and possibly resulting in an inability to report findings as promised to funding and sponsoring sources at year's end. The lead person is often the only person who has an overview of all of the activities that are going on simultaneously, and therefore has responsibility for integrating component parts of the change effort.

In monitoring technical activities, it may be useful to add several columns to the activity chart, such as the following: Was the activity completed? Was it completed on time? What was the quality of the product? What adjustments are needed for this activity? What adjustments are needed for subsequent activities? By tracking each of these factors, the lead person will be in a position to be more proactive in anticipating problems and needs and making the necessary adjustments.

Monitor Interpersonal Activities. Questions to be explored for this activity include:

- How enthusiastic and supportive are the designated implementers?
- Is there a formal or informal system for evaluating the performance of implementers?
- Is there a strategy for dealing with poor performance, apathy, or resistance?

Monitoring the implementation of a plan can be a highly rewarding experience when persons carrying out the plan are enthusiastic, hard working, competent, compatible, cooperative, and committed to a common vision. Unfortunately, such a scenario is not always the case. Some participants may have been assigned without their consent. Personalities and styles of working may clash. Competition may emerge.

Interpersonal tensions can often be traced to uncertainty about roles and responsibilities or to feelings of being overly controlled. Good management practices should be promoted, encouraging participants to use their talents and abilities to the greatest extent while the designated point person focuses on removing barriers to implementation activities. However, in spite of the manager's best efforts, competition and conflict are likely to surface at some point.

A strategy for dealing with performance problems, including interpersonal tensions, should be established and communicated to all participants. Within an organizational arena, performance should be evaluated regularly and consistently. In a larger, more permanent program, a formal appraisal will be conducted and placed in a personnel file. In a less formally structured effort (particularly with community change), regularly scheduled conferences, staff meetings, or peer review sessions can be encouraged in the interest of airing concerns before they affect morale and performance. Rewards and incentives should be commensurate with performance. Identifying all of these motivational factors for each participant at the point of selection and hiring can go a long way toward preempting interpersonal problems.

Community change efforts may involve coalitions of organizations or groups of people who do not work for one organization. Change efforts might be almost totally dependent on volunteer commitment. Policy approaches to change may pull together disparate groups who are concerned about an issue but who are not formally related and who disperse once approval of the policy occurs. In these situations, implementation is complicated in that the persons responsible for implementing the change may not agree with the change. Advocates may have to select point persons who literally oversee the implementation process when resources are not put in place for policy implementation. In some cases, employees of the organization responsible for implementing a change could not have been involved in the change process because they are not allowed to participate in advocacy efforts as part of their employment status. In these circumstances, it may be difficult to determine just how much resistance or support one has from the implementing system until the implementation process begins. This is why vigilance in the implementation process is critical if the full extent of the change effort is to be realized.

Task 7: Evaluate the Effectiveness of the Intervention

To evaluate effectiveness, it is necessary to refer to the result or outcome specified in the outcome objectives. Recall that the plan includes a goal, one or more outcome objectives, a set of process objectives for each outcome objective, and a set of activities for each process objective. When the work specified in the activities has been completed, the process objective should be completed, and when all process objectives have been achieved, the outcome objective should have been achieved.

Once all activities and processes have been completed, it is time to return to outcome objectives to determine whether the intervention has been successful. In planning for change, the "bottom line" for an intervention is whether the intervention improved the condition or quality of life of the people it set out to help. This is the focus when evaluating the intervention.

Compile Periodic Evaluation Reports.   Questions to be explored for this activity include:

- What outcome(s) or result(s) were specified in the intervention plan?
- What quantitative data and other types of information are available for evaluative purposes?
- How shall data be aggregated and displayed in evaluation reports?

Evaluation requires collecting and compiling data and information. The performance of each client or participant needs to be tracked in a way that allows for establishment of a baseline at the outset of the intervention and periodic measurement of progress. This may involve some type of pre- and posttest, for example, to measure learning, or it may require a tracking of a single indicator such as a client being hired into a new job.

Documenting performance and progress will require some type of data collection. If the intervention involves initiation of a large-scale program with many clients or participants, forms must be designed and data entered into a computerized system. For a small project, it is possible that records may be maintained by hand in a notebook.

The focus of the evaluation is on outcomes or results specified in outcome objectives. These expected outcomes had a great deal to do with why the change effort was supported, sponsored, and funded in the first place. It is critically important that current participants honor the commitments made, and report back to sponsors and supporters their findings about the effectiveness of the intervention.

Recall that the outcome objectives for the preschool program (Example 1) and for caregiver participation in medically related decision making (Example 2) were stated as follows:

Example 1: The Single Moms' Program

Outcome Objective 1: By June 30, 20XX, at least 10 preschool children of single mothers who are part of the program and have received child-care services will demonstrate ability to perform 10 age-appropriate tasks at minimum standards or better as measured by a standardized performance test for preschool children.

Example 2: A New Policy for Caregivers

By October 1, 20XX, at least 30 caregivers of nonblood-related patients admitted for treatment within hospitals in Region I of the state will have participated to their satisfaction in the patient care decision-making process as measured by a confidential follow-up caregiver survey.

What the outcome in Example 1 means is that the performance of the 10 children admitted to the preschool program will be tested periodically, using the standardized performance test selected for the project. Their scores will be recorded, and the progress that they demonstrate on each of the 10 measures will become the basis for evaluation of outcomes. The outcome in Example 2 will be measured by a confidential caregiver satisfaction survey designed to determine whether a satisfactory level of participation has been achieved for at least 30 caregivers. Charts similar to those illustrated in Figure 11.4 could be used to display the findings from these two interventions.

When data for all outcome objectives have been collected, aggregated and compiled, a brief end-of-the-year report should be prepared for funding sources and other stakeholders. This report would include information such as the following:

I   Overview (Rationale behind the change effort)

II   Description (What interventions are being provided?)

FIGURE 11.4   Display of Findings from the Evaluation of the Preschool Program

Preschool Program
Pre- and Postprogram Performance Levels

Beginning Date: _____   Date of Evaluation:_____

Child No.	Pre- and Postscore	Performance Skills										Mean Score
		1	2	3	4	5	6	7	8	9	10	
1	Pre Post											
2	Pre Post											
3	Pre Post											
4	Pre Post											
5	Pre Post											
6	Pre Post											
7	Pre Post											
8	Pre Post											
9	Pre Post											
10	Pre Post											

Mean Pretest Scores: _____
Mean Posttest Scores: _____
Number of children who successfully completed the program: _____

III   Goals and Objectives (Briefly stated)
IV   First-Year Findings (Tables, graphs, and charts plus explanations)
V   Recommendations (What should be changed in the second and succeeding years?)

Rapp and Poertner (1992) offer some useful suggestions for report writing:

1. *Establish a standard.* Numbers are meaningless if there are no standards for comparison.
2. *Avoid too much information.* Limit the presentation to major findings. Present it in an uncluttered format.
3. *Pay attention to aesthetics.* Use simple, attractive graphs, charts, and tables wherever possible.
4. *Explain tables, graphs, and charts in simple English.* Avoid using jargon. Write for the uninformed reader.
5. *Make aggregation meaningful.* Make sure that users of the report will be able to identify data and information that are meaningful to them at their level in the organization or community.

Using sound techniques for collecting and aggregating data and information, clearly displaying outcomes, and reporting in a way that is useful to the intended audience will help to solidify and build support for the change effort from key stakeholders. Continual feedback and reassessment, as well as steady communication with all participants and supporters, will go a long way toward stabilizing the change effort in a way that it becomes a permanent, well-integrated part of the organization or community. This, in the end, is what the change agent hoped for when the change effort was initiated, and is an indicator that the intervention has been successful.

Summary

If all the planning described in the first 10 chapters is followed, the change agent should have all the ingredients necessary to develop the final, written plan, and to implement, monitor, and evaluate the intervention. The working intervention hypothesis establishes the direction and the parameters for goals and objectives. Writing goals and objectives makes the whole change effort become proactive, which is to say that the action system is in a position to make things happen rather than simply to hope that they happen.

A goal statement provides the general sense of direction for the planned change effort. It is stated in terms of expected outcomes for the target population. As the intervention is implemented, there should be some general sense of positive movement toward the goal, but goals as used in this context are not actually measured.

An outcome objective is a statement of expected outcomes that is intended to operationalize the goal, and is written in a way that the outcome can be measured, monitored, and evaluated. An objective includes four parts: time, target, result, and criterion. Process objectives are used to describe the major components of the intervention that will be necessary in order to achieve the outcome objective. Once the outcome expectations are clear, phases or components necessary to successful achievement of the outcomes should be itemized, and a complete process objective written for each phase or component. When examining all process objectives taken together, the planner should be convinced that, if they are all completed as planned, their completion will add up to successful achievement of the outcome objective.

Activities are then written for each process objective. Activities or tasks should be planned sequentially so that, when all activities are completed, the process objective will have been achieved. For each activity a time frame and the person responsible for completion of the activity should be specified. Thus, the overall plan becomes a very intricate set of goals, objectives, and activities, designed to work together. If the plan is carefully devised in this manner, the chances for success are greatly increased. If all the activities are completed within the specified time frame, then process objectives should be achieved. If process objectives are achieved, then outcome objectives should be achieved. And finally, if outcome objectives are achieved, the change effort will have moved toward its goal.

Implementing the intervention involves managing the logistics specified in the plan, and ensuring that all technical and interpersonal problems are addressed. Evaluating the effectiveness of the intervention focuses on outcome objectives, and requires data collection and aggregation for the purpose of reporting back to funding sources and other sponsors and stakeholders. Once a complete cycle of monitoring and evaluation has been completed (usually by the end of the first year), efforts should be focused on making necessary adjustments to improve the program based on findings from the evaluation, and looking for ways to solidify the project and to ensure ongoing support.

DISCUSSION QUESTIONS AND EXERCISES

1. Using either Example 1, the Single Moms' Program, or Example 2, the Caregivers' Initiative, write outcome objectives for the after-school program and the career development program or for the hospital staff sensitivity training and the social support group.

	After-School **Component**	**Career Development** **Component**

Time Frame:

Target:

Result:

Criterion:

	Hospital Staff **Training Component**	**Social Support** **Group Component**

Time Frame:

Target:

Result:

Criterion:

2. Are the time frames consistent with Outcome Objective 1 for each program? How many participants did you include in each of the above programs? Why? Have you stated the results in terms of a quality-of-life change for the target populations? Were you able to specify observable, measurable criteria for use in determining whether the result has been achieved?

3. Using the two outcome objectives you have written above, write at least one process objective for each outcome objective.

	After-School **Component**	**Career Development** **Component**

Time Frame:

Target:

Result:

Criterion:

	Hospital Staff **Training Component**	**Social Support** **Group Component**

Time Frame:

Target:

Result:

Criterion:

4. Are the time frames consistent with the dates specified in the respective outcome objectives? If the result of the process objective is achieved, is it reasonable to expect that the outcome objective will be achieved? What criteria will you use to document completion of the process specified?

5. Identify some of the activities that must be completed in order to achieve each process objective.

6. Suppose some of the early activities are not completed on time. What actions might you, as lead person, consider taking in order to ensure success for the intervention?

7. If interpersonal tensions should arise among three or four of the target individuals or families, and they were serious enough to threaten continuation of the change effort, how would you propose to address these concerns?

8. Monitoring the change process involves tracking activities to make sure they have been accomplished, and that the work is being done at an acceptable level of quality. Looking at some of the activities you identified above, how would you satisfy yourself that the work had been done, and how would you determine the level of quality?

9. List data elements that you might use in documenting achievement of outcomes. Prepare a table, chart, or graph that you might use to illustrate the results of your outcome objectives.

APPENDIX A
Framework for Planning, Implementing, Monitoring, and Evaluating the Intervention

Task 1: Set a Goal for the Intervention
- What is the overall outcome that is expected if the intervention is successful?

Task 2: Write Outcome Objectives

Establish a Time Frame for the Objective
- At what point in the future is it reasonable to expect to see measurable results from this intervention?
- Is it possible to establish a day, month, and year when the first results should be evident?

Define the Target Population
- Who are the expected primary beneficiaries of the intervention?

Specify a Result or Outcome
- What quality-of-life changes are expected for the target population from this intervention?

Define a Criterion for Measuring Success
- How will the result as stated in the objective be measured?
- Are there observable criteria readily available for measurement, or will criteria need to be designed?

Task 3: Develop Process Objectives

Establish a Time Frame for the Process Objective
■ When will the actions specified in this objective begin and end?

Define the Target
■ Who will be the participants in the process named in this objective?

Specify a Result for the Process Objective
■ What result will provide evidence that the objective has been achieved?

Define a Criterion to Be Used for Documentation Purposes
■ What observable or measurable factor(s) can be used to determine whether the process objective has been achieved?

Task 4: List Activities for Process Objectives

Format Activities for Easy Monitoring
■ What activities or tasks must be successfully completed in order to achieve the process objective?
■ When should each activity begin and end?
■ Who should be assigned responsibility for completion of the activity?

Task 5: Initiate the Action Plan

Manage Logistics
■ What facilities, equipment, and other resources will need to be made available prior to implementation?
■ If needed, where will new personnel, including volunteers, be housed?
■ How can the steps or phases be depicted in flowchart form?

Select and Train Participants
■ Who will have overall leadership and management responsibilities for the intervention?
■ Will existing or new staff and/or volunteers be used in the intervention?
■ What preparations need to be made to bring participants on board?
■ What type of orientation and training will be needed?

Task 6: Monitor and Evaluate the Intervention

Monitor Technical Activities
■ What is the appropriate sequencing for the activities that must be completed in order to achieve the process objective?
■ Who will be assigned responsibility for completion of each activity?

- When must each activity be completed in order for the process objective to be achieved on time?

Monitor Interpersonal Activities
- How enthusiastic and supportive are the designated implementers?
- Is there a formal or informal system for evaluating the performance of implementers?
- Is there a strategy for dealing with poor performance, apathy, or resistance?

Task 7: Evaluate the Effectiveness of the Intervention

Compile Periodic Evaluation Reports
- What outcome(s) or result(s) were specified in the intervention plan?
- What quantitative data and other types of information are available for evaluative purposes?
- How shall data be aggregated and displayed in evaluation reports?

APPENDIX B
Case Example—Jackson County Foster Care

The following example illustrates the major components of a written plan for a macro-change effort.

Background

Jackson County incorporates a major city, several medium-sized suburbs, and a small amount of rural area. The Child Welfare Services Division of its Department of Social Services recently undertook an analysis of foster children for which it had responsibility during the past five years. The findings revealed that there was a disproportionately low number of white children in this population and a disproportionately high number of children from other racial or ethnic groups.

In response to a newspaper article that reported these results, over 30 representatives of various ethnic communities attended an open hearing held by the County Board of Supervisors. They expressed serious concerns about the findings. The County Director of Child Welfare Services was instructed to appoint a task force to study the situation and to make recommendations. The 14-member task force included:

- Three parents of ethnic minority foster children
- Four leaders from minority communities
- Two foster parents
- Two foster care social workers
- A foster-home recruitment coordinator

- A child welfare researcher from the local university
- The top administrator from the foster care program

Analysis of the Problem

The group began with an initial statement of the problem that focused on the fact that ethnic minority children comprised a higher proportion of children in foster care than would be expected based on the overall proportion of these children in the county. Group members then began to review available literature to familiarize themselves with issues associated with foster care and return to natural families. The literature review they conducted uncovered the following facts:

1. Children of color are overrepresented in foster care not only in Jackson County but elsewhere in the country as well.
2. Racial or ethnic minority children can become overrepresented in foster care in two ways: (a) They can be placed in foster care at a higher rate than white children and/or (b) they can leave foster care at a slower rate than white children and thus account for a greater number in care at any given point in time.
3. Research reports suggest that ethnic minority children, once placed in foster care, are adopted or placed in other permanent arrangements at the same rate as white children. However, ethnic minority children who are returned to their biological parents' homes do so much more slowly than do white children.
4. Placing children in foster care may be necessary if it is the only way to ensure their safety, but all possible efforts should be made by workers to avoid the need for foster care by facilitating solutions to family problems while the child is still in the home.
5. If it still becomes necessary, foster care is supposed to be temporary. Workers should attempt to facilitate solutions to problems in the family in order to allow the child to return home as quickly as possible. If this cannot be done, the next best option is to find some other permanent placement, such as an adoptive home.

Analysis of the Population

The task force members then directed their efforts toward gaining a better understanding of the population of interest, which they defined as ethnic minority children in foster care. To accomplish this, they reviewed five-year statistics from the department's child welfare division, studied in detail the findings of the division's recent report, and examined other research on minority children and families. The most important results they found were:

1. Foster care that is intended to be temporary but that continues indefinitely is harmful to children. This is because it jeopardizes their ability to form developmentally critical attachments with a parent or permanent parent surrogate.

2. For healthy development, children need to go through a series of stages and successfully complete developmental tasks. Completion of these tasks can be interrupted by going into foster care. This can result in delayed development for the child.
3. Placement of a child from an ethnic group with a foster family from another ethnic group can be detrimental to the child if the foster family is unaware of or insensitive to important cultural factors.

Based on these findings, the task force refined its problem statement to focus on the specific concerns of children of color being too likely to be placed in foster care and too unlikely to be reunited with their biological families in a timely fashion.

Analysis of the Arena

Initial findings of the research efforts of the task force also implied that the arena in which a change effort would need to take place was not the community as a whole but the Jackson County Social Services organization. Under this assumption, the task force collected the following information from records within the Department and from interviews with current and former clients and professionals in other agencies in the community:

1. The proportion of persons of color who hold professional positions in Jackson County's foster care services division is much lower than the proportion of children of color who are placed in foster care in the county.
2. Foster parents licensed by the division are much less racially and ethnically diverse than the population of foster children in the county.
3. Many child welfare workers and foster parents lack an in-depth understanding of the meaning of culture and tradition to ethnic minority families. This means that children's behavior tends to be interpreted from a white perspective, which might be inconsistent with norms established and understood in minority communities.
4. After child welfare services in Jackson County had commenced, white children were less likely to be placed in foster care than nonwhite children.
5. Support services to help families deal with problems when a child is removed lack the cultural sensitivity necessary to help strengthen ethnic minority families.

As per Figure 1.1 in Chapter 1, the change effort that task force members began planning therefore assumed that the situation was one involving an overlap of problem (too great a likelihood of children entering foster care and staying too long), population (children of color), and arena (Jackson County Social Services, its employees, its foster parents, and its clients). It was thought that biological families served by the department's foster care division needed more resources and supportive services. Also, the division's professional staff and its foster parents needed a better understanding of family norms and the variables critical to healthy family environments for minority children.

Hypothesis of Etiology

Based on the preceding findings, the task force developed the following hypothesis of etiology:

Because of the following factors:
1. The low number of staff from ethnic minority populations;
2. The low number of foster parents from ethnic minority populations;
3. The limited knowledge of culture on the part of staff and foster parents; and
4. The high number of ethnic minority children being removed from their homes.

The result has been:
1. An organizational insensitivity to and unawareness of the importance of culture in foster care;
2. A preference on the part of foster parents for white children;
3. Low levels of cultural competence throughout the agency; and
4. A disproportionate number of ethnic minority children in foster care.

Intervention Hypothesis

Based on the preceding analysis, the task force proposed the following as their intervention hypothesis:

If we can do the following:
1. Recruit a more diverse child welfare staff;
2. Recruit more ethnic minority foster parents;
3. Train staff and foster parents; and
4. Support ethnic minority families in the home.

Then we would expect the following results:
1. Improved communication and understanding between ethnic minority families and staff;
2. Families better able to meet the cultural and ethnic needs of ethnic minority foster children;
3. Increased cultural competence on the part of white staff and foster parents; and
4. Increased number of successful returns of ethnic minority children to biological families.

After proceeding through each of the tasks outlined in the earlier chapters of this book, the task force produced the following written plan.

Part I: The Problem and the Proposed Change

In the Jackson County Division of Child Welfare Services it was recently discovered that the rate of return of minority children from foster care to their natural families was significantly less than the rates for white children. A task force was appointed and a study was undertaken. A number of causal factors have emerged from the study.

Evidence shows that minority families whose children go into foster care have more serious economic, social, and emotional problems and are in need of a network of supportive services that will enable them to strengthen the family and better parent the child. On the whole, such services, with a special emphasis on serving ethnic minority families, have generally not been available to these families.

Study results also show that child welfare workers and foster parents lack knowledge about culture that could be important in the decision-making process about the needs of ethnic minority children and what should be considered realistic behavioral and performance expectations for return to natural families.

The task force proposes a series of interventions aimed at improving the cultural sensitivity of child-care workers and foster parents and strengthening families who place children in foster care.

The first set of interventions will be directed toward child welfare workers and foster care parents. Recruitment activities will include:

- Contact with graduate schools of social work
- Advertising in urban agencies where there are large numbers of ethnic minority child welfare workers

Cultural sensitivity training for child welfare workers and foster parents will include:

- Assessing one's values and perceptions as they relate to work with minority children and their families
- Understanding African American families and children
- Understanding Hispanic American families and children
- Understanding Native American families and children
- Understanding Asian American families and children

Foster parents who complete cultural sensitivity training courses will:

- Receive a higher level of payment
- Be certified to receive ethnic minority foster children

The second set of interventions will include support services, under contract with agencies that have demonstrated an understanding of and sensitivity to ethnic minority cultures. These services will be directed toward minority families. They are:

- Individual and family assessment and counseling
- Case management
- Economic incentives
- Parent training
- Self-help groups

Part II: Key Actors and Systems

System Representative	Definition	System
Initiator	Those who first brought the problem to attention	Black Families United, a community organization that organized the effort to meet with the County Board of Supervisors.
Change Agent	The professional social worker, agency, and others coordinating the change effort	The Task Force, staffed by an experienced child welfare supervisor.
Client	Primary and secondary beneficiaries	Ethnic minority children who are placed in foster care, and their parents.
Support	Others who may be expected to support the change effort	At least eight ethnic community organizations, two child welfare advocacy groups, several ethnic minority clergy and their congregations, many child welfare professionals, and the foster parents' association.
Controlling	The person or persons who have the power and the authority to approve the change and direct that it be implemented	The County Board of Supervisors.
Host	The part of the organization or community that will provide auspices for administration of the intervention	The Jackson County Division of Child Welfare.
Implementing	The staff and/or volunteers who will carry out the intervention	Three units within the Jackson County Division of Child Welfare: (1) the foster care unit, (2) the staff development and training unit, and (3) the purchase of services contracting unit.

| Target | That which must be changed for the intervention to be successful | Since this will be a multiphase process, there will be phase-specific targets. The initial target will be the funding sources needed to underwrite the proposed interventions. This includes the Board of Supervisors and several local foundations. Subsequent targets include (1) child welfare workers and foster parents who need to become more ethnic-sensitive and (2) ethnic minority families with children in foster care. |
| Action | The expanded planning and coordinating committee responsible for seeing the change effort through to completion | The Task Force, together with key representatives from the Division of Child Welfare and potential service providers. |

Part III: Goals, Objectives, and Activities

This change effort is proposed as a three-year pilot project, during which time the Division of Child Welfare will experiment and correct any problems discovered in implementing the original design. Following the three-year trial period, it is to be implemented as a permanent part of Jackson County Child Welfare Services.

Goal
To reduce the disproportionate number of ethnic minority children in foster care in the Jackson County Child Welfare system.

Outcome Objective 1
By December 31, 20XX, to increase the knowledge of four ethnic minority cultures of at least 50 trainees (including child welfare workers and foster parents), as measured by a 50 percent increase between pretest and posttest scores on tests developed for the training course.

Process Objectives

1.1 By July 31, 20XX, to present a proposal to the County Board of Supervisors for funds to develop culturally sensitive curriculum for child welfare workers and foster parents in Jackson County.

1.2 By September 30, 20XX, to develop four training courses on understanding African American, Hispanic American, Native American, and Asian American families designed for child welfare workers and foster parents who serve ethnic minority children.

1.3 By October 31, 20XX, to produce 50 copies of all handouts associated with the training courses and distribute them to the Child Welfare Staff Development and Training Unit.

1.4 By November 30, 20XX, to recruit at least 50 child welfare workers and foster parents to take the training courses.

1.5 By January 31, 20XX, to administer pretests and to train at least 50 child welfare workers and foster parents in cultural sensitivity.

1.6 By March 31, 20XX, to administer posttests to trainees and to analyze the pretest/posttest results.

Outcome Objective 2

By September 30, 20XX, at least 100 ethnic minority families with children in foster care will demonstrate improved family strength and parenting skills as measured by at least 30 percent higher scores on the Multidimensional Parenting and Family Assessment Inventory.

Process Objectives

2.1 By November 30, 20XX, economic, social, emotional, and family support resources needed to serve African American, Hispanic American, Native American, and Asian American families in Jackson County will be inventoried.

2.2 By April 30, 20XX, at least 100 ethnic minority families with children in foster care will have been initially assessed to determine what resources are currently used and what resources are needed but not available or accessible.

2.3 By June 30, 20XX, gaps between available and needed resources for minority families will be documented in writing.

2.4 By September 30, 20XX, formal proposals for funding services designed for minority families will be presented to the Jackson County Board of Supervisors and at least two local foundations.

Activity Chart for Process Objective 2.1 By November 30, 20XX, economic, social, emotional, and family support resources needed to serve African American, Hispanic American, Native American, and Asian American families in Jackson County will be inventoried.

Activity Number	Activity	Person Responsible	J	F	M	A	M	J	J	A	S	O	N	D
1.	Form task force to identify resources.	Change agent	█											
2.	Hold meeting of task force.	Change agent		█										
3.	Develop subcommittee.	Members of task force		█	█									
4.	Conduct inventory of resources: a. Economic b. Social c. Emotional d. Support	Members of task force				█	█	█	█	█	█			
5.	Prepare final report.	Change agent										█	█	
6.	Report results along with identified gaps in available resources.	Change agent												█

Part IV: Tactics

It is anticipated that this change effort will proceed through a series of phases, as follows:

Phase 1   The purpose of Phase 1 is to get the change accepted by potential funding sources. The focus of this phase is on the County Board of Supervisors, several private foundations interested in minority concerns, and people capable of influencing their decisions. Campaign tactics will include education, persuasion, and lobbying. In the event that campaign tactics are not successful and that funding sources are not open to change, contest tactics may be used. These tactics would include mass media appeals to mobilize the support system as well as bargaining and negotiation and large group social action.

Phase 2   The purpose of Phase 2, if the project is funded, is to increase cultural awareness, knowledge, and competence. The focus of this phase is on child welfare staff and foster parents who serve minority children and their families. Collaborative tactics will include joint action, capacity building, and education.

Phase 3   The purpose of Phase 3 is to ensure that improved services are provided to minority families who have placed children in foster care. Services should be adapted to the unique needs, concerns, interests, and traditions of each ethnic group, and will involve application of knowledge and skill gained in Phase 2. The focus of this effort will be on child welfare workers, foster parents, and contracted service providers. Collaborative tactics will include capacity building and joint action.

Monitoring and Evaluation

The child welfare supervisor who served on the task force will be assigned the responsibility of monitoring the implementation of the project and producing evaluation reports. She will use the project's goal, outcome objectives, and activities as a basis for ensuring that all tasks and activities are carried out on time and at an acceptable level of quality.

The evaluation report will focus on outcomes related to (1) increased cultural awareness, knowledge, and competence of workers and foster parents; (2) improved levels of comfort and understanding between ethnic minority families and child welfare workers; (3) strengthened families and parenting skills on the part of participating ethnic minority families; and (4) increasing rates of successful return of ethnic minority children in foster care to their biological families.

SUGGESTED READINGS

Gabor, P. A., and R. M. Grinnell, Jr. (1994). *Evaluation and quality improvement in the human services.* Boston: Allyn and Bacon.

Kirst-Ashman, K. K., and G. H. Hull, Jr. (2002). *Understanding generalist practice* (3rd ed.). Monterey, CA: Brooks/Cole.

Lewis, J. A., M. D. Lewis, T. Packard, and F. Souflee, Jr. (2001). *Management of human service programs* (3rd ed.). Monterey, CA: Brooks/Cole.

Meenaghan, T. M., and W. E. Gibbons. (2000). *Generalist practice in larger settings.* Chicago: Lyceum Books.

Posavac, E. J., and R. G. Carey. (1997). *Program evaluation methods and case studies* (5th ed.). Upper Saddle River, NJ: Prentice-Hall.

Rubin, H. J., and I. Rubin. (2001). *Community organizing and development* (3rd ed.). Boston: Allyn and Bacon.

van Breda, A. D. (2000). The practical value of strategic direction. *Administration in Social Work,* 24(3): 1–16.

REFERENCES

Bardach, E. (1979). *The implementation game: What happens after a bill becomes a law.* Cambridge, MA: MIT Press.

Brody, R. (1993). *Effectively managing human service organizations.* Newbury Park, CA: Sage.

Dessler, G. (1997). *Human resources management* (7th ed.). Upper Saddle River, NJ: Prentice-Hall.

Gantt, H. (1919). *Organizing for work.* New York: Harcourt, Brace and Howe.

Hardina, D. (2002). *Analytical skills for community organization practice.* New York: Columbia University Press.

Hash, K. (2001). Preliminary study of caregiving and postcaregiving of older gay men and lesbians. *Journal of Gay and Lesbian Social Services, 13*(4): 87–94.

Hudson, W. (1982). *The clinical measurement package.* Homewood, IL: Dorsey.

Kettner, P. M. (2002). *Achieving excellence in the management of human service organizations.* Boston: Allyn and Bacon.

Kettner, P. M., J. M. Daley, and A. W. Nichols. (1985). *Initiating change in organizations and communities: A macro practice model.* Monterey, CA: Brooks/Cole.

Kettner, P. M, R. M. Moroney, and L. L. Martin. (1999). *Designing and managing programs: An effectiveness-based approach* (2nd ed.). Thousand Oaks, CA: Sage.

Montana, P. J., and B. H. Charnov. (1993). *Management.* Hauppauge, NY: Barron's Educational Series.

Rapp, C. A., and J. Poertner. (1992). *Social administration: A client-centered approach.* New York: Longman.

Weinbach, R. W. (1998). *The social worker as manager: A practical guide to success.* Boston: Allyn and Bacon.

INDEX